VOL. 17
Action Edition

Story and Art by
RUMIKO TAKAHASHI

English Adaptation by Gerard Jones

Translation/Mari Morimoto
Touch-Up Art & Lettering/Bill Schuch
Cover and Interior Graphics & Design/Yuki Ameda
Supervising Editor/Julie Davis
Editor/Avery Gotoh
Assistant Editor/Michelle Pangilinan

Managing Editor/Annette Roman
Editor in Chief/Alvin Lu
Production Manager/Noboru Watanabe
Sr. Dir. of Licensing and Acquisitions/Rika Inouye
VP of Marketing/Liza Coppola
Sr. VP of Editorial/Hyoe Narita
Publisher/Seiji Horibuchi

Printed in Canada.

Published by VIZ, LLC
P.O. Box 77010
San Francisco, CA 94107

Action Edition
10 9 8 7 6 5 4 3 2 1
First printing, March 2004

store.viz.com

www.viz.com

INUYASHA

VOL. 17 Action Edition

STORY AND ART BY
RUMIKO TAKAHASHI

CONTENTS

SCROLL ONE
TOKIJIN
7

SCROLL TWO
TETSUSAIGA REBORN
25

SCROLL THREE
TOKIJIN'S CHOICE
43

SCROLL FOUR
THE SCENT OF BLOOD
61

SCROLL FIVE
TRUE STRENGTH
77

SCROLL SIX
THE FOURTH ONE
97

SCROLL SEVEN
JUROMARU, THE BEAST BOY
115

SCROLL EIGHT
WITHOUT SHIELDS
133

SCROLL NINE
SHADOW BOY
151

SCROLL TEN
TWO AGAINST TWO
169

THE STORY THUS FAR

Long ago, in the "Warring States" era of Japan's Muromachi period (Sengoku-jidai, approximately 1467-1568 CE), a legendary doglike half-demon called "Inu-Yasha" attempted to steal the Shikon Jewel, or "Jewel of Four Souls," from a village, but was stopped by the enchanted arrow of the village priestess, Kikyo. Inu-Yasha fell into a deep sleep, pinned to a tree by Kikyo's arrow, while the mortally wounded Kikyo took the Shikon Jewel with her into the fires of her funeral pyre. Years passed.

Fast forward to the present day. Kagome, a Japanese high school girl, is pulled into a well one day by a mysterious centipede monster and finds herself transported into the past, only to come face to face with the trapped Inu-Yasha. She frees him, and Inu-Yasha easily defeats the centipede monster.

The residents of the village, now fifty years older, readily accept Kagome as the reincarnation of their deceased priestess Kikyo, a claim supported by the fact that the Shikon Jewel emerges from a cut on Kagome's body. Unfortunately, the jewel's rediscovery means that the village is soon under attack by a variety of demons in search of this treasure. Then, the jewel is accidentally shattered into many shards, each of which may have the fearsome power of the entire jewel.

Although Inu-Yasha says he hates Kagome because of her resemblance to Kikyo, the woman who "killed" him, he is forced to team up with her when Kaede, the village leader, binds him to Kagome with a powerful spell. Now the two grudging companions must fight to reclaim and reassemble the shattered shards of the Shikon Jewel before they fall into the wrong hands.

THIS VOLUME As Kagura tests the bounds of Naraku's patience, a new evil enters upon the land— Juromaru, the Beast Boy...and the terrifying secret he holds within!

CHARACTERS

KAGOME
Modern Japanese schoolgirl who can travel back and forth between the past and present through an enchanted well.

INU-YASHA
Half-demon hybrid, son of a human mother and a demon father. His necklace is enchanted, allowing Kagome to control him with a word.

SANGO
"Demon Slayer" from the village where the Shikon Jewel was first born.

MIROKU
Lecherous Buddhist priest cursed with a mystical "hellhole" in his hand that is slowly killing him.

NARAKU
Enigmatic demon-mastermind who's caused the miseries of nearly everyone in the story.

SHIPPO
Orphaned young kitsune or "fox-demon" who likes to play shape-changing tricks.

SESSHŌ-MARU
Inu-Yasha's half-brother, Sesshō-Maru is the full-demon son of the same father.

KAGURA
Created by Naraku to be his puppet, Kagura can manipulate the dead.

SCROLL ONE

TOKIJIN

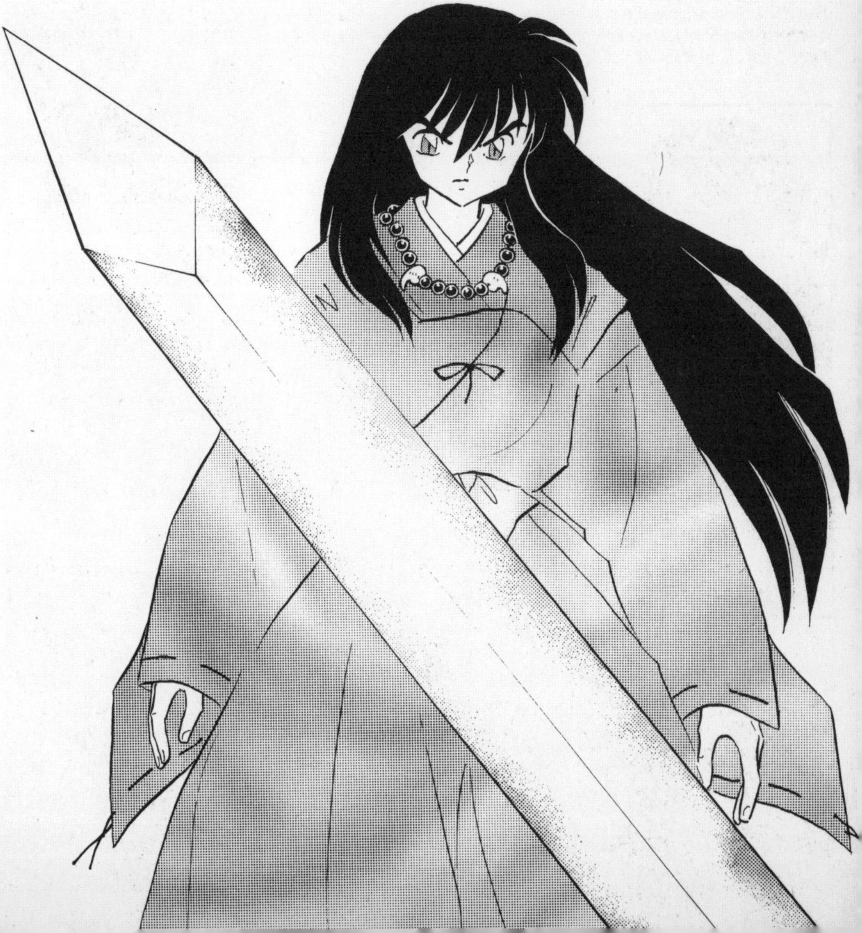

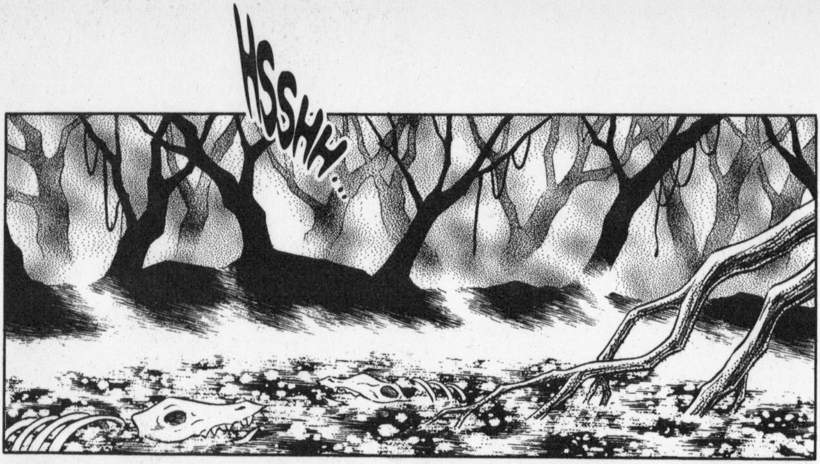
HSSHH...
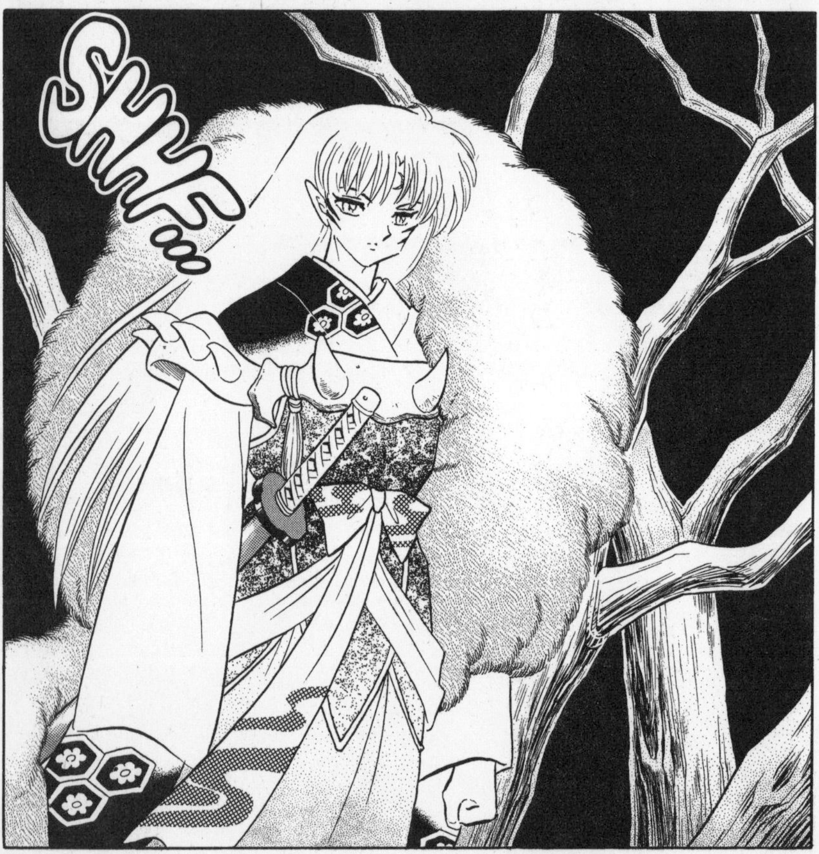
SHF...

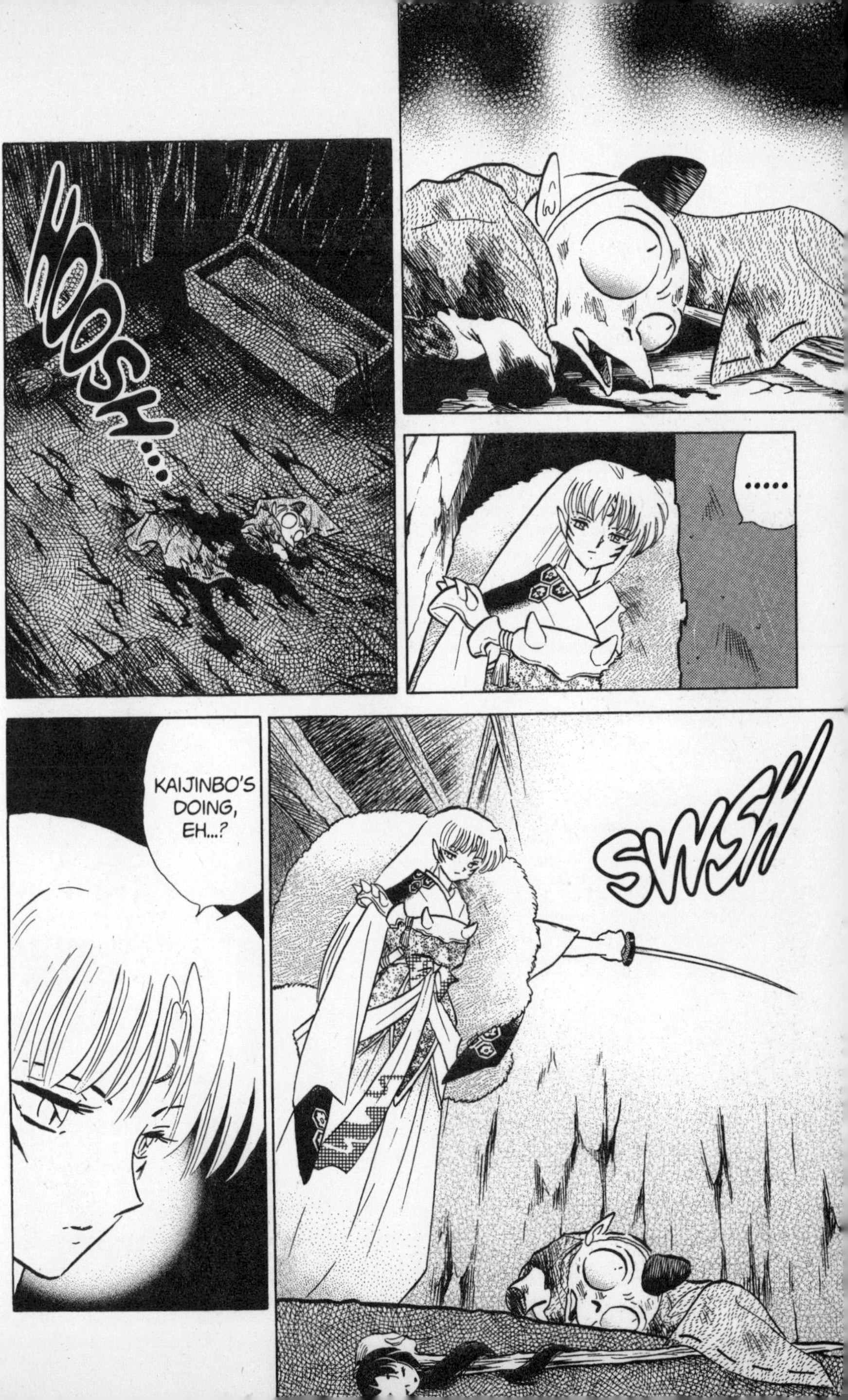
WHOOSH...
......
KAIJINBO'S DOING, EH...?
SWSH

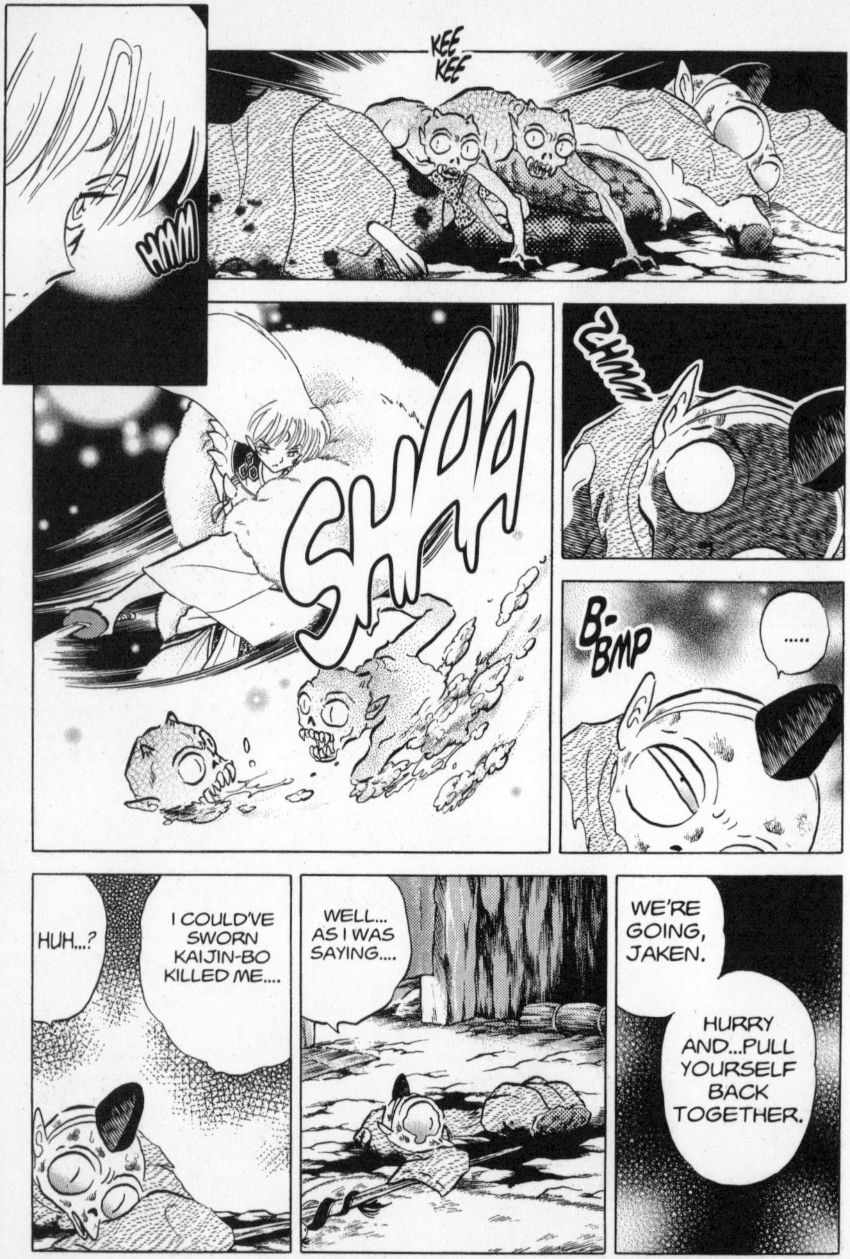
HMM
KEE KEE
SHAA
ZHMM
B-BMP
.....
HUH...?
I COULD'VE SWORN KAIJIN-BO KILLED ME....
WELL... AS I WAS SAYING....
WE'RE GOING, JAKEN.
HURRY AND...PULL YOURSELF BACK TOGETHER.

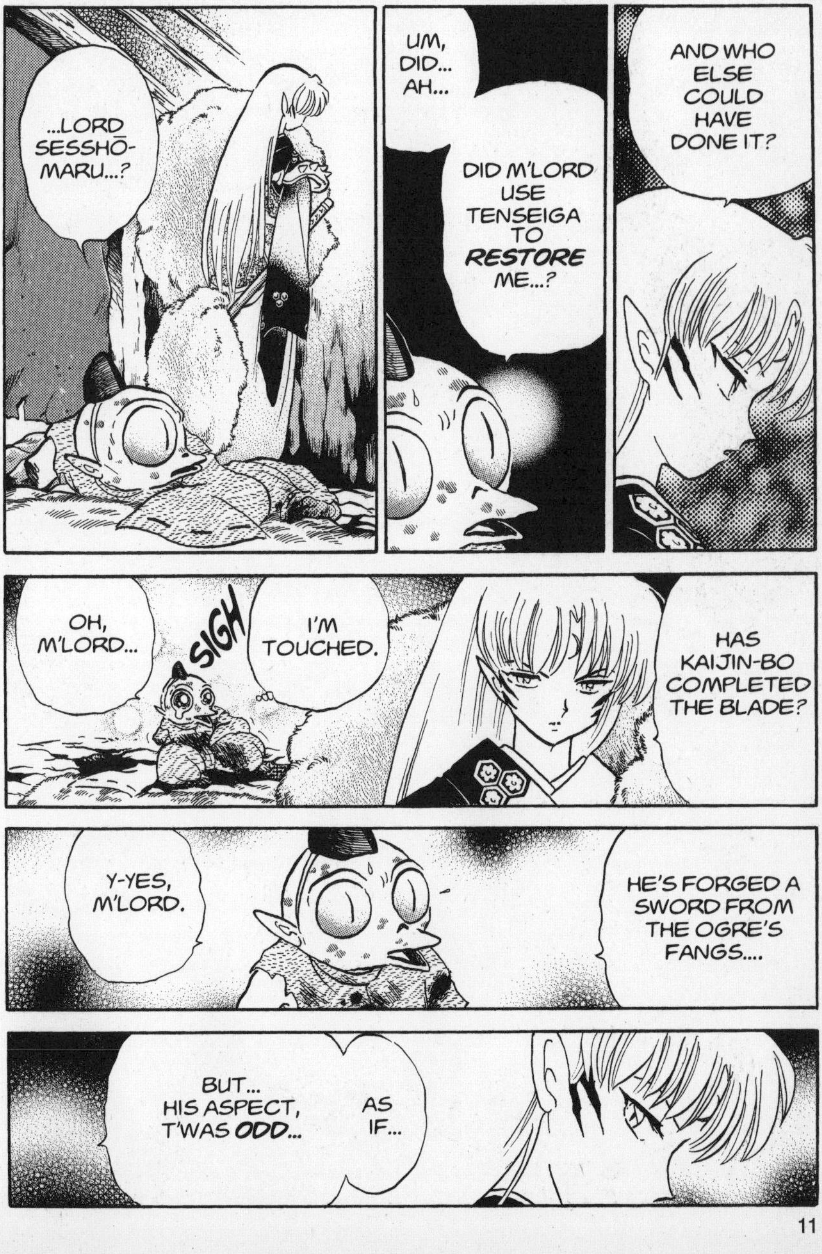

...LORD SESSHŌ-MARU...?
UM, DID... AH...
DID M'LORD USE TENSEIGA TO **RESTORE** ME...?
AND WHO ELSE COULD HAVE DONE IT?
OH, M'LORD...
SIGH
I'M TOUCHED.
HAS KAIJIN-BO COMPLETED THE BLADE?
Y-YES, M'LORD.
HE'S FORGED A SWORD FROM THE OGRE'S FANGS....
BUT... HIS ASPECT, T'WAS **ODD**...
AS IF...

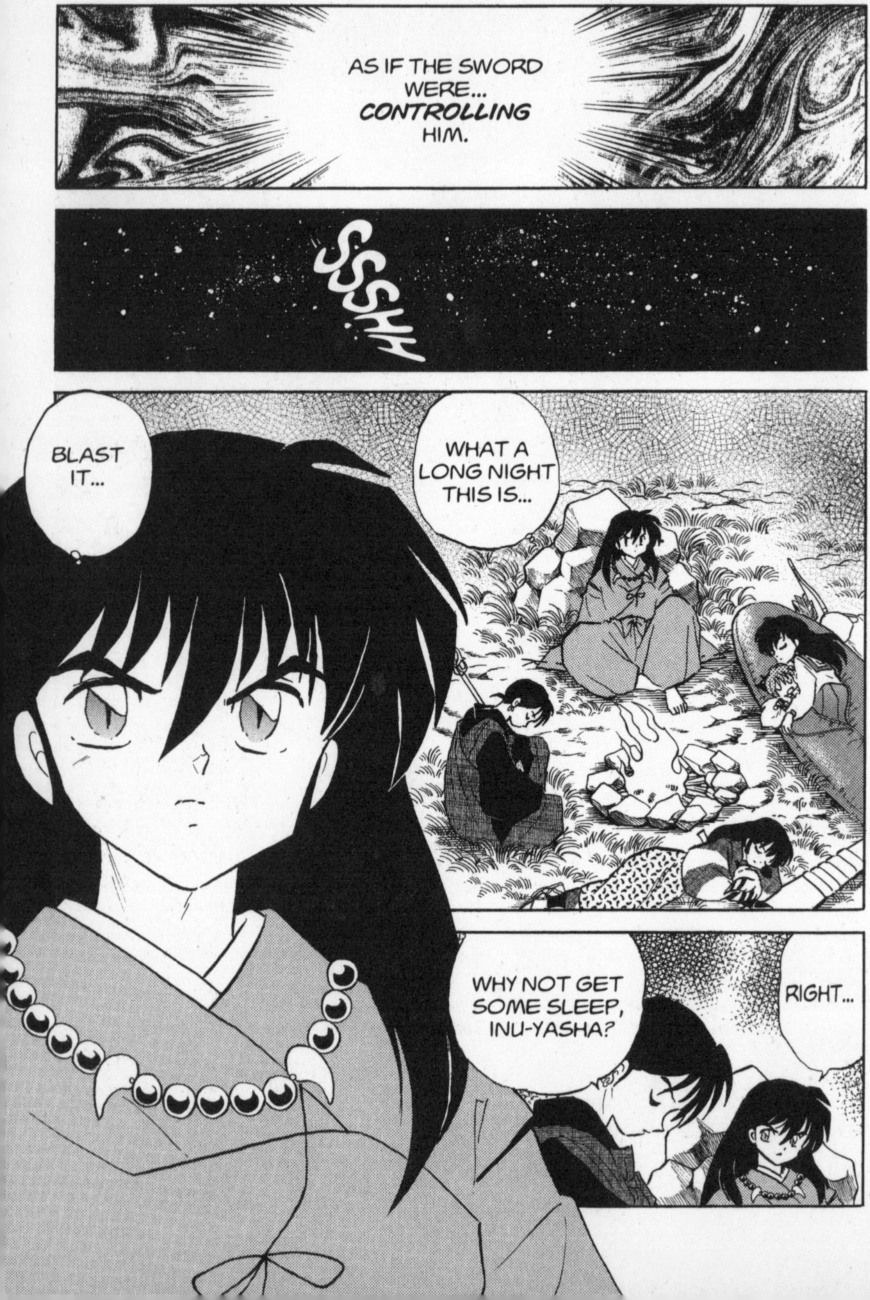
AS IF THE SWORD WERE... CONTROLLING HIM.
SSSHH
BLAST IT...
WHAT A LONG NIGHT THIS IS...
WHY NOT GET SOME SLEEP, INU-YASHA?
RIGHT...

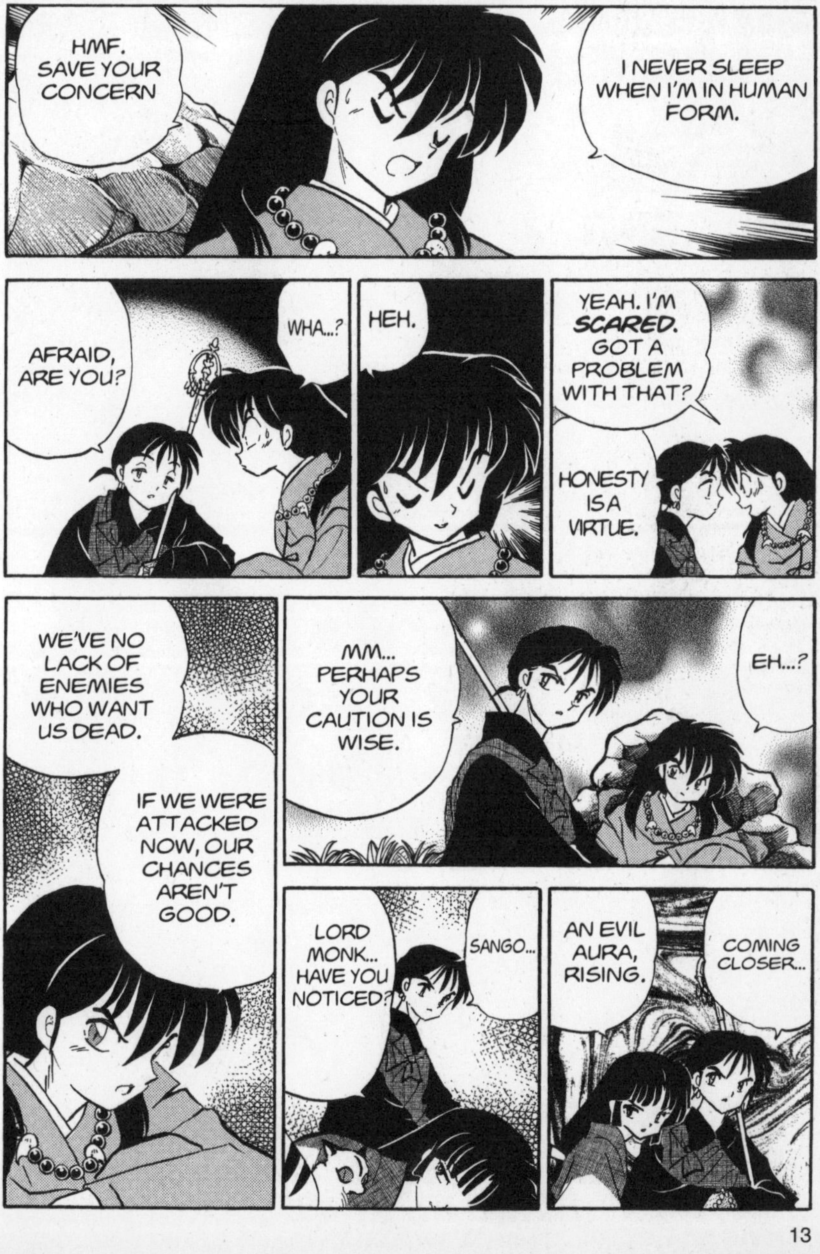
HMF. SAVE YOUR CONCERN
I NEVER SLEEP WHEN I'M IN HUMAN FORM.
AFRAID, ARE YOU?
WHA...?
HEH.
YEAH. I'M *SCARED.* GOT A PROBLEM WITH THAT?
HONESTY IS A VIRTUE.
WE'VE NO LACK OF ENEMIES WHO WANT US DEAD.
IF WE WERE ATTACKED NOW, OUR CHANCES AREN'T GOOD.
MM... PERHAPS YOUR CAUTION IS WISE.
EH...?
LORD MONK... HAVE YOU NOTICED?
SANGO...
AN EVIL AURA, RISING.
COMING CLOSER...

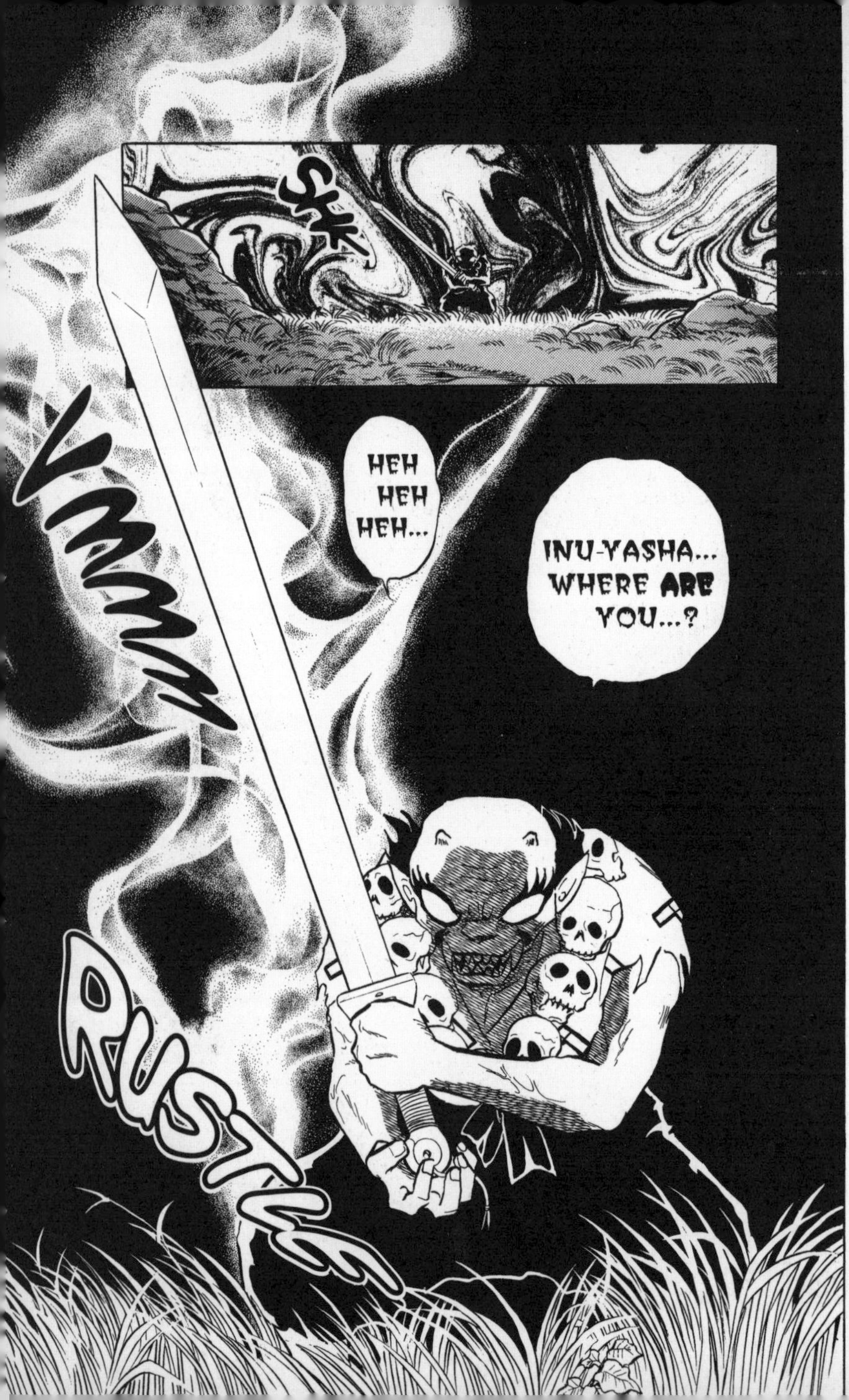
SHK
VMMM
HEH HEH HEH...
INU-YASHA... WHERE ARE YOU...?
RUSTLE

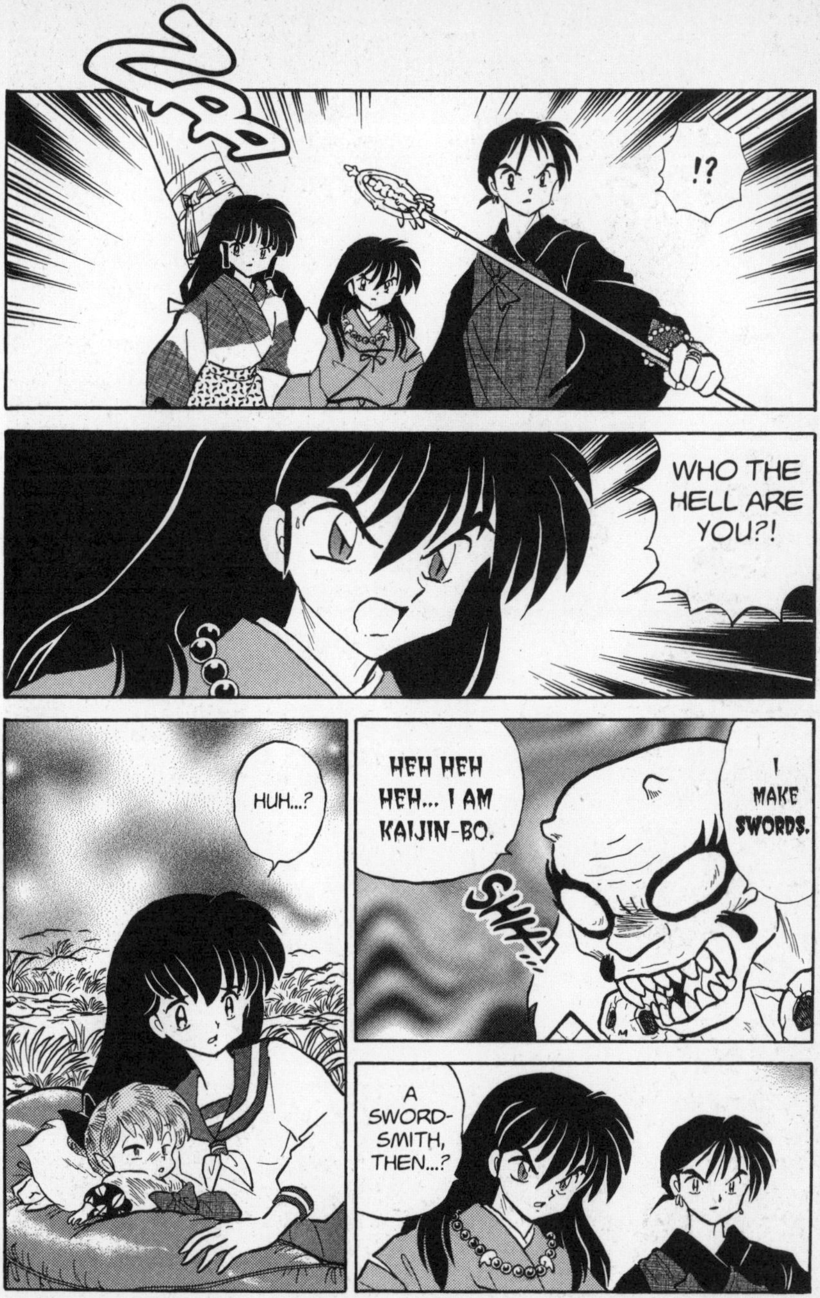
ZPA
!?
WHO THE HELL ARE YOU?!
HUH...?
HEH HEH HEH... I AM KAIJIN-BO.
I MAKE SWORDS.
SHIK
A SWORD-SMITH, THEN...?

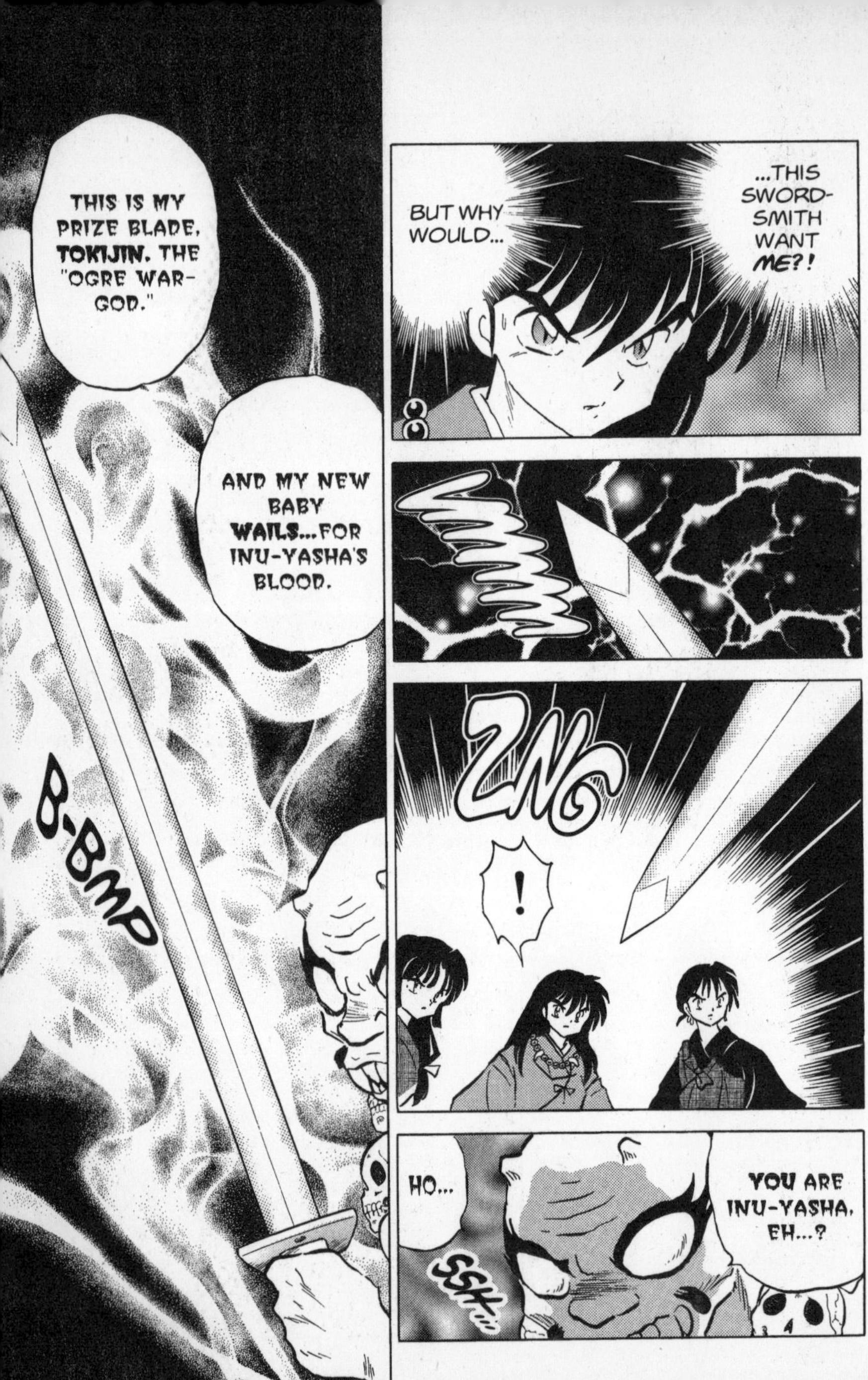
THIS IS MY PRIZE BLADE, TOKIJIN. THE "OGRE WAR-GOD."
AND MY NEW BABY WAILS...FOR INU-YASHA'S BLOOD.
B-BMP
BUT WHY WOULD...
...THIS SWORD-SMITH WANT ME?!
VMMMMM
ZNG
!
HO...
SSK...
YOU ARE INU-YASHA, EH...?

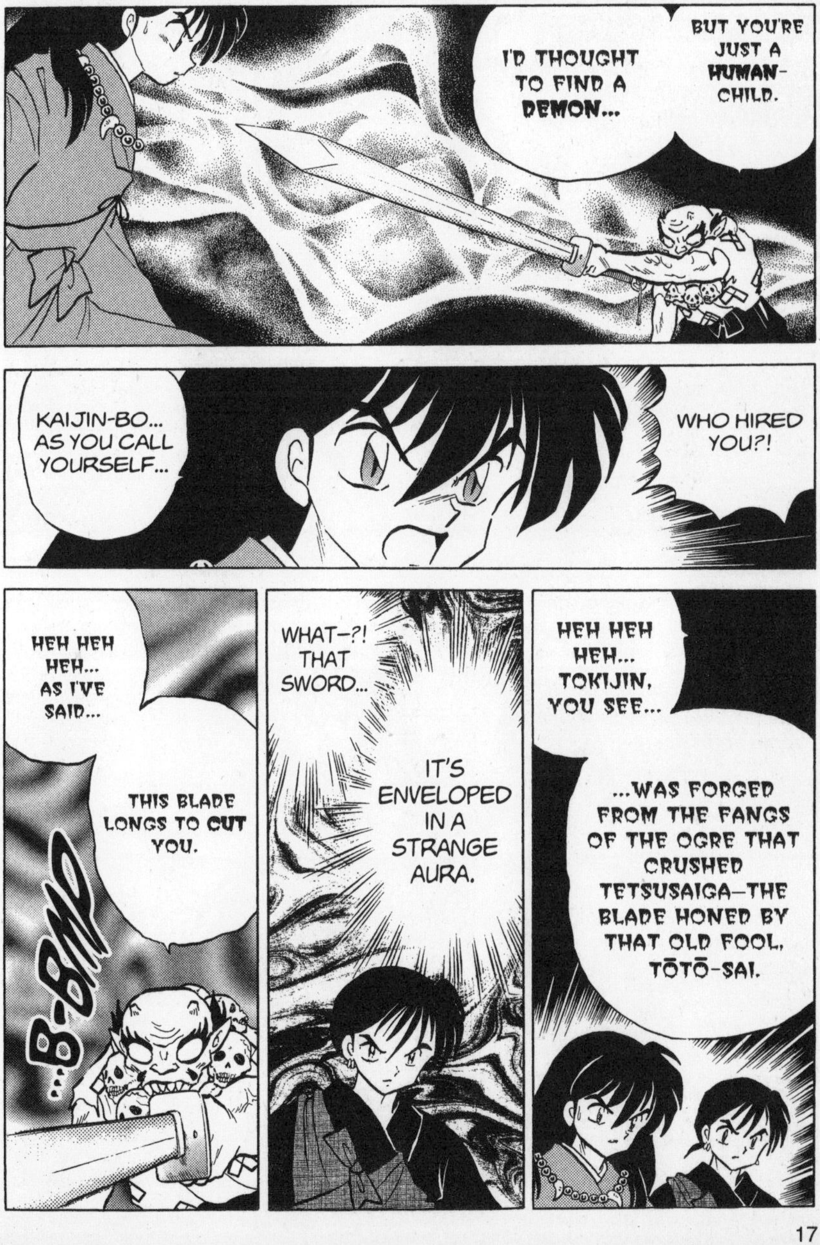
I'D THOUGHT TO FIND A DEMON...
BUT YOU'RE JUST A HUMAN-CHILD.
KAIJIN-BO... AS YOU CALL YOURSELF...
WHO HIRED YOU?!
HEH HEH HEH... AS I'VE SAID...
THIS BLADE LONGS TO CUT YOU.
...B-BMP
WHAT-?! THAT SWORD...
IT'S ENVELOPED IN A STRANGE AURA.
HEH HEH HEH... TOKIJIN, YOU SEE...
...WAS FORGED FROM THE FANGS OF THE OGRE THAT CRUSHED TETSUSAIGA—THE BLADE HONED BY THAT OLD FOOL, TŌTŌ-SAI.

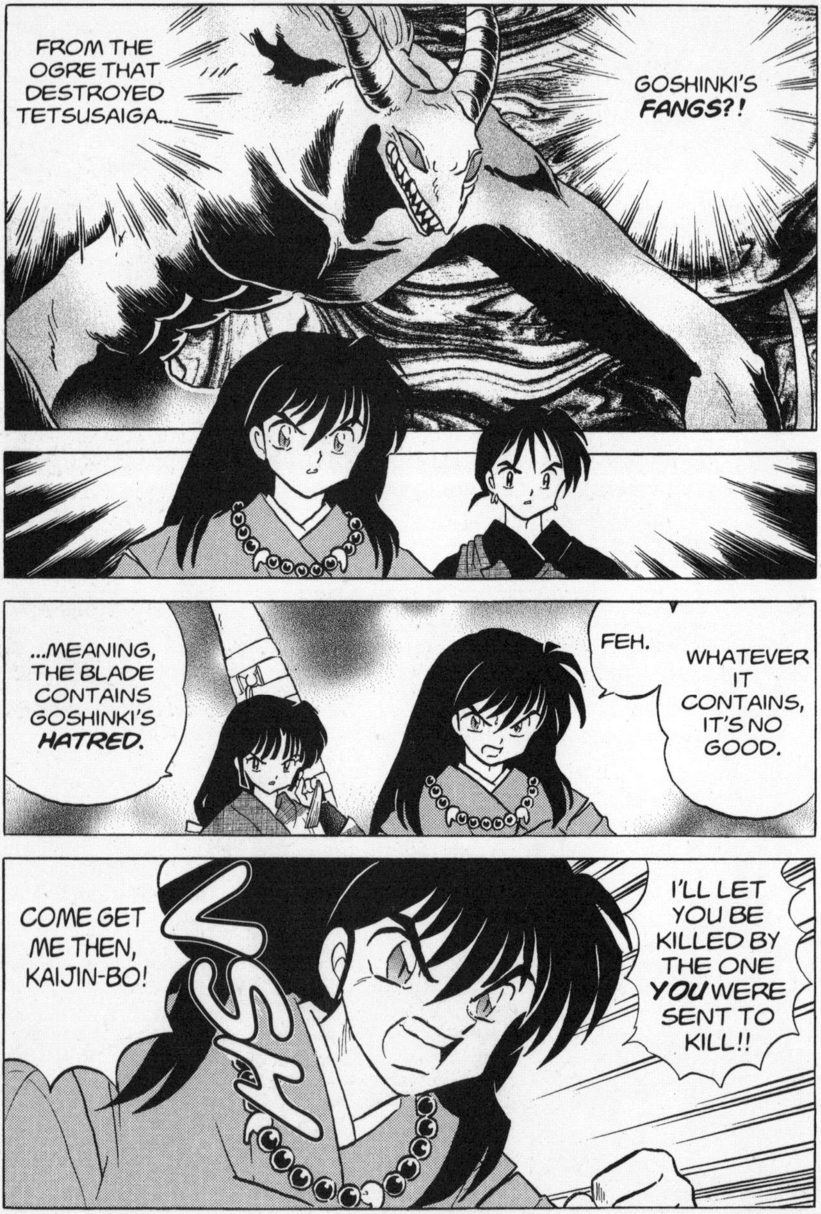
FROM THE OGRE THAT DESTROYED TETSUSAIGA...
GOSHINKI'S FANGS?!
...MEANING, THE BLADE CONTAINS GOSHINKI'S HATRED.
FEH.
WHATEVER IT CONTAINS, IT'S NO GOOD.
COME GET ME THEN, KAIJIN-BO!
I'LL LET YOU BE KILLED BY THE ONE YOU WERE SENT TO KILL!!

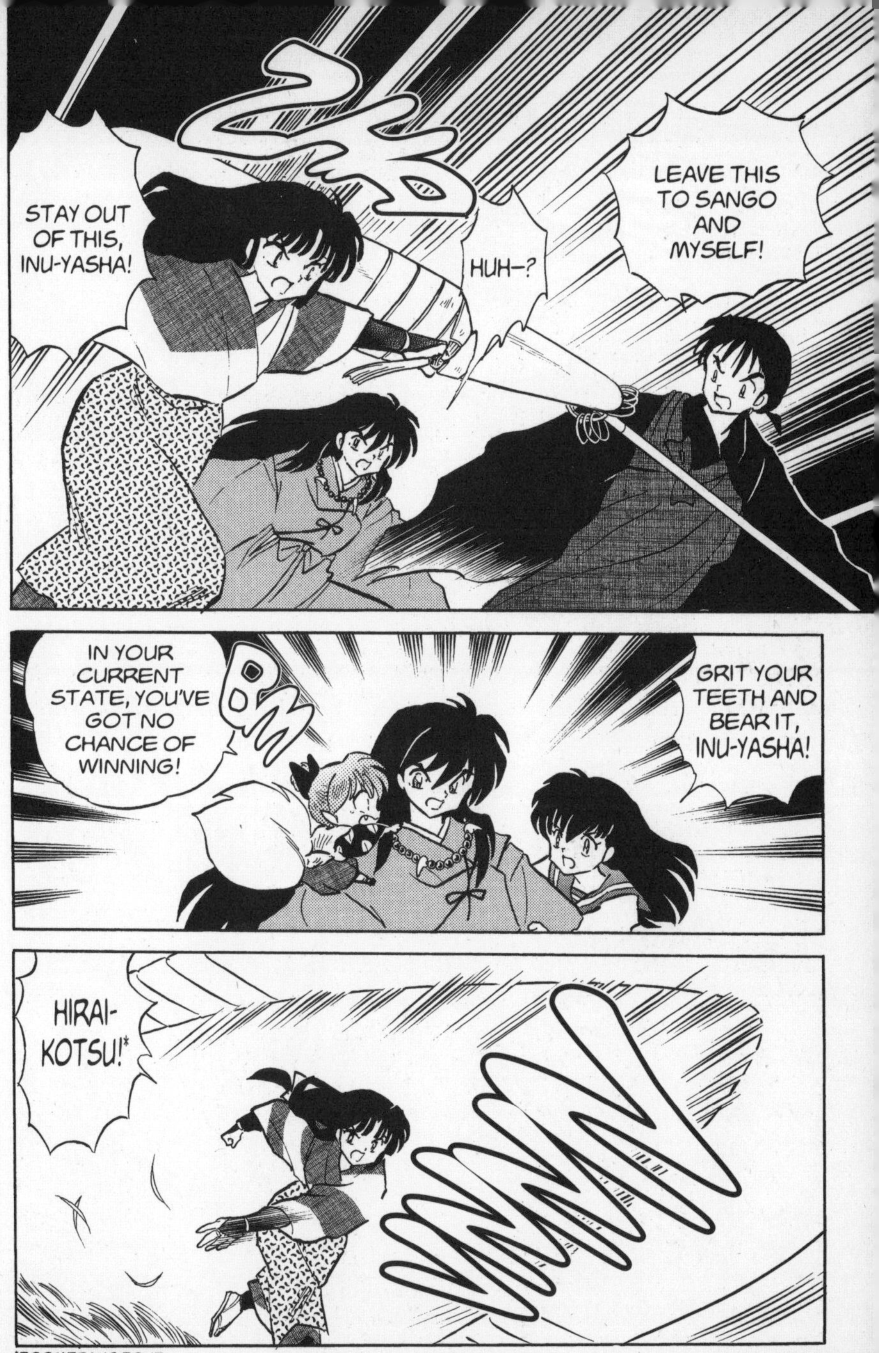
STAY OUT OF THIS, INU-YASHA!
HUH-?
LEAVE THIS TO SANGO AND MYSELF!
IN YOUR CURRENT STATE, YOU'VE GOT NO CHANCE OF WINNING!
GRIT YOUR TEETH AND BEAR IT, INU-YASHA!
HIRAI-KOTSU!*

*BOOMERANG BONE

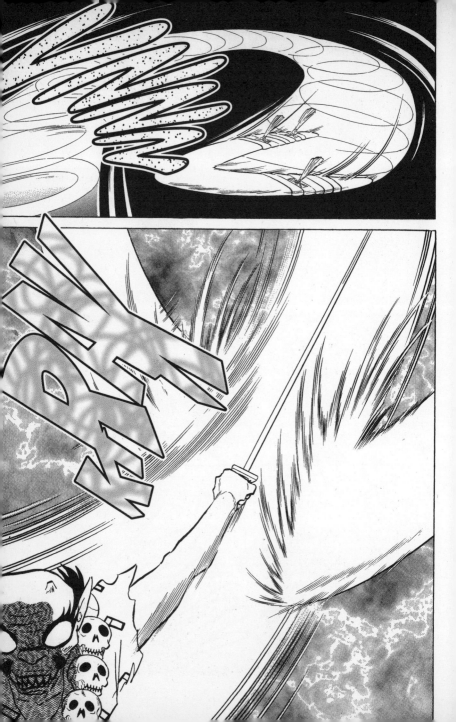

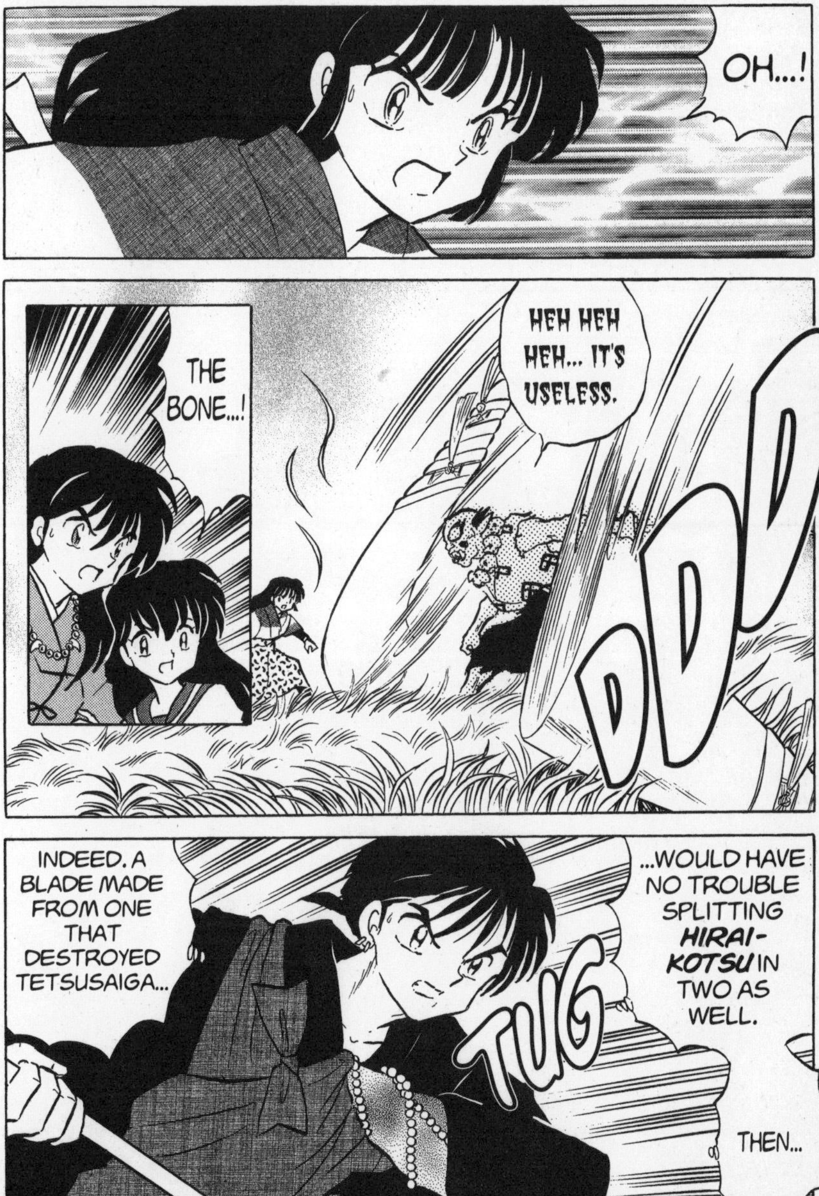
OH...!
THE BONE...!
HEH HEH HEH... IT'S USELESS.
DDDD
INDEED. A BLADE MADE FROM ONE THAT DESTROYED TETSUSAIGA...
...WOULD HAVE NO TROUBLE SPLITTING HIRAI-KOTSU IN TWO AS WELL.
TUG
THEN...

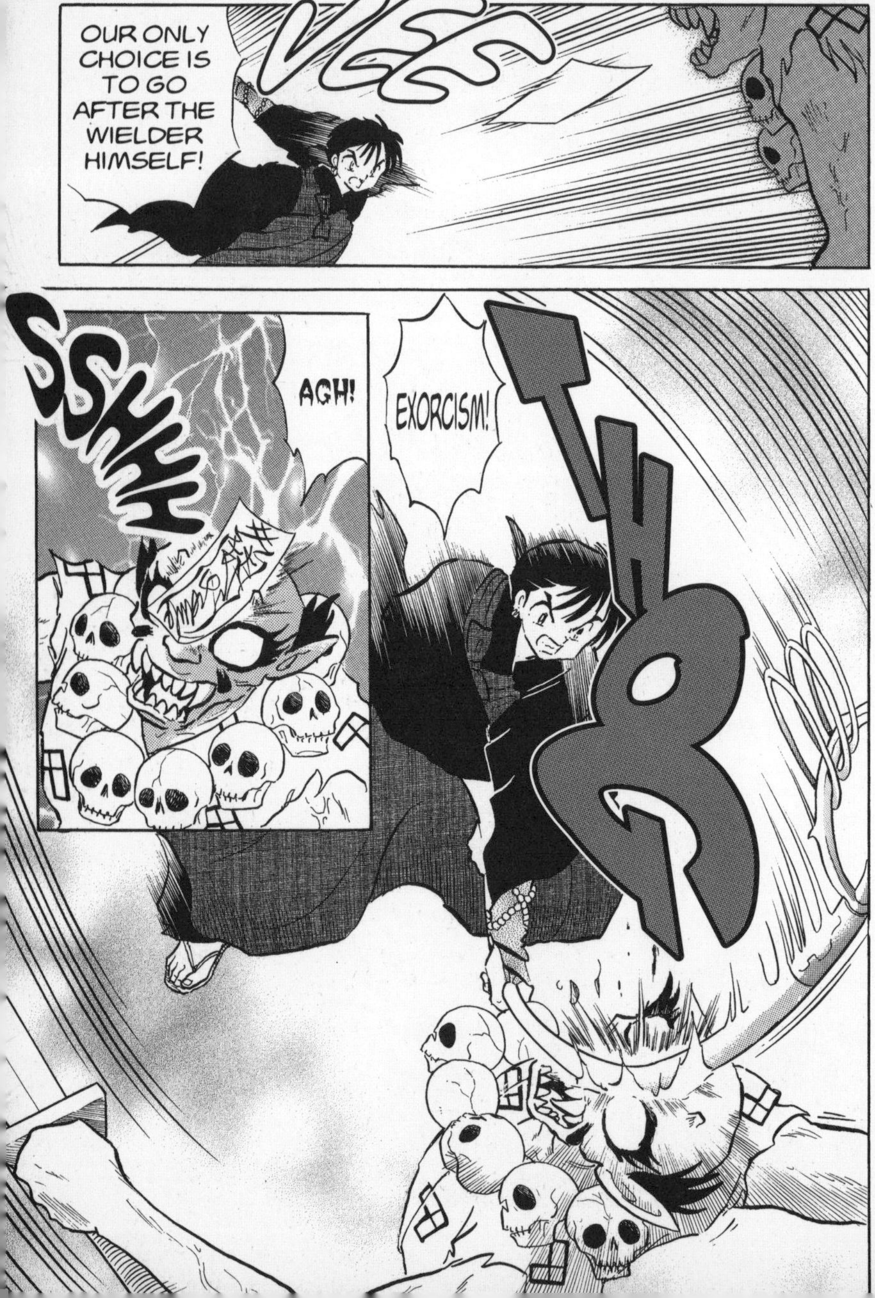
OUR ONLY CHOICE IS TO GO AFTER THE WIELDER HIMSELF!
AGH!
EXORCISM!

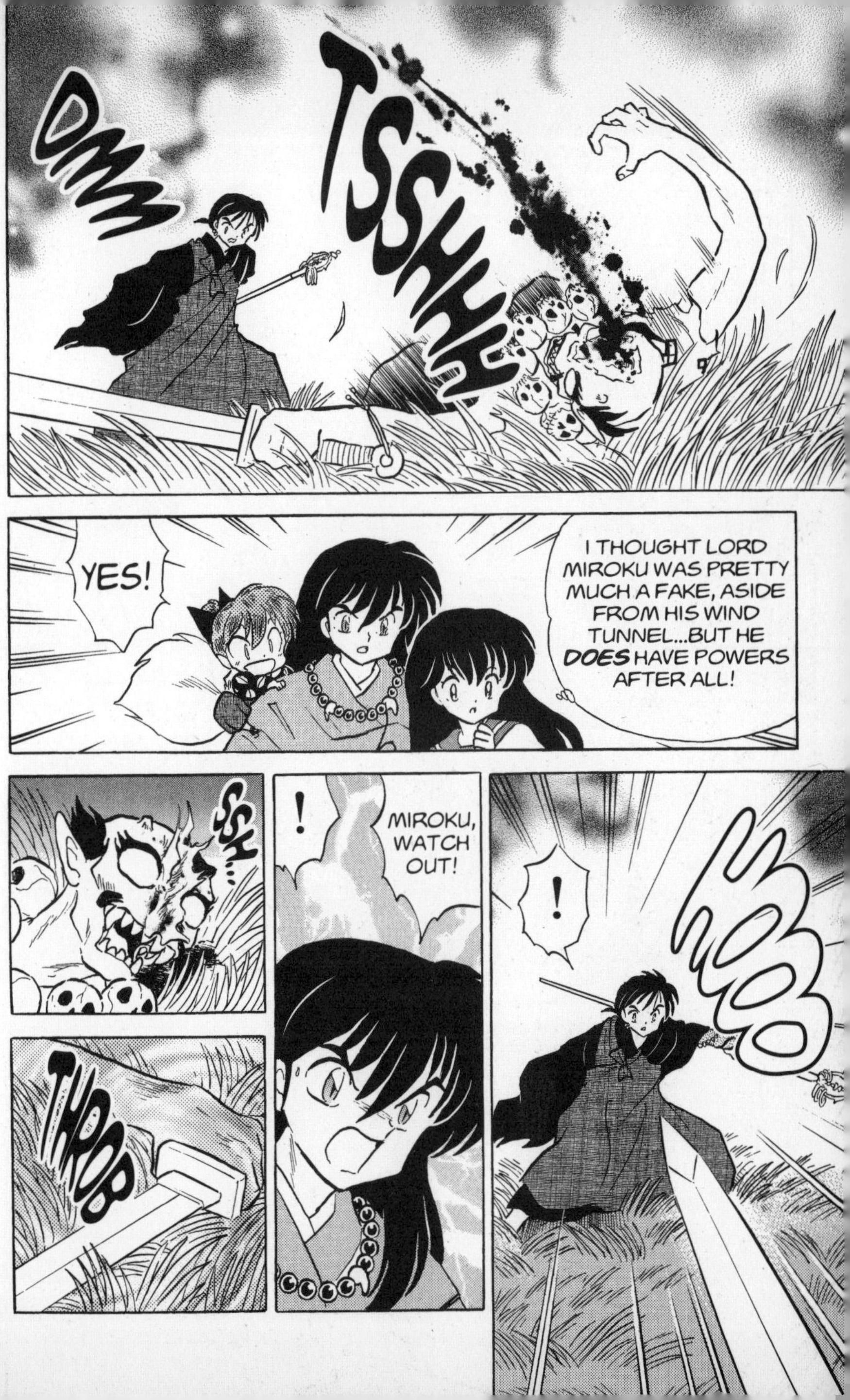
DMM
TSSHHHH
YES!
I THOUGHT LORD MIROKU WAS PRETTY MUCH A FAKE, ASIDE FROM HIS WIND TUNNEL...BUT HE DOES HAVE POWERS AFTER ALL!
SSH...
!
MIROKU, WATCH OUT!
THROB
!
WOOO

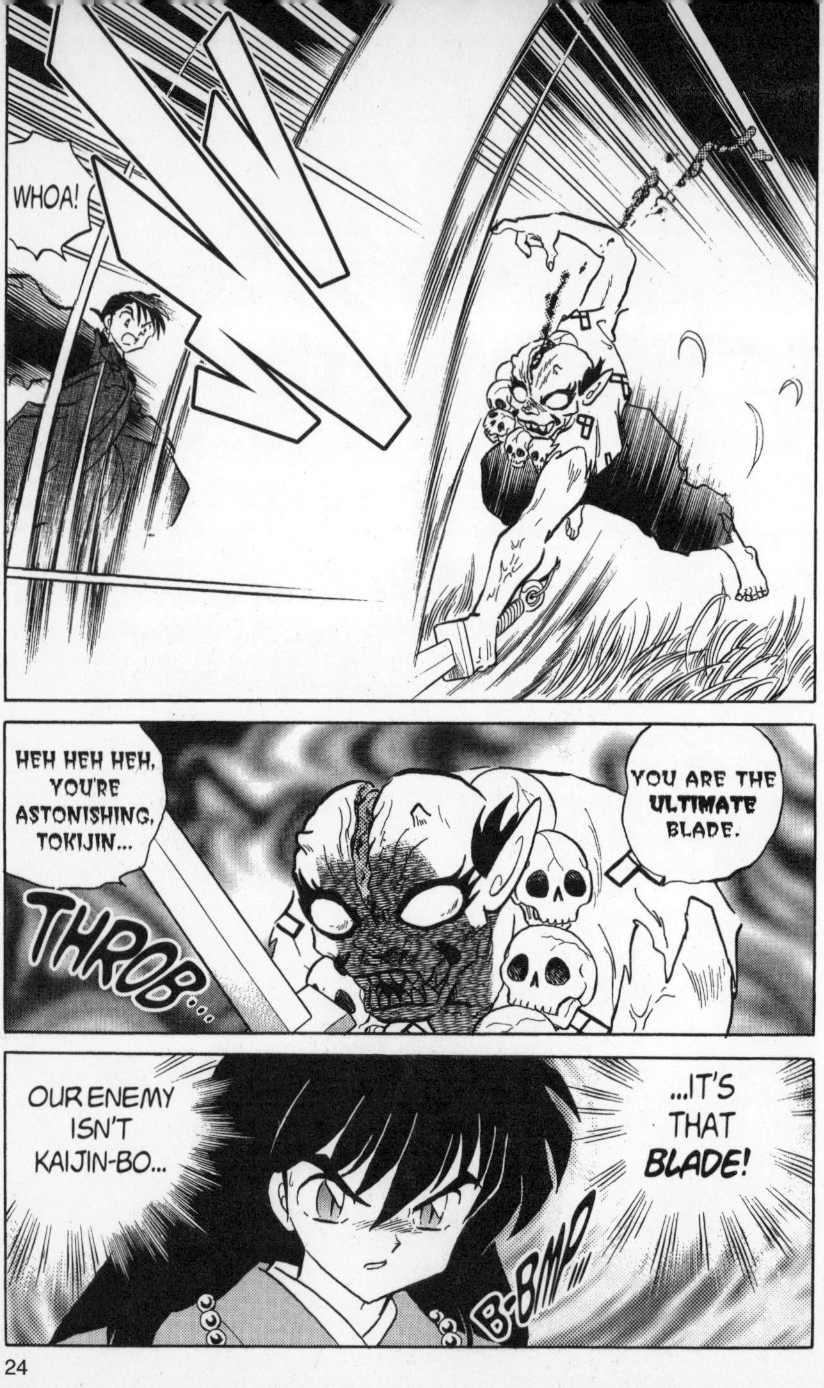
WHOA!
HEH HEH HEH, YOU'RE ASTONISHING, TOKIJIN...
THROB...
YOU ARE THE ULTIMATE BLADE.
OUR ENEMY ISN'T KAIJIN-BO...
...IT'S THAT BLADE!
B-BMP...

SCROLL TWO

TETSUSAIGA REBORN

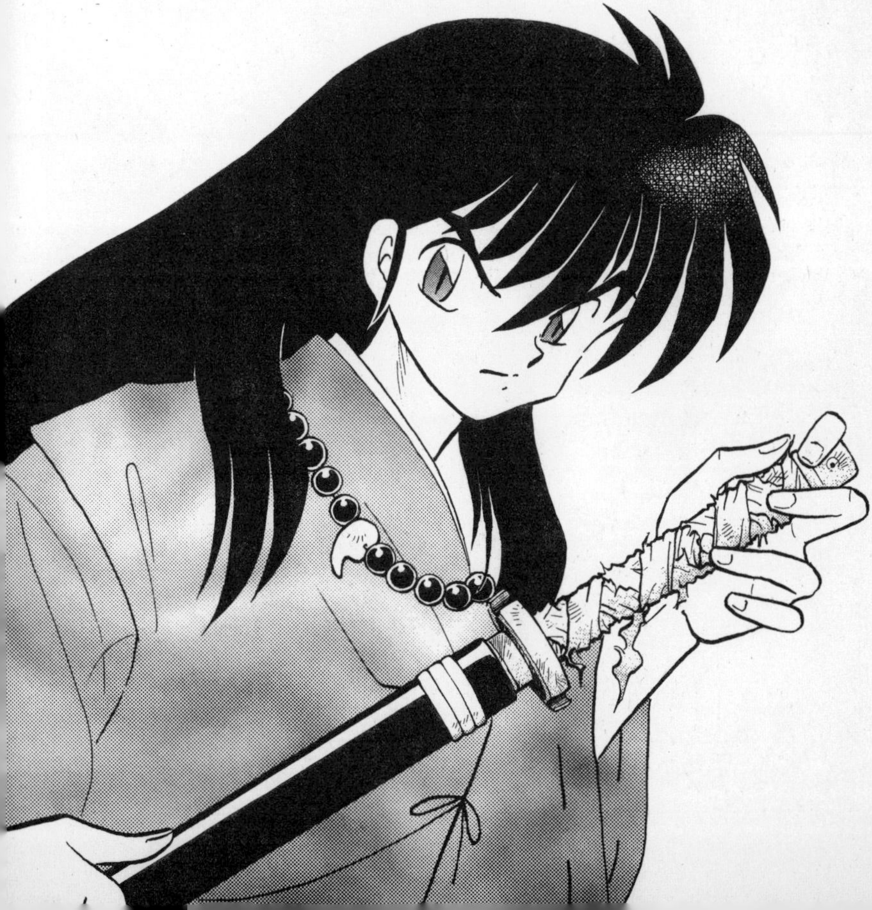

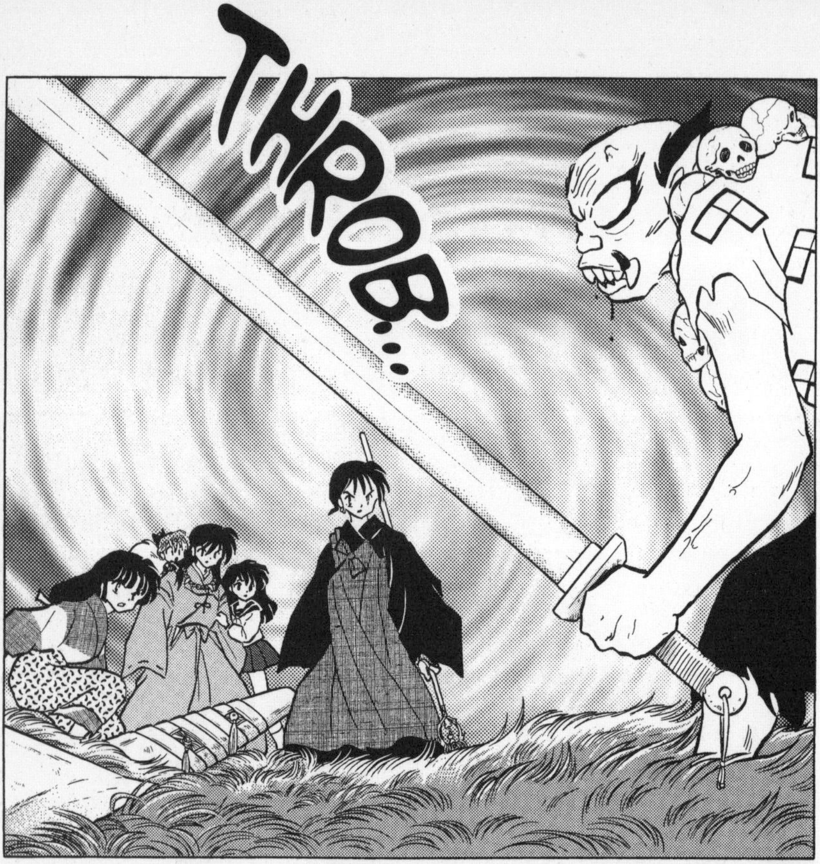
THROB...

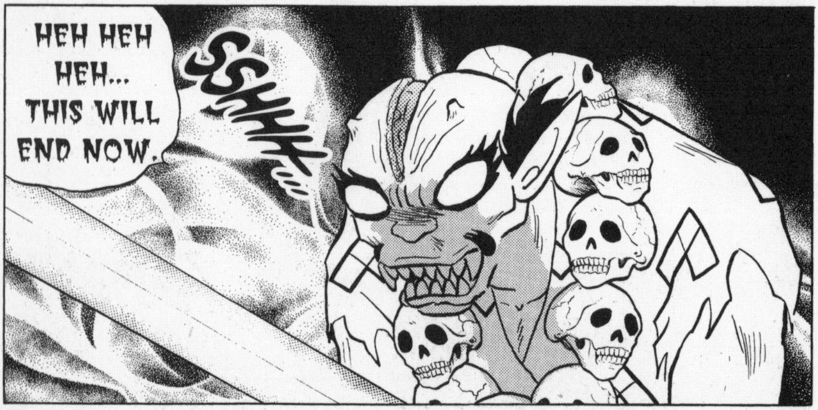
HEH HEH HEH... THIS WILL END NOW.
SSHHH...

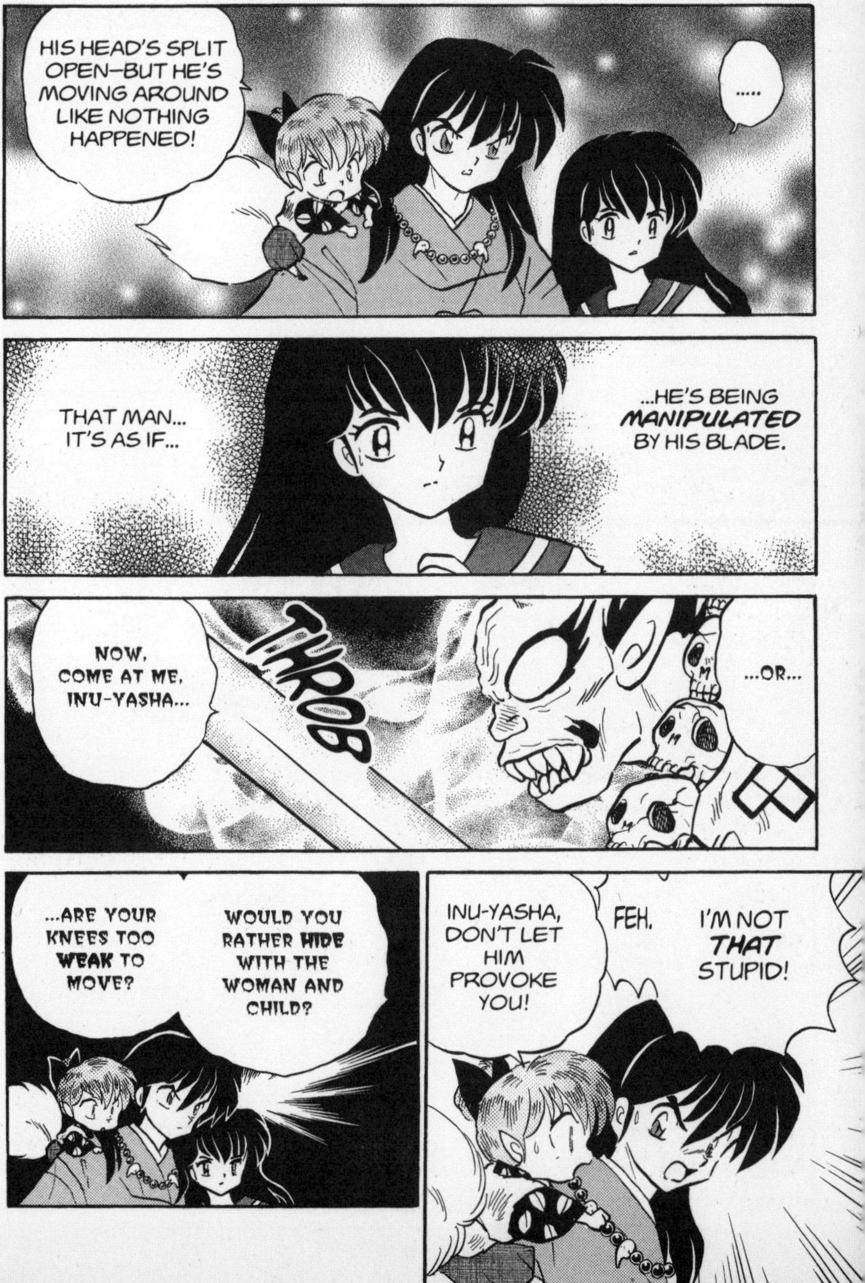
HIS HEAD'S SPLIT OPEN—BUT HE'S MOVING AROUND LIKE NOTHING HAPPENED!
.....
THAT MAN... IT'S AS IF...
...HE'S BEING MANIPULATED BY HIS BLADE.
NOW, COME AT ME, INU-YASHA...
THROB
...OR...
...ARE YOUR KNEES TOO WEAK TO MOVE?
WOULD YOU RATHER HIDE WITH THE WOMAN AND CHILD?
INU-YASHA, DON'T LET HIM PROVOKE YOU!
FEH.
I'M NOT THAT STUPID!

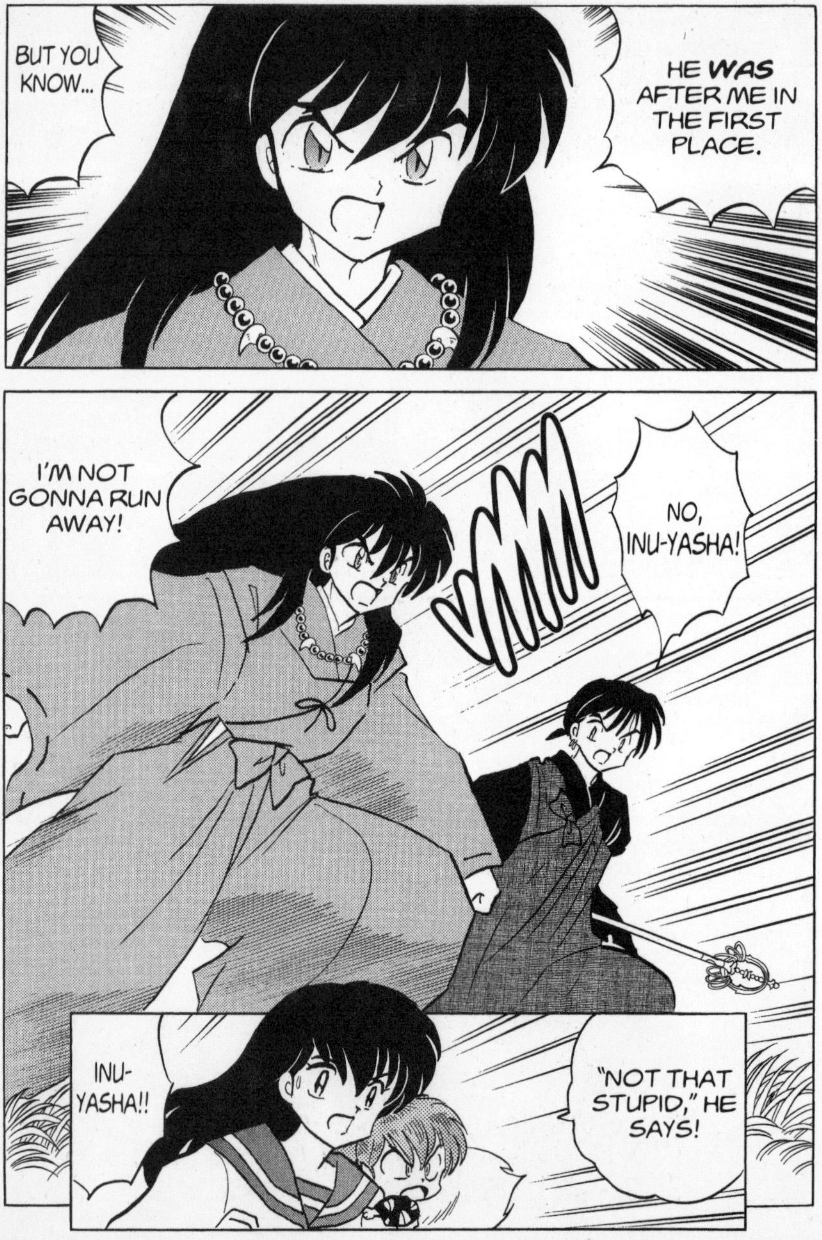
BUT YOU KNOW...
HE **WAS** AFTER ME IN THE FIRST PLACE.
I'M NOT GONNA RUN AWAY!
NO, INU-YASHA!
INU-YASHA!!
"NOT THAT STUPID," HE SAYS!

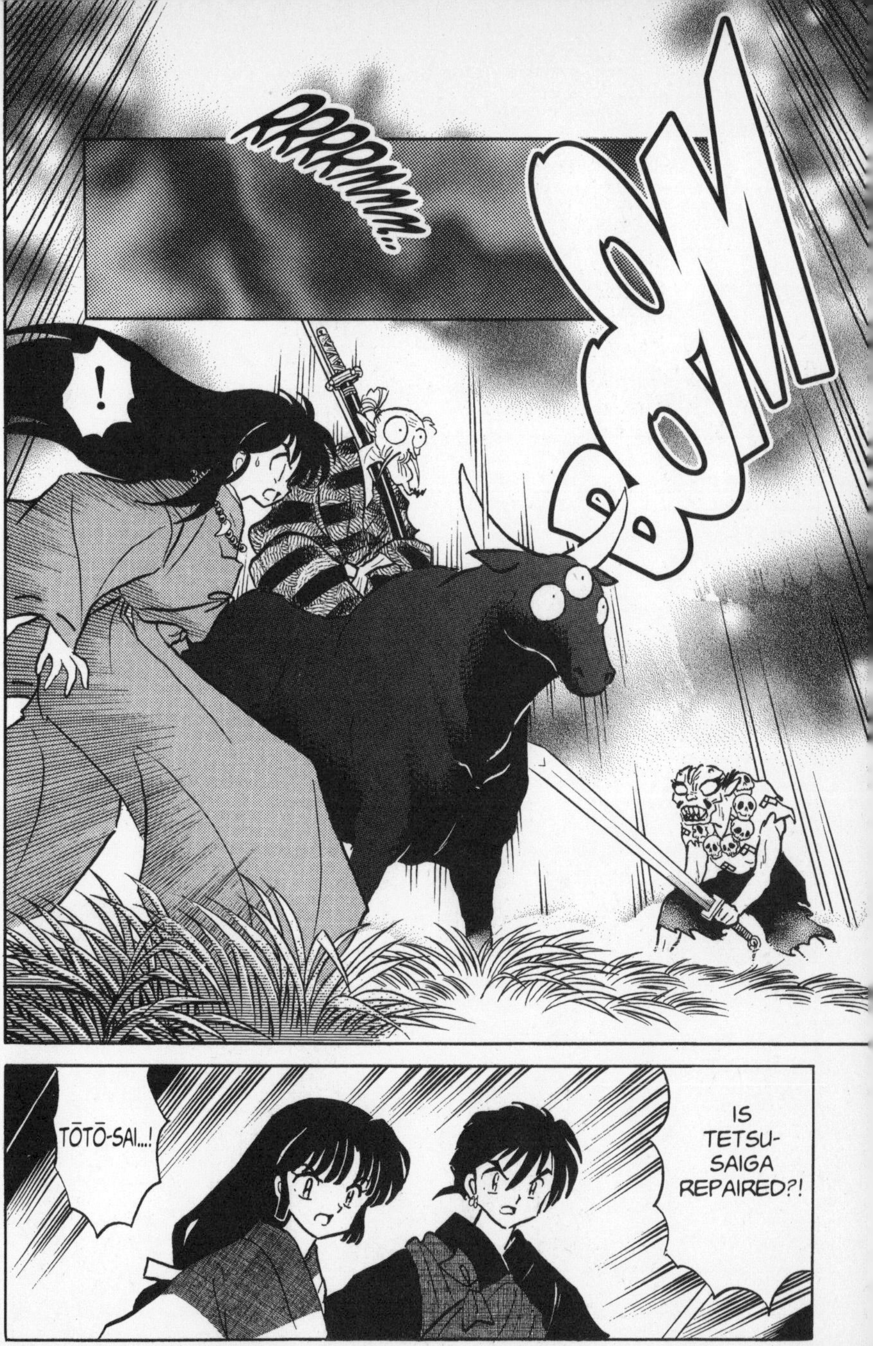
RRRRMMMM...
BOOM
!
TŌTŌ-SAI...!
IS TETSU-SAIGA REPAIRED?!

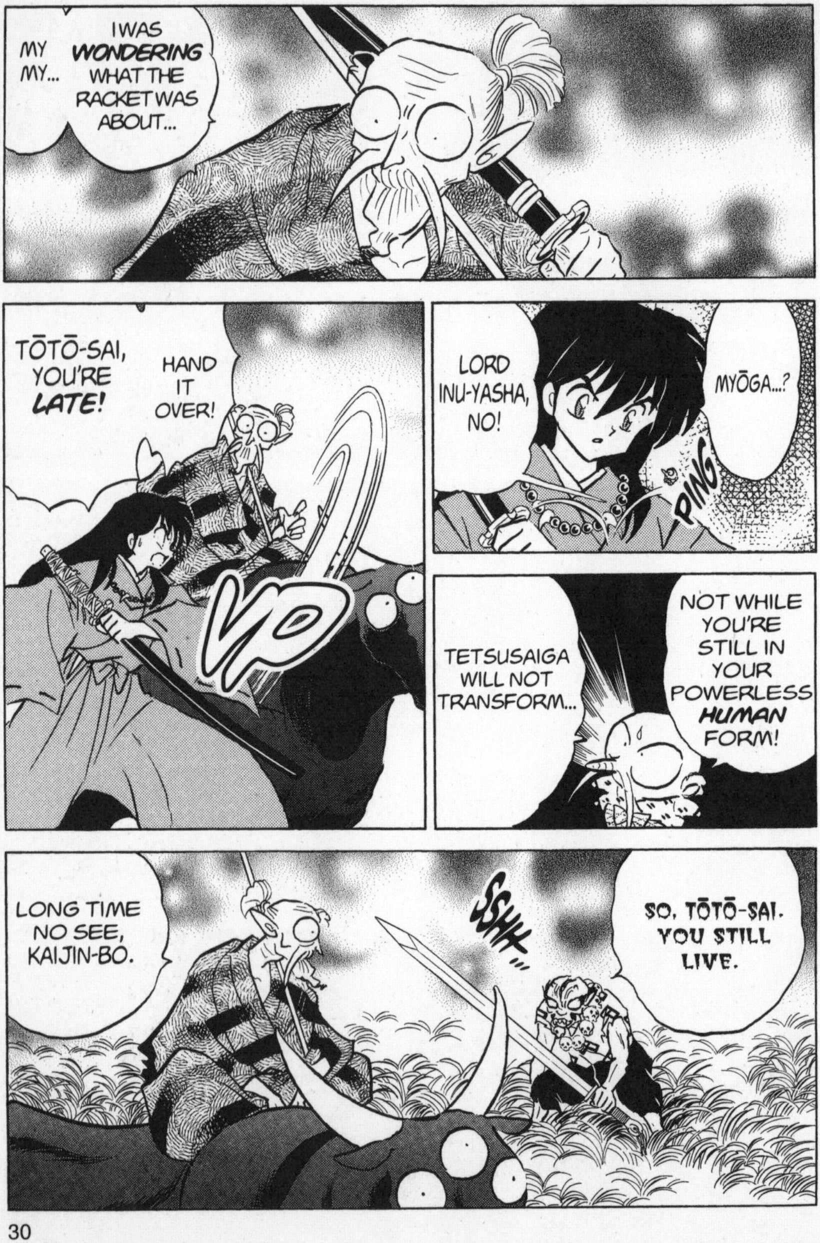
MY MY...
I WAS **WONDERING** WHAT THE RACKET WAS ABOUT...
TŌTŌ-SAI, YOU'RE **LATE!**
HAND IT OVER!
VP
LORD INU-YASHA, NO!
MYŌGA...?
PING
TETSUSAIGA WILL NOT TRANSFORM...
NOT WHILE YOU'RE STILL IN YOUR POWERLESS **HUMAN** FORM!
LONG TIME NO SEE, KAIJIN-BO.
SSHK
SO, TŌTŌ-SAI. YOU STILL LIVE.

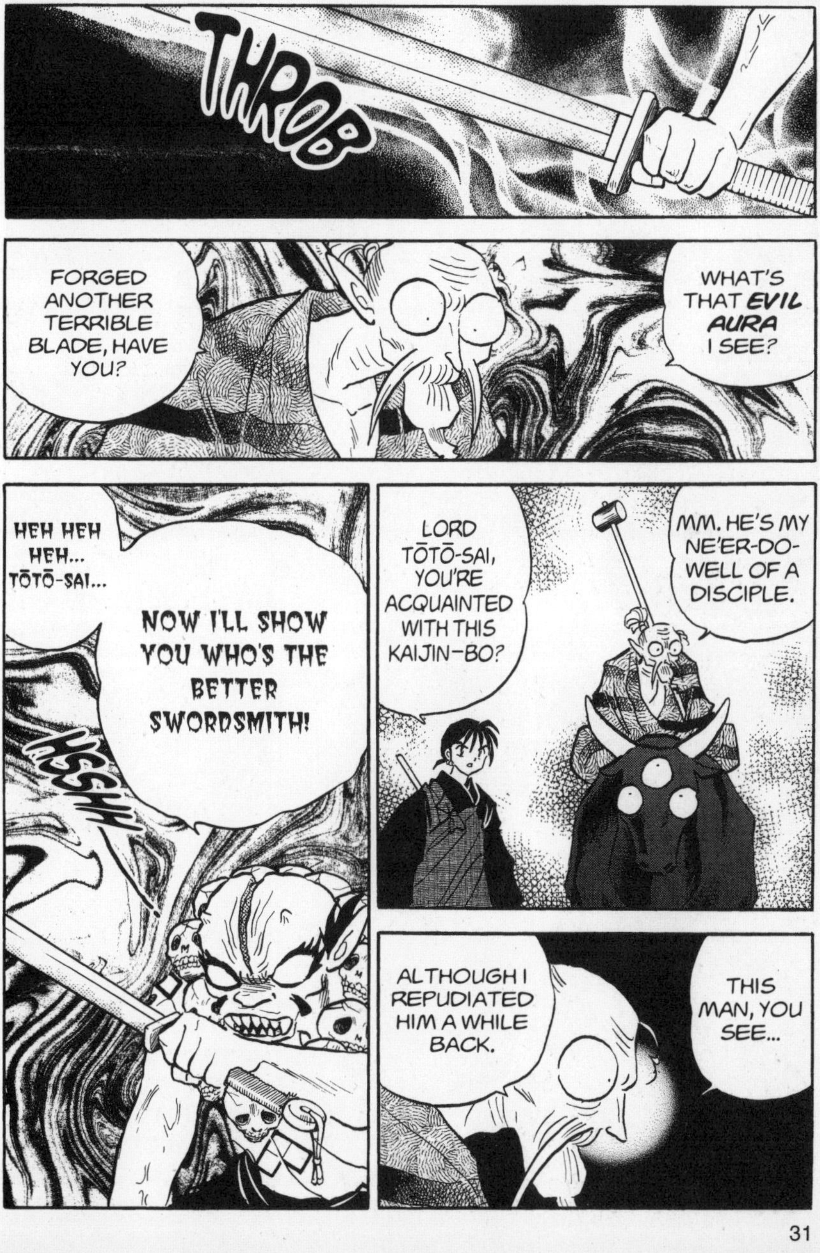
THROB
FORGED ANOTHER TERRIBLE BLADE, HAVE YOU?
WHAT'S THAT EVIL AURA I SEE?
HEH HEH HEH... TŌTŌ-SAI...
NOW I'LL SHOW YOU WHO'S THE BETTER SWORDSMITH!
HSSHH
LORD TŌTŌ-SAI, YOU'RE ACQUAINTED WITH THIS KAIJIN-BO?
MM. HE'S MY NE'ER-DO-WELL OF A DISCIPLE.
ALTHOUGH I REPUDIATED HIM A WHILE BACK.
THIS MAN, YOU SEE...

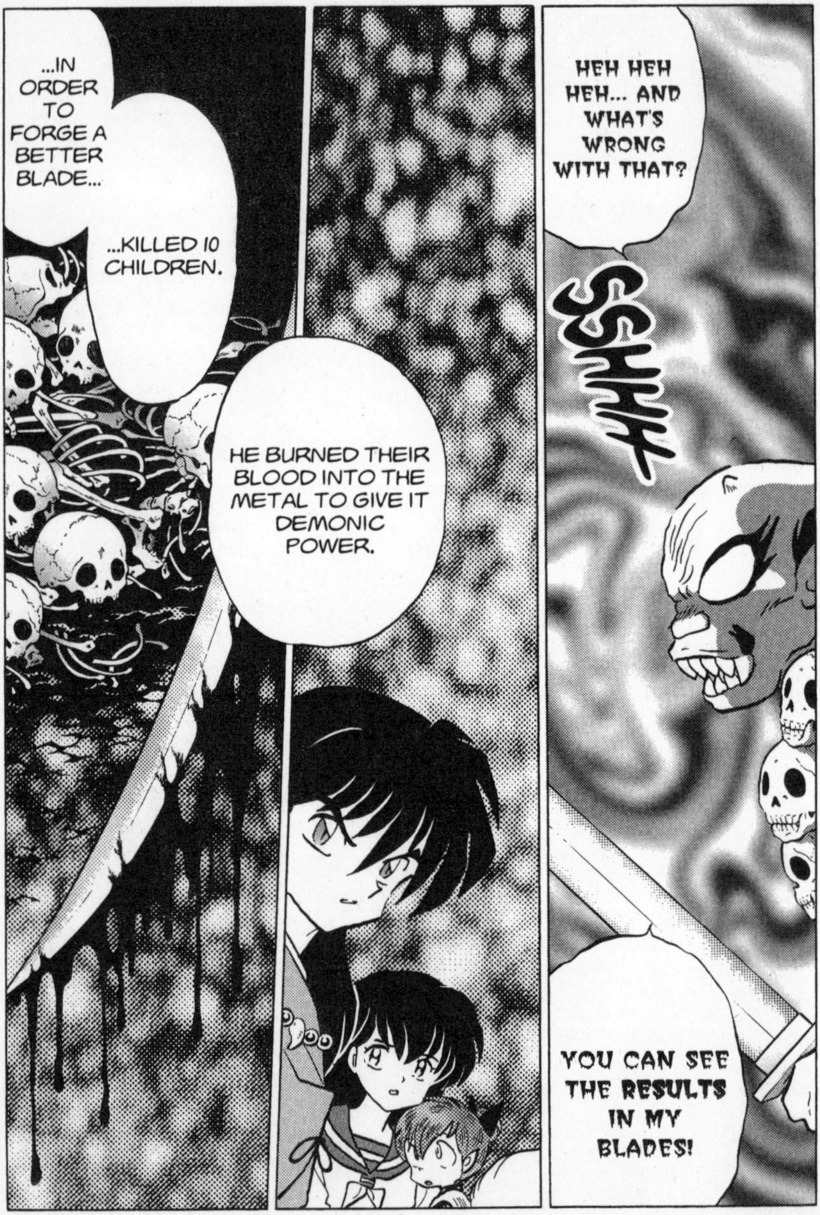
...IN ORDER TO FORGE A BETTER BLADE...
...KILLED 10 CHILDREN.
HE BURNED THEIR BLOOD INTO THE METAL TO GIVE IT DEMONIC POWER.
HEH HEH HEH... AND WHAT'S WRONG WITH THAT?
SSHHH
YOU CAN SEE THE RESULTS IN MY BLADES!

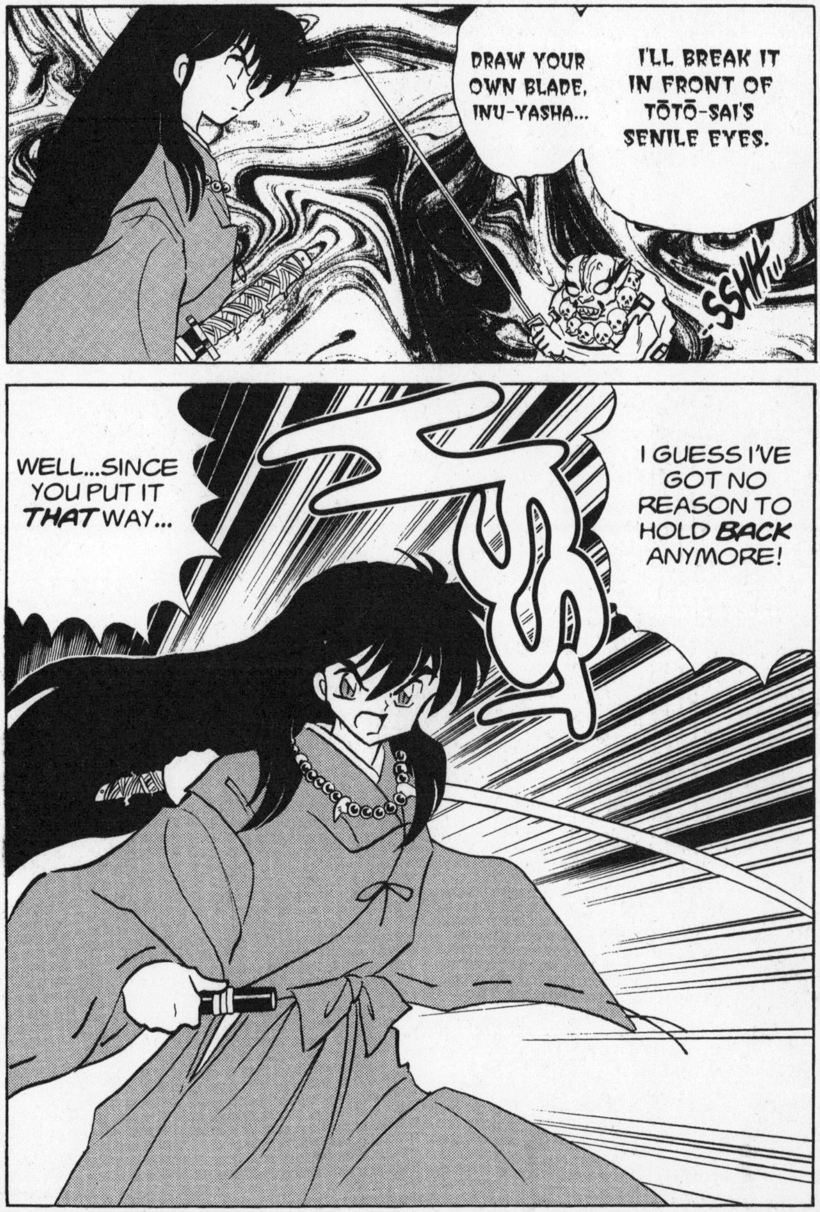
DRAW YOUR OWN BLADE, INU-YASHA...
I'LL BREAK IT IN FRONT OF TŌTŌ-SAI'S SENILE EYES.
SSHH...
WELL...SINCE YOU PUT IT *THAT* WAY...
I GUESS I'VE GOT NO REASON TO HOLD *BACK* ANYMORE!

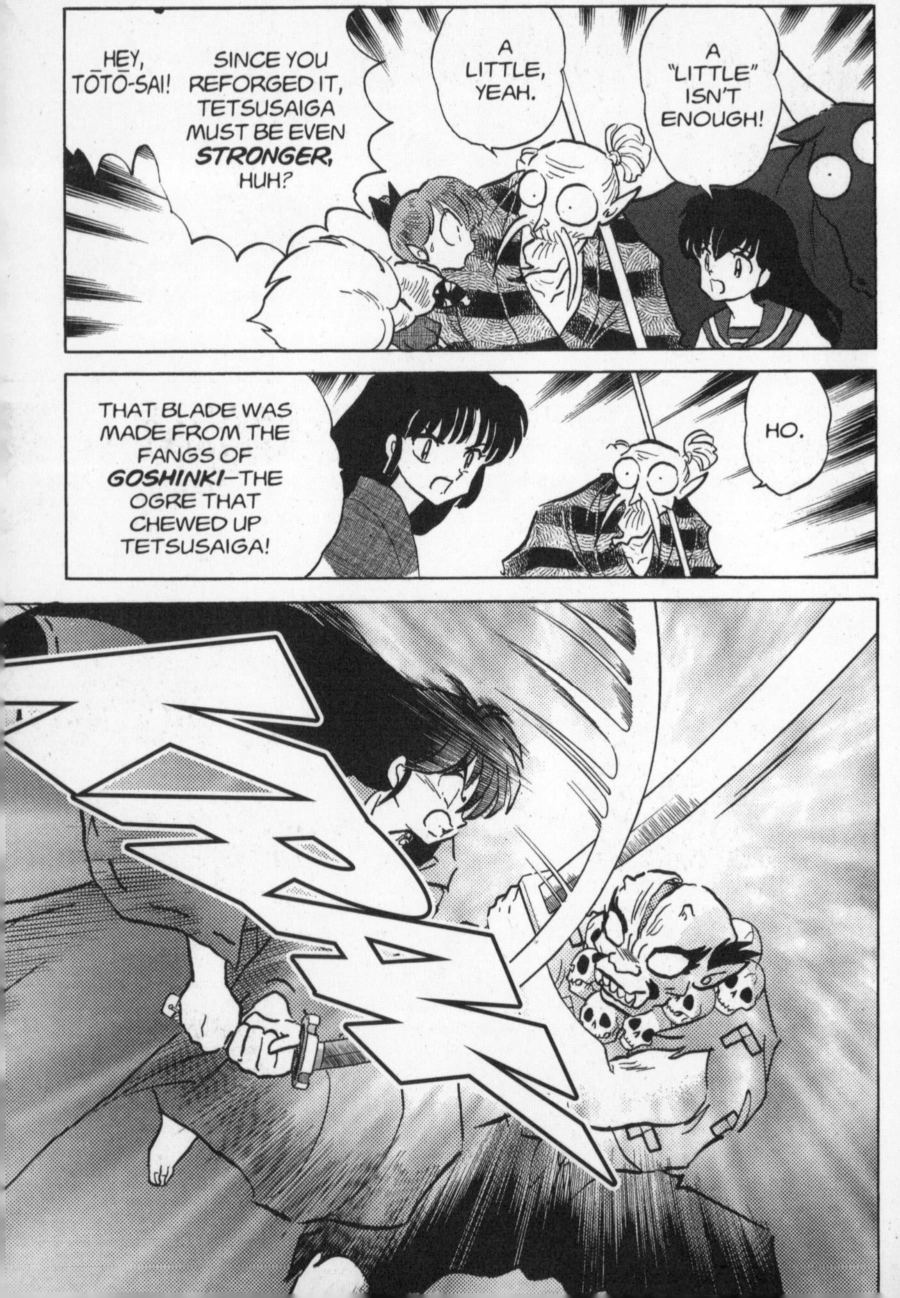
HEY, TŌTŌ-SAI!
SINCE YOU REFORGED IT, TETSUSAIGA MUST BE EVEN STRONGER, HUH?
A LITTLE, YEAH.
A "LITTLE" ISN'T ENOUGH!
THAT BLADE WAS MADE FROM THE FANGS OF GOSHINKI—THE OGRE THAT CHEWED UP TETSUSAIGA!
HO.

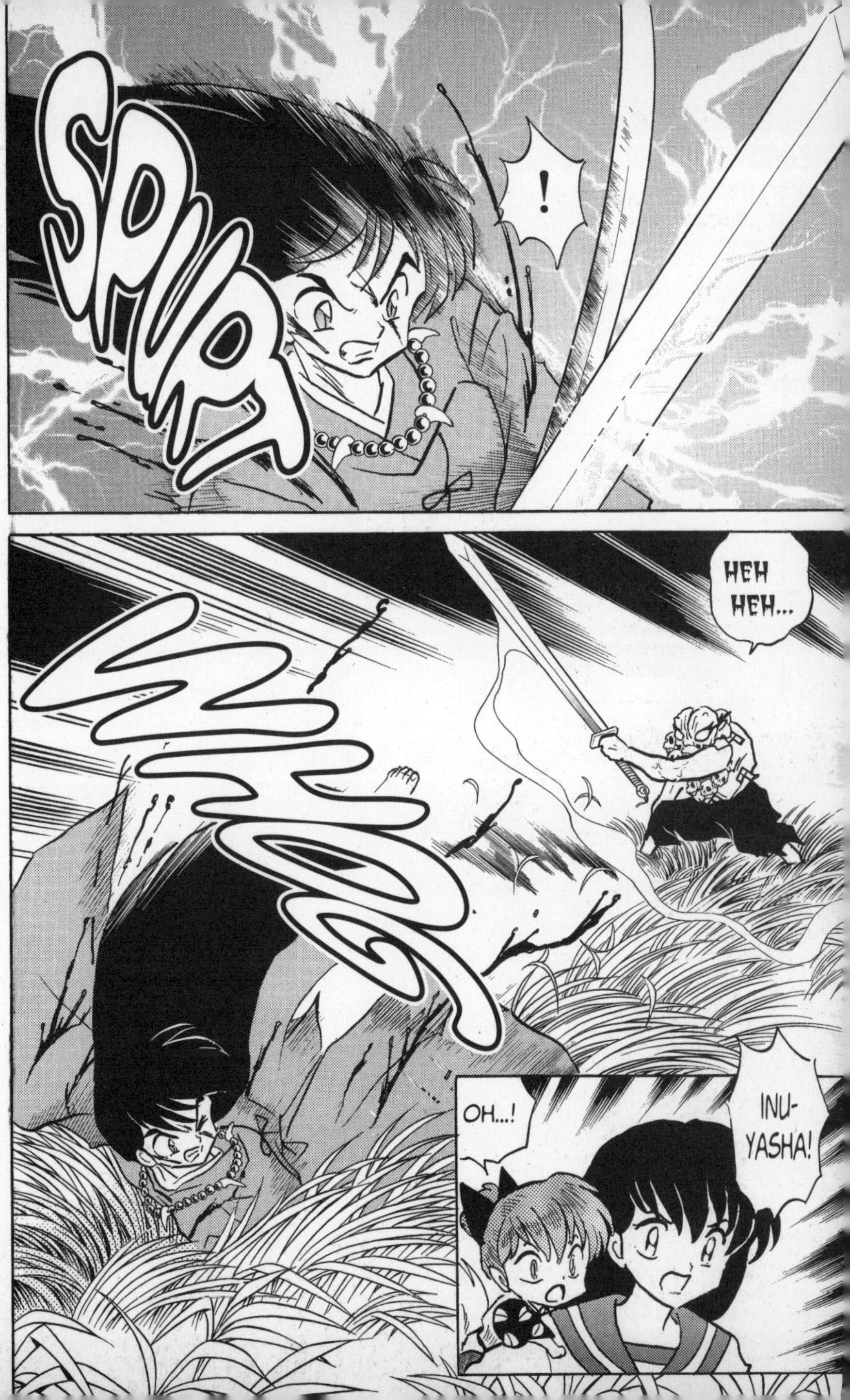
SPLORT
!
HEH HEH...
OH...!
INU-YASHA!

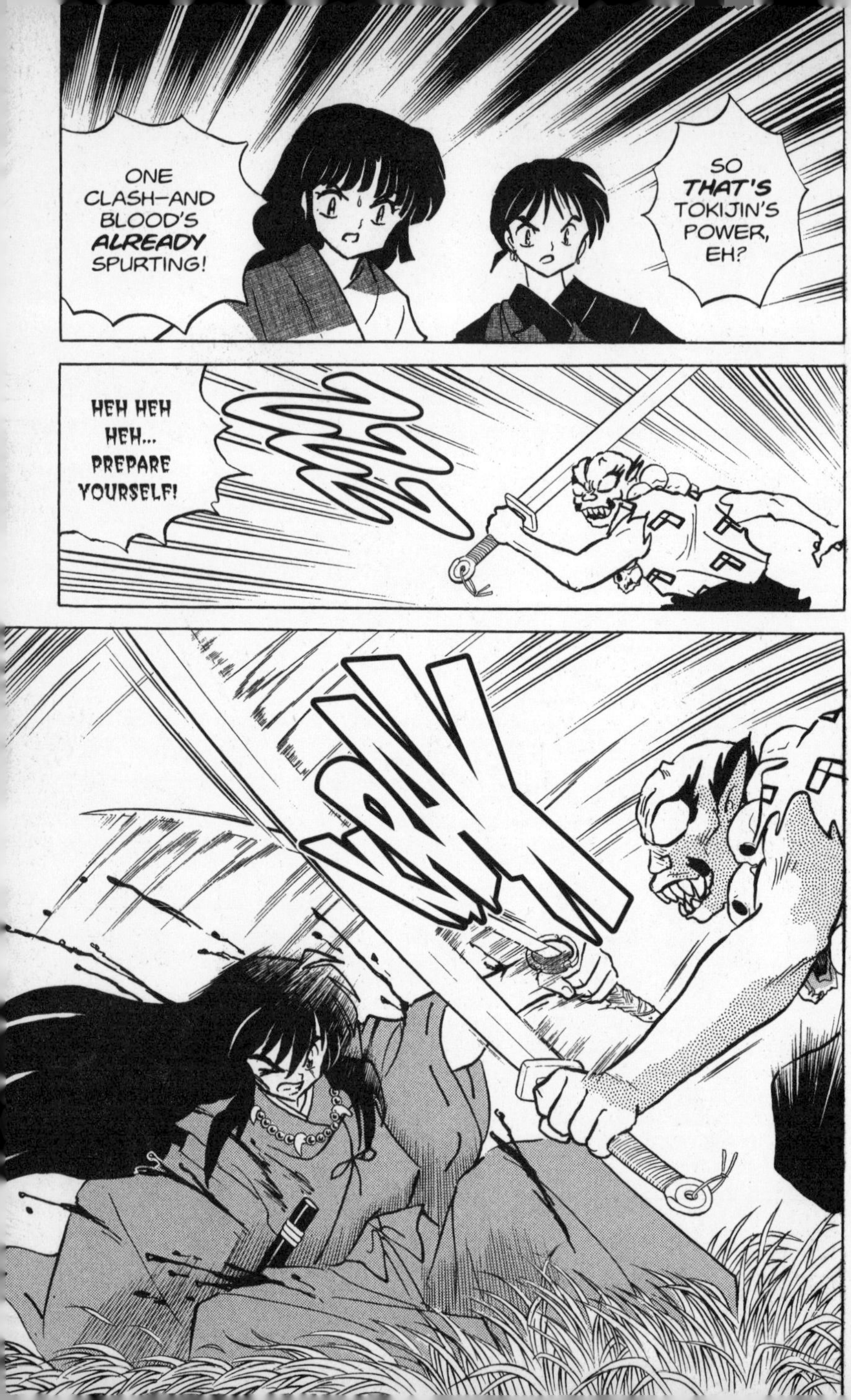
ONE CLASH—AND BLOOD'S ALREADY SPURTING!
SO THAT'S TOKIJIN'S POWER, EH?
HEH HEH HEH... PREPARE YOURSELF!

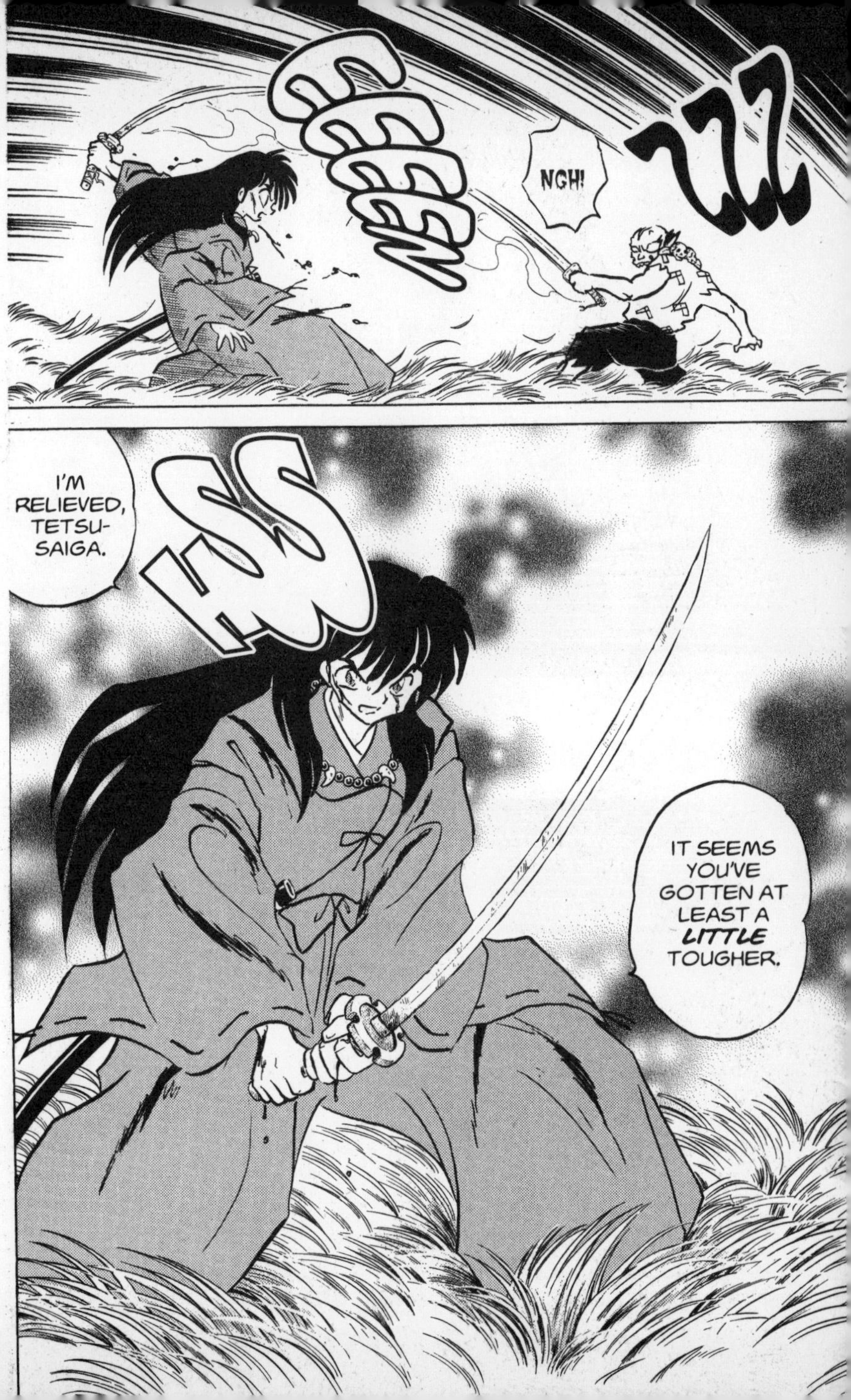
NGH!
ZZZ
I'M RELIEVED, TETSU-SAIGA.
IT SEEMS YOU'VE GOTTEN AT LEAST A *LITTLE* TOUGHER.

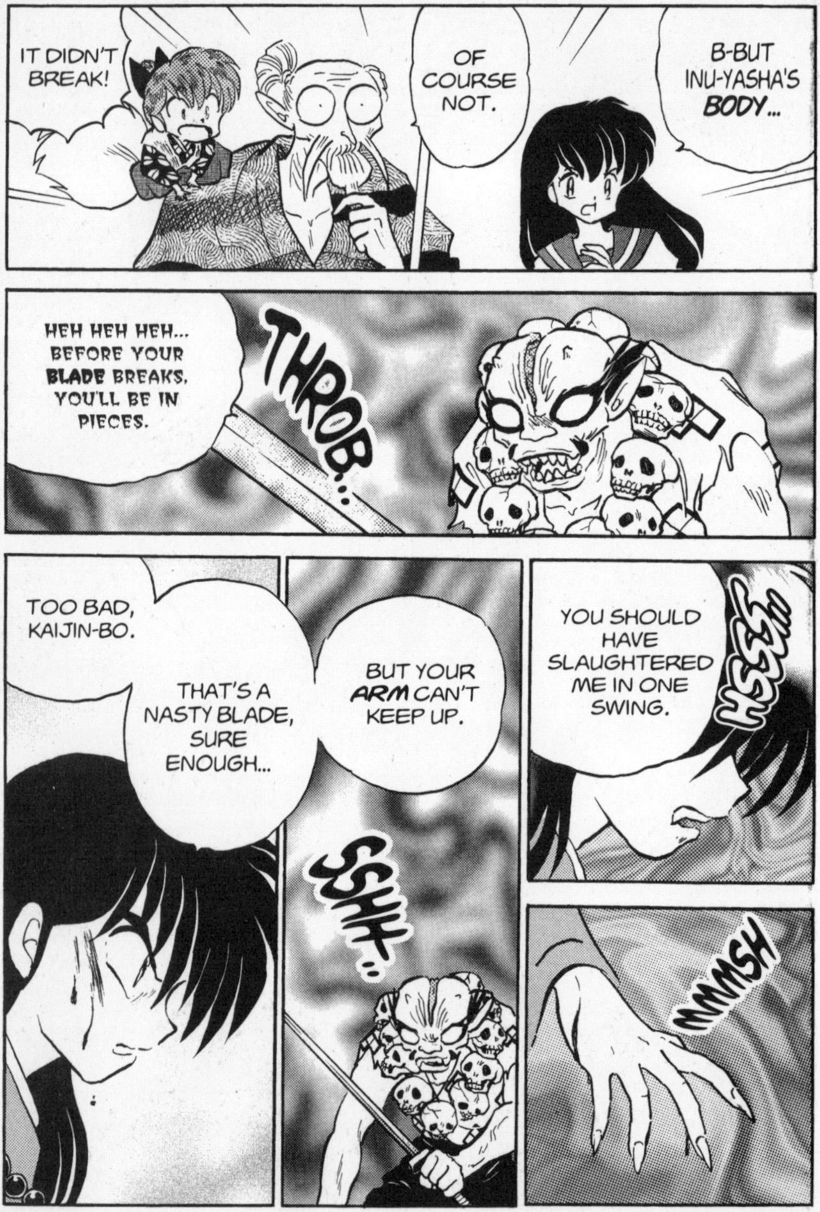
IT DIDN'T BREAK!
OF COURSE NOT.
B-BUT INU-YASHA'S BODY...
HEH HEH HEH... BEFORE YOUR BLADE BREAKS, YOU'LL BE IN PIECES.
THROB...
TOO BAD, KAIJIN-BO.
THAT'S A NASTY BLADE, SURE ENOUGH...
BUT YOUR ARM CAN'T KEEP UP.
SSHH...
YOU SHOULD HAVE SLAUGHTERED ME IN ONE SWING.
HSSSS...
MMMSH

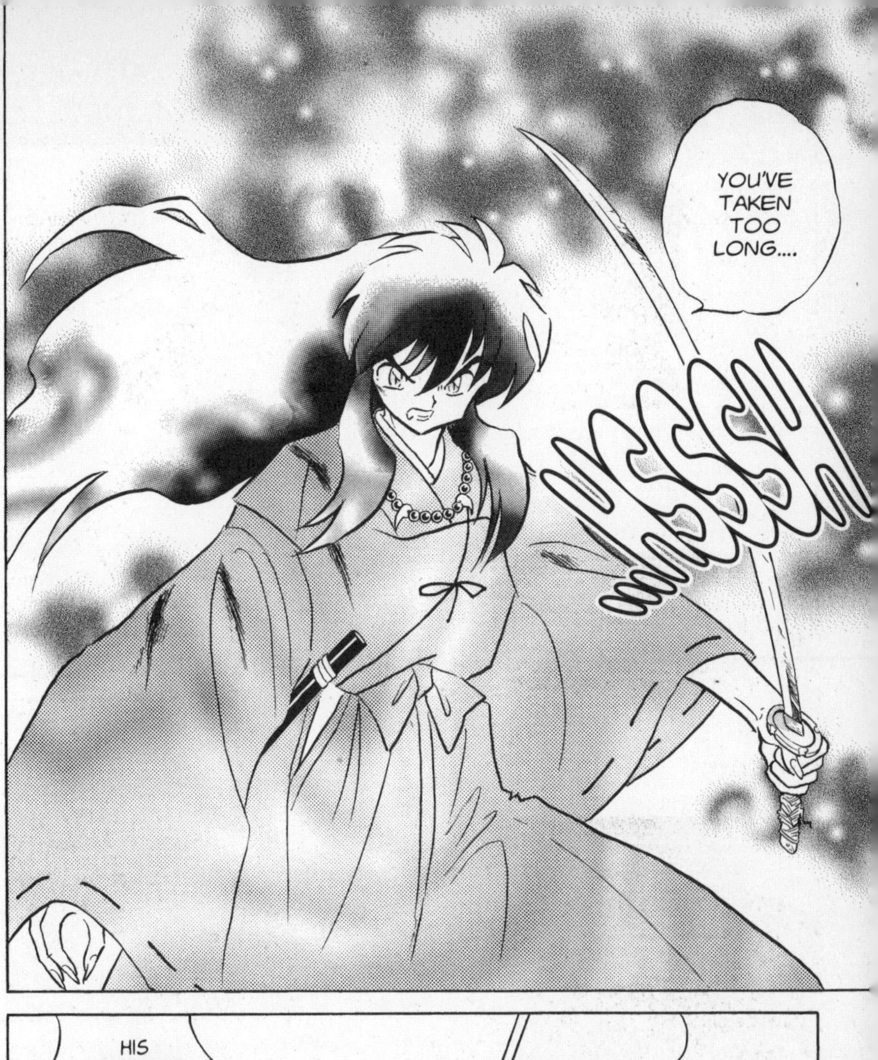
YOU'VE TAKEN TOO LONG....
WHSSSH!

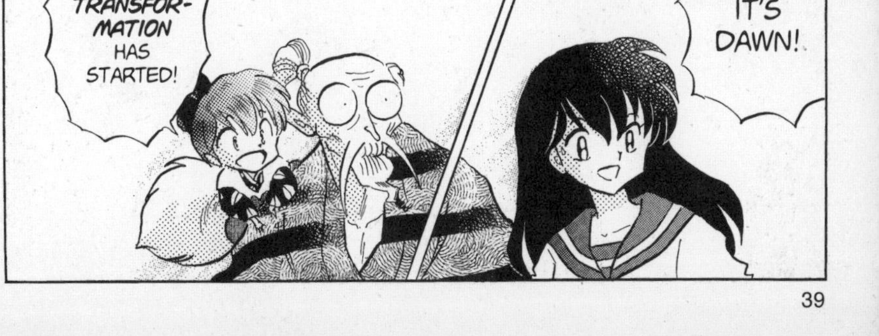
HIS *TRANSFORMATION* HAS STARTED!
IT'S DAWN!

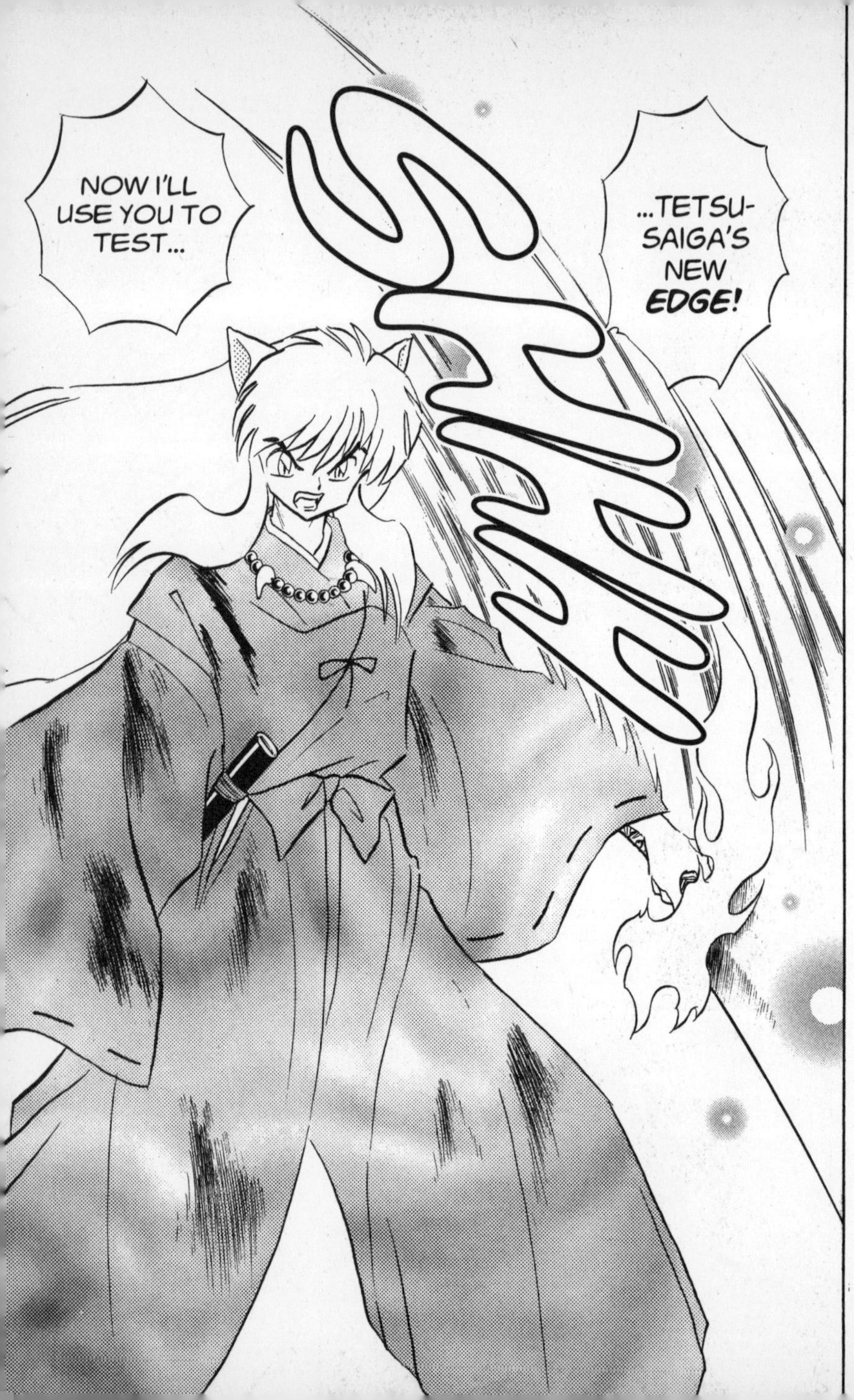
NOW I'LL USE YOU TO TEST...
...TETSU-SAIGA'S NEW EDGE!

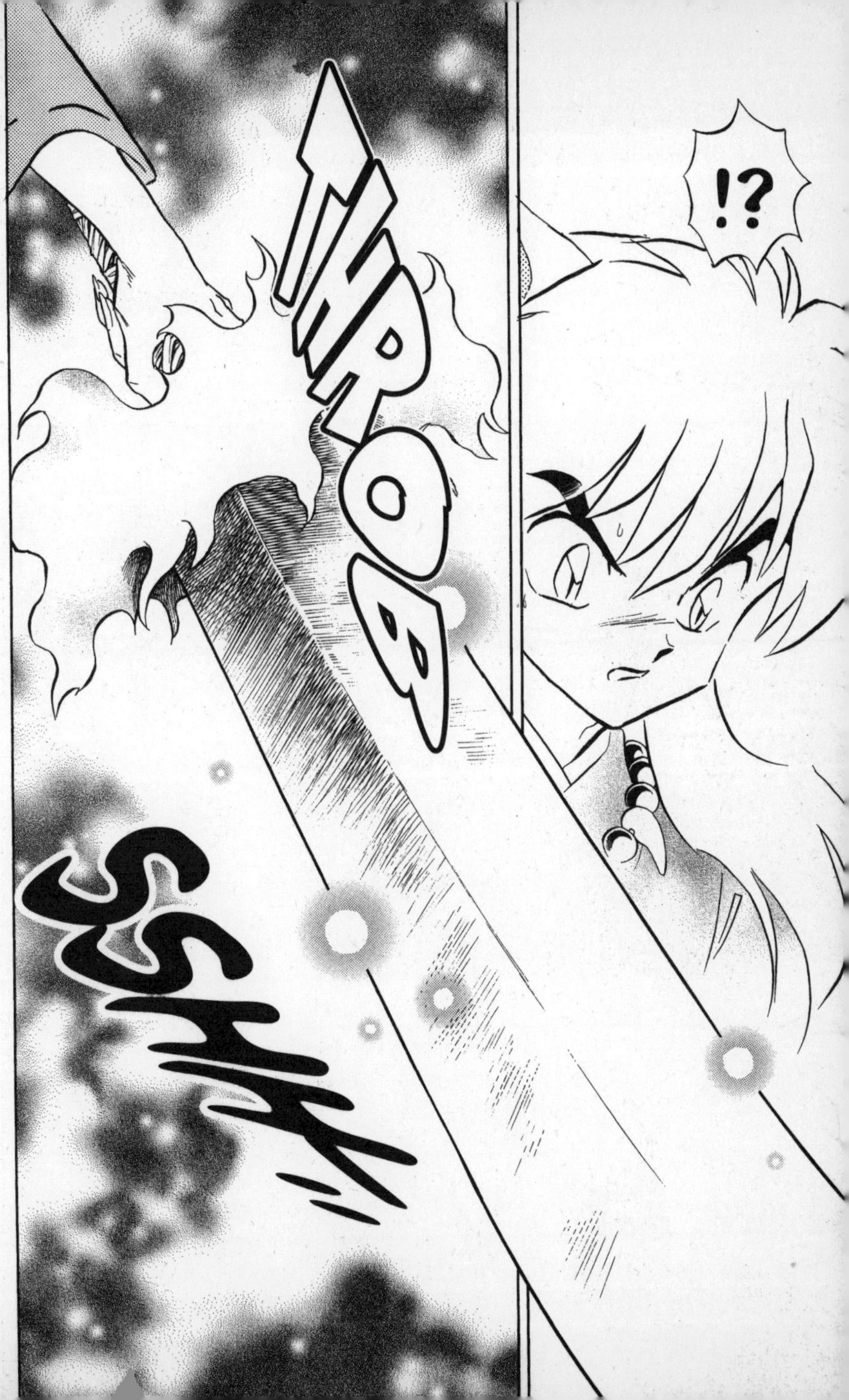
THROB
!?
SSHH!!

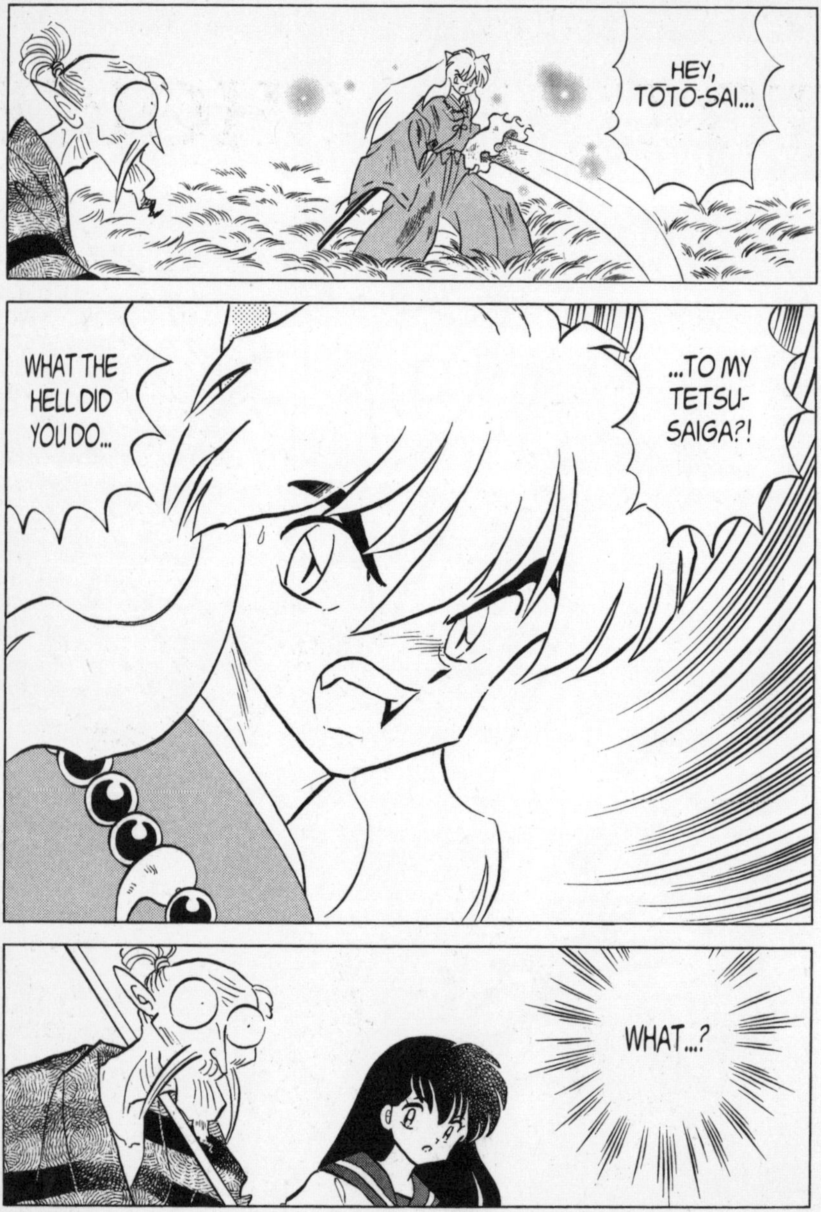
HEY, TŌTŌ-SAI...
WHAT THE HELL DID YOU DO...
...TO MY TETSU-SAIGA?!
WHAT...?

SCROLL THREE

TOKIJIN'S CHOICE

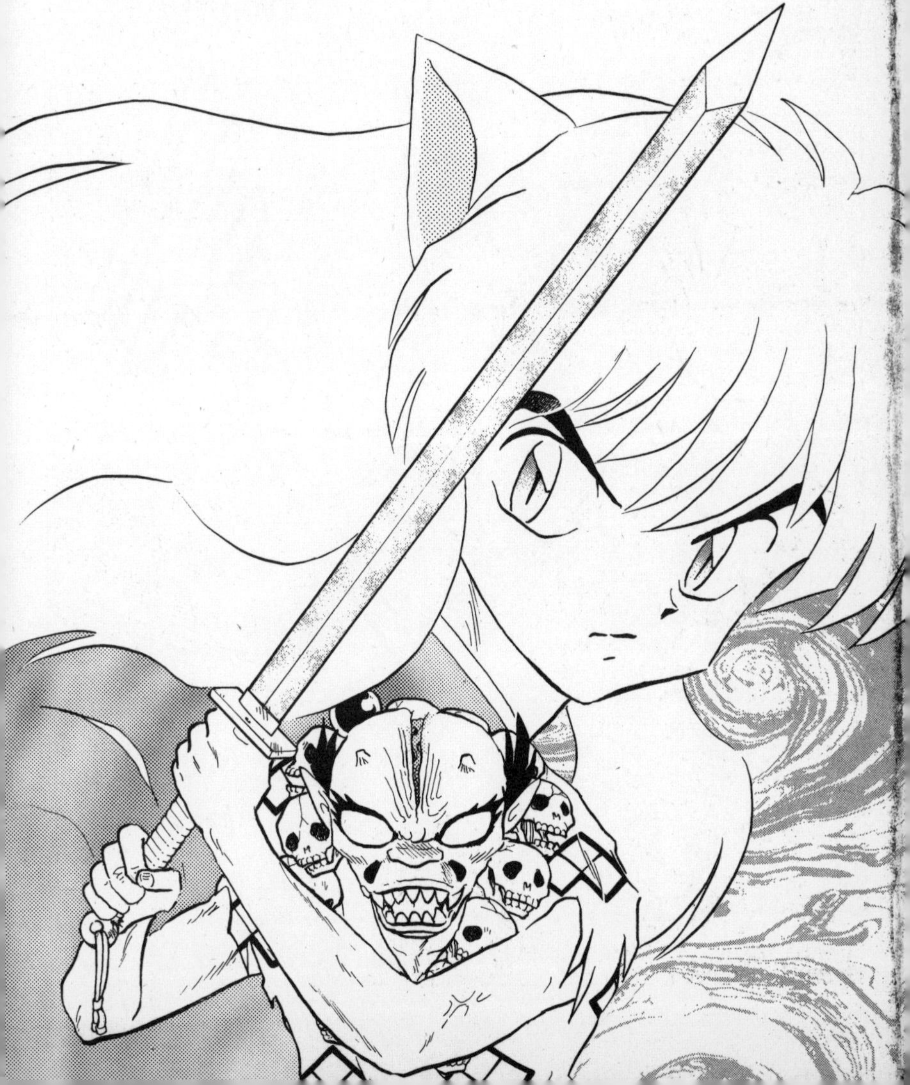

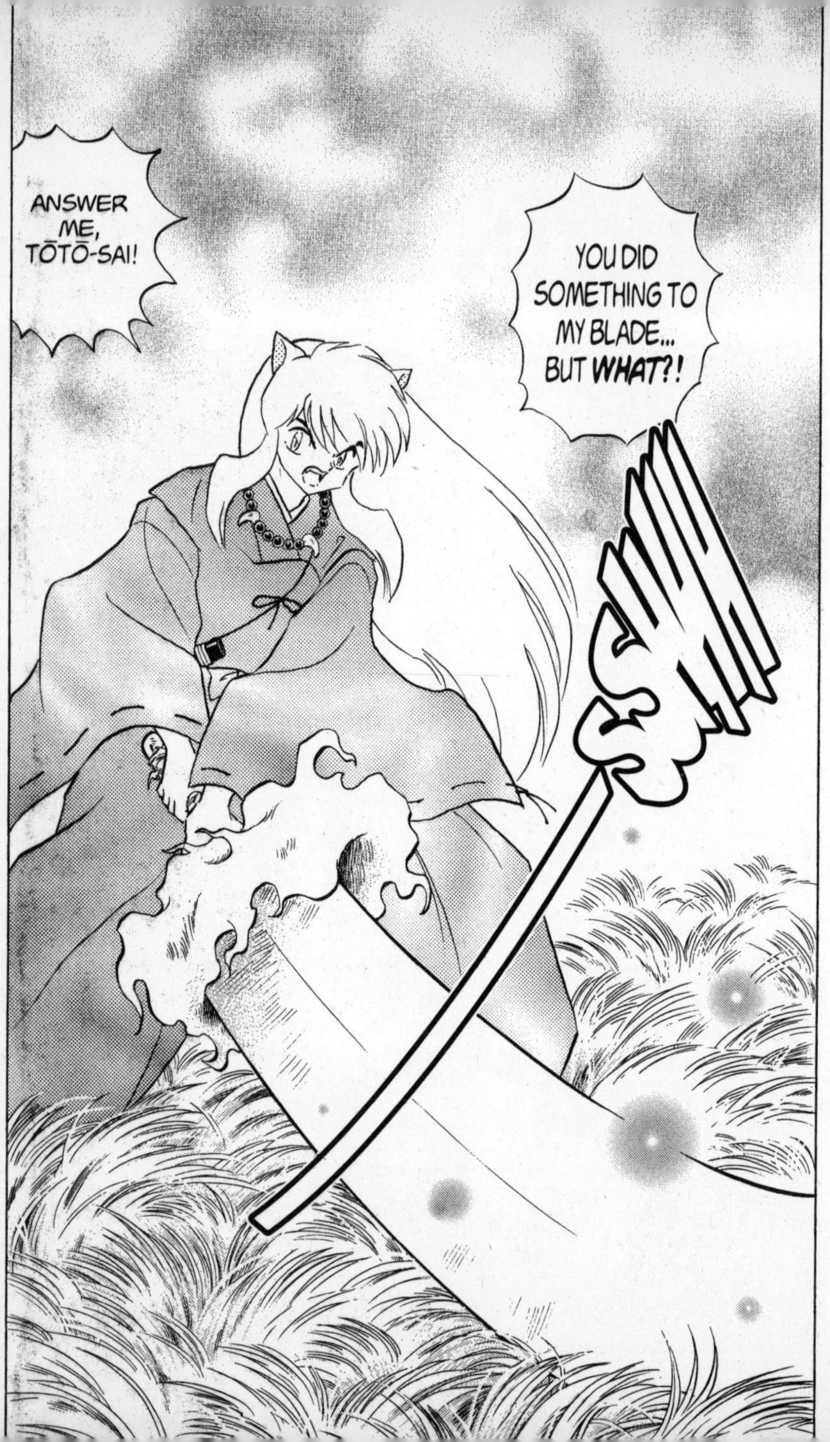
ANSWER ME, TŌTŌ-SAI!
YOU DID SOMETHING TO MY BLADE... BUT **WHAT?!**
SCHWAAA

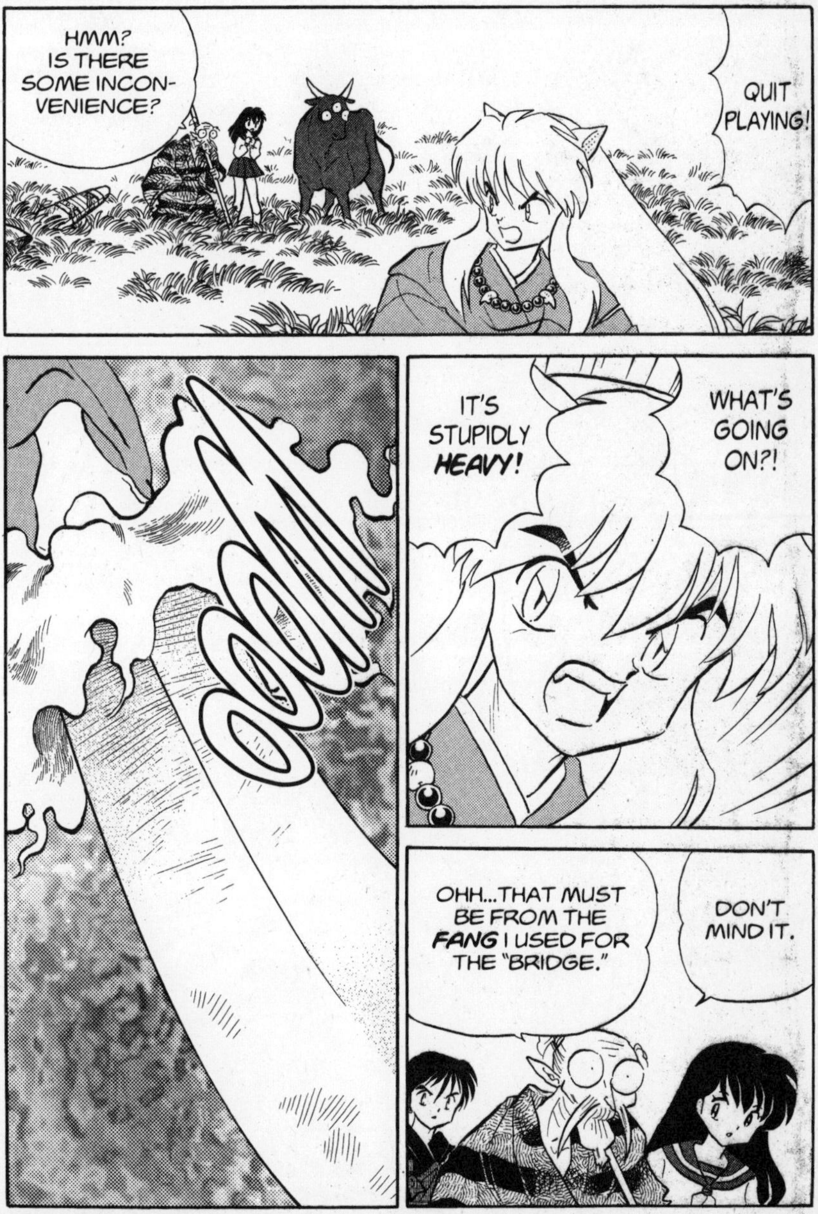
HMM? IS THERE SOME INCON- VENIENCE?
QUIT PLAYING!
IT'S STUPIDLY **HEAVY!**
WHAT'S GOING ON?!
OHH...THAT MUST BE FROM THE **FANG** I USED FOR THE "BRIDGE."
DON'T MIND IT.

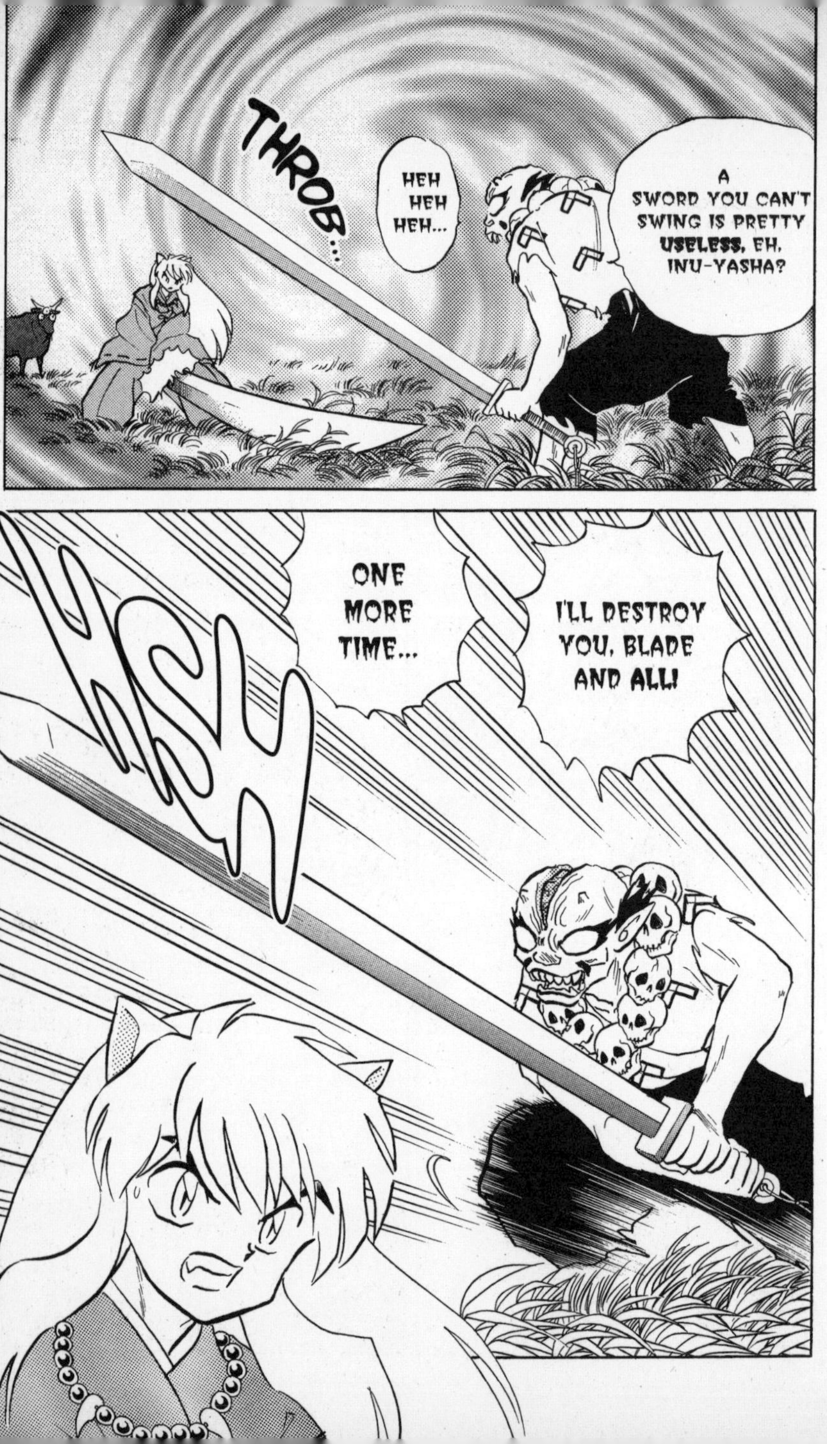

THROB...
HEH HEH HEH...
A SWORD YOU CAN'T SWING IS PRETTY USELESS, EH, INU-YASHA?
ONE MORE TIME...
I'LL DESTROY YOU, BLADE AND ALL!

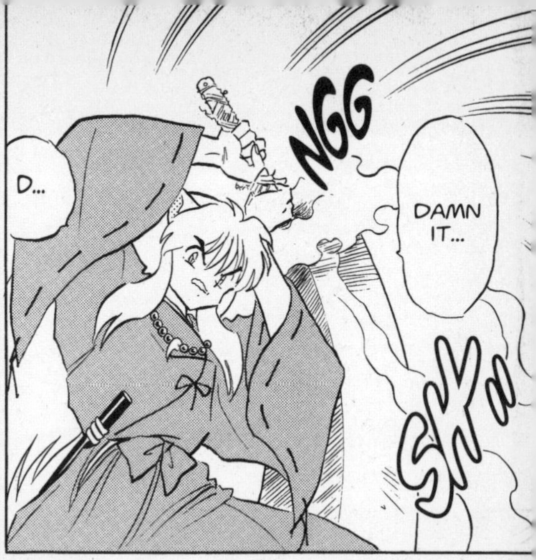
NGG
D...
DAMN IT...
SHK
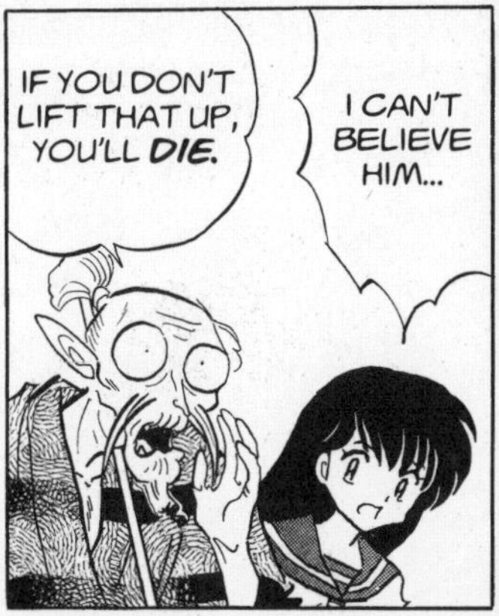
I CAN'T BELIEVE HIM...
IF YOU DON'T LIFT THAT UP, YOU'LL **DIE.**
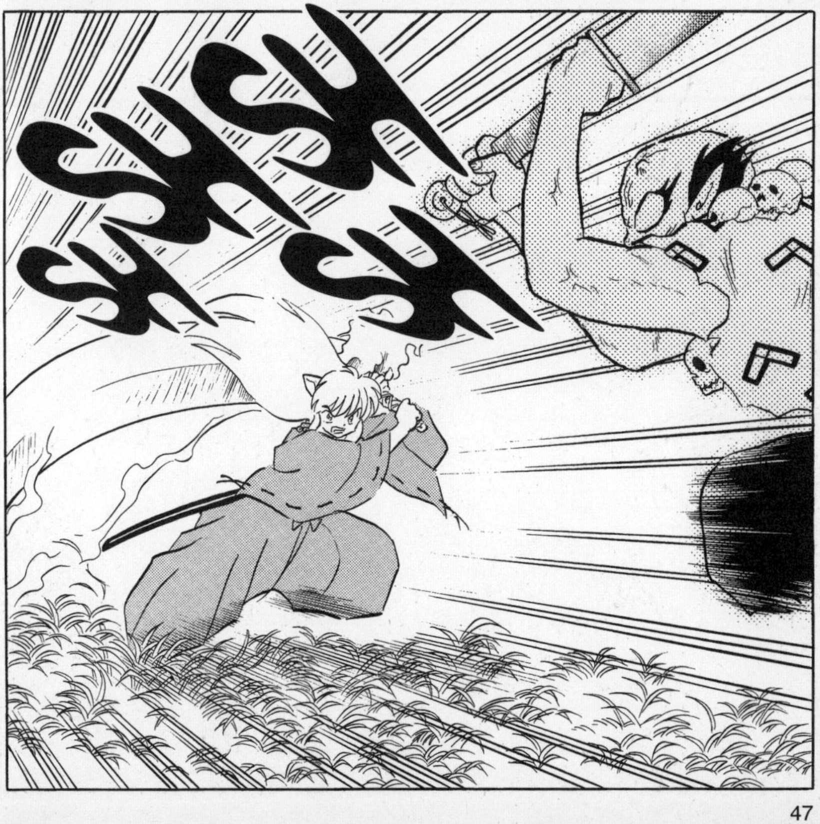
SHSH
SHSH

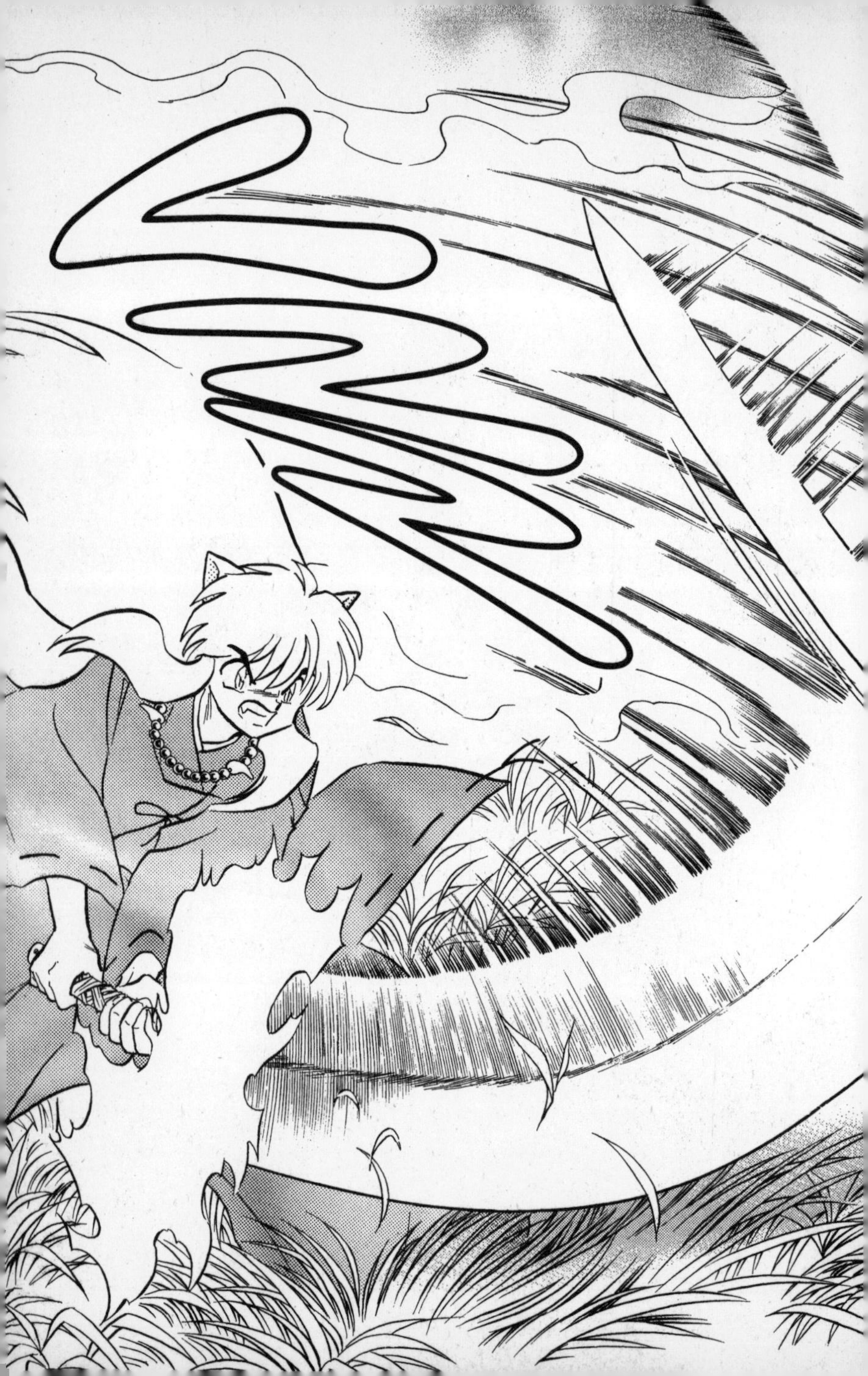

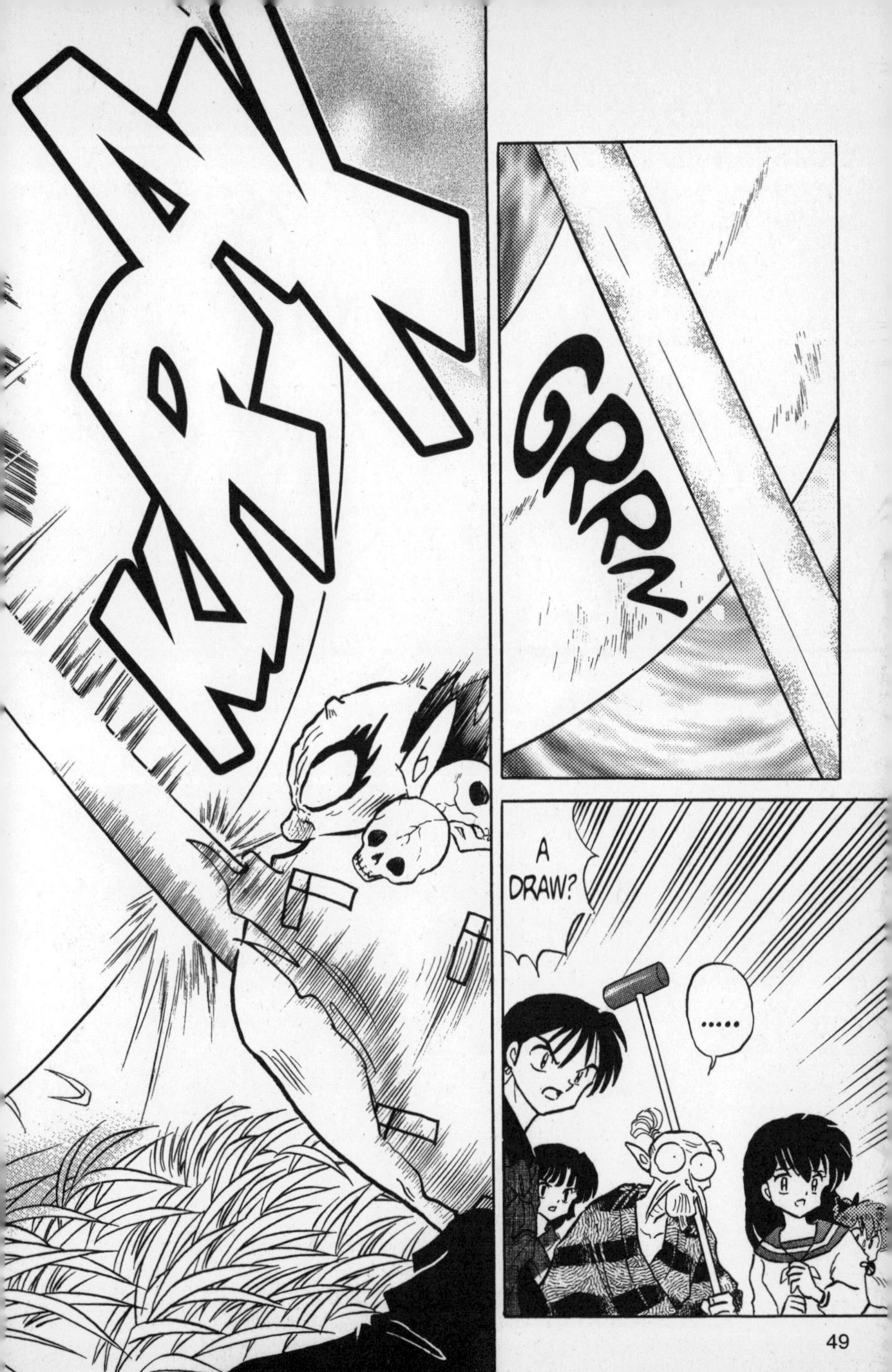
GRRN
A DRAW?
......

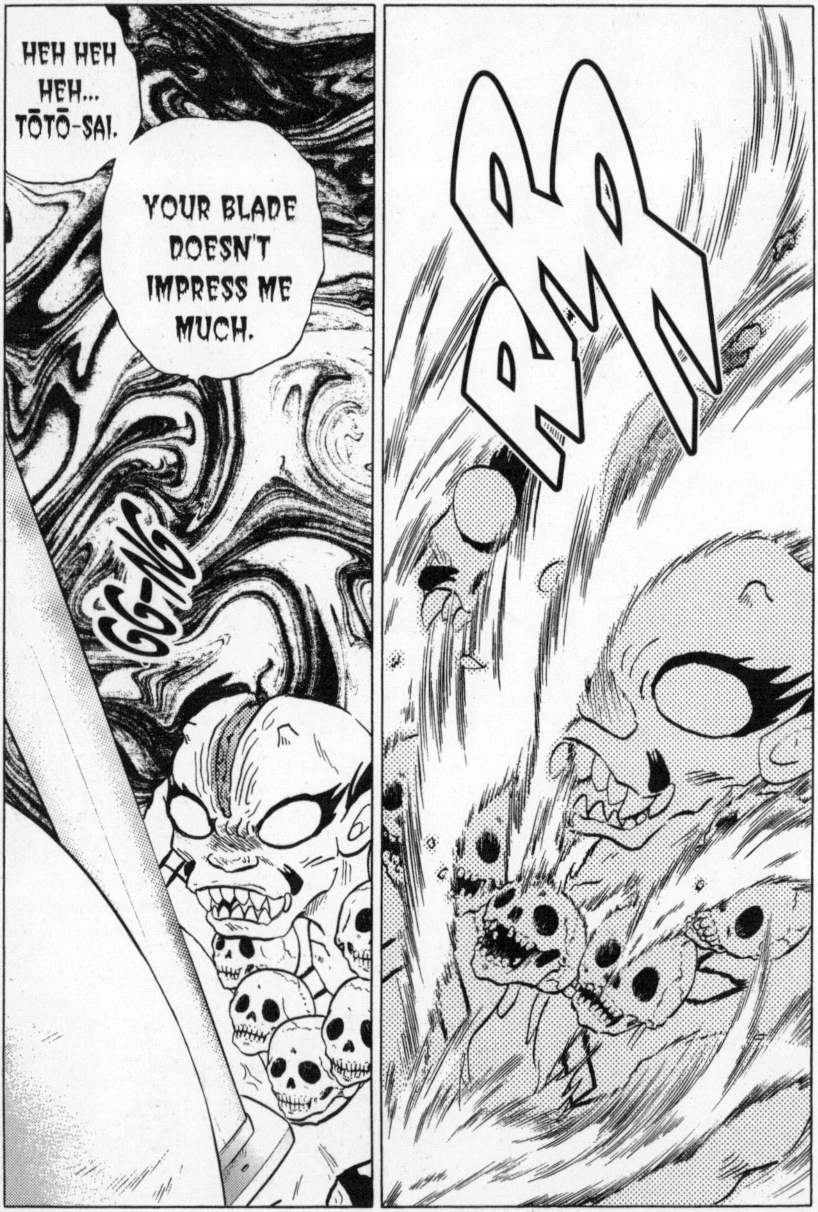
HEH HEH HEH... TŌTŌ-SAI.
YOUR BLADE DOESN'T IMPRESS ME MUCH.
GG-NG
RIP

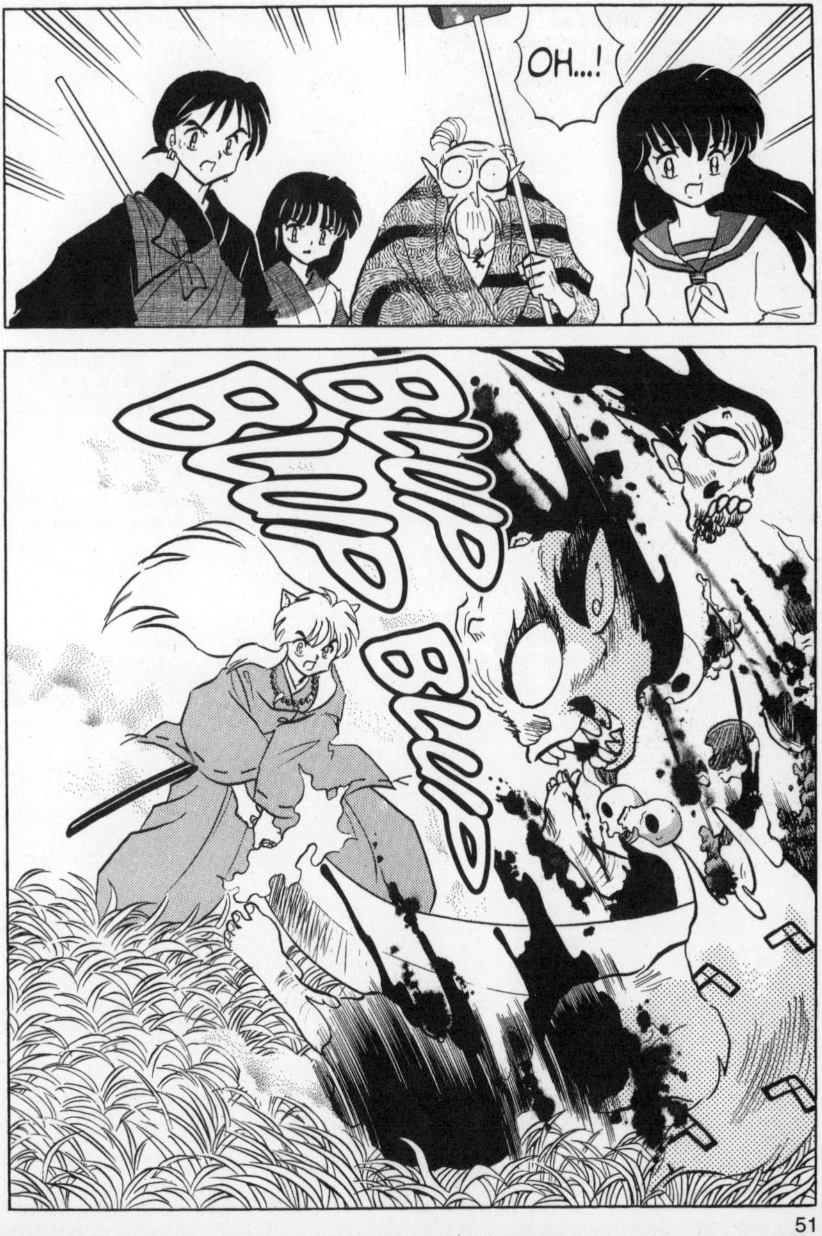
OH...!
BLUP
BLUP
BLUP

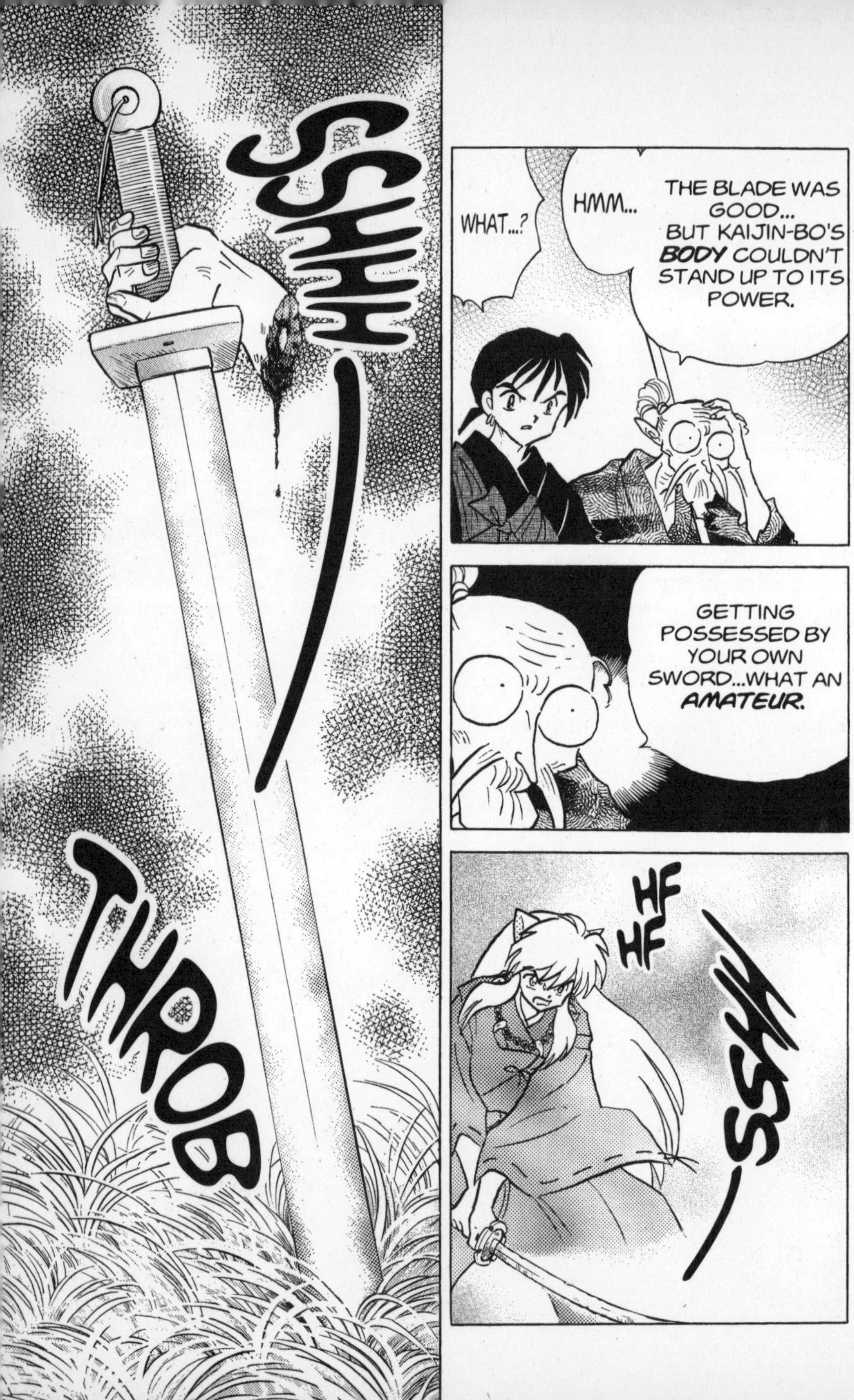
SSHHH
THROB
WHAT...?
HMM...
THE BLADE WAS GOOD... BUT KAIJIN-BO'S **BODY** COULDN'T STAND UP TO ITS POWER.
GETTING POSSESSED BY YOUR OWN SWORD...WHAT AN ***AMATEUR.***
HF HF
SSHH

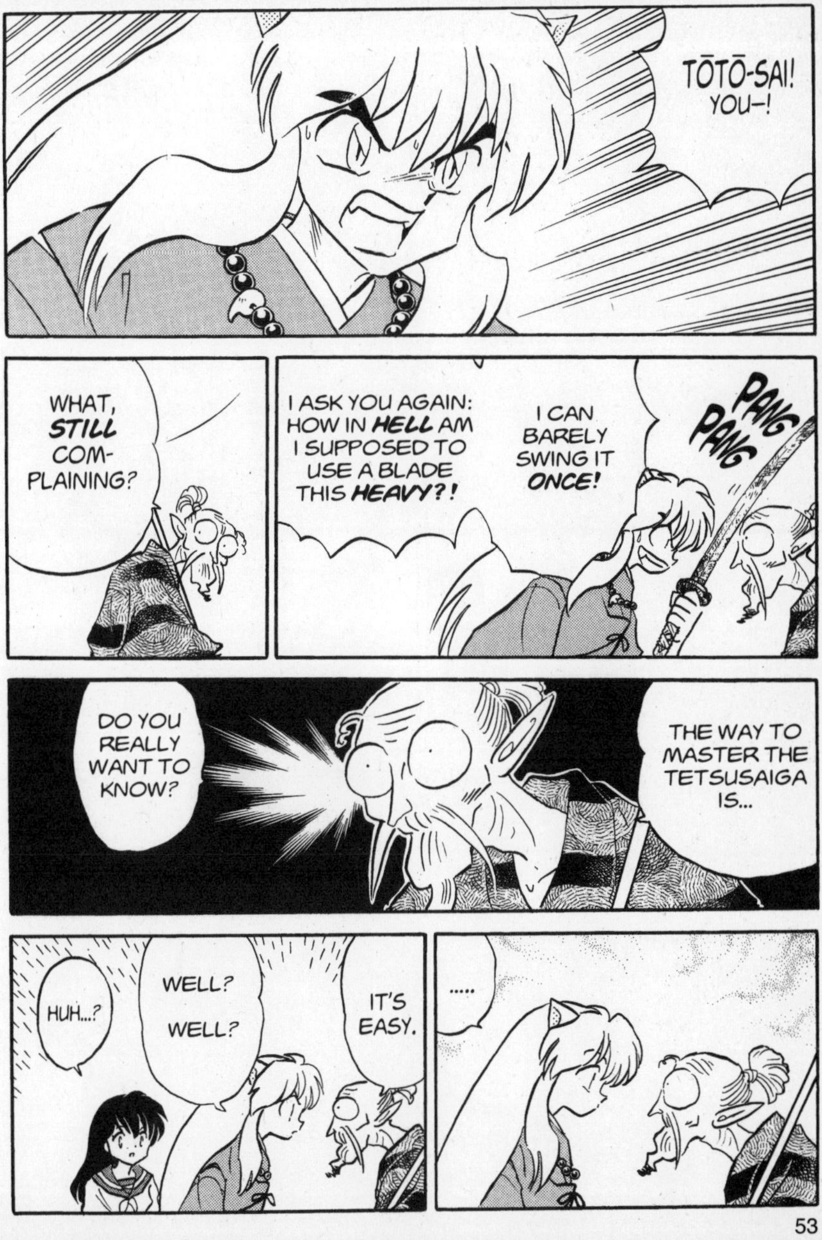
TŌTŌ-SAI! YOU–!
WHAT, STILL COM-PLAINING?
I ASK YOU AGAIN: HOW IN HELL AM I SUPPOSED TO USE A BLADE THIS HEAVY?!
I CAN BARELY SWING IT ONCE!
PANG PANG
DO YOU REALLY WANT TO KNOW?
THE WAY TO MASTER THE TETSUSAIGA IS...
HUH...?
WELL? WELL?
IT'S EASY.
.....

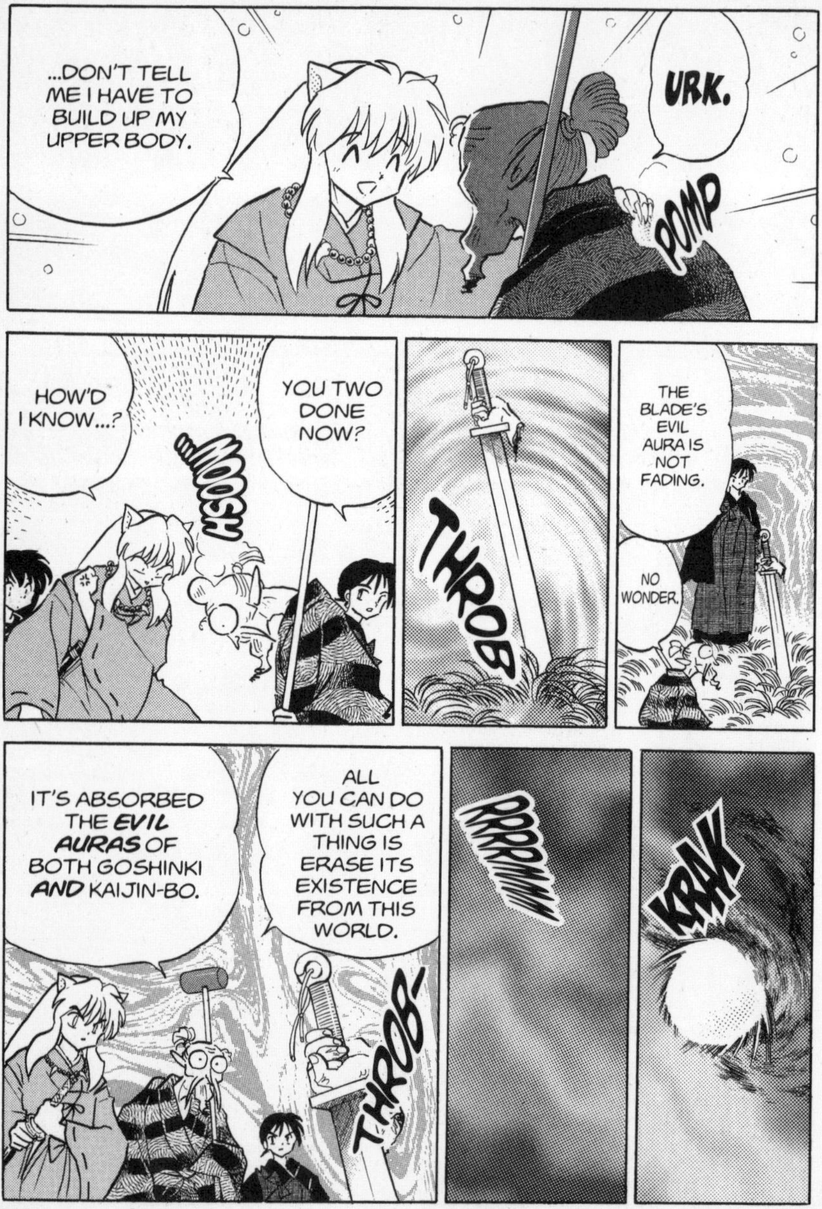
...DON'T TELL ME I HAVE TO BUILD UP MY UPPER BODY.
URK.
POMP
HOW'D I KNOW...?
YOU TWO DONE NOW?
WHOOSH
THROB
THE BLADE'S EVIL AURA IS NOT FADING.
NO WONDER.
IT'S ABSORBED THE ***EVIL AURAS*** OF BOTH GOSHINKI ***AND*** KAIJIN-BO.
ALL YOU CAN DO WITH SUCH A THING IS ERASE ITS EXISTENCE FROM THIS WORLD.
THROB-
RRRRMMMM
KRAK

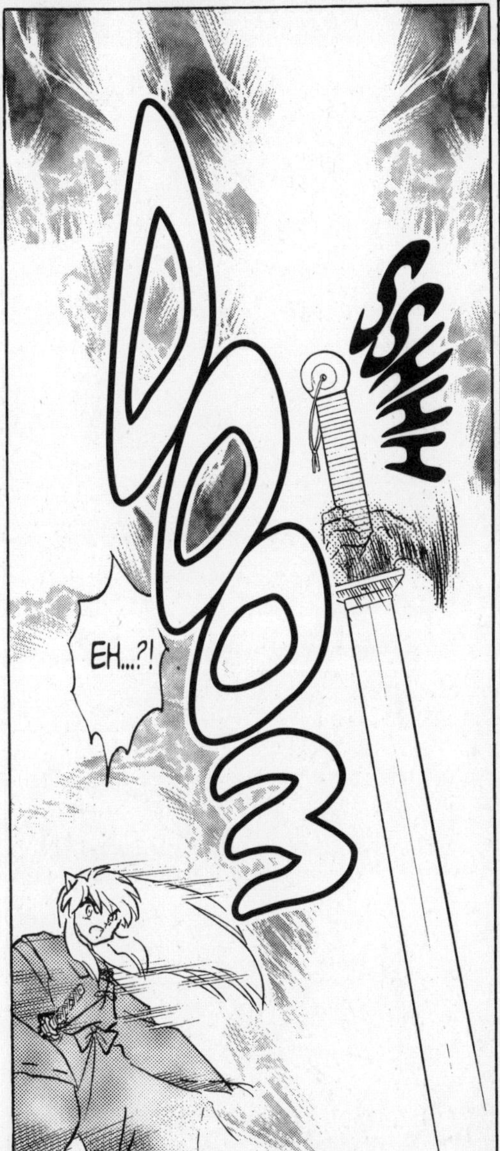
DOOOM
SSHHH
EH...?!
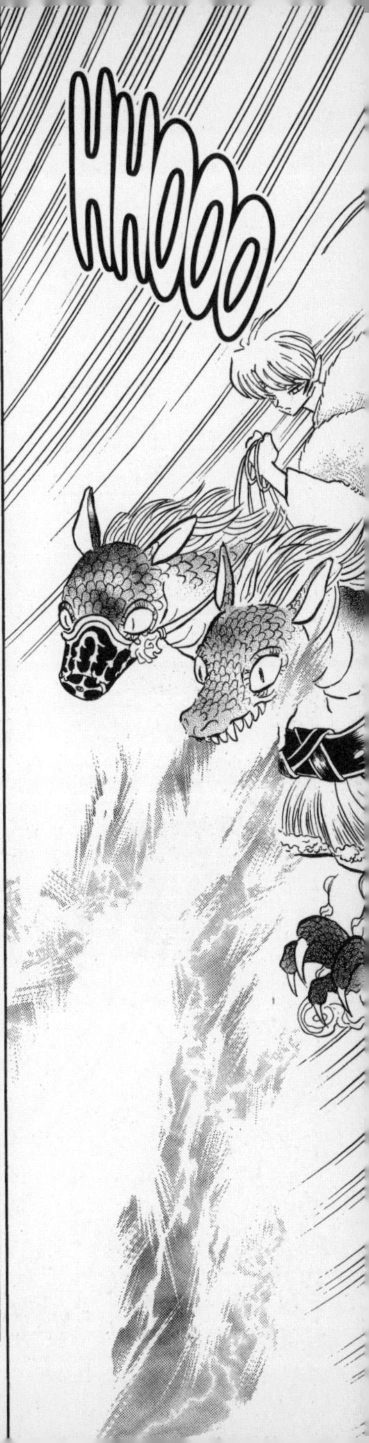
HHOOO

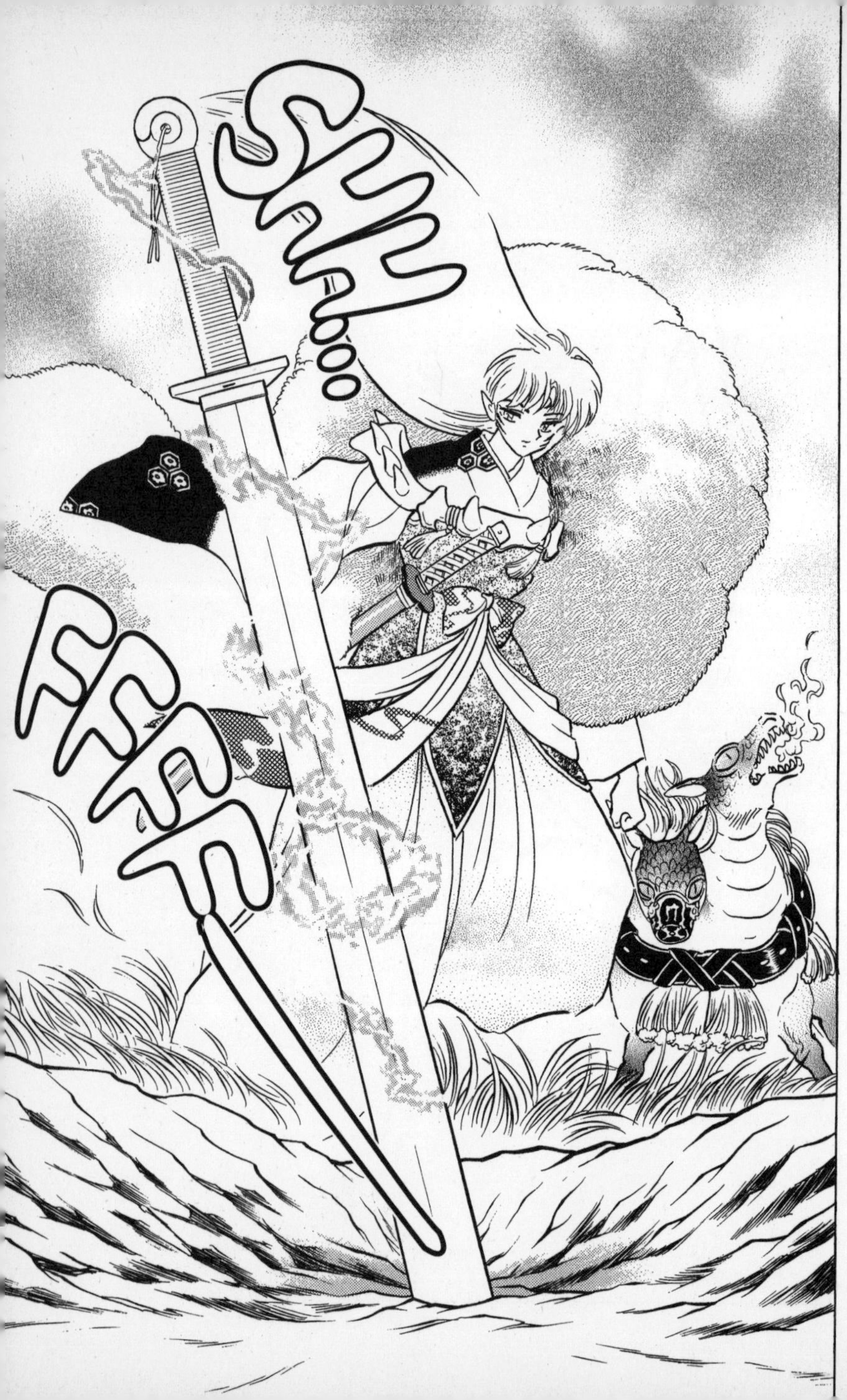
SHHHhooo
EEEEE

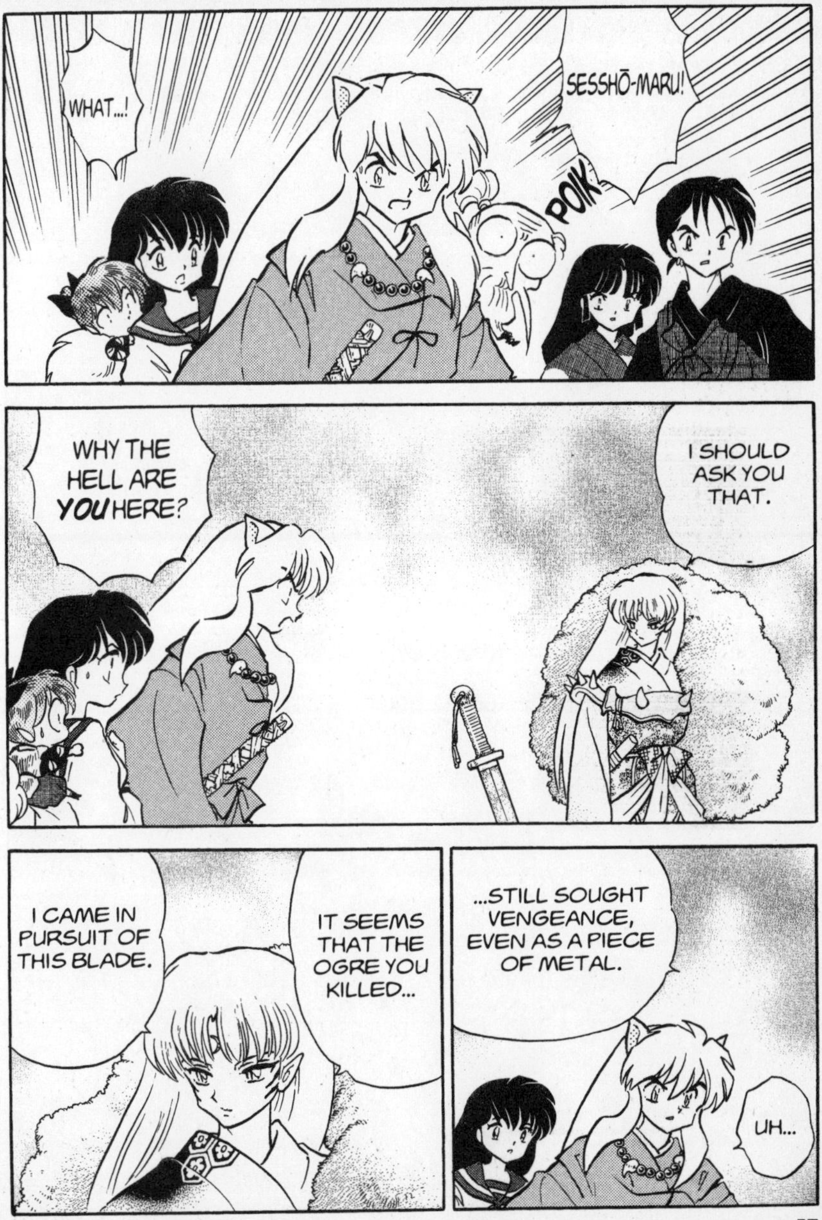
WHAT...!
SESSHŌ-MARU!
POIK
WHY THE HELL ARE YOU HERE?
I SHOULD ASK YOU THAT.
I CAME IN PURSUIT OF THIS BLADE.
IT SEEMS THAT THE OGRE YOU KILLED...
...STILL SOUGHT VENGEANCE, EVEN AS A PIECE OF METAL.
UH...

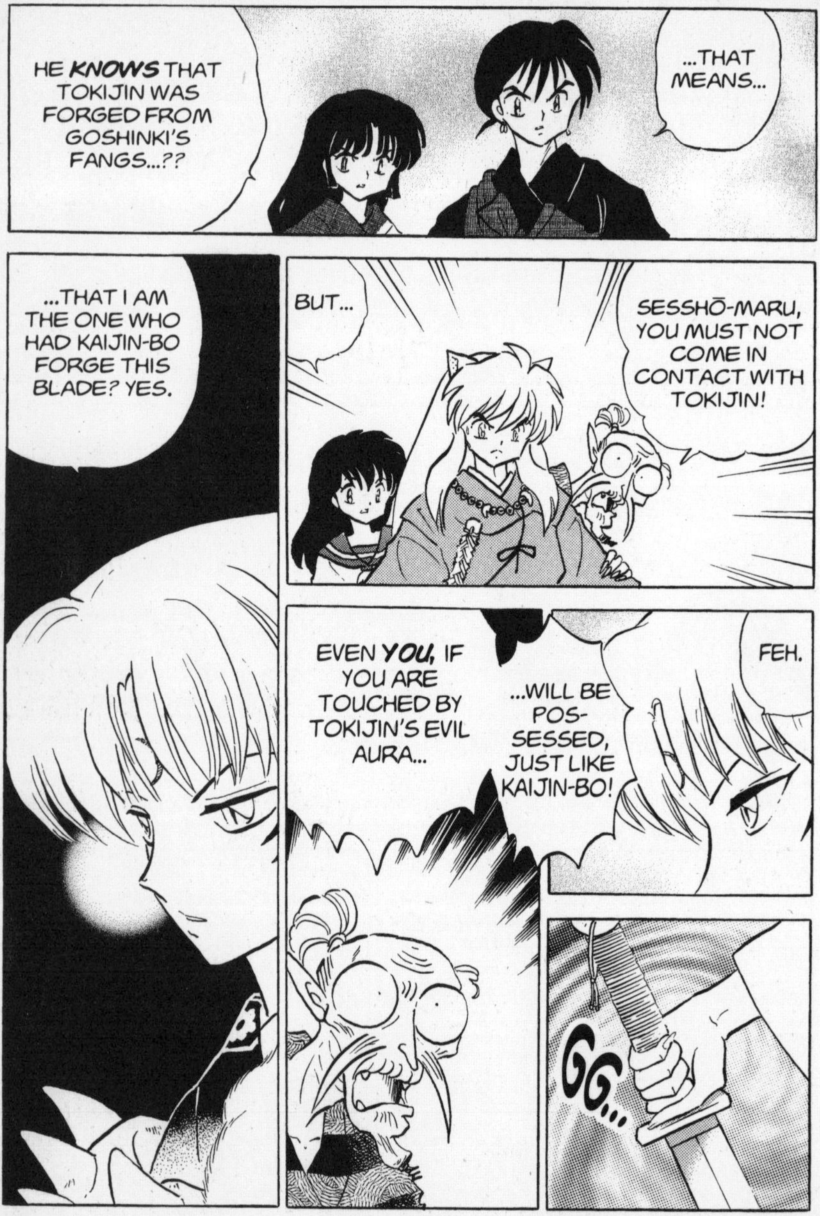
HE KNOWS THAT TOKIJIN WAS FORGED FROM GOSHINKI'S FANGS...??
...THAT MEANS...
...THAT I AM THE ONE WHO HAD KAIJIN-BO FORGE THIS BLADE? YES.
BUT...
SESSHŌ-MARU, YOU MUST NOT COME IN CONTACT WITH TOKIJIN!
EVEN YOU, IF YOU ARE TOUCHED BY TOKIJIN'S EVIL AURA...
...WILL BE POS-SESSED, JUST LIKE KAIJIN-BO!
FEH.
GG...

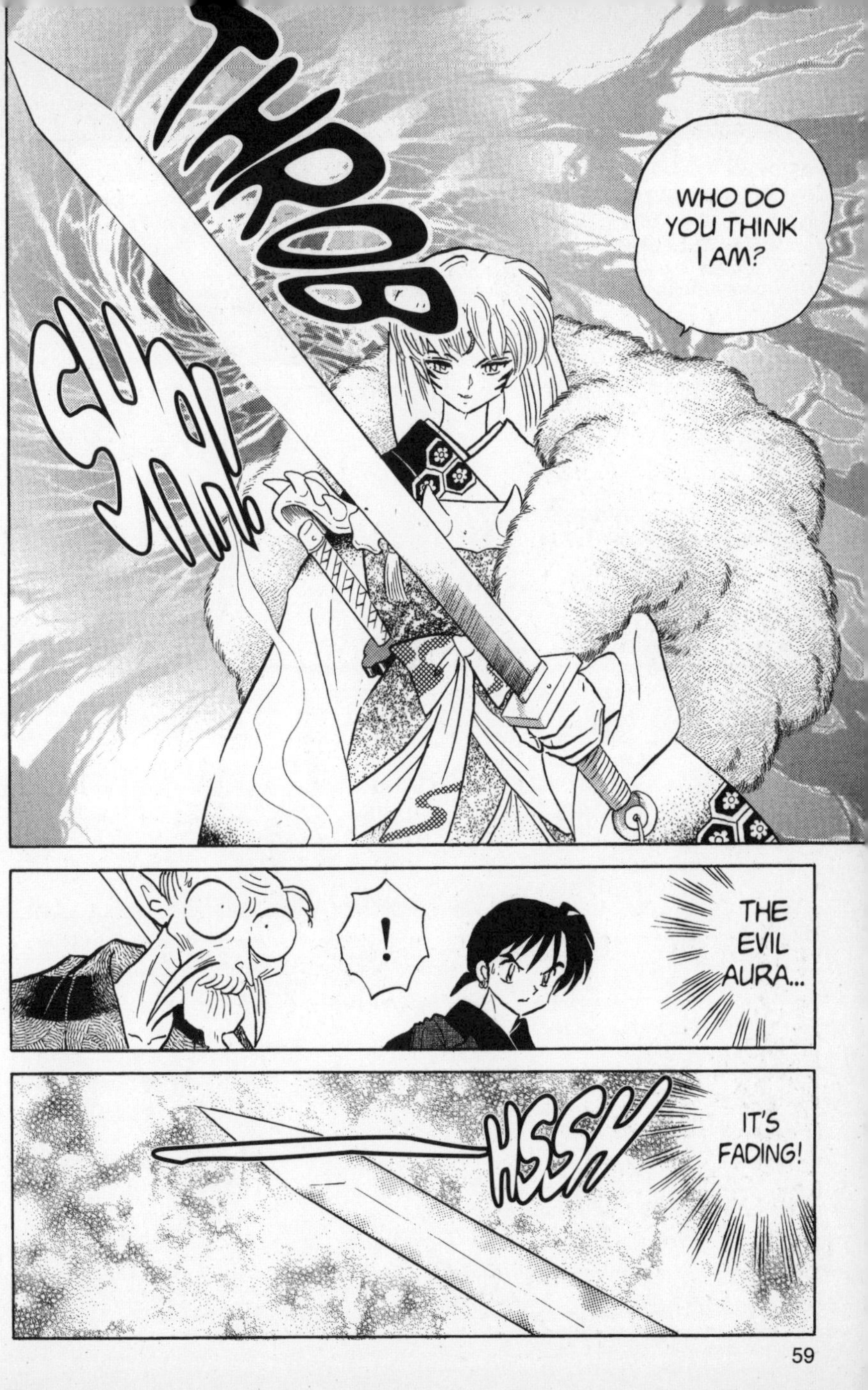
THROB
SHING!
WHO DO YOU THINK I AM?
!
THE EVIL AURA...
HSSH
IT'S FADING!

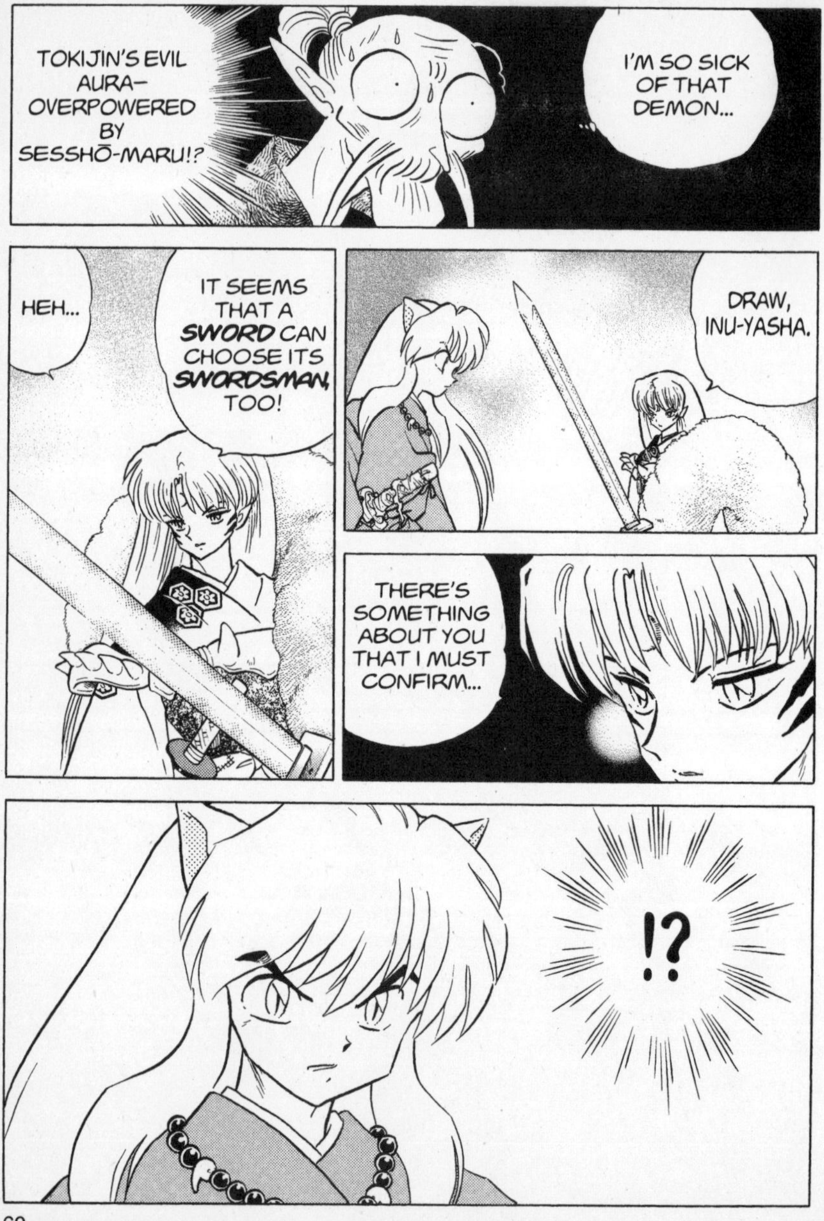
TOKIJIN'S EVIL AURA— OVERPOWERED BY SESSHŌ-MARU!?
I'M SO SICK OF THAT DEMON...
HEH...
IT SEEMS THAT A SWORD CAN CHOOSE ITS SWORDSMAN, TOO!
DRAW, INU-YASHA.
THERE'S SOMETHING ABOUT YOU THAT I MUST CONFIRM...
!?

SCROLL FOUR

THE SCENT OF BLOOD

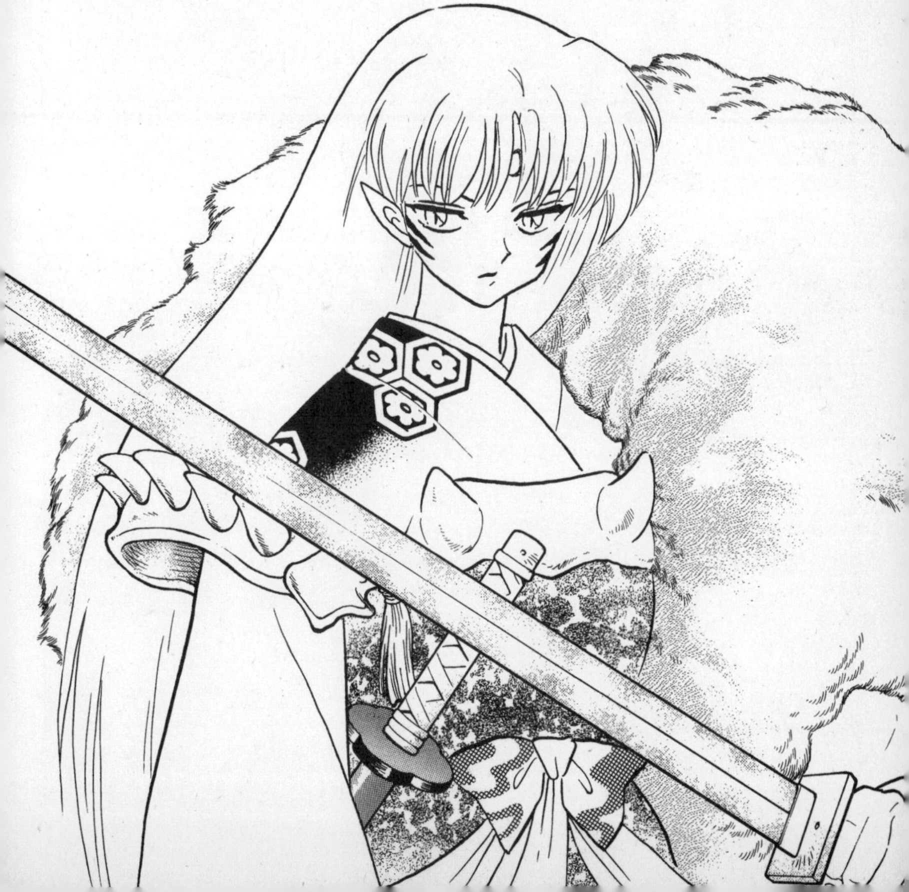

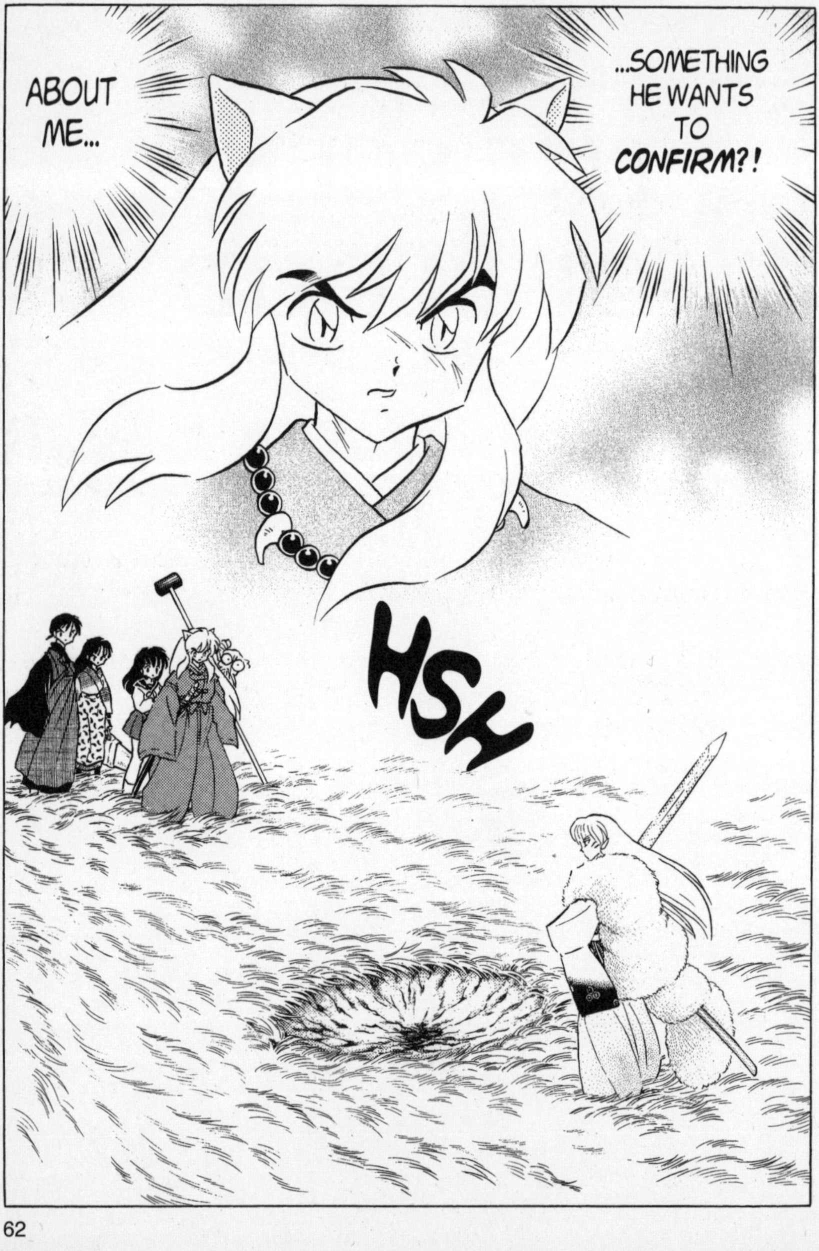
ABOUT ME...
...SOMETHING HE WANTS TO CONFIRM?!
HSH

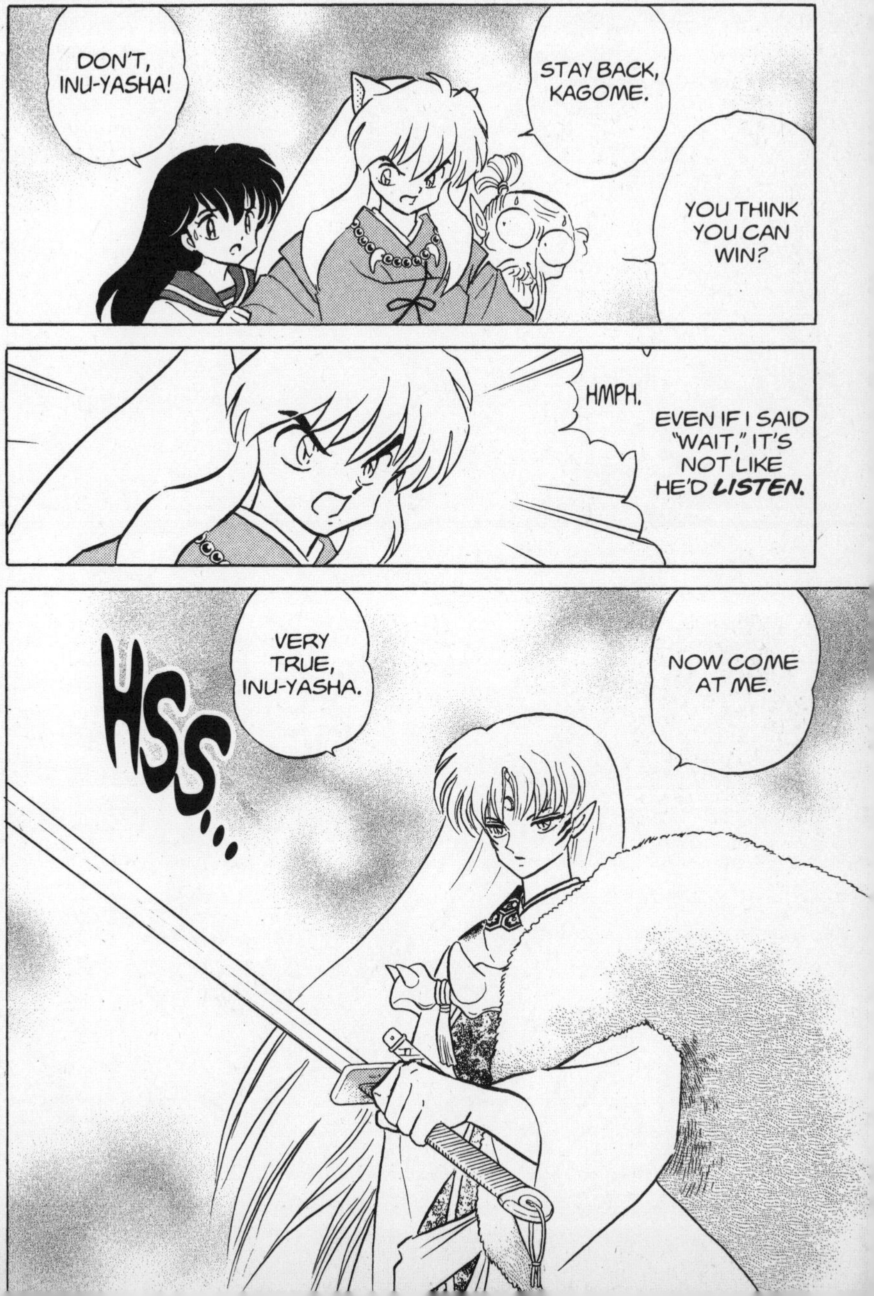
DON'T, INU-YASHA!
STAY BACK, KAGOME.
YOU THINK YOU CAN WIN?
HMPH.
EVEN IF I SAID "WAIT," IT'S NOT LIKE HE'D **LISTEN.**
HSS...
VERY TRUE, INU-YASHA.
NOW COME AT ME.

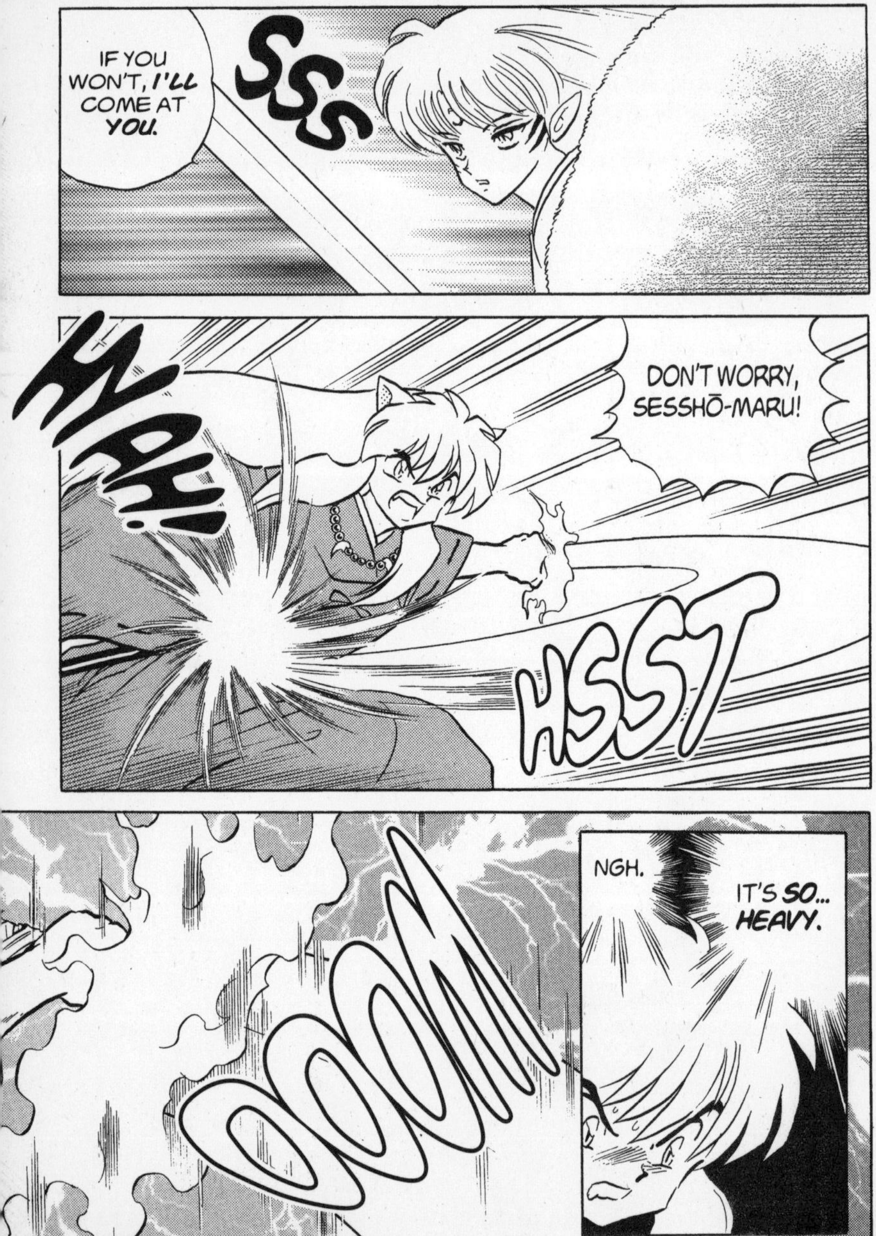
IF YOU WON'T, I'LL COME AT YOU.
SSS
HYAAH!
DON'T WORRY, SESSHŌ-MARU!
HSSST
DOOOM
NGH.
IT'S SO... HEAVY.

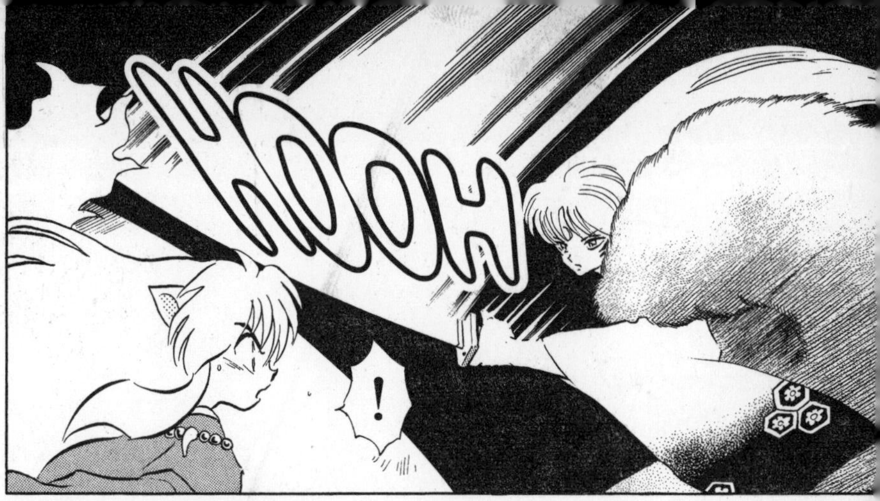
!

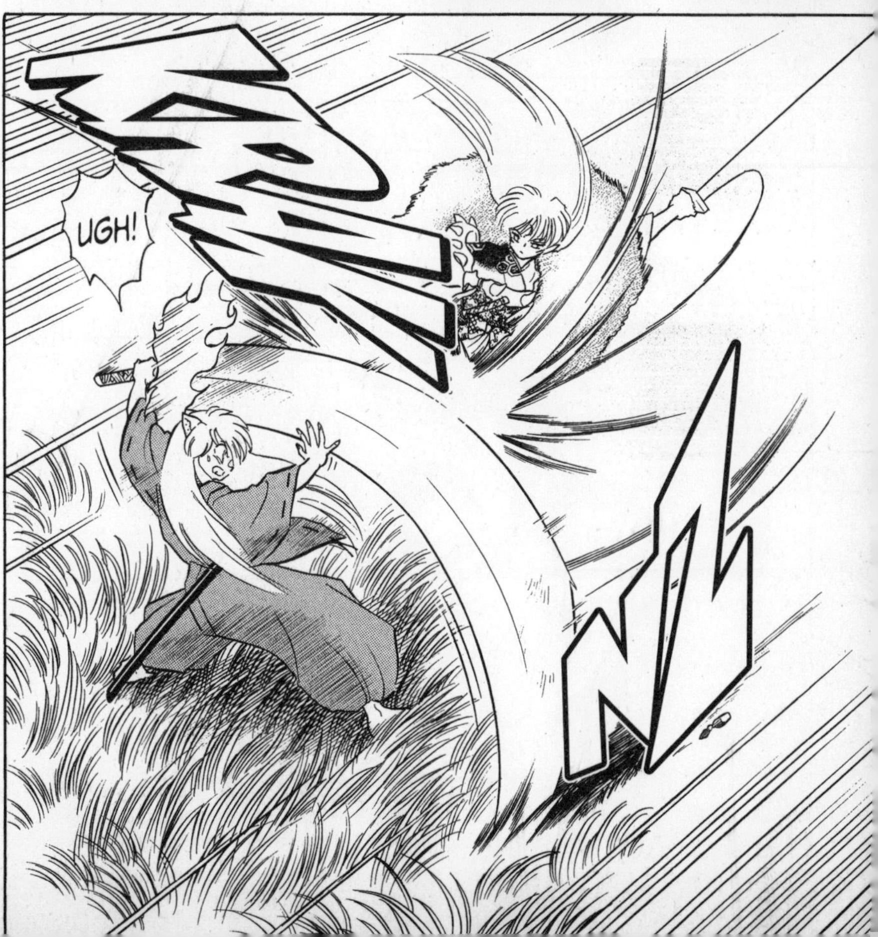
UGH!

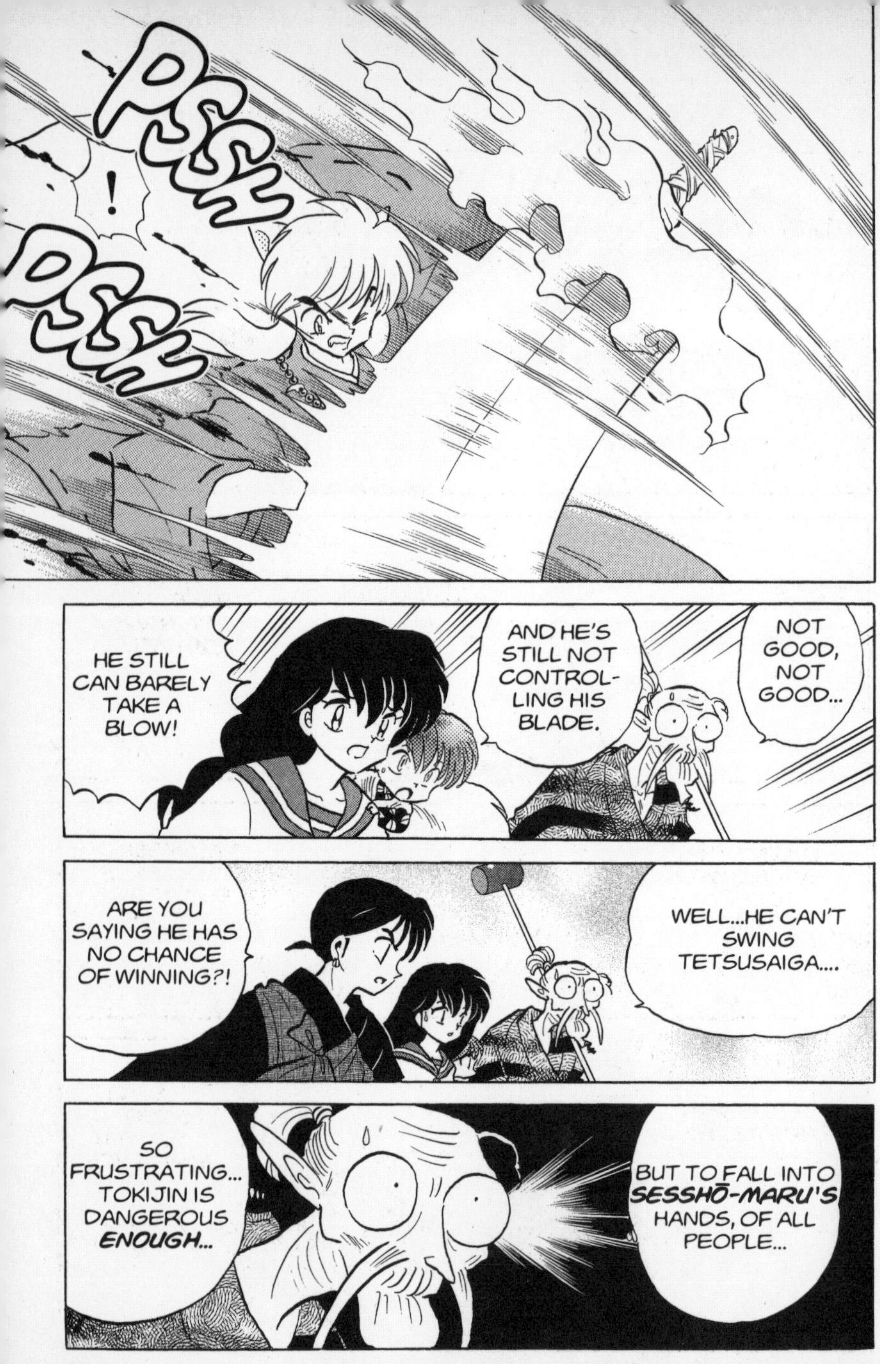
PSSH
!
PSSH
HE STILL CAN BARELY TAKE A BLOW!
AND HE'S STILL NOT CONTROL-LING HIS BLADE.
NOT GOOD, NOT GOOD...
ARE YOU SAYING HE HAS NO CHANCE OF WINNING?!
WELL...HE CAN'T SWING TETSUSAIGA....
SO FRUSTRATING... TOKIJIN IS DANGEROUS ***ENOUGH***...
BUT TO FALL INTO ***SESSHŌ-MARU'S*** HANDS, OF ALL PEOPLE...

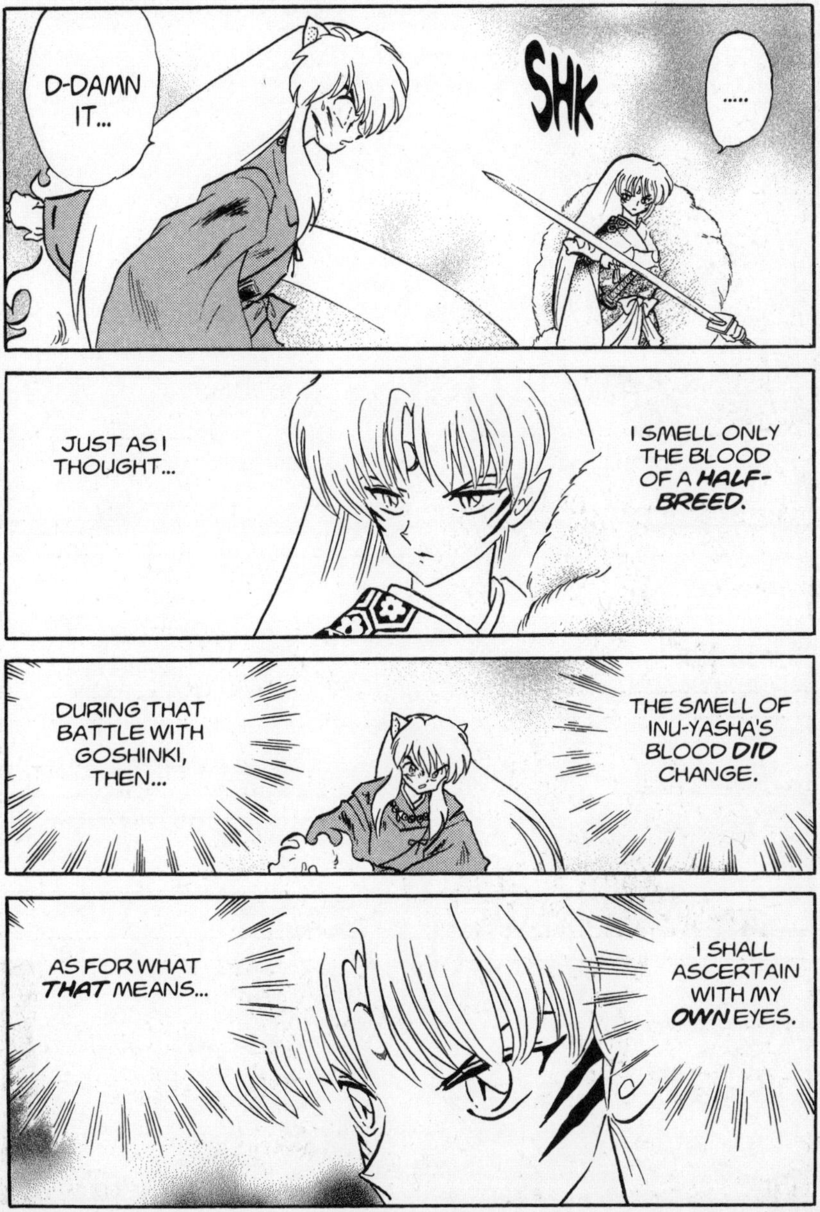
D-DAMN IT...
SHK
......
JUST AS I THOUGHT...
I SMELL ONLY THE BLOOD OF A HALF-BREED.
DURING THAT BATTLE WITH GOSHINKI, THEN...
THE SMELL OF INU-YASHA'S BLOOD DID CHANGE.
AS FOR WHAT THAT MEANS...
I SHALL ASCERTAIN WITH MY OWN EYES.

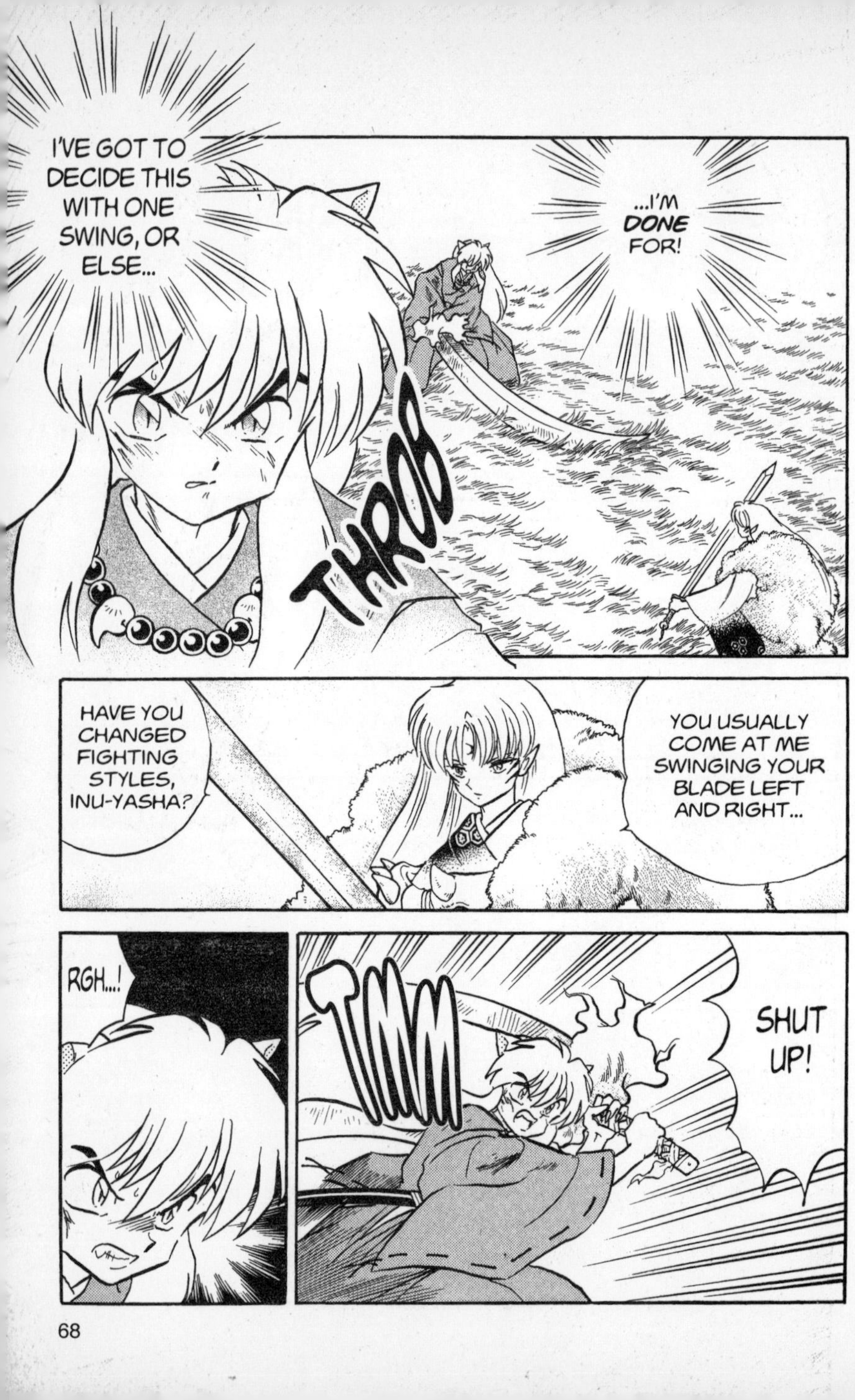
I'VE GOT TO DECIDE THIS WITH ONE SWING, OR ELSE...
THROB
...I'M DONE FOR!
HAVE YOU CHANGED FIGHTING STYLES, INU-YASHA?
YOU USUALLY COME AT ME SWINGING YOUR BLADE LEFT AND RIGHT...
RGH...!
TMM
SHUT UP!

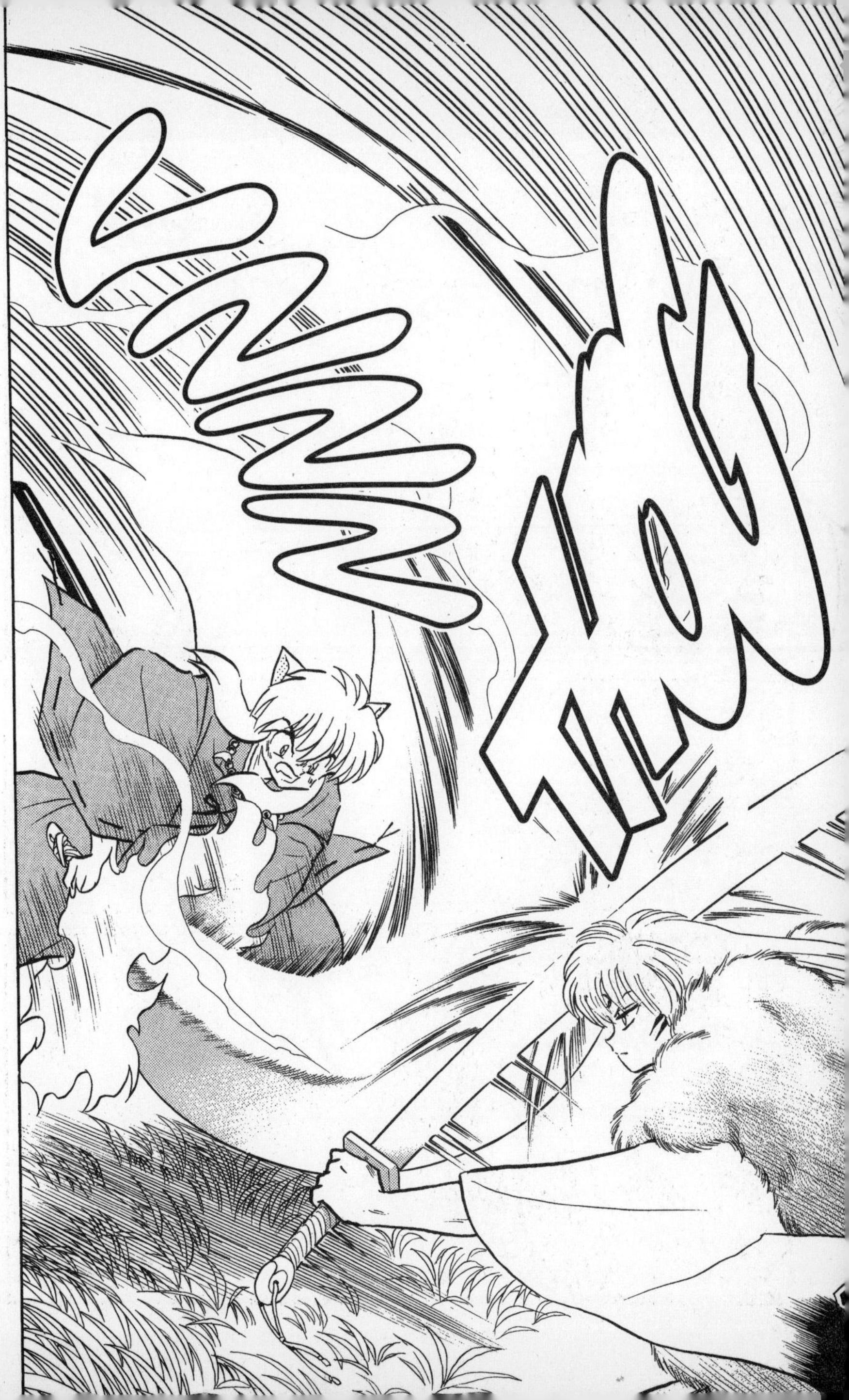

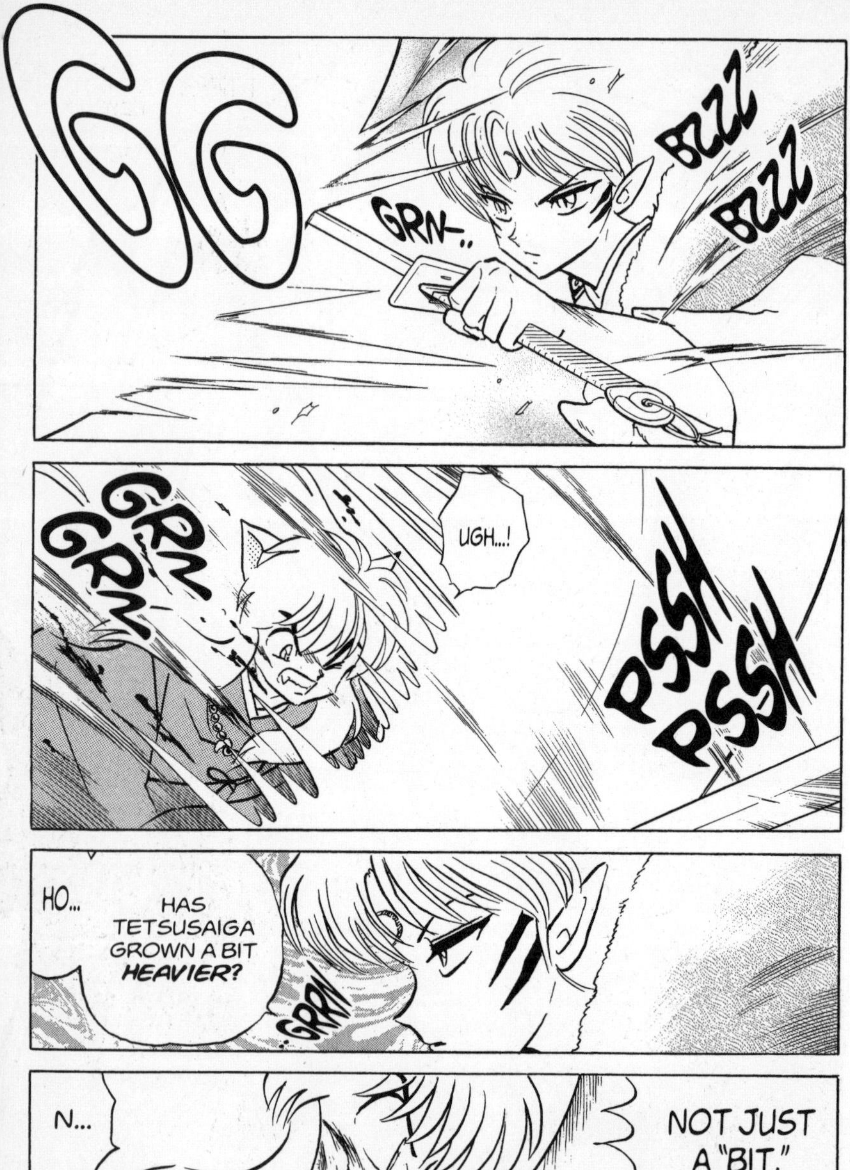
GG
GRN..
BZZZ
BZZZ
GRN
GRN
UGH...!
PSSH
PSSH
HO...
HAS TETSUSAIGA GROWN A BIT HEAVIER?
GRR
N...
NOT JUST A "BIT," IDIOT!

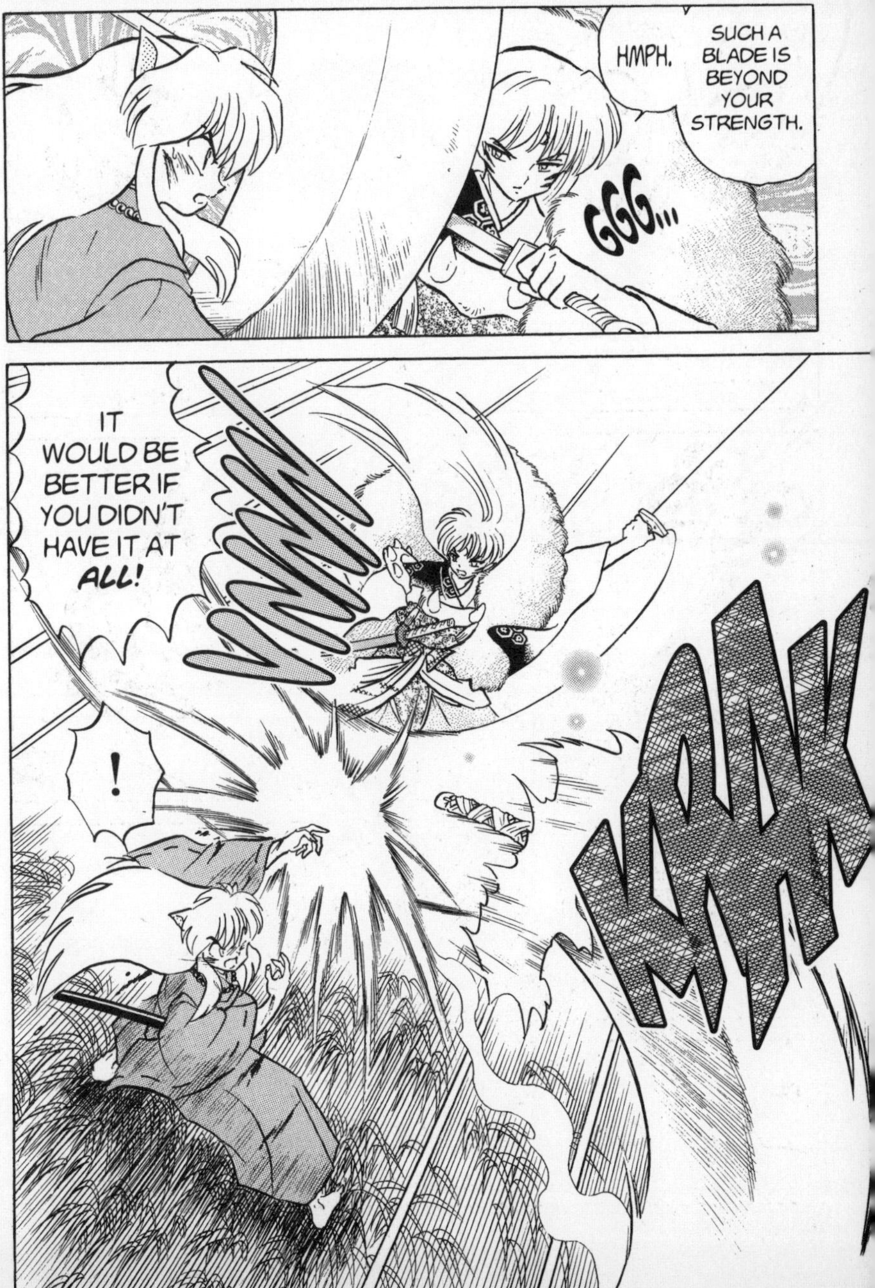
HMPH.
SUCH A BLADE IS BEYOND YOUR STRENGTH.
GGG...
IT WOULD BE BETTER IF YOU DIDN'T HAVE IT AT ALL!
!

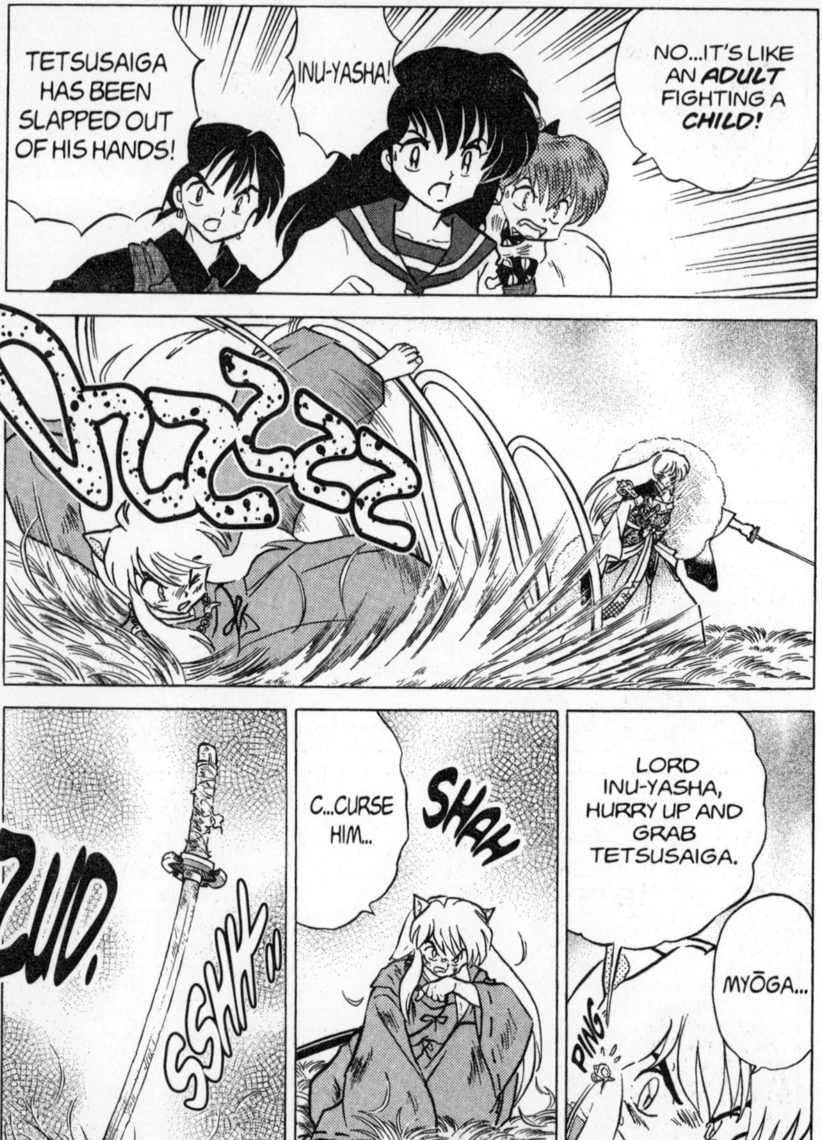
TETSUSAIGA HAS BEEN SLAPPED OUT OF HIS HANDS!
INU-YASHA!
NO...IT'S LIKE AN ADULT FIGHTING A CHILD!
ZUD.
SSHH...
C...CURSE HIM...
SHAH
LORD INU-YASHA, HURRY UP AND GRAB TETSUSAIGA.
PING
MYŌGA...

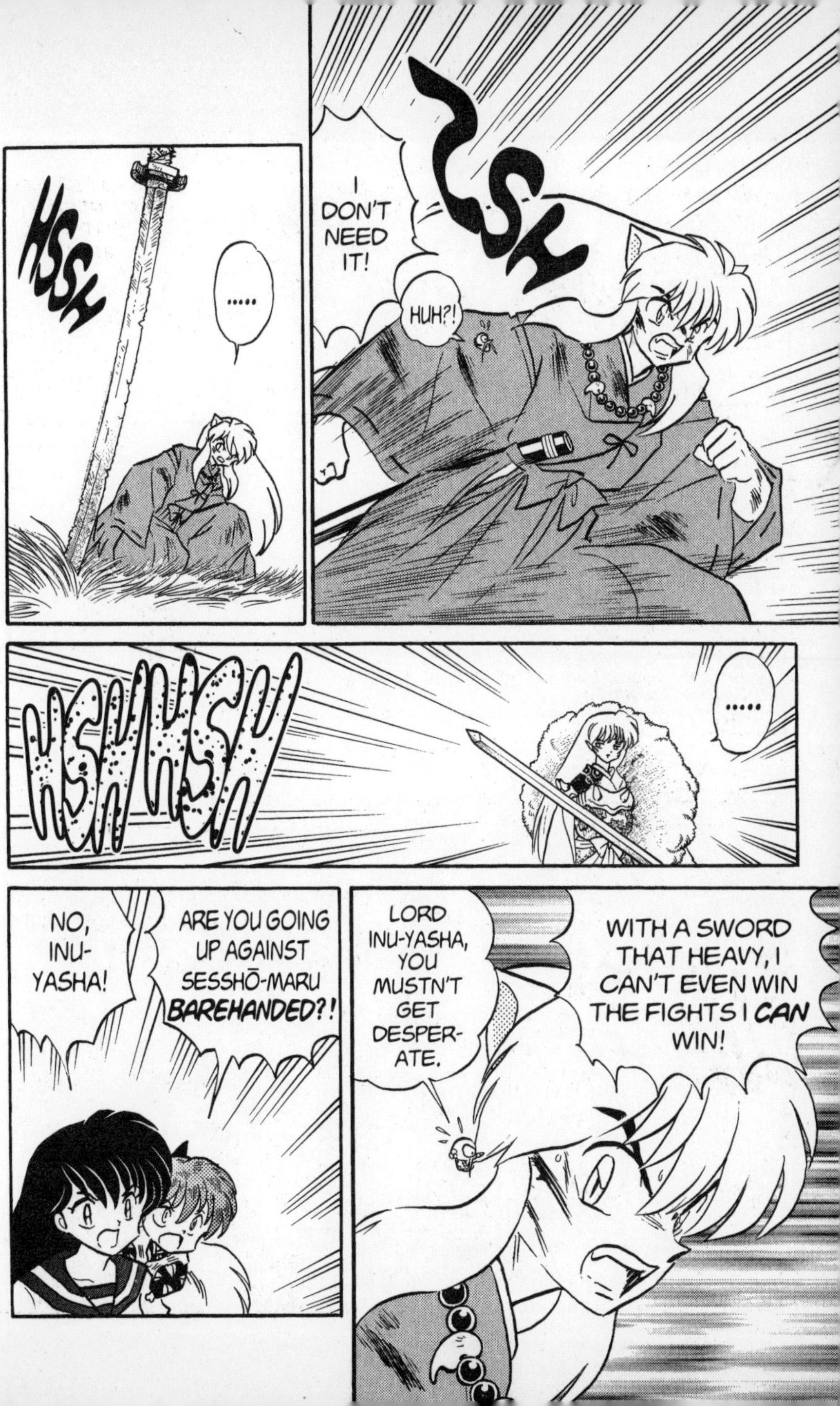
HSSH
......
I DON'T NEED IT!
HUH?!
HSHHSH
......
NO, INU-YASHA!
ARE YOU GOING UP AGAINST SESSHŌ-MARU **BAREHANDED**?!
LORD INU-YASHA, YOU MUSTN'T GET DESPER-ATE.
WITH A SWORD THAT HEAVY, I CAN'T EVEN WIN THE FIGHTS I **CAN** WIN!

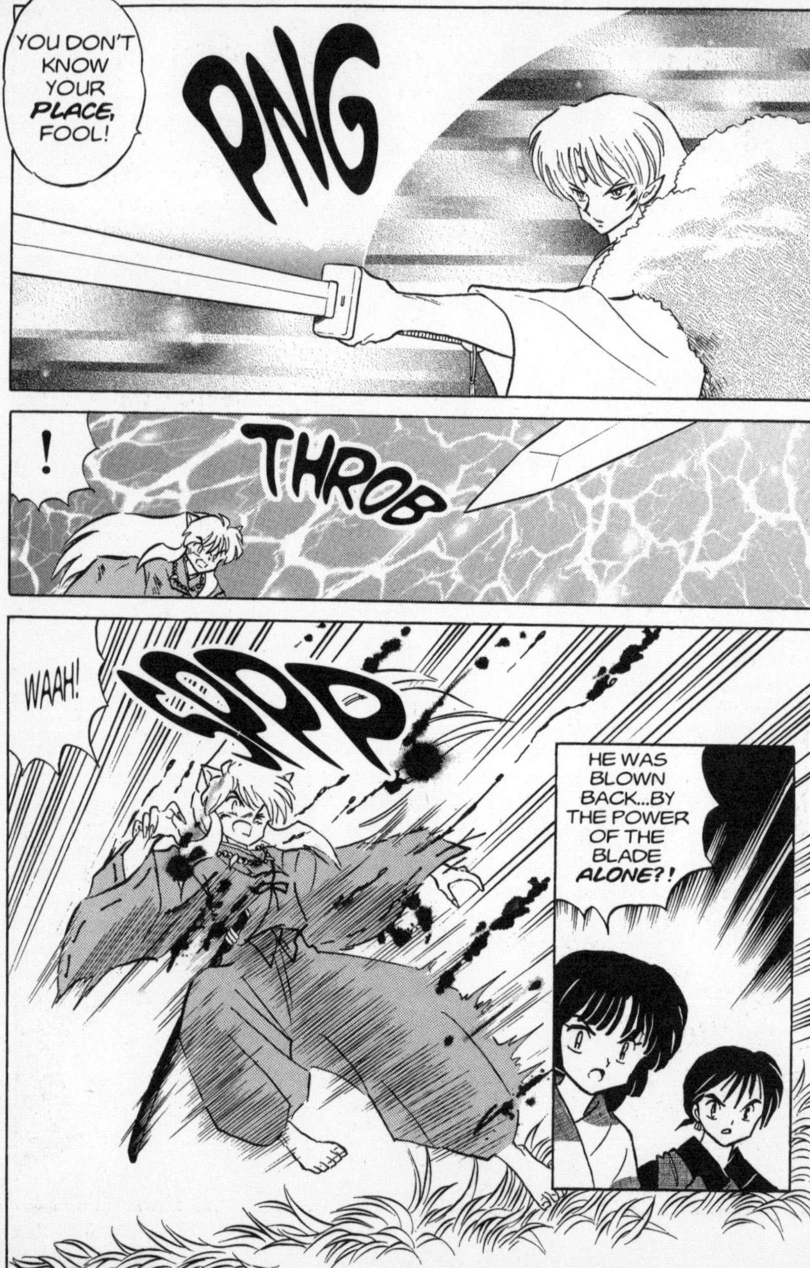
YOU DON'T KNOW YOUR PLACE, FOOL!
PNG
!
THROB
WAAH!
HE WAS BLOWN BACK...BY THE POWER OF THE BLADE ALONE?!

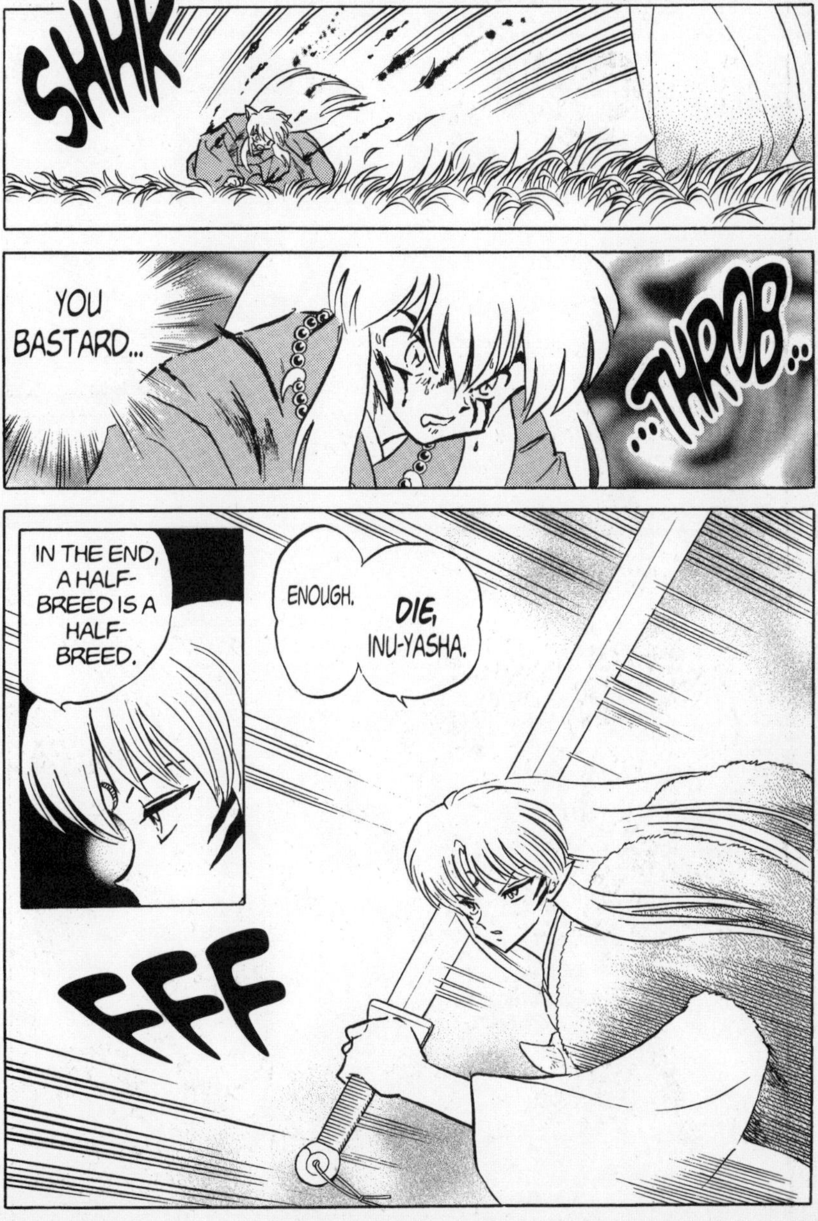
SHHK
YOU BASTARD...
...THROB...
IN THE END, A HALF-BREED IS A HALF-BREED.
ENOUGH.
DIE, INU-YASHA.
FFF

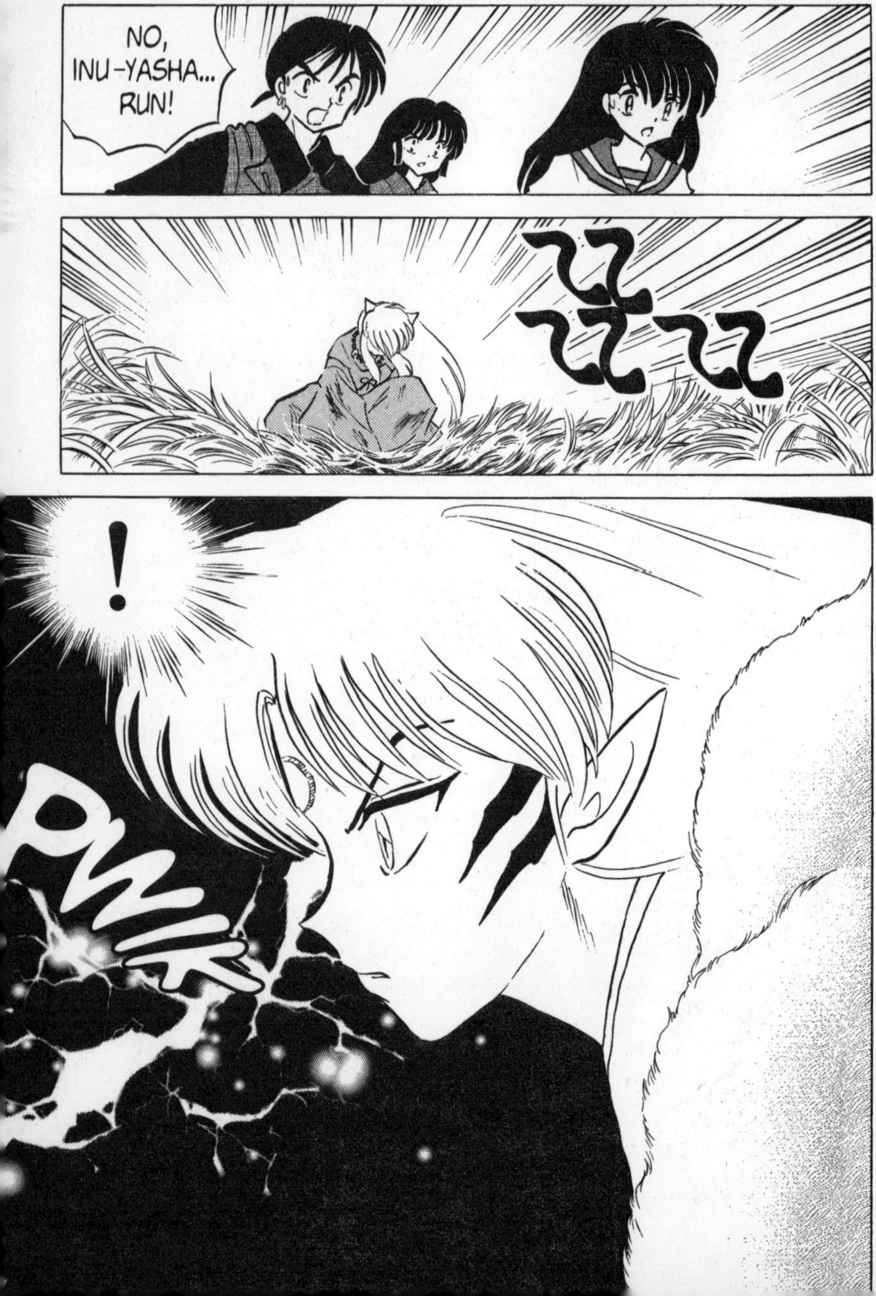
NO, INU-YASHA... RUN!
ZZZ ZZZ ZZZ
!
PWIK

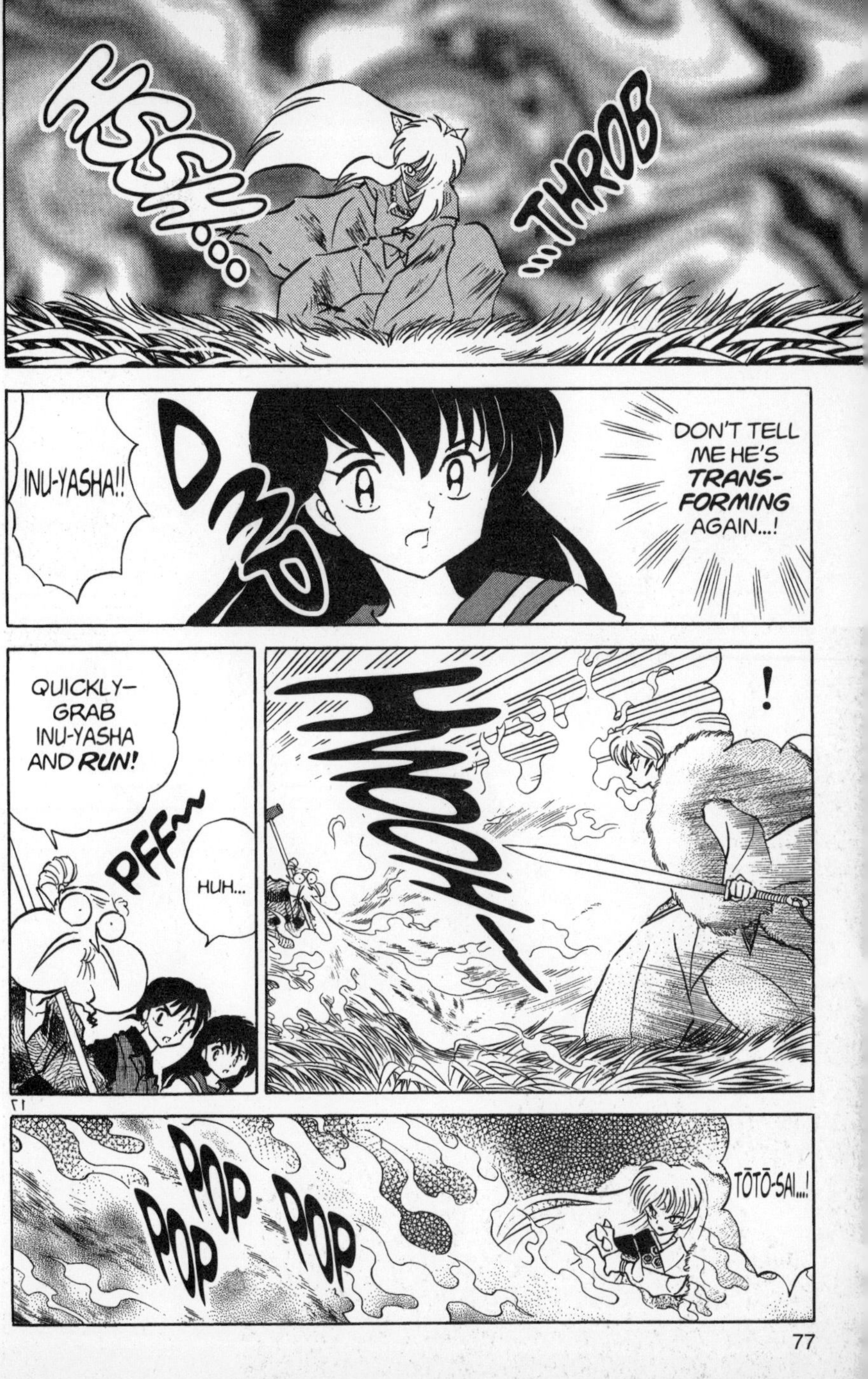
HSSH...
...THROB
INU-YASHA!!
DMP
DON'T TELL ME HE'S TRANSFORMING AGAIN...!
QUICKLY— GRAB INU-YASHA AND RUN!
PFF...
HUH...
WHOOSH
!
POP POP POP POP
TŌTŌ-SAI...!

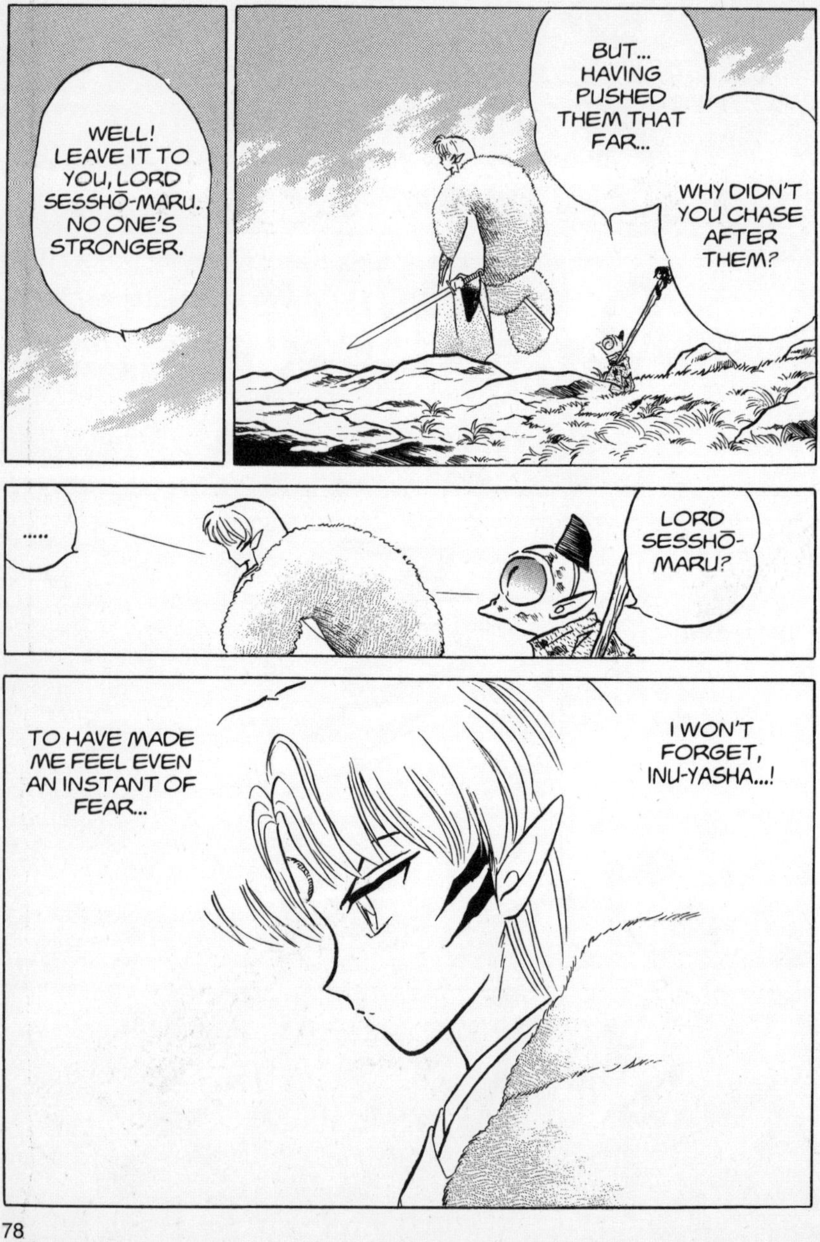
WELL! LEAVE IT TO YOU, LORD SESSHŌ-MARU. NO ONE'S STRONGER.
BUT... HAVING PUSHED THEM THAT FAR...
WHY DIDN'T YOU CHASE AFTER THEM?
.....
LORD SESSHŌ-MARU?
TO HAVE MADE ME FEEL EVEN AN INSTANT OF FEAR...
I WON'T FORGET, INU-YASHA...!

SCROLL FIVE

TRUE STRENGTH

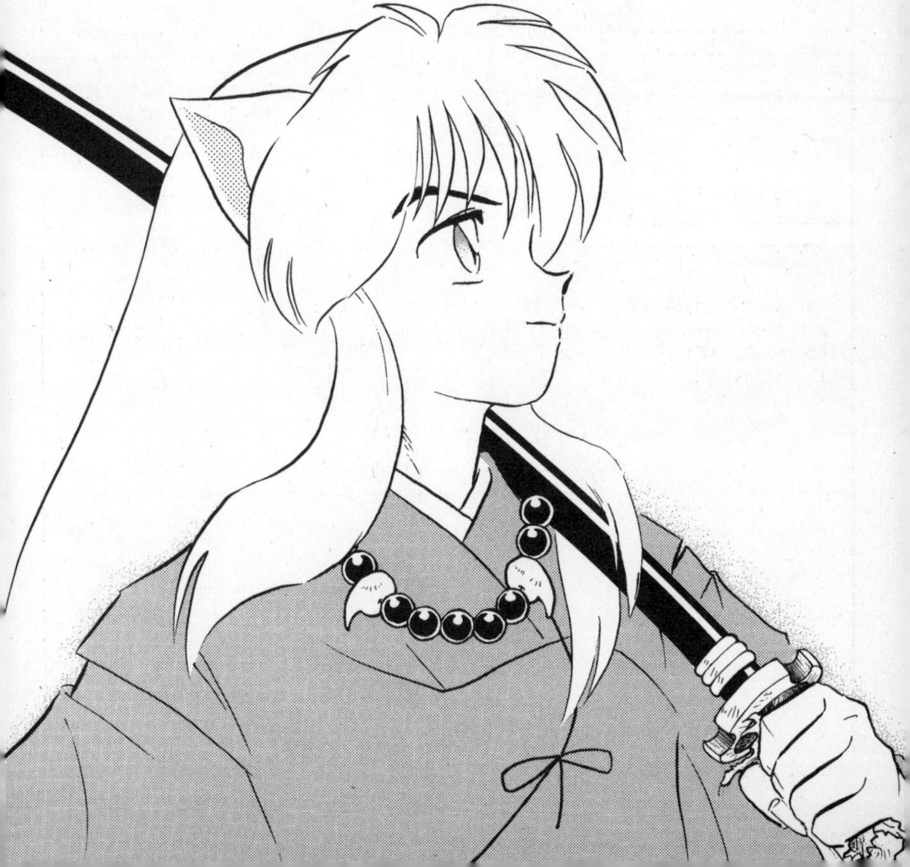

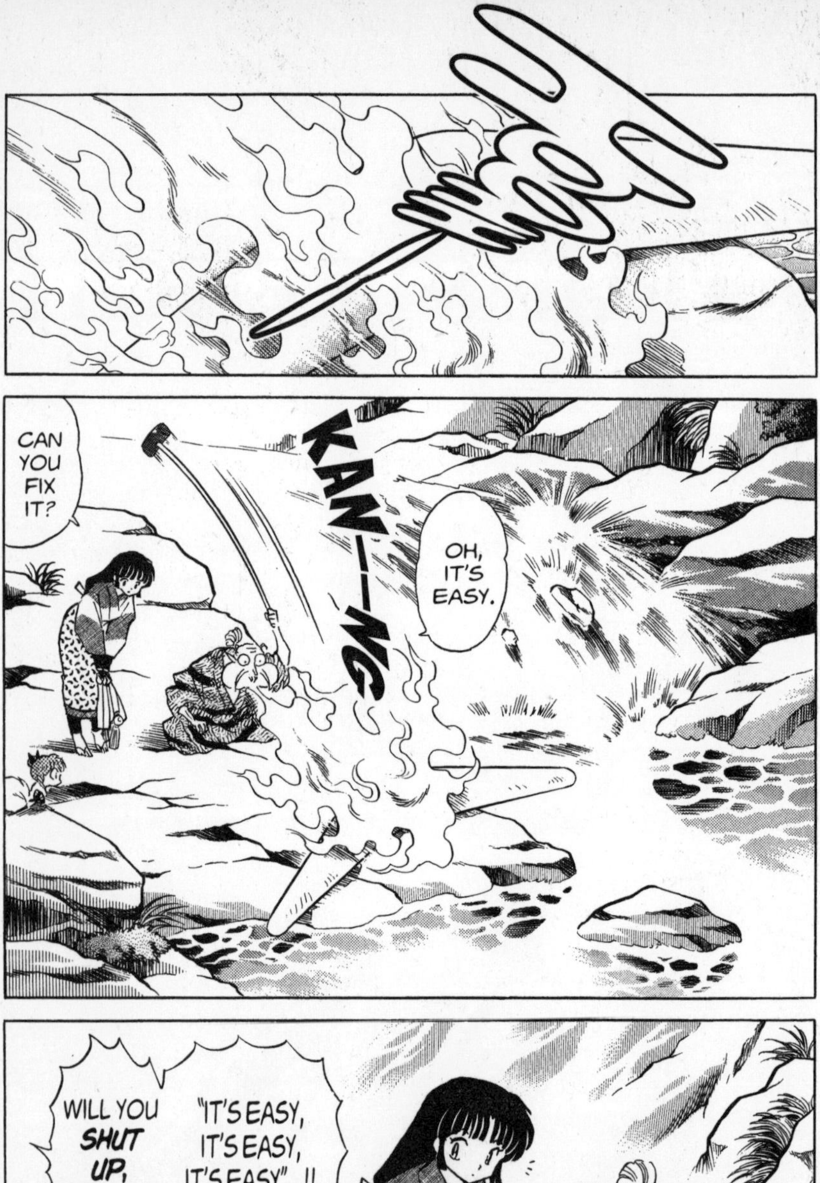
CAN YOU FIX IT?
KAN—NG
OH, IT'S EASY.
WILL YOU **SHUT UP,** FOOL?!
"IT'S EASY, IT'S EASY, IT'S EASY"...!!

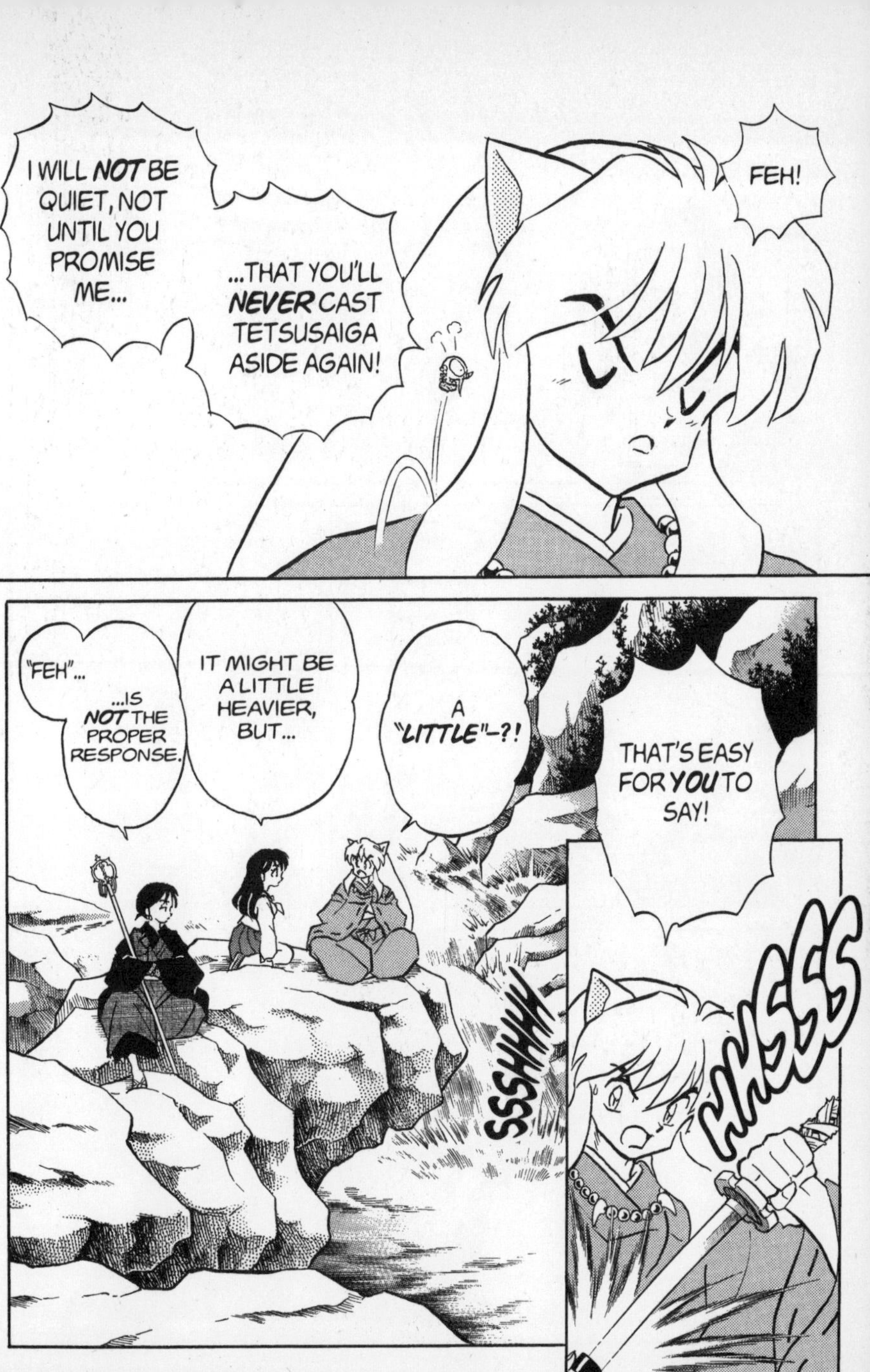
I WILL **NOT** BE QUIET, NOT UNTIL YOU PROMISE ME...
...THAT YOU'LL **NEVER** CAST TETSUSAIGA ASIDE AGAIN!
FEH!
"FEH"... ...IS **NOT** THE PROPER RESPONSE.
IT MIGHT BE A LITTLE HEAVIER, BUT...
A "***LITTLE***"–?!
THAT'S EASY FOR **YOU** TO SAY!
SSSHHHH
WHSSS

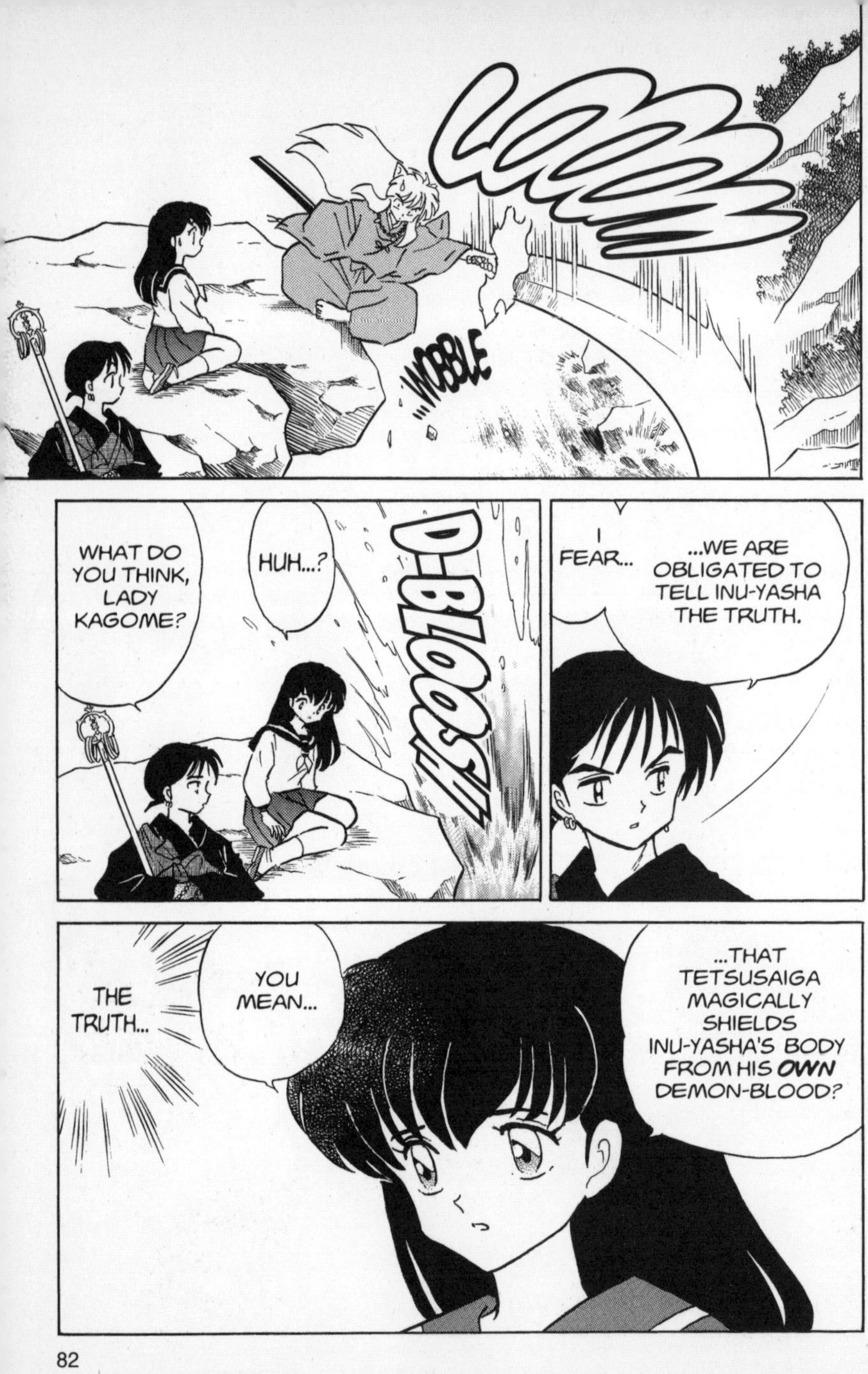
...WOBBLE
WHAT DO YOU THINK, LADY KAGOME?
HUH...?
D-BLOOSH!!
I FEAR...
...WE ARE OBLIGATED TO TELL INU-YASHA THE TRUTH.
THE TRUTH...
YOU MEAN...
...THAT TETSUSAIGA MAGICALLY SHIELDS INU-YASHA'S BODY FROM HIS ***OWN*** DEMON-BLOOD?

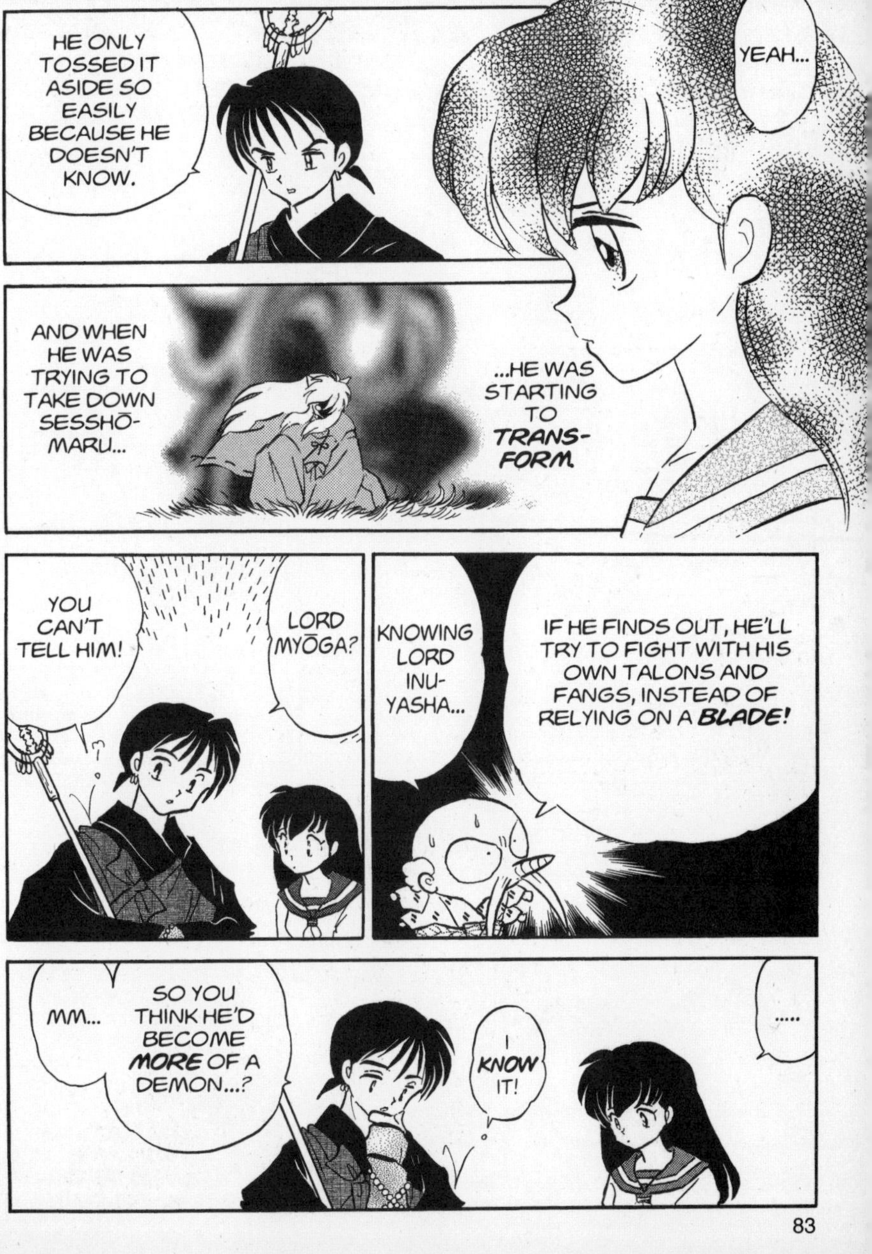
HE ONLY TOSSED IT ASIDE SO EASILY BECAUSE HE DOESN'T KNOW.
YEAH...
AND WHEN HE WAS TRYING TO TAKE DOWN SESSHŌ-MARU...
...HE WAS STARTING TO ***TRANS-FORM.***
YOU CAN'T TELL HIM!
LORD MYŌGA?
KNOWING LORD INU-YASHA...
IF HE FINDS OUT, HE'LL TRY TO FIGHT WITH HIS OWN TALONS AND FANGS, INSTEAD OF RELYING ON A ***BLADE!***
MM...
SO YOU THINK HE'D BECOME ***MORE*** OF A DEMON...?
I ***KNOW*** IT!
.....

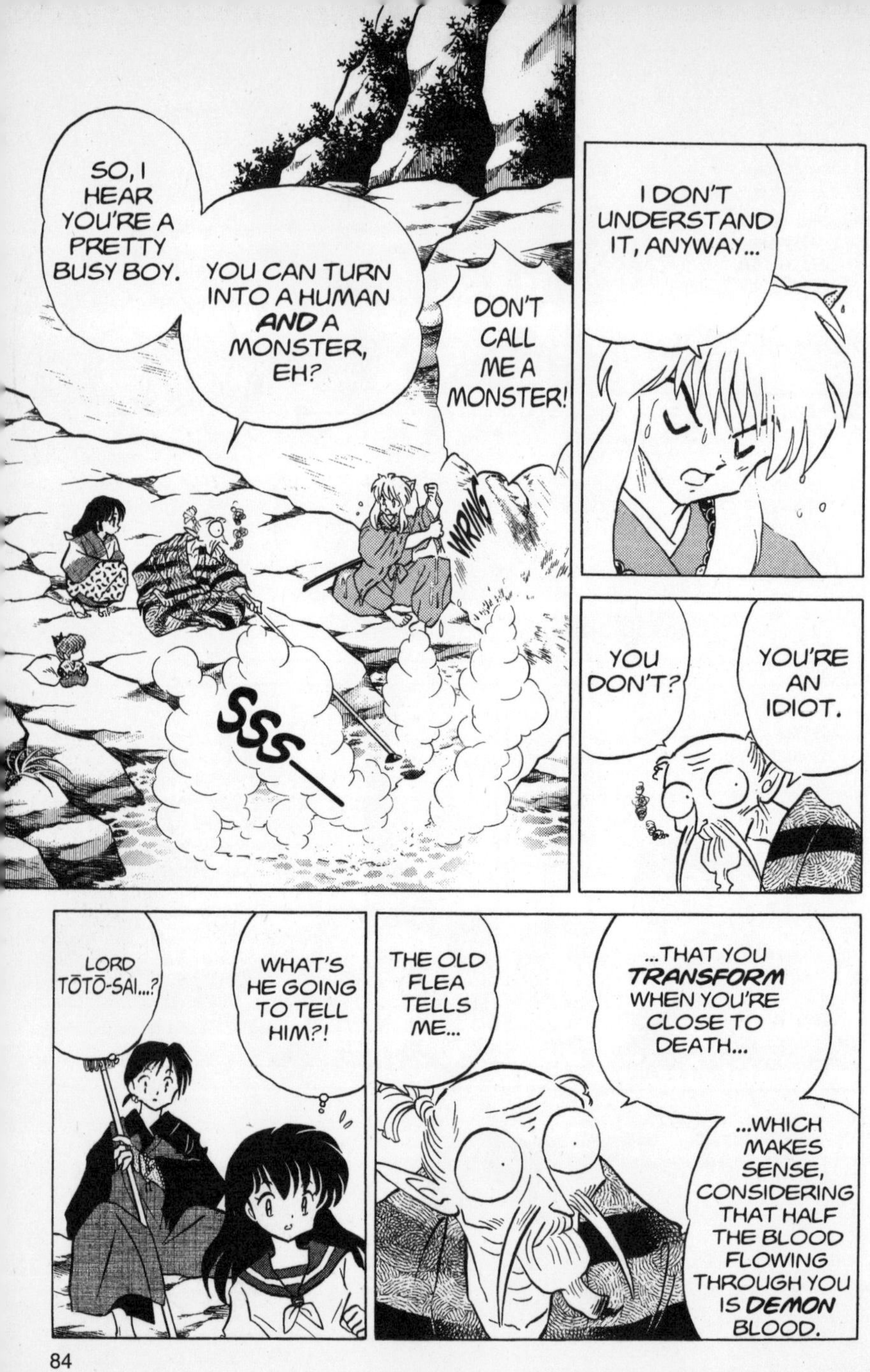
SO, I HEAR YOU'RE A PRETTY BUSY BOY.
YOU CAN TURN INTO A HUMAN AND A MONSTER, EH?
DON'T CALL ME A MONSTER!
WRING
SSS—
I DON'T UNDERSTAND IT, ANYWAY...
YOU DON'T?
YOU'RE AN IDIOT.
LORD TŌTŌ-SAI...?
WHAT'S HE GOING TO TELL HIM?!
THE OLD FLEA TELLS ME...
...THAT YOU TRANSFORM WHEN YOU'RE CLOSE TO DEATH...
...WHICH MAKES SENSE, CONSIDERING THAT HALF THE BLOOD FLOWING THROUGH YOU IS DEMON BLOOD.

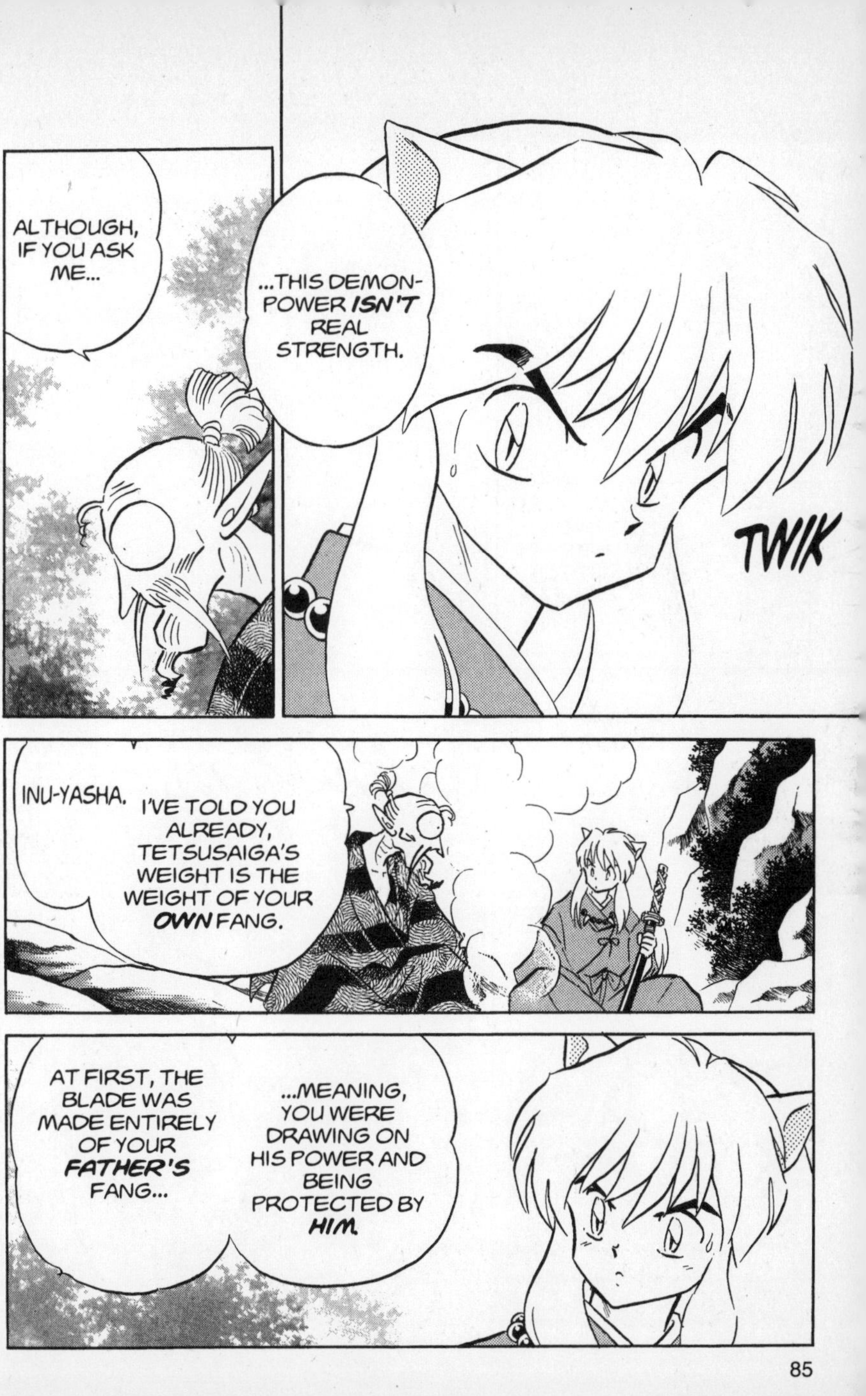

ALTHOUGH, IF YOU ASK ME...
...THIS DEMON-POWER ISN'T REAL STRENGTH.
TWIK
INU-YASHA.
I'VE TOLD YOU ALREADY, TETSUSAIGA'S WEIGHT IS THE WEIGHT OF YOUR OWN FANG.
AT FIRST, THE BLADE WAS MADE ENTIRELY OF YOUR FATHER'S FANG...
...MEANING, YOU WERE DRAWING ON HIS POWER AND BEING PROTECTED BY HIM.

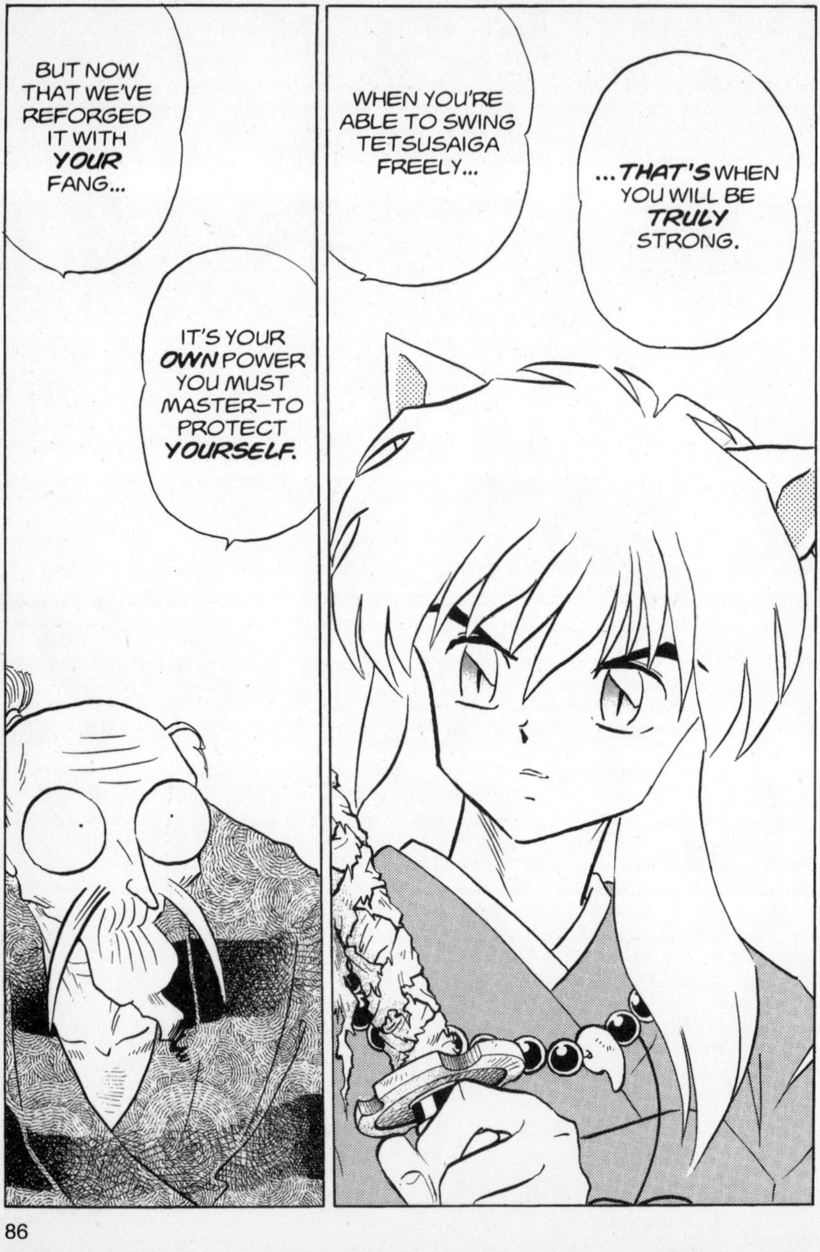
BUT NOW THAT WE'VE REFORGED IT WITH YOUR FANG...
IT'S YOUR OWN POWER YOU MUST MASTER—TO PROTECT YOURSELF.
WHEN YOU'RE ABLE TO SWING TETSUSAIGA FREELY...
...THAT'S WHEN YOU WILL BE TRULY STRONG.

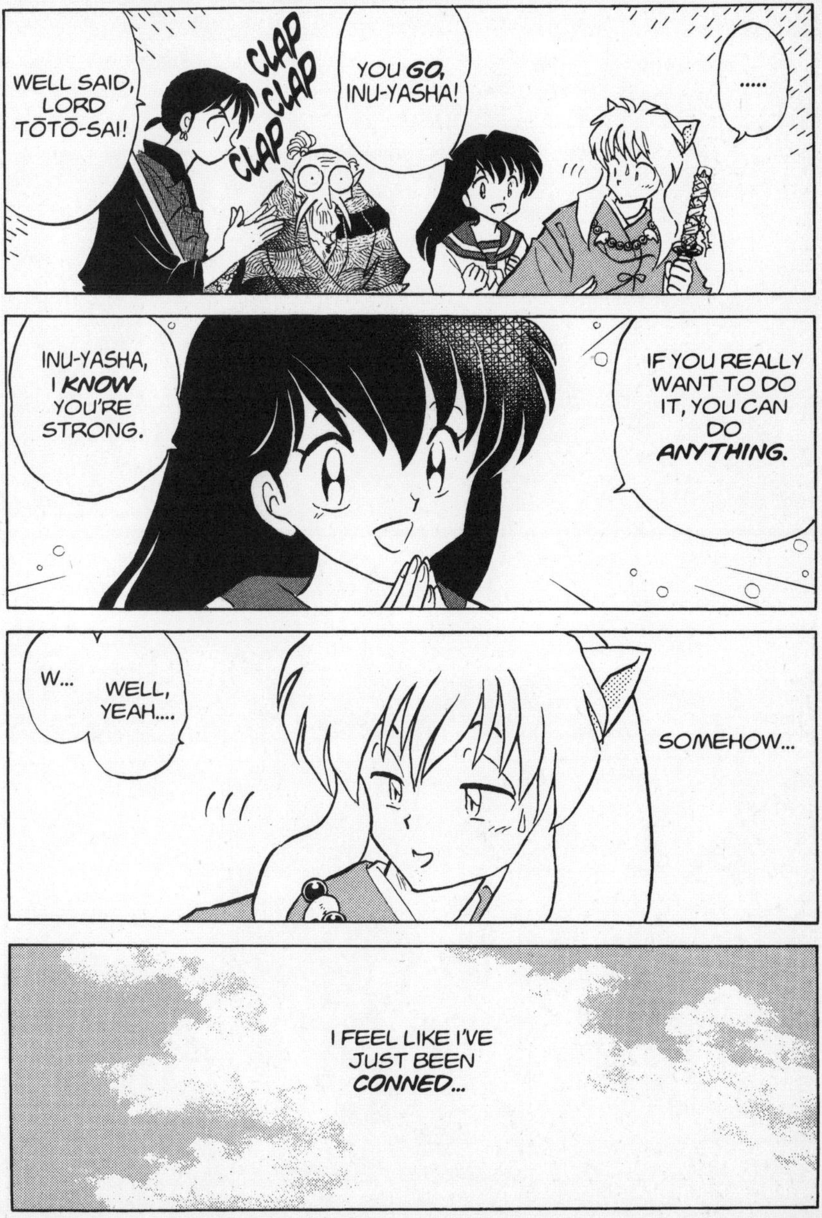
WELL SAID, LORD TŌTŌ-SAI!
CLAP CLAP CLAP
YOU GO, INU-YASHA!
.....
INU-YASHA, I KNOW YOU'RE STRONG.
IF YOU REALLY WANT TO DO IT, YOU CAN DO ANYTHING.
W... WELL, YEAH....
SOMEHOW...
I FEEL LIKE I'VE JUST BEEN CONNED...

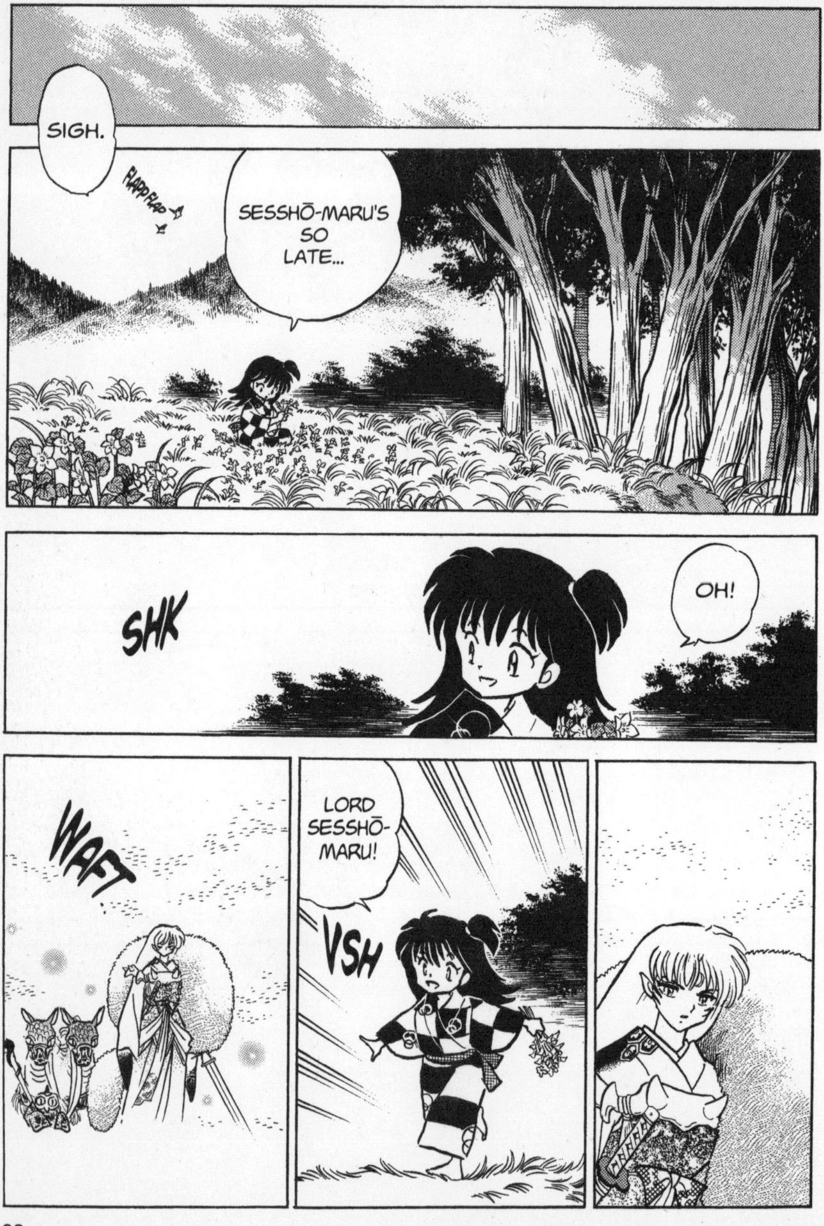
SIGH.
FLAPP FLAP
SESSHŌ-MARU'S SO LATE...
SHK
OH!
WAFT
LORD SESSHŌ-MARU!
VSH

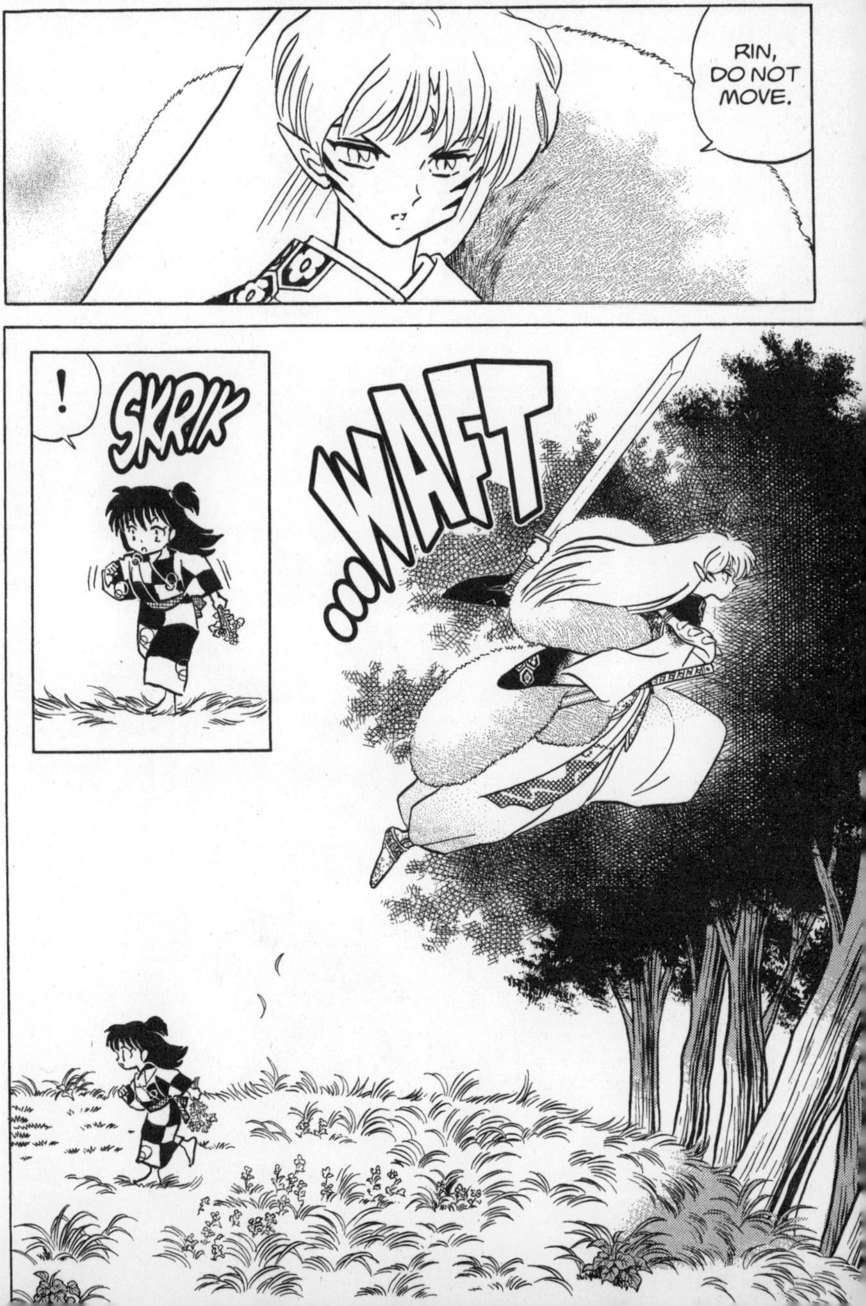
RIN, DO NOT MOVE.
!
SKRIK
...WAFT

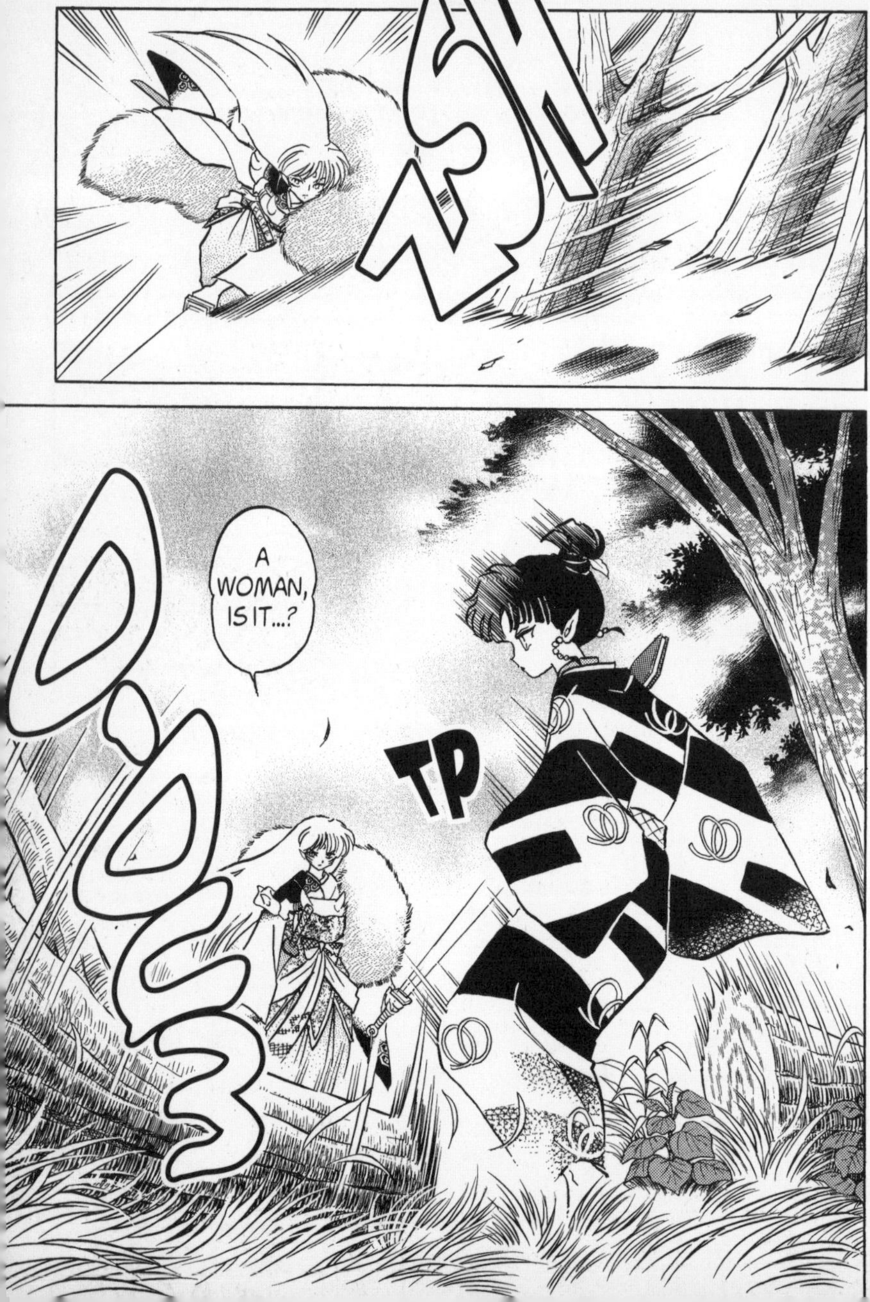
ZSH
D-DUM
A WOMAN, IS IT...?
TP

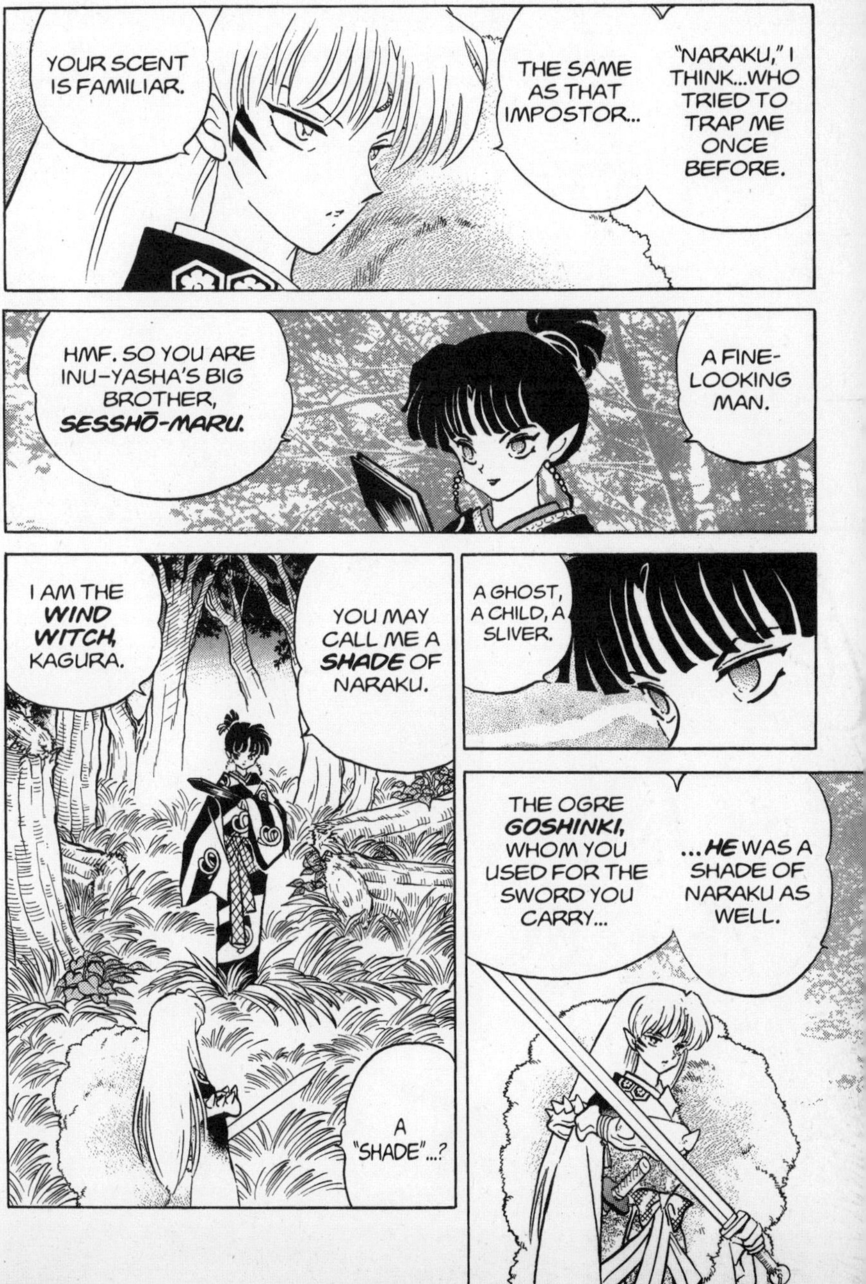
YOUR SCENT IS FAMILIAR.
THE SAME AS THAT IMPOSTOR...
"NARAKU," I THINK...WHO TRIED TO TRAP ME ONCE BEFORE.
HMF. SO YOU ARE INU-YASHA'S BIG BROTHER, ***SESSHŌ-MARU.***
A FINE-LOOKING MAN.
I AM THE ***WIND WITCH,*** KAGURA.
YOU MAY CALL ME A ***SHADE*** OF NARAKU.
A "SHADE"...?
A GHOST, A CHILD, A SLIVER.
THE OGRE ***GOSHINKI,*** WHOM YOU USED FOR THE SWORD YOU CARRY...
...***HE*** WAS A SHADE OF NARAKU AS WELL.

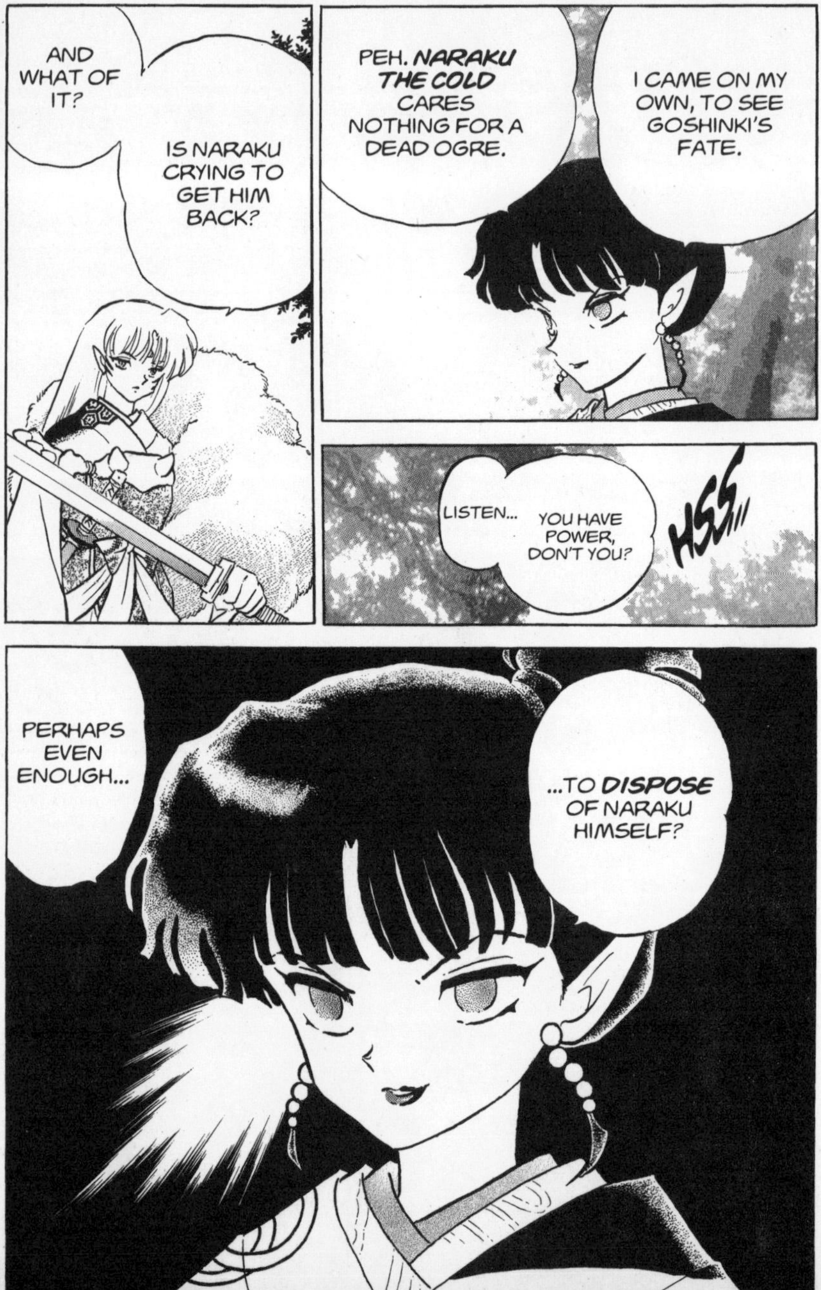
AND WHAT OF IT?
IS NARAKU CRYING TO GET HIM BACK?
PEH. ***NARAKU THE COLD*** CARES NOTHING FOR A DEAD OGRE.
I CAME ON MY OWN, TO SEE GOSHINKI'S FATE.
LISTEN...
YOU HAVE POWER, DON'T YOU?
HSS
PERHAPS EVEN ENOUGH...
...TO ***DISPOSE*** OF NARAKU HIMSELF?

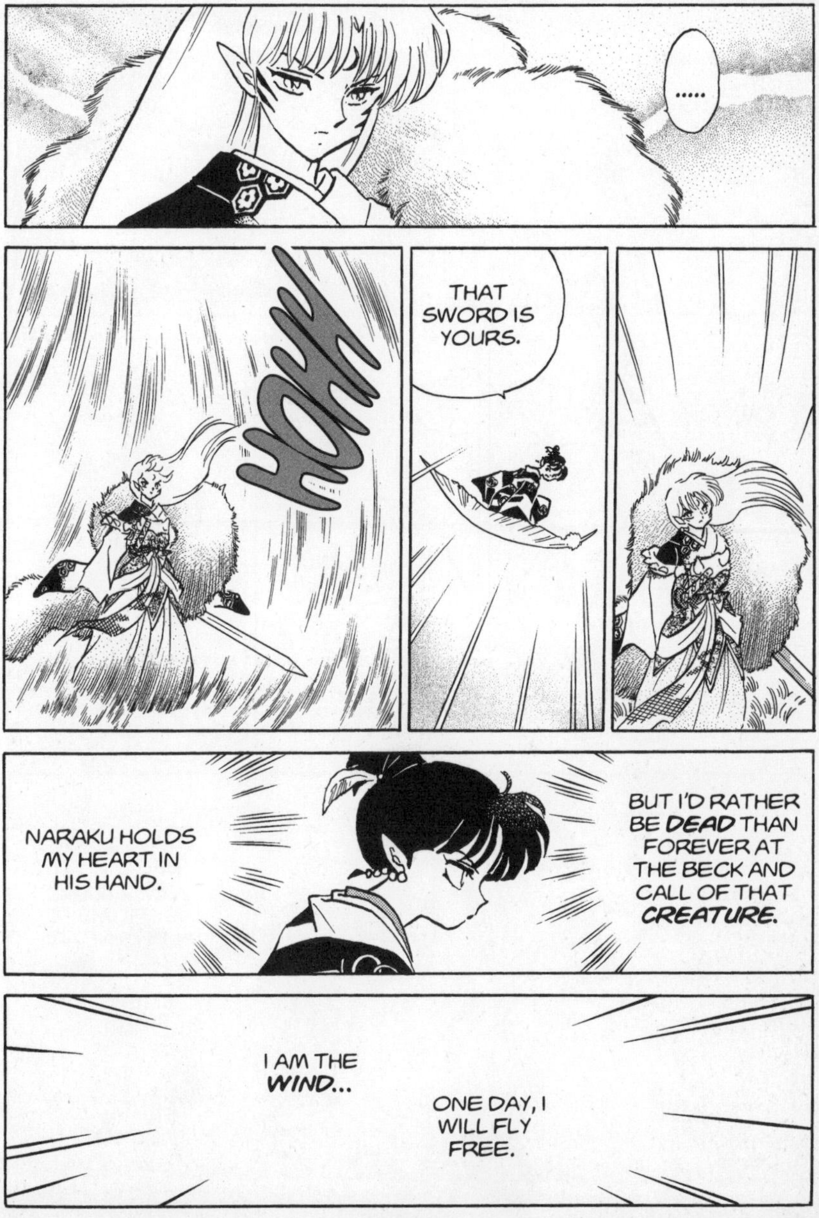
......
THAT SWORD IS YOURS.
NARAKU HOLDS MY HEART IN HIS HAND.
BUT I'D RATHER BE **DEAD** THAN FOREVER AT THE BECK AND CALL OF THAT **CREATURE.**
I AM THE **WIND...**
ONE DAY, I WILL FLY FREE.

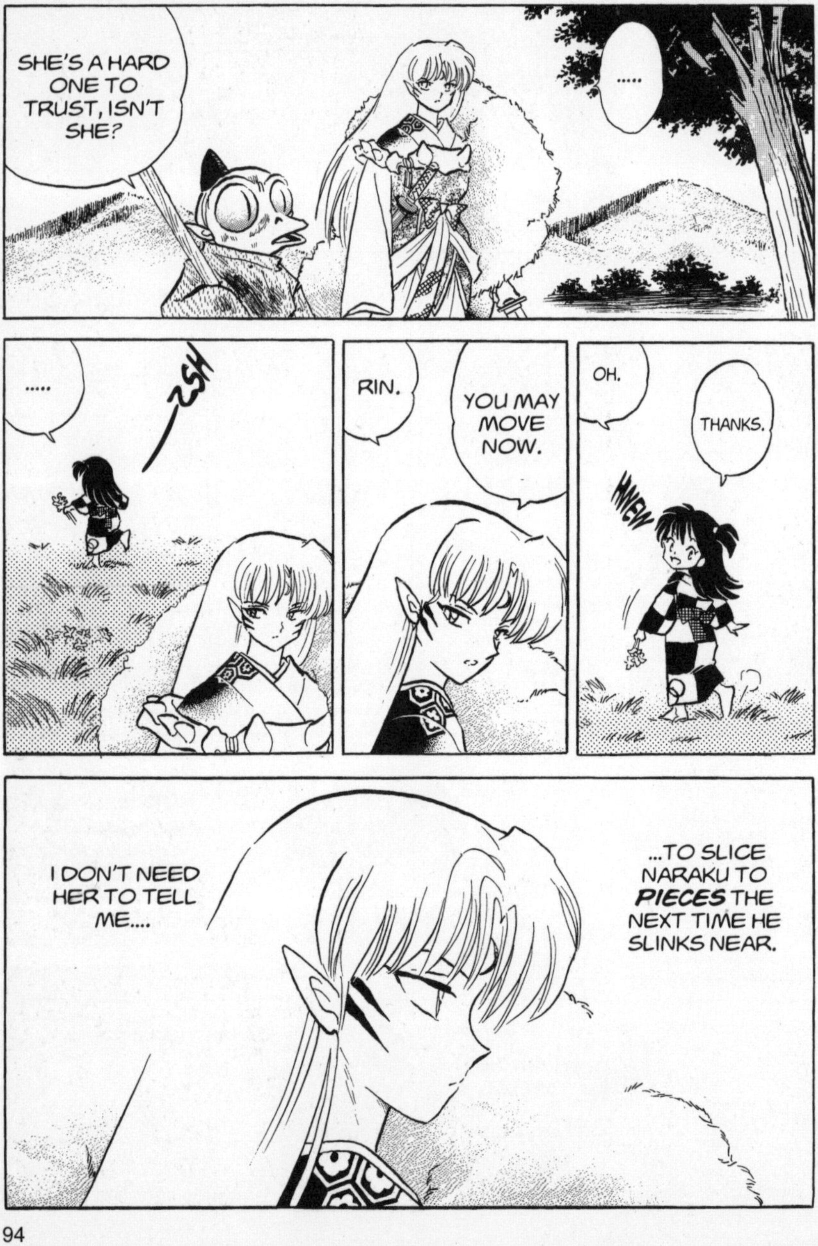
SHE'S A HARD ONE TO TRUST, ISN'T SHE?
.....
.....
ZSH
RIN.
YOU MAY MOVE NOW.
OH.
THANKS.
HNEW
I DON'T NEED HER TO TELL ME....
...TO SLICE NARAKU TO **PIECES** THE NEXT TIME HE SLINKS NEAR.

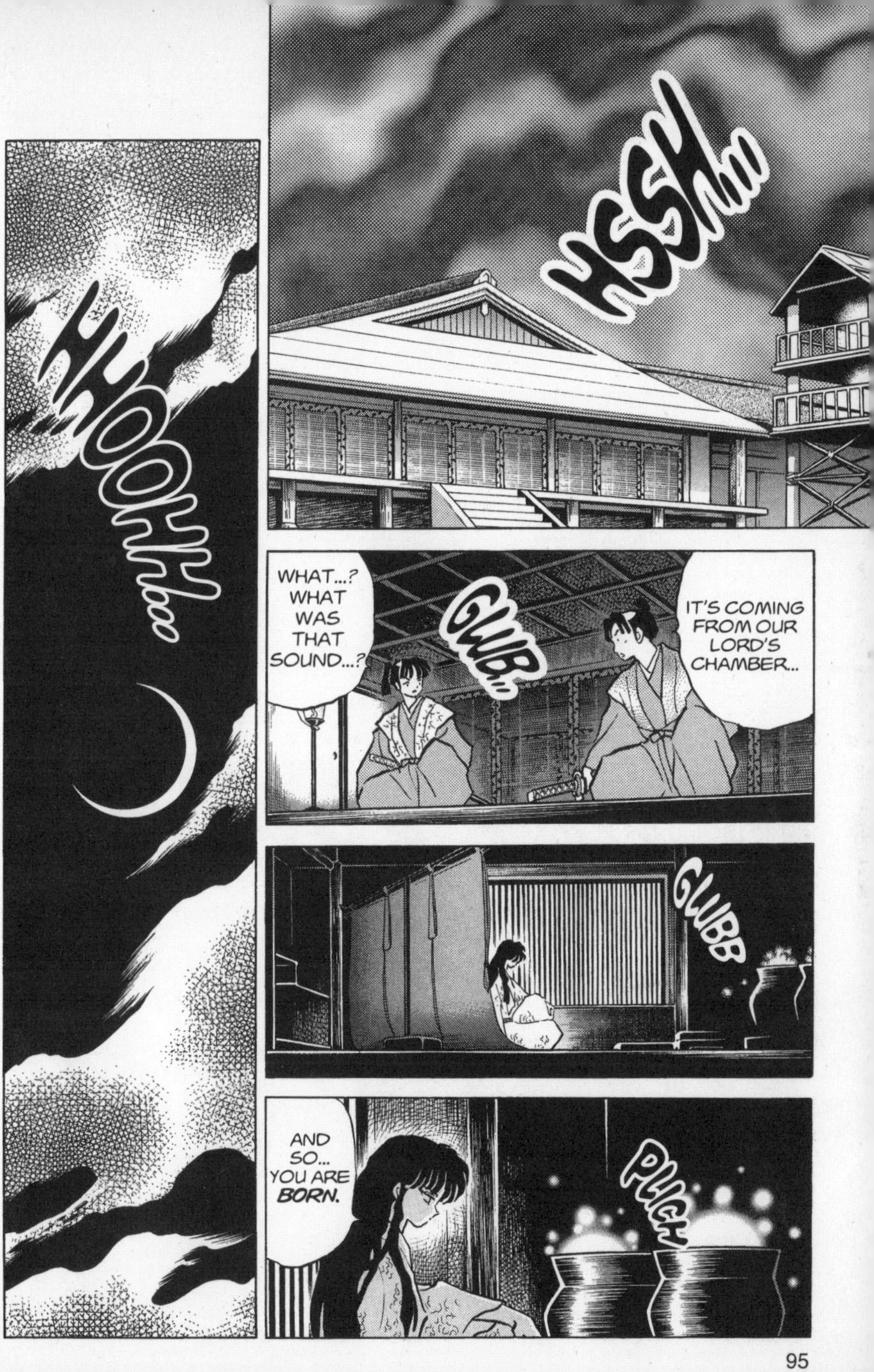
HHOOHHhooo
HSSH...
WHAT...? WHAT WAS THAT SOUND...?
GWUB...
IT'S COMING FROM OUR LORD'S CHAMBER...
GWUBB
AND SO... YOU ARE **BORN.**
PLOCH

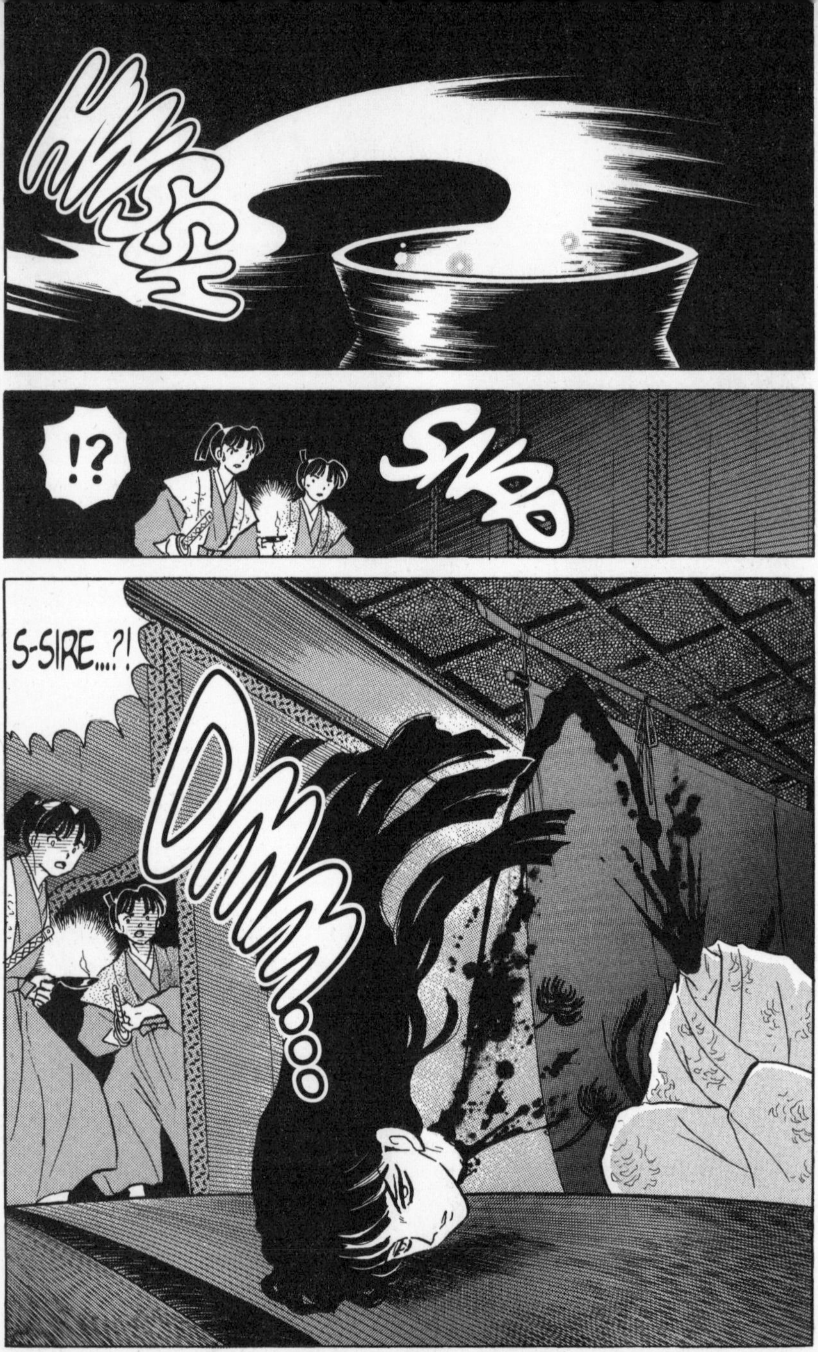

HWSSH
!?
SNAP
S-SIRE...?!
DMM...

SCROLL SIX

THE FOURTH ONE

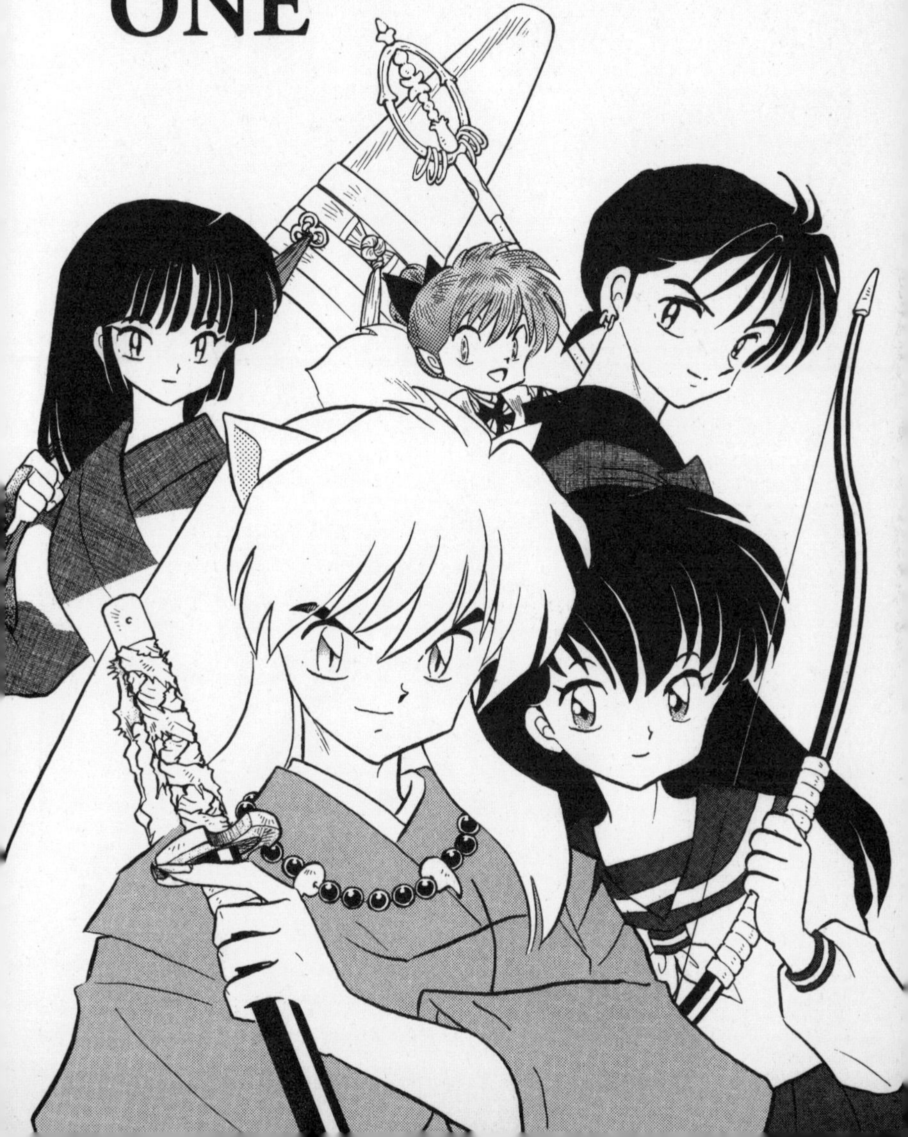

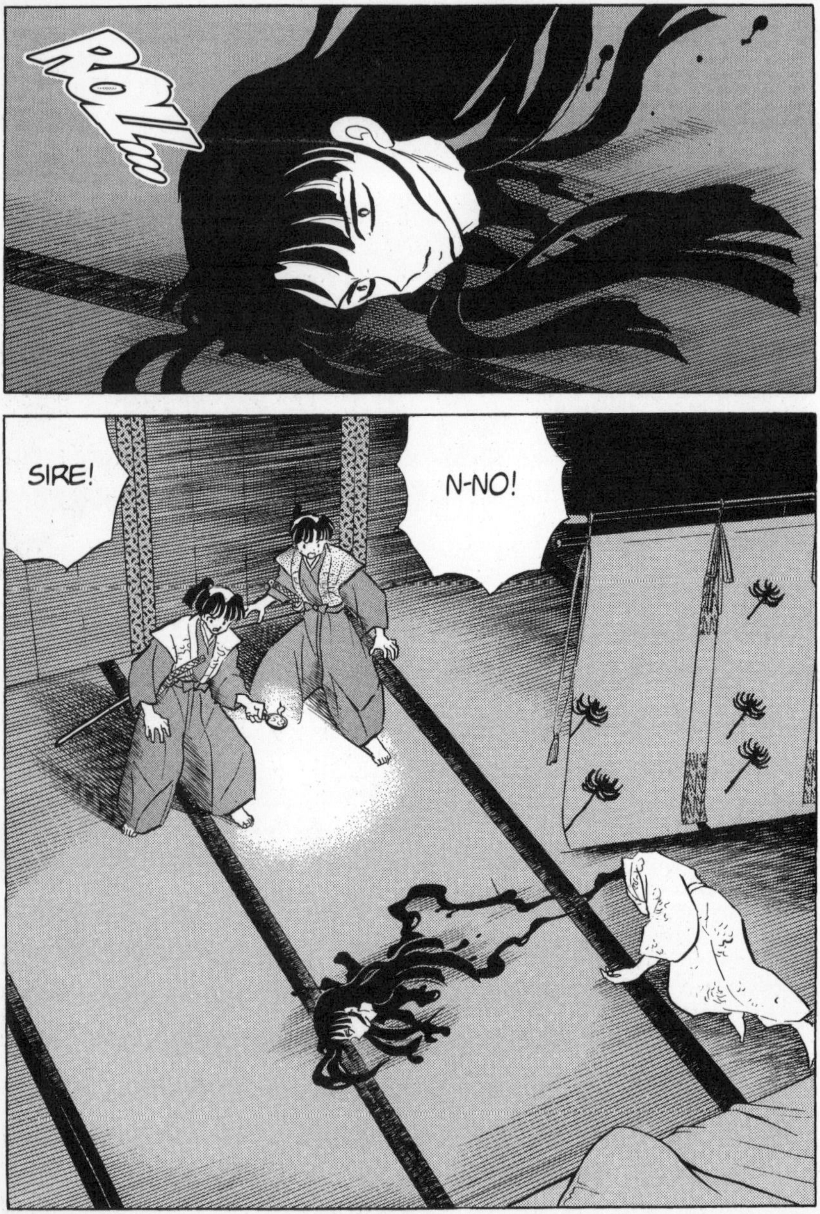
ROLL...
SIRE!
N-NO!

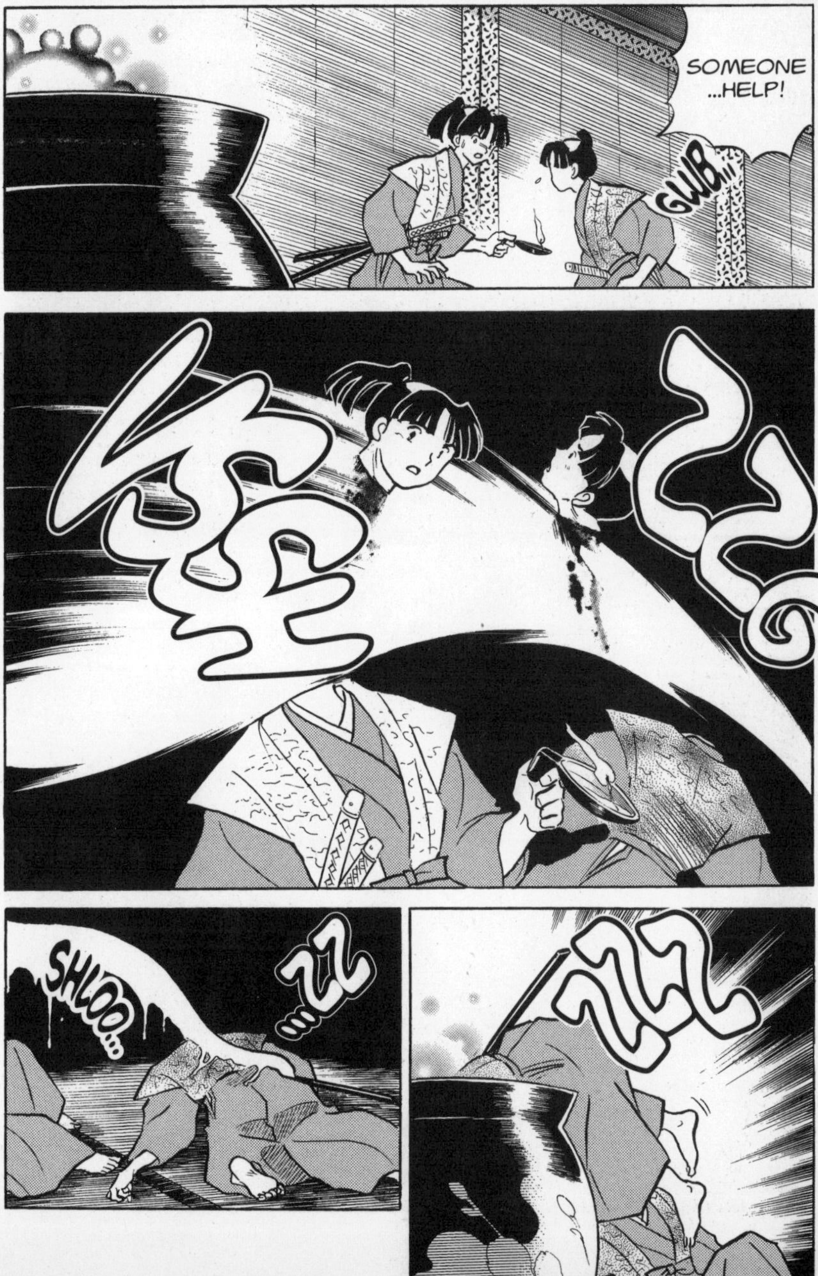
SOMEONE ...HELP!
GWB...
SHLOO...
...ZZ
ZZZ

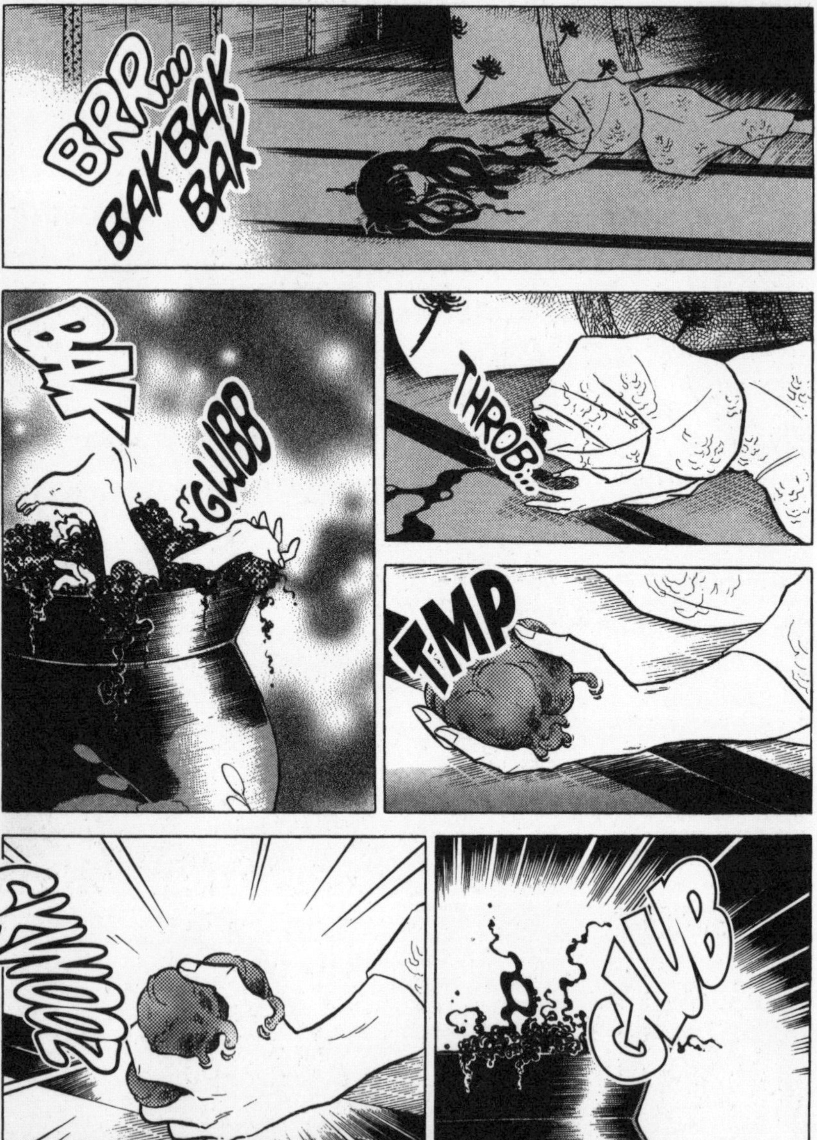
BRR...
BAK BAK BAK
BAK
GWBB
THROB...
TMP
SKWOOZ
GLUB

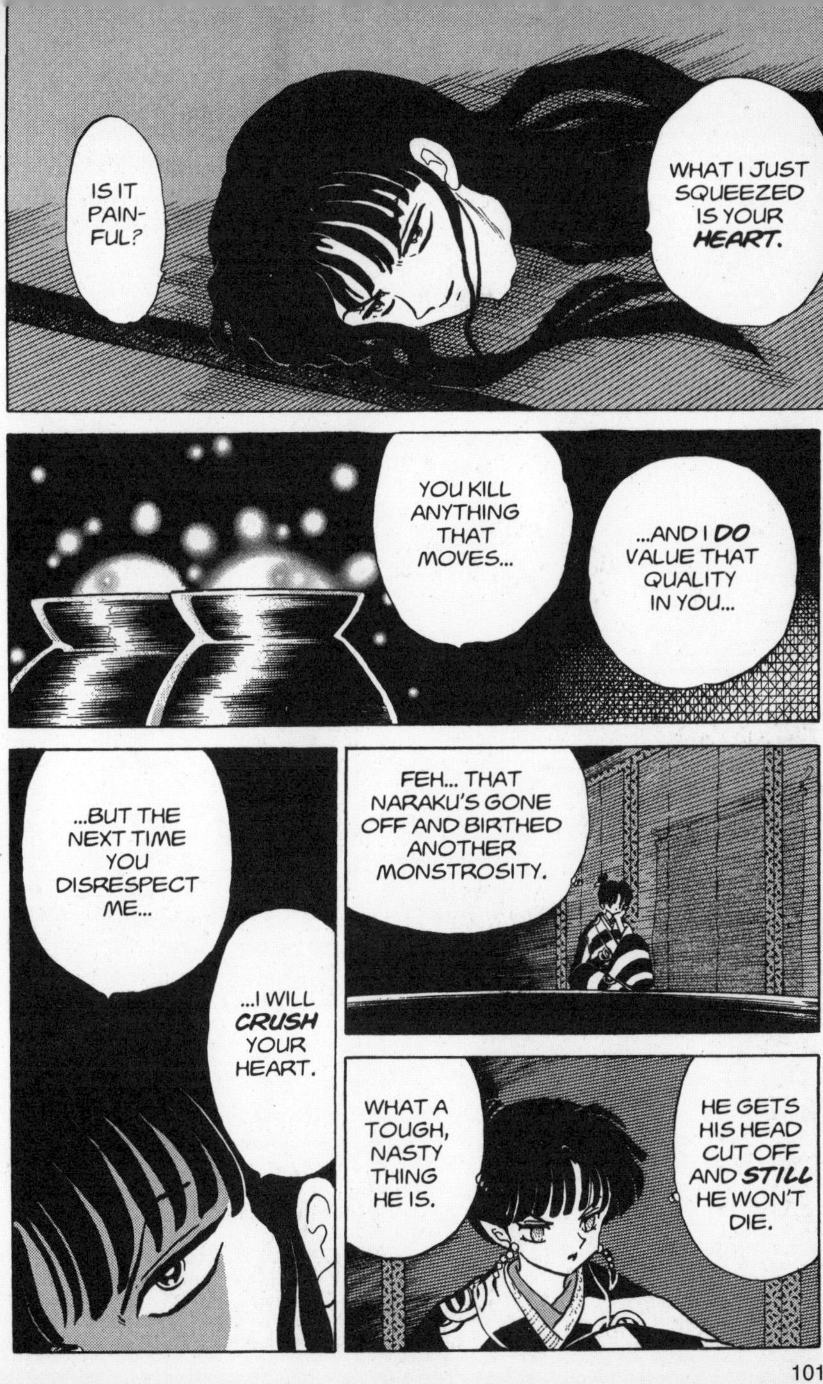
IS IT PAIN-FUL?
WHAT I JUST SQUEEZED IS YOUR **HEART.**
YOU KILL ANYTHING THAT MOVES...
...AND I **DO** VALUE THAT QUALITY IN YOU...
...BUT THE NEXT TIME YOU DISRESPECT ME...
...I WILL **CRUSH** YOUR HEART.
FEH... THAT NARAKU'S GONE OFF AND BIRTHED ANOTHER MONSTROSITY.
WHAT A TOUGH, NASTY THING HE IS.
HE GETS HIS HEAD CUT OFF AND **STILL** HE WON'T DIE.

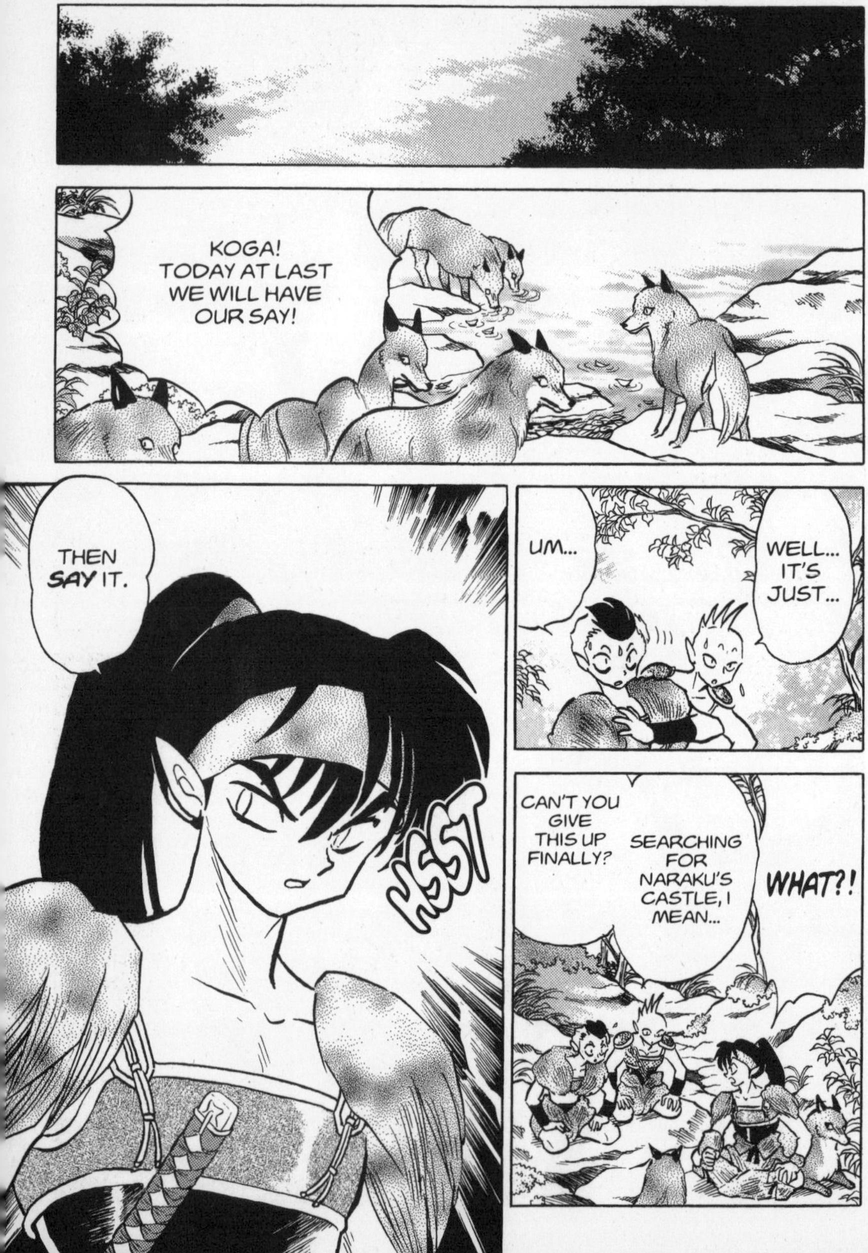
KOGA! TODAY AT LAST WE WILL HAVE OUR SAY!
THEN SAY IT.
HSST
UM...
WELL... IT'S JUST...
CAN'T YOU GIVE THIS UP FINALLY?
SEARCHING FOR NARAKU'S CASTLE, I MEAN...
WHAT?!

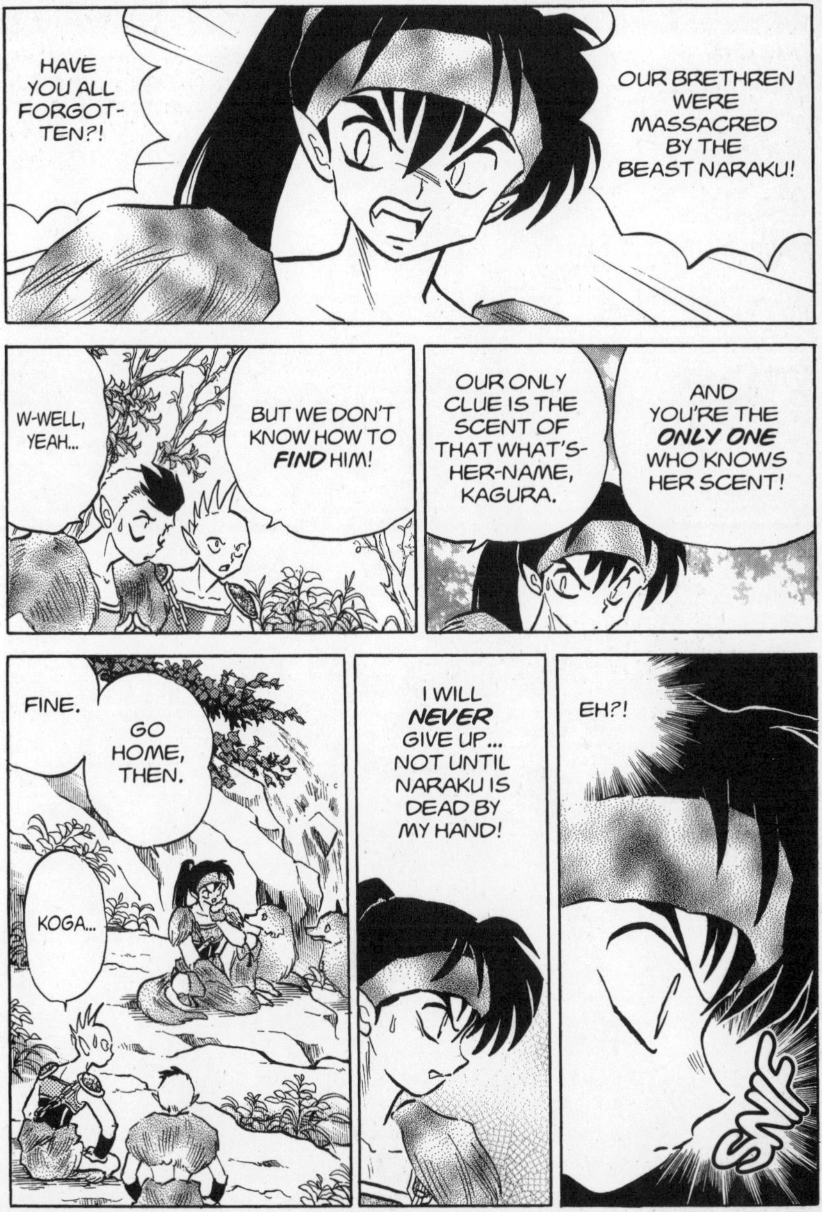
HAVE YOU ALL FORGOT-TEN?!
OUR BRETHREN WERE MASSACRED BY THE BEAST NARAKU!
W-WELL, YEAH...
BUT WE DON'T KNOW HOW TO **FIND** HIM!
OUR ONLY CLUE IS THE SCENT OF THAT WHAT'S-HER-NAME, KAGURA.
AND YOU'RE THE **ONLY ONE** WHO KNOWS HER SCENT!
FINE.
GO HOME, THEN.
KOGA...
I WILL **NEVER** GIVE UP... NOT UNTIL NARAKU IS DEAD BY MY HAND!
EH?!
SNIF

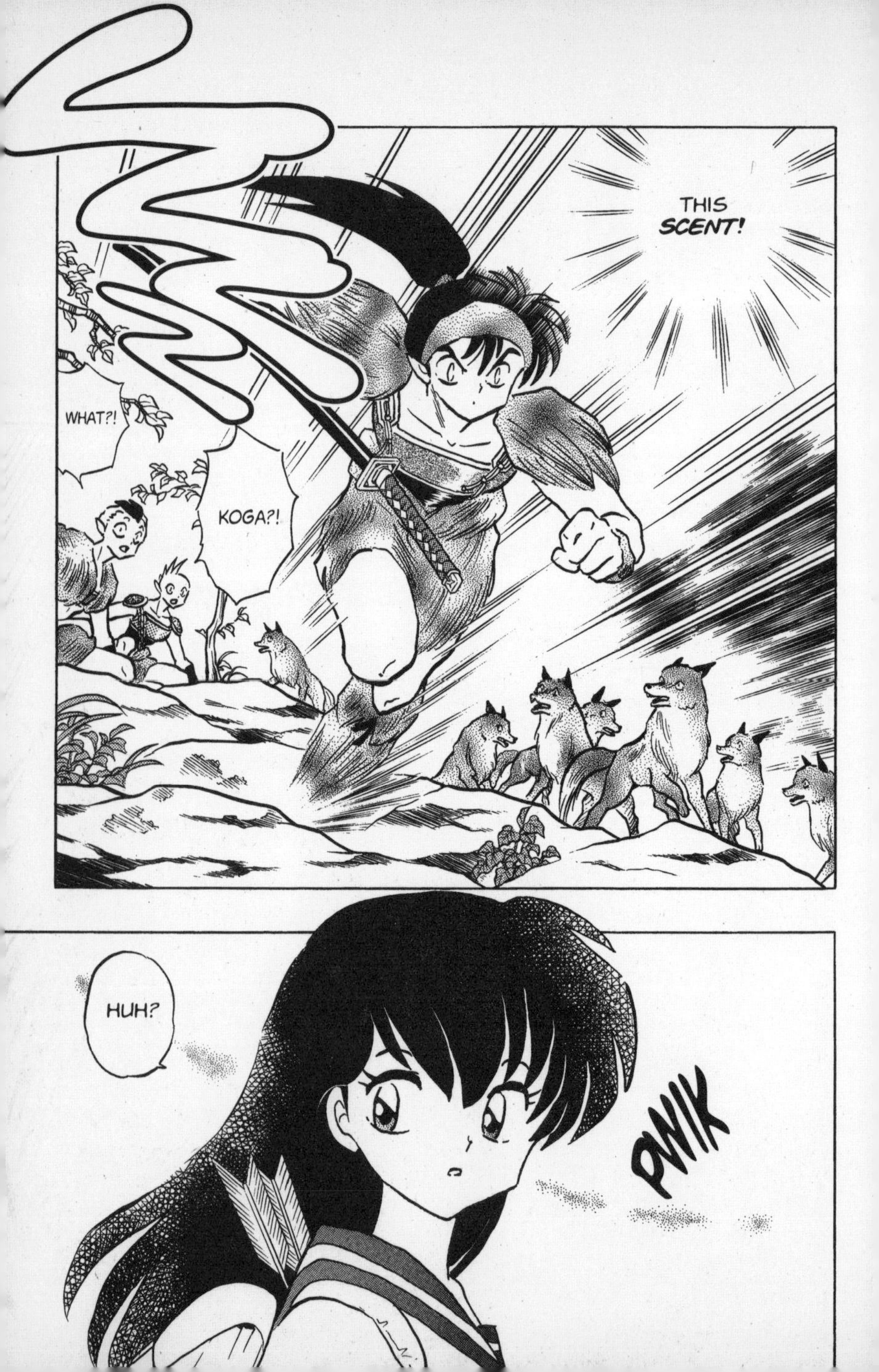
THIS SCENT!
WHAT?!
KOGA?!
HUH?
PWIK

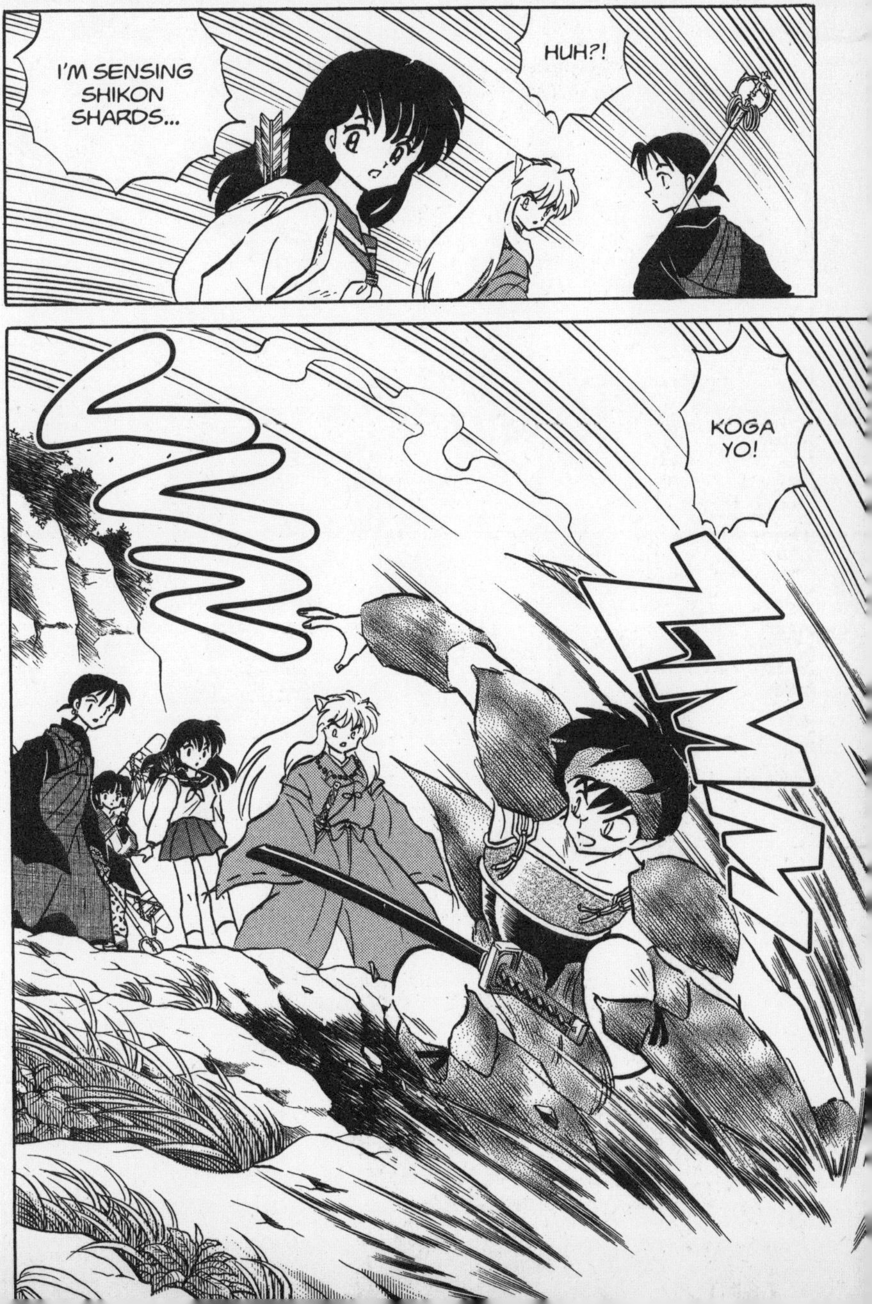
I'M SENSING SHIKON SHARDS...
HUH?!
KOGA YO!

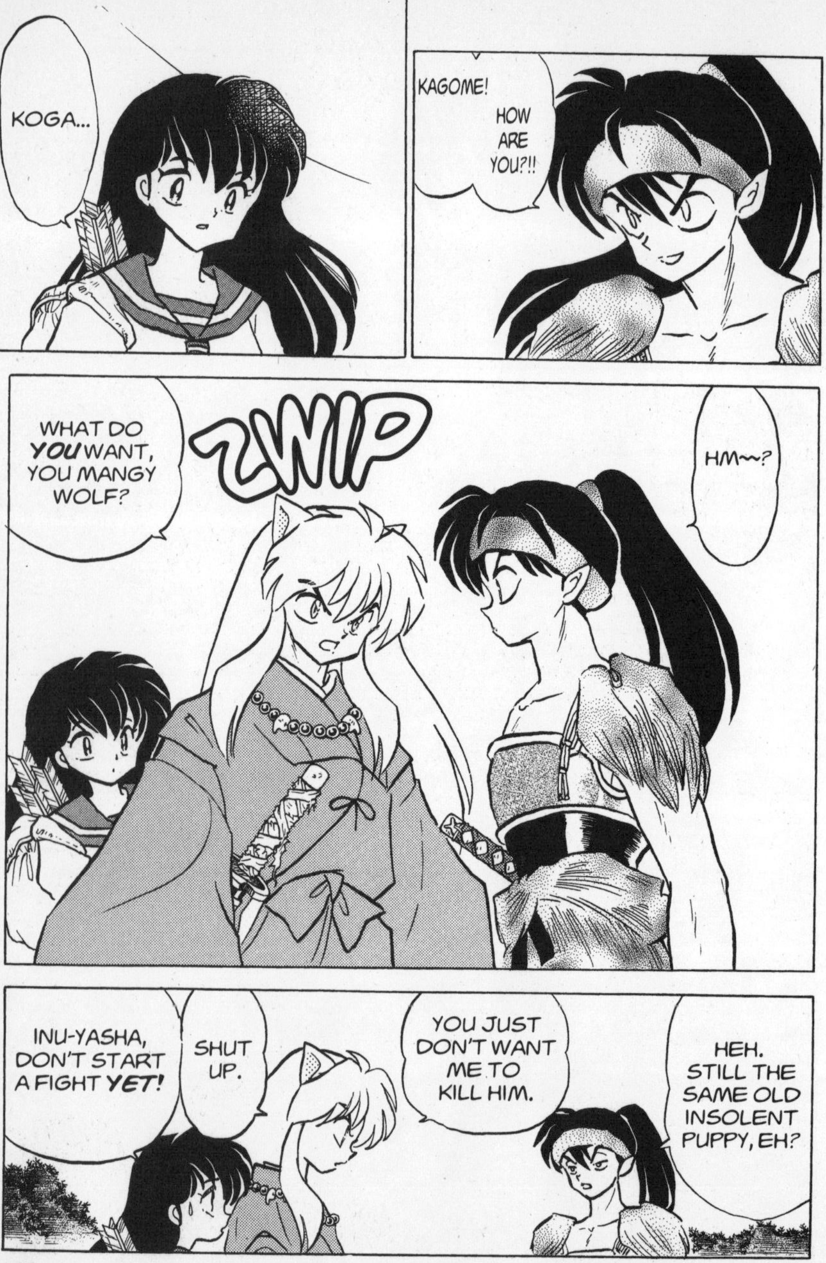
KOGA...
KAGOME!
HOW ARE YOU?!!
WHAT DO YOU WANT, YOU MANGY WOLF?
ZWIP
HM~~?
INU-YASHA, DON'T START A FIGHT YET!
SHUT UP.
YOU JUST DON'T WANT ME TO KILL HIM.
HEH. STILL THE SAME OLD INSOLENT PUPPY, EH?

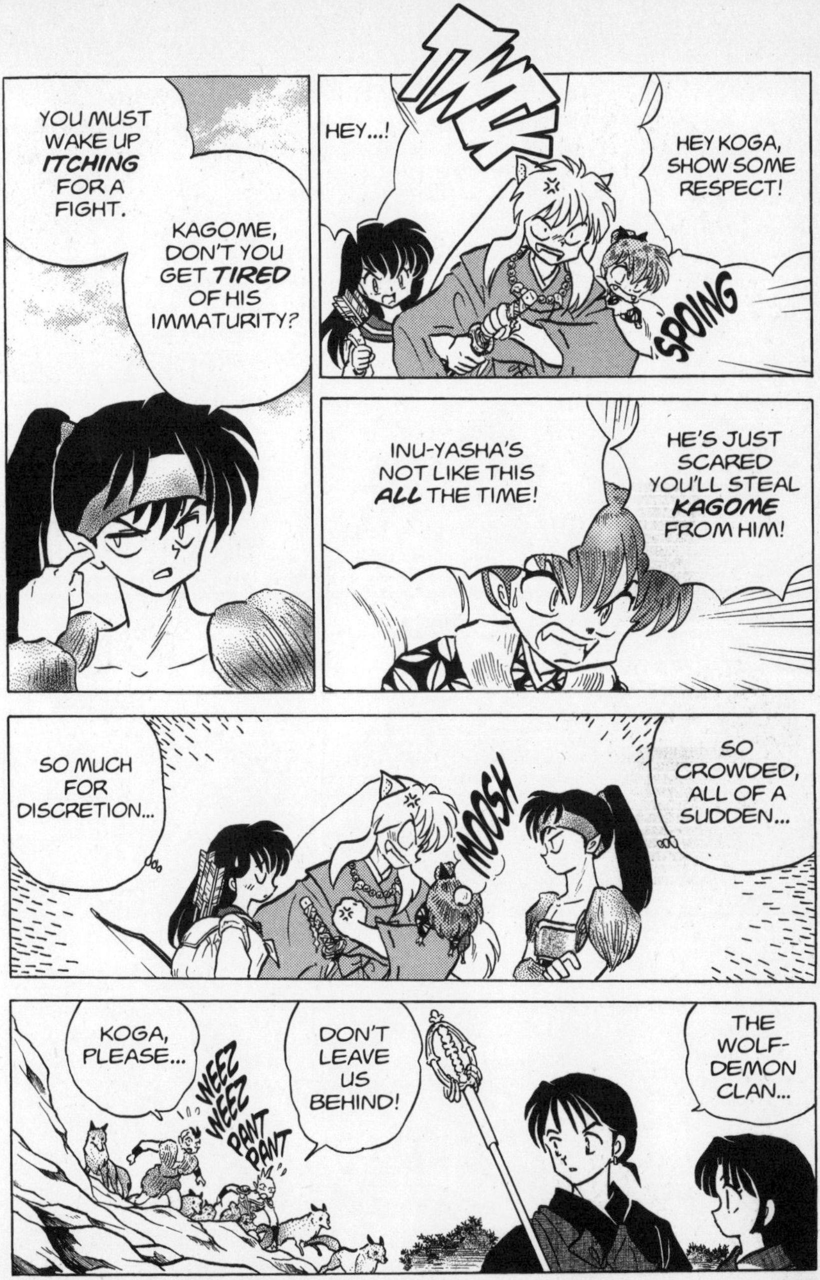
YOU MUST WAKE UP ITCHING FOR A FIGHT.
KAGOME, DON'T YOU GET TIRED OF HIS IMMATURITY?
HEY...!
TWAK
HEY KOGA, SHOW SOME RESPECT!
SPOING
INU-YASHA'S NOT LIKE THIS ALL THE TIME!
HE'S JUST SCARED YOU'LL STEAL KAGOME FROM HIM!
SO MUCH FOR DISCRETION...
MOOSH
SO CROWDED, ALL OF A SUDDEN...
KOGA, PLEASE...
WEEZ WEEZ
PANT PANT
DON'T LEAVE US BEHIND!
THE WOLF-DEMON CLAN...

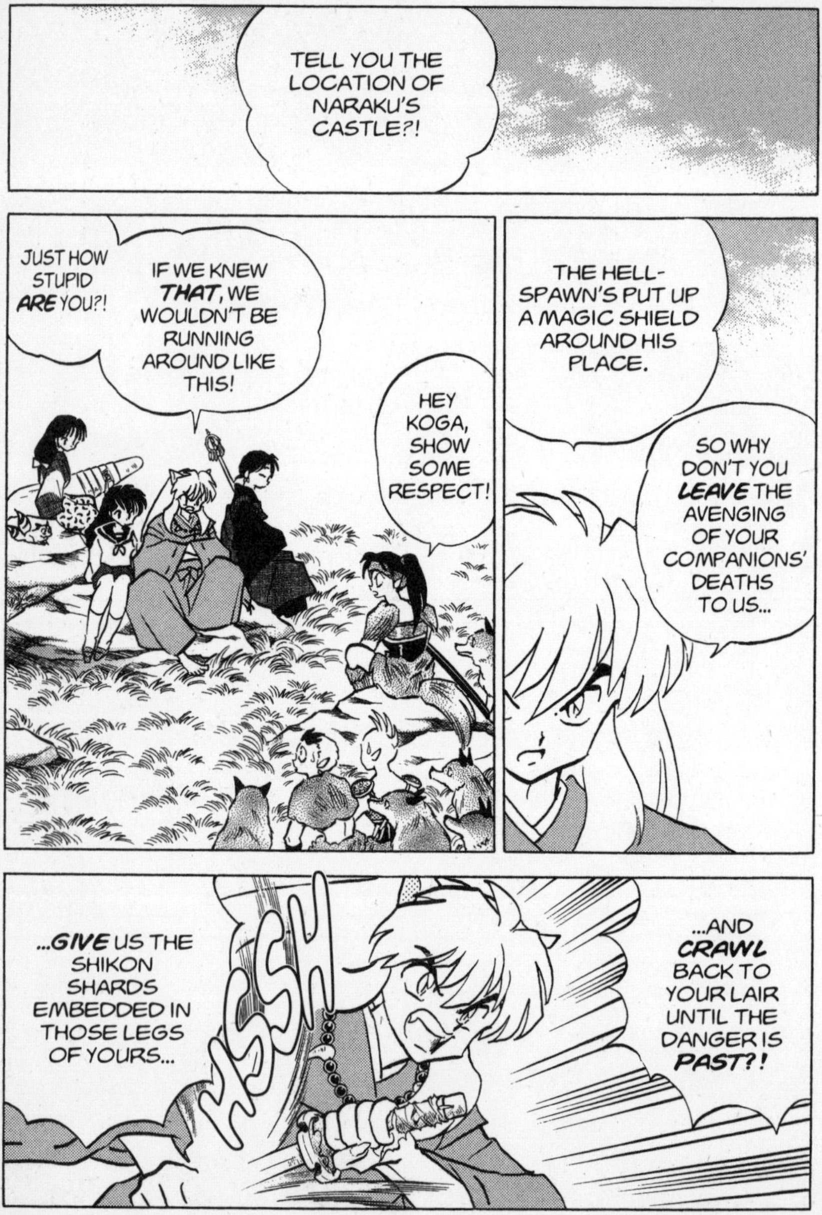
TELL YOU THE LOCATION OF NARAKU'S CASTLE?!
JUST HOW STUPID ARE YOU?!
IF WE KNEW THAT, WE WOULDN'T BE RUNNING AROUND LIKE THIS!
HEY KOGA, SHOW SOME RESPECT!
THE HELL-SPAWN'S PUT UP A MAGIC SHIELD AROUND HIS PLACE.
SO WHY DON'T YOU LEAVE THE AVENGING OF YOUR COMPANIONS' DEATHS TO US...
...GIVE US THE SHIKON SHARDS EMBEDDED IN THOSE LEGS OF YOURS...
HSSH
...AND CRAWL BACK TO YOUR LAIR UNTIL THE DANGER IS PAST?!

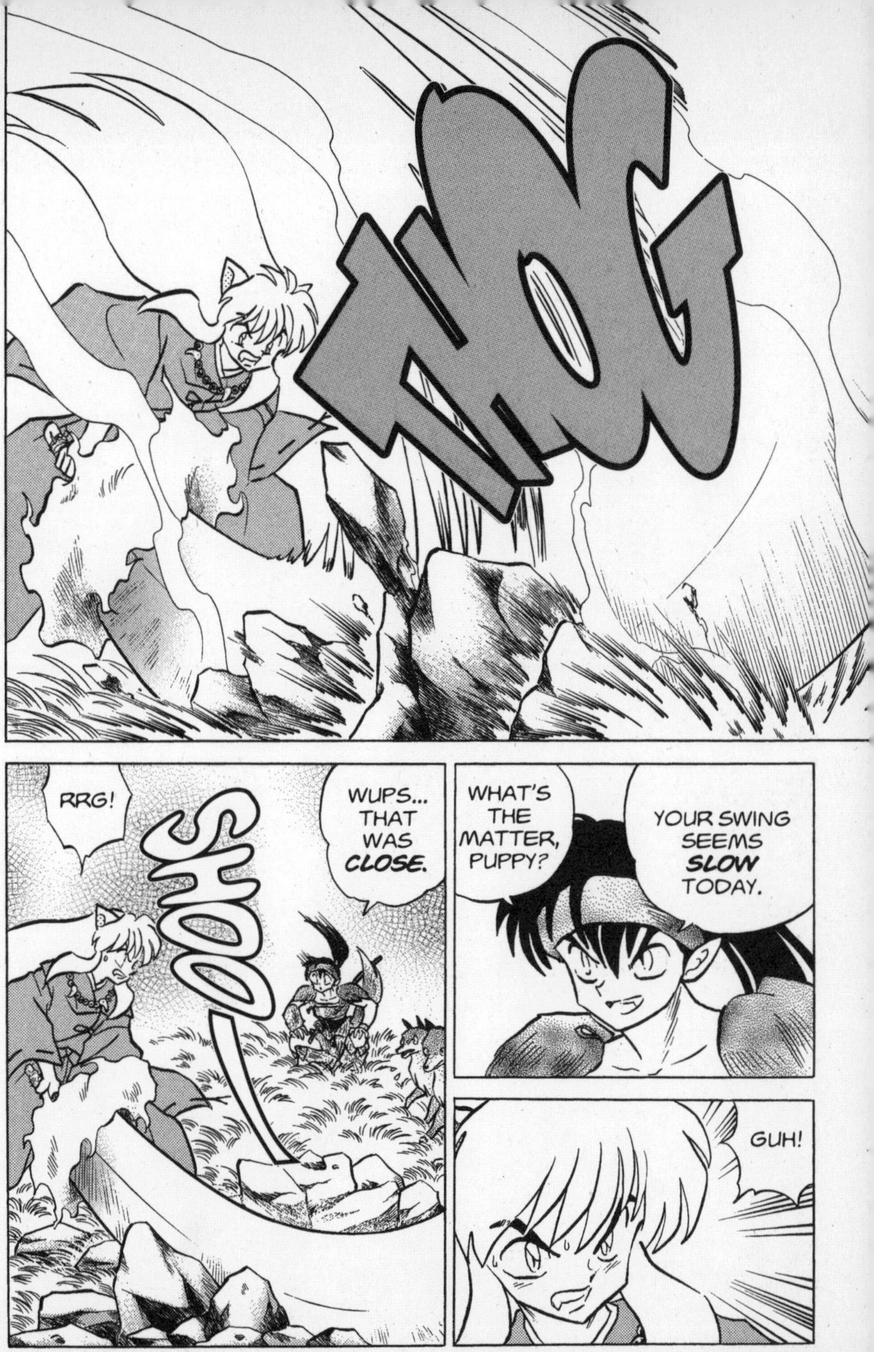

THOG
RRG!
SHOO
WUPS... THAT WAS CLOSE.
WHAT'S THE MATTER, PUPPY?
YOUR SWING SEEMS SLOW TODAY.
GUH!

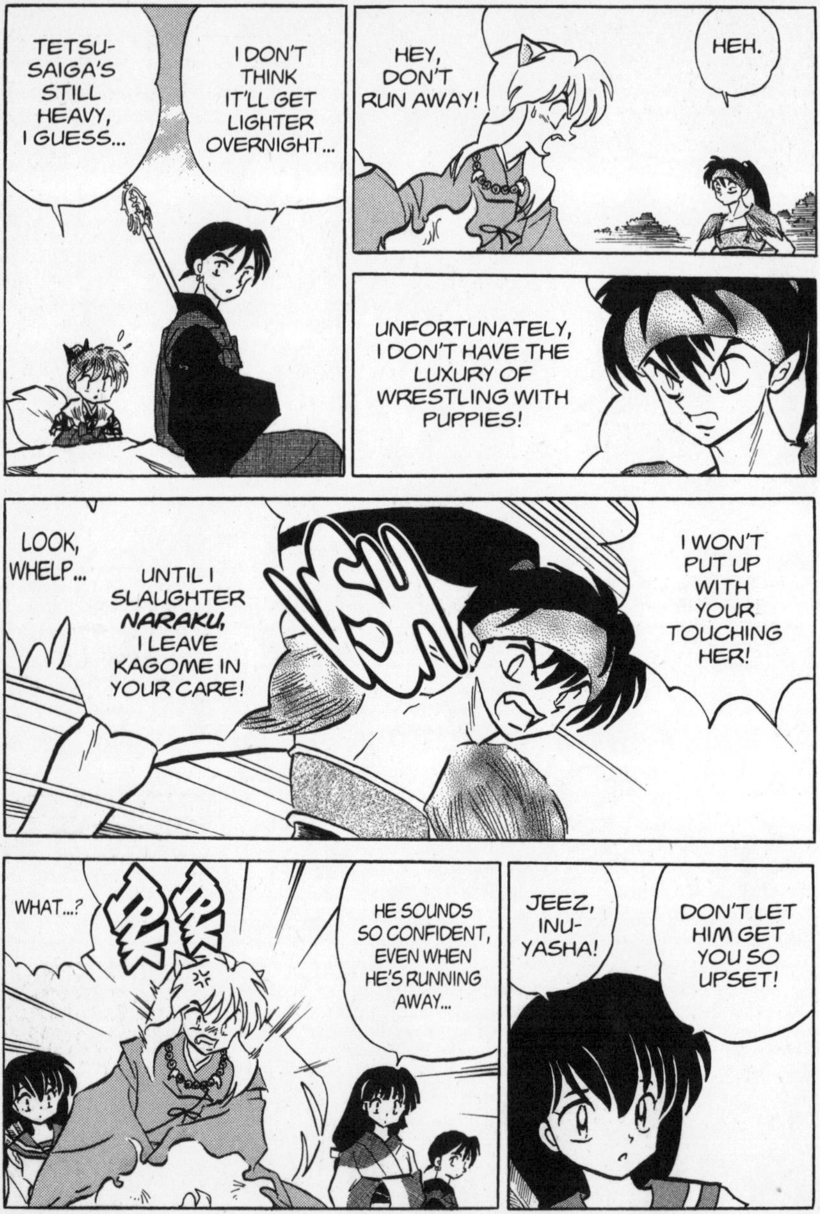
TETSU-SAIGA'S STILL HEAVY, I GUESS...
I DON'T THINK IT'LL GET LIGHTER OVERNIGHT...
HEY, DON'T RUN AWAY!
HEH.
UNFORTUNATELY, I DON'T HAVE THE LUXURY OF WRESTLING WITH PUPPIES!
LOOK, WHELP...
UNTIL I SLAUGHTER NARAKU, I LEAVE KAGOME IN YOUR CARE!
WSH
I WON'T PUT UP WITH YOUR TOUCHING HER!
WHAT...?
TRK TRK
HE SOUNDS SO CONFIDENT, EVEN WHEN HE'S RUNNING AWAY...
JEEZ, INU-YASHA!
DON'T LET HIM GET YOU SO UPSET!

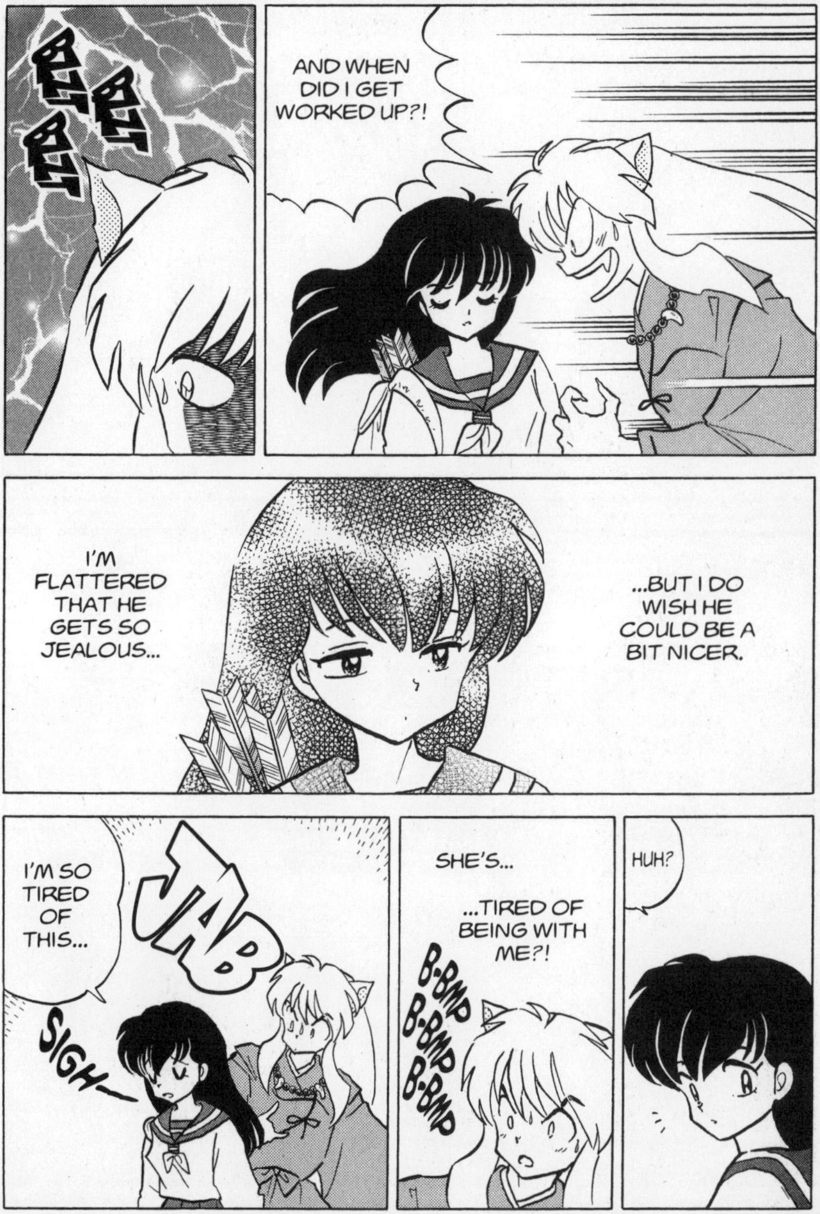
BZZT
BZZT
BZZT
AND WHEN DID I GET WORKED UP?!
I'M FLATTERED THAT HE GETS SO JEALOUS...
...BUT I DO WISH HE COULD BE A BIT NICER.
I'M SO TIRED OF THIS...
JAB
SIGH—
SHE'S...
...TIRED OF BEING WITH ME?!
B-BMP B-BMP B-BMP B-BMP
HUH?

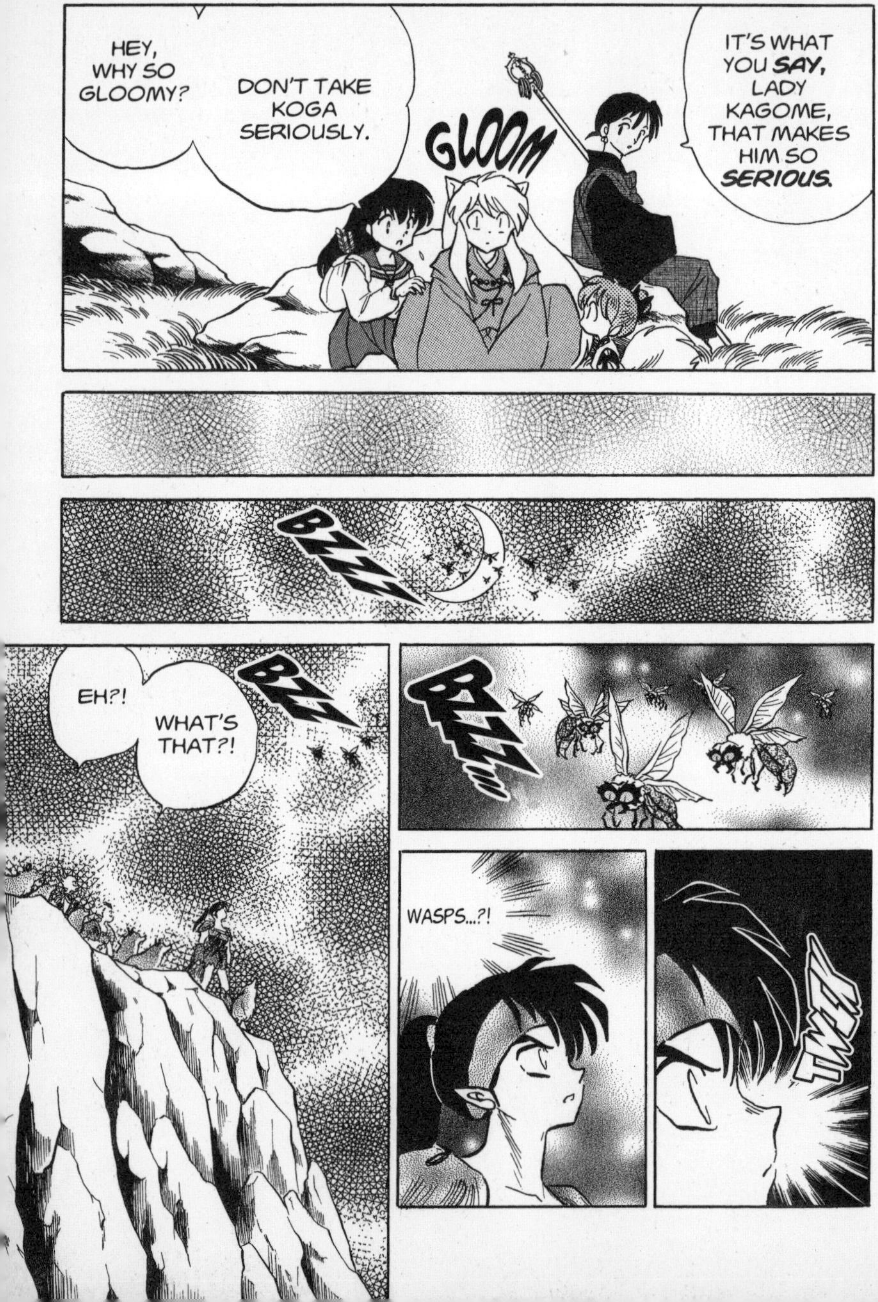
HEY, WHY SO GLOOMY?
DON'T TAKE KOGA SERIOUSLY.
GLOOM
IT'S WHAT YOU **SAY,** LADY KAGOME, THAT MAKES HIM SO **SERIOUS.**
EH?!
WHAT'S THAT?!
WASPS...?!

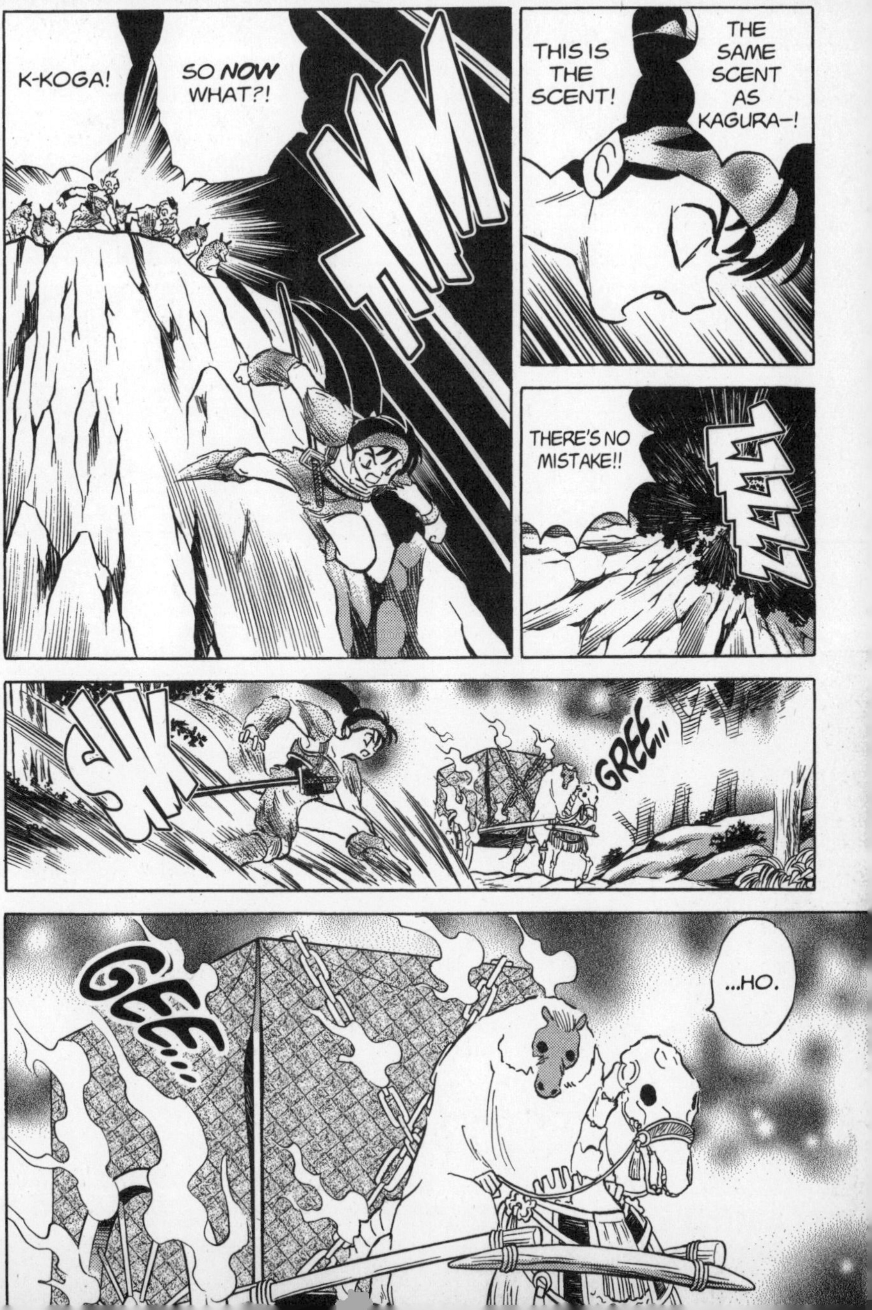
K-KOGA!
SO NOW WHAT?!
WM
THIS IS THE SCENT!
THE SAME SCENT AS KAGURA-!
THERE'S NO MISTAKE!!
SHK
GREE...
GEE...
...HO.

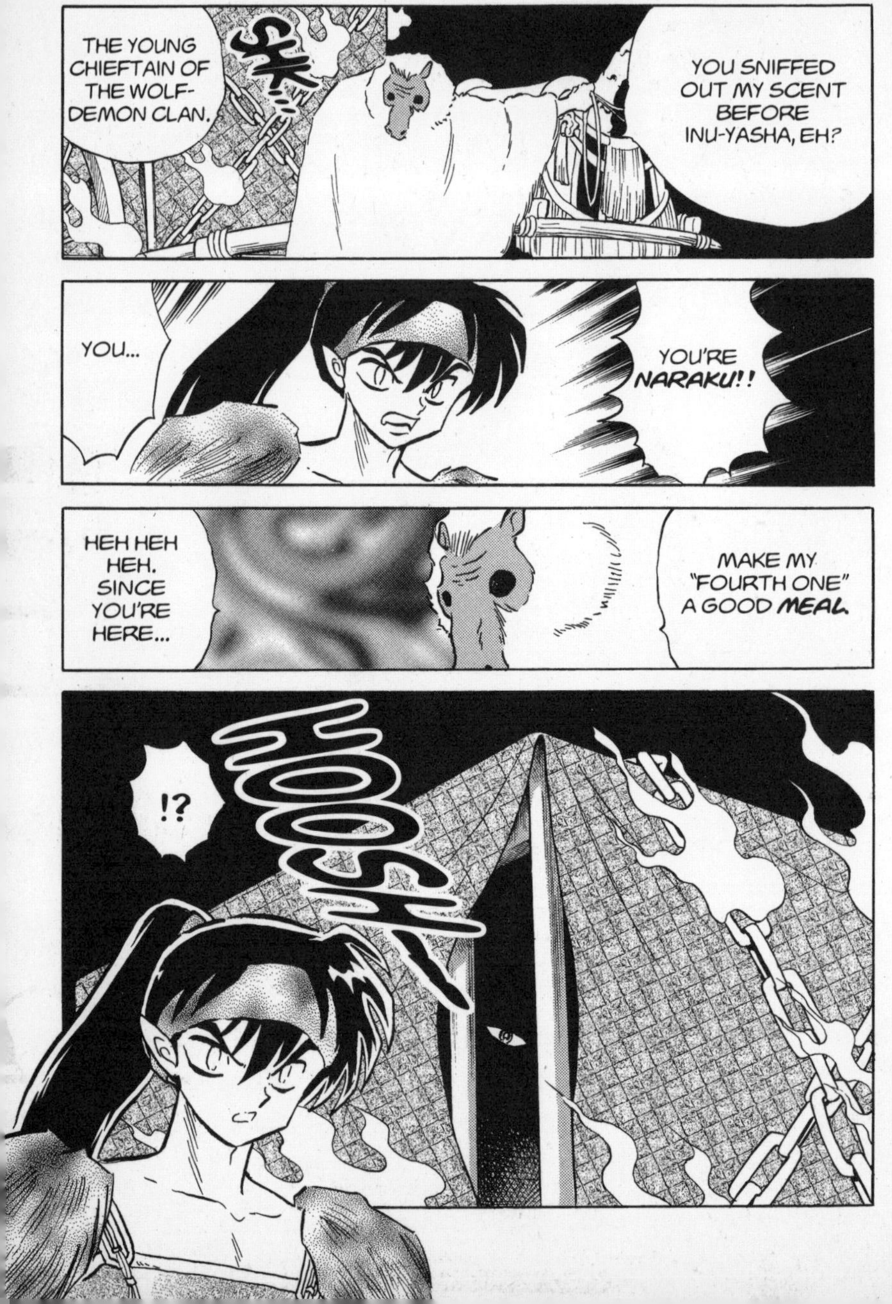
THE YOUNG CHIEFTAIN OF THE WOLF-DEMON CLAN.
SSK...
YOU SNIFFED OUT MY SCENT BEFORE INU-YASHA, EH?
YOU...
YOU'RE NARAKU!!
HEH HEH HEH. SINCE YOU'RE HERE...
MAKE MY "FOURTH ONE" A GOOD MEAL.
!?
WHOOSH

SCROLL SEVEN

JUROMARU, THE BEAST BOY

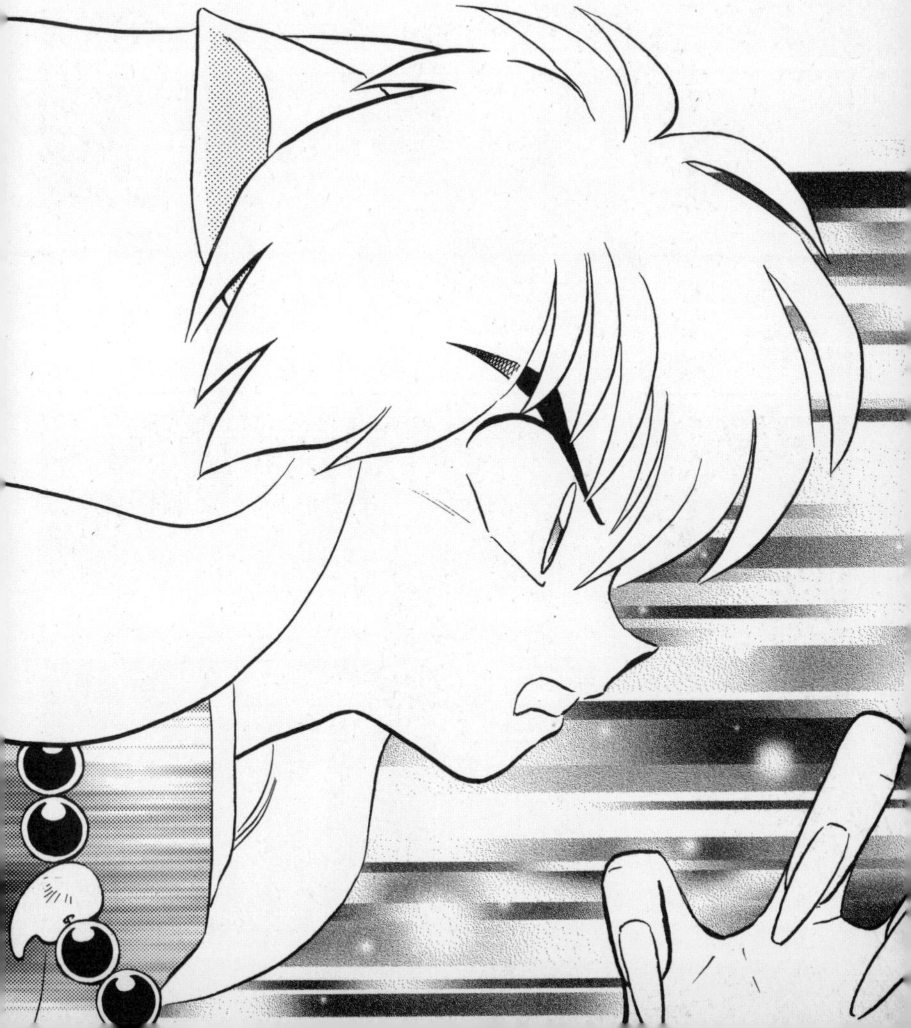

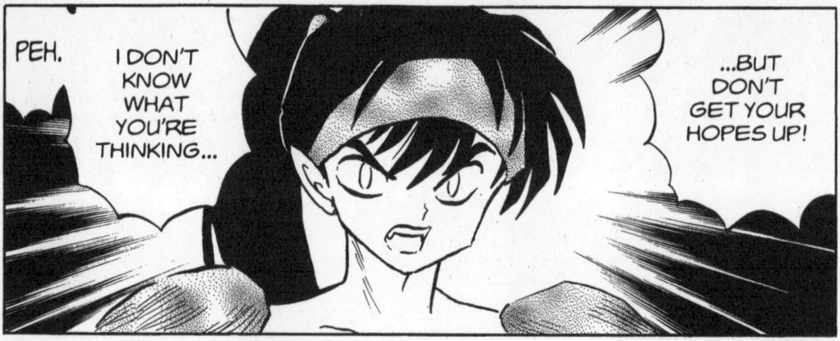
PEH.
I DON'T KNOW WHAT YOU'RE THINKING...
...BUT DON'T GET YOUR HOPES UP!

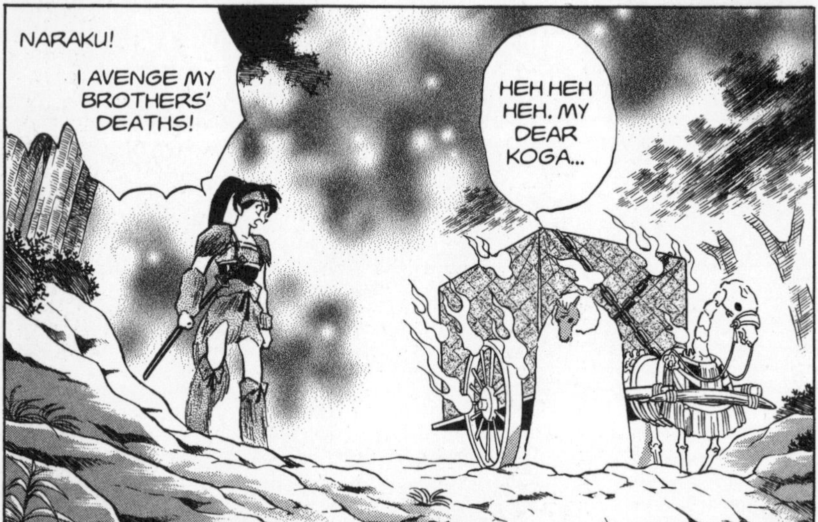
NARAKU!
I AVENGE MY BROTHERS' DEATHS!
HEH HEH HEH. MY DEAR KOGA...

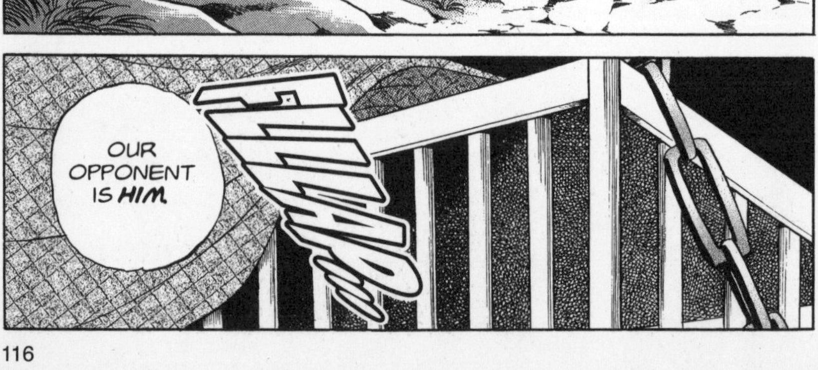
OUR OPPONENT IS *HIM*.

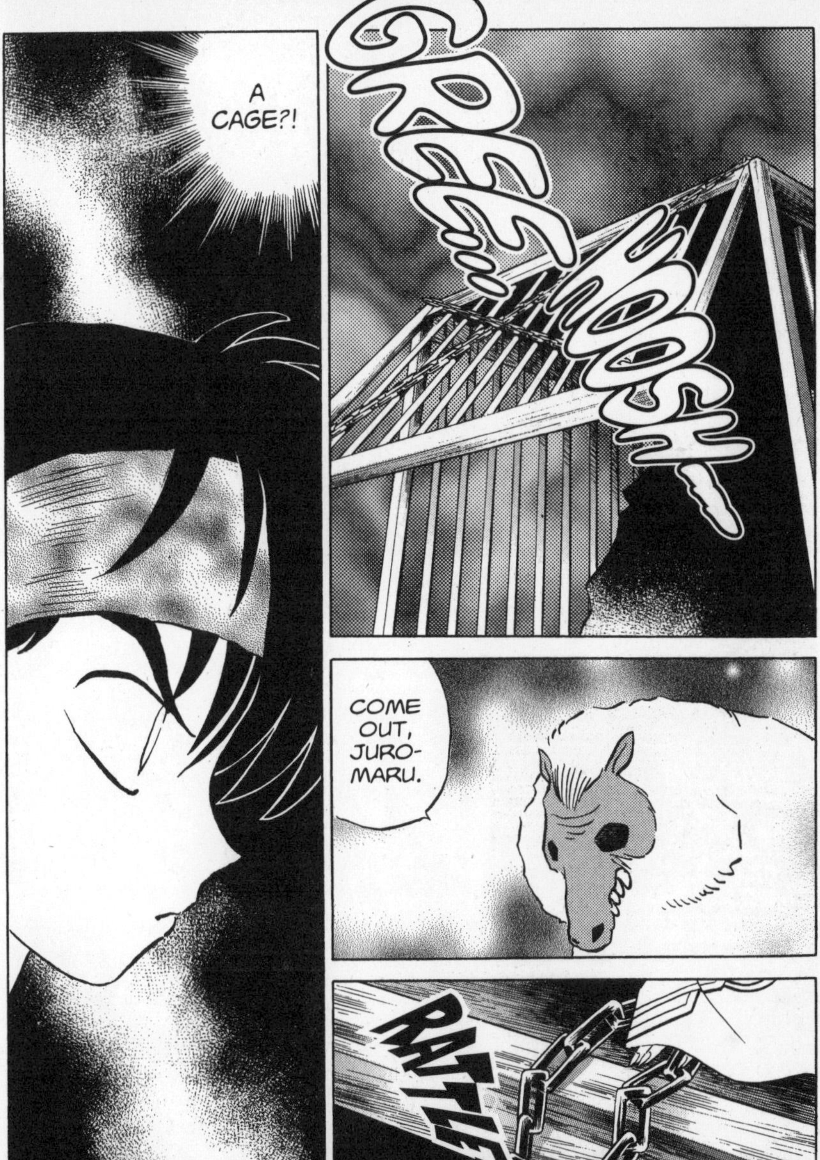
A CAGE?!
GREE...
WHOOSH
COME OUT, JURO-MARU.
RATTLE

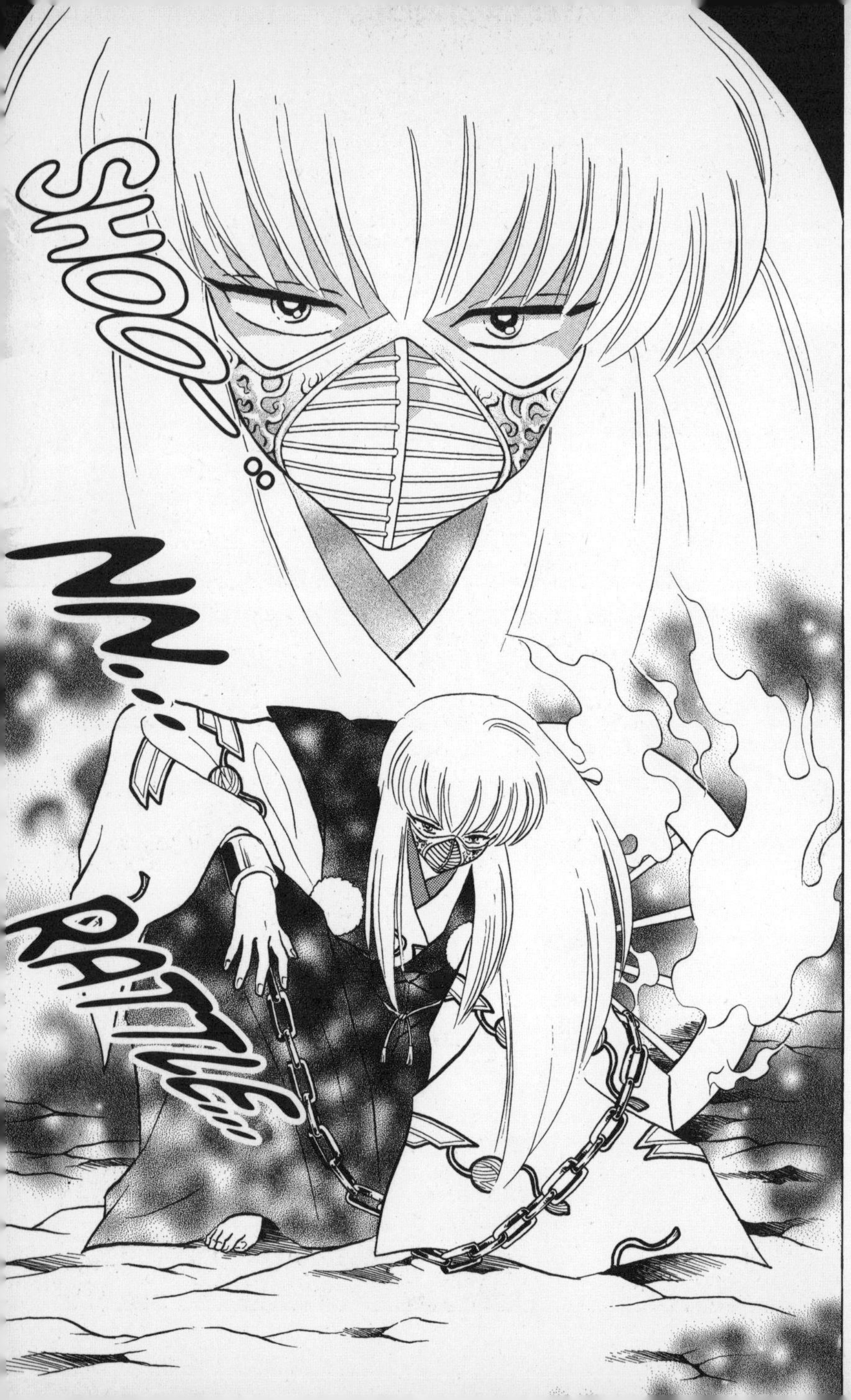
SHOO..
NN...
RATTLE!!

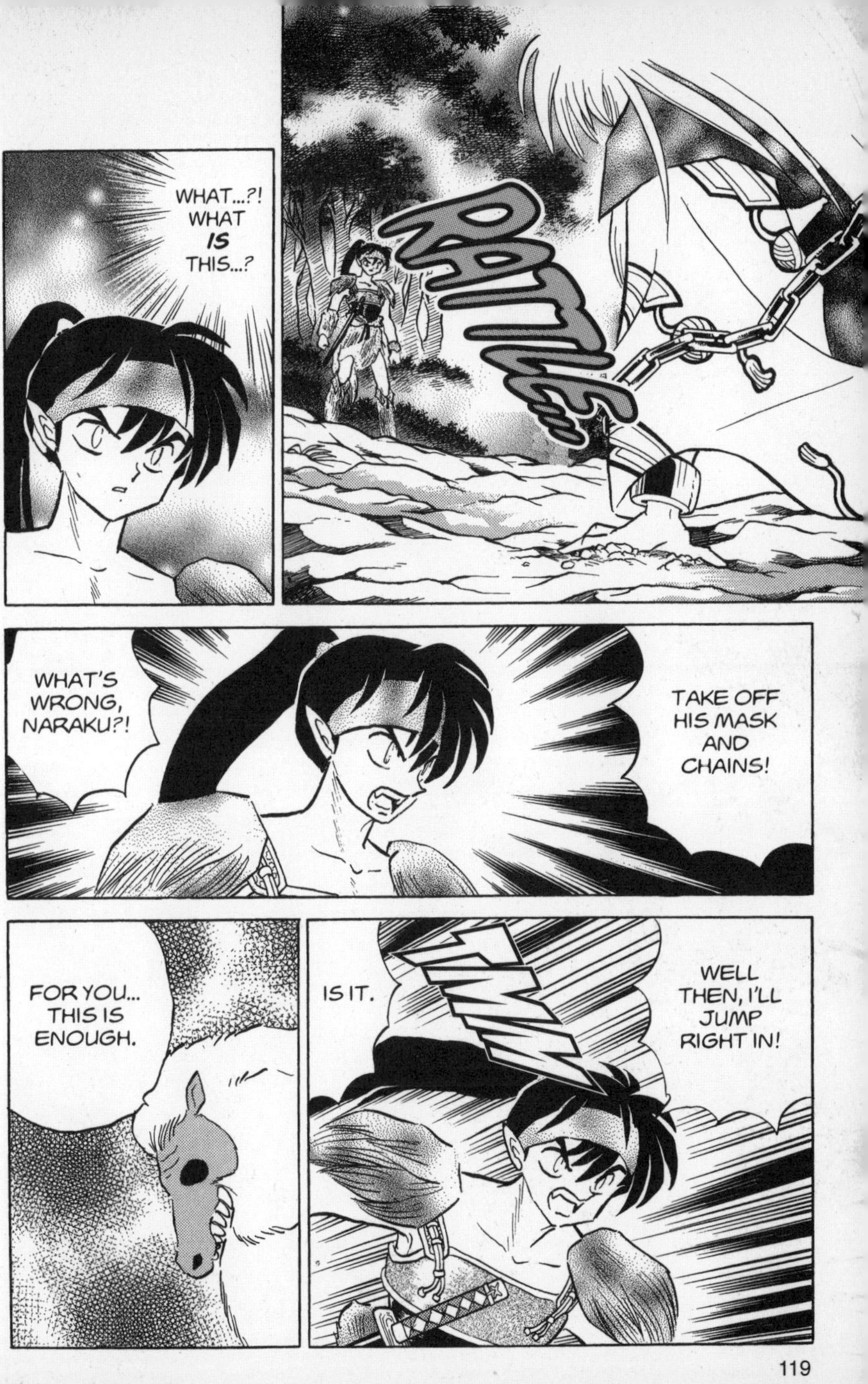
WHAT...?! WHAT *IS* THIS...?
RATTLE...
WHAT'S WRONG, NARAKU?!
TAKE OFF HIS MASK AND CHAINS!
FOR YOU... THIS IS ENOUGH.
IS IT.
WELL THEN, I'LL JUMP RIGHT IN!

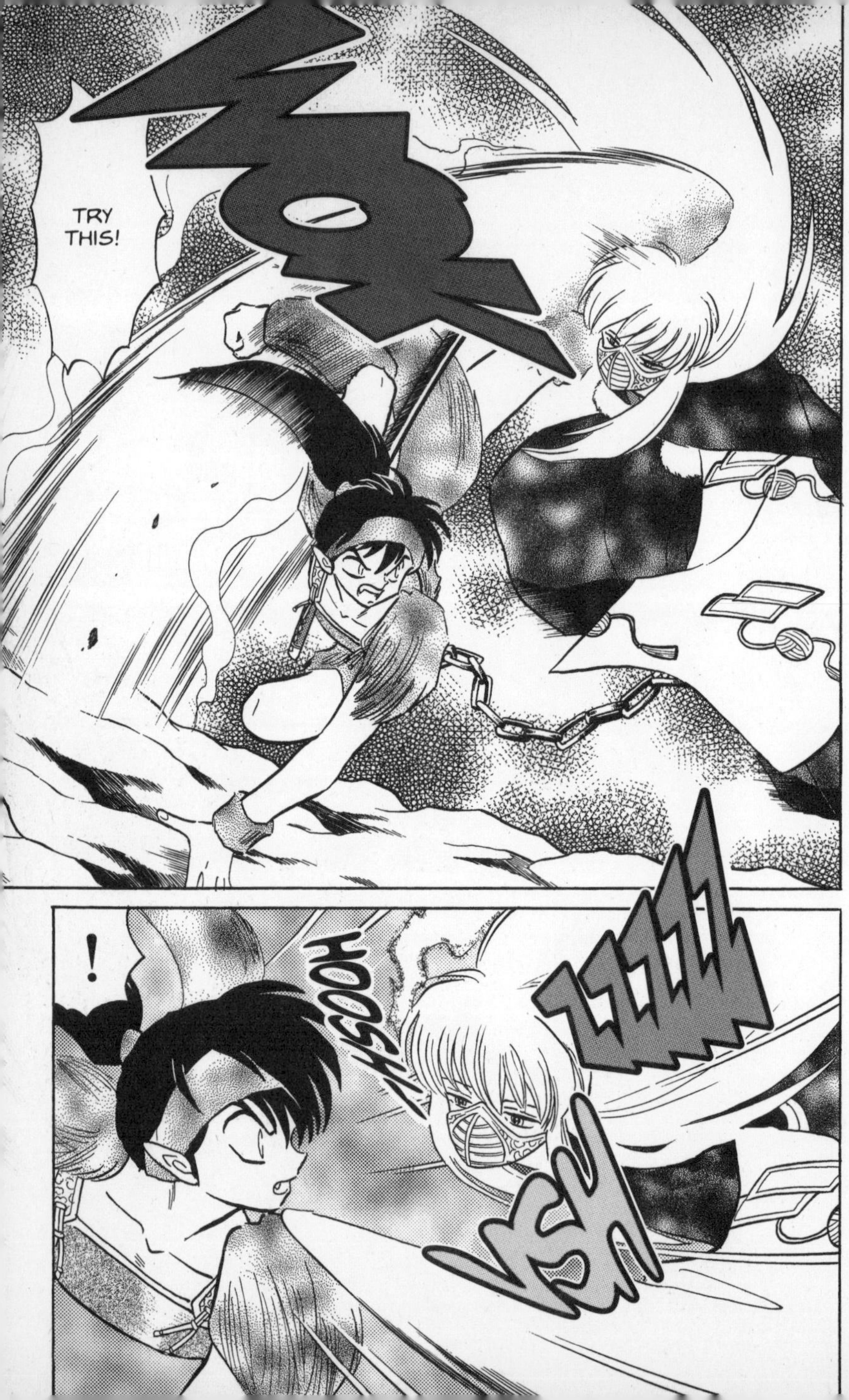
TRY THIS!
!

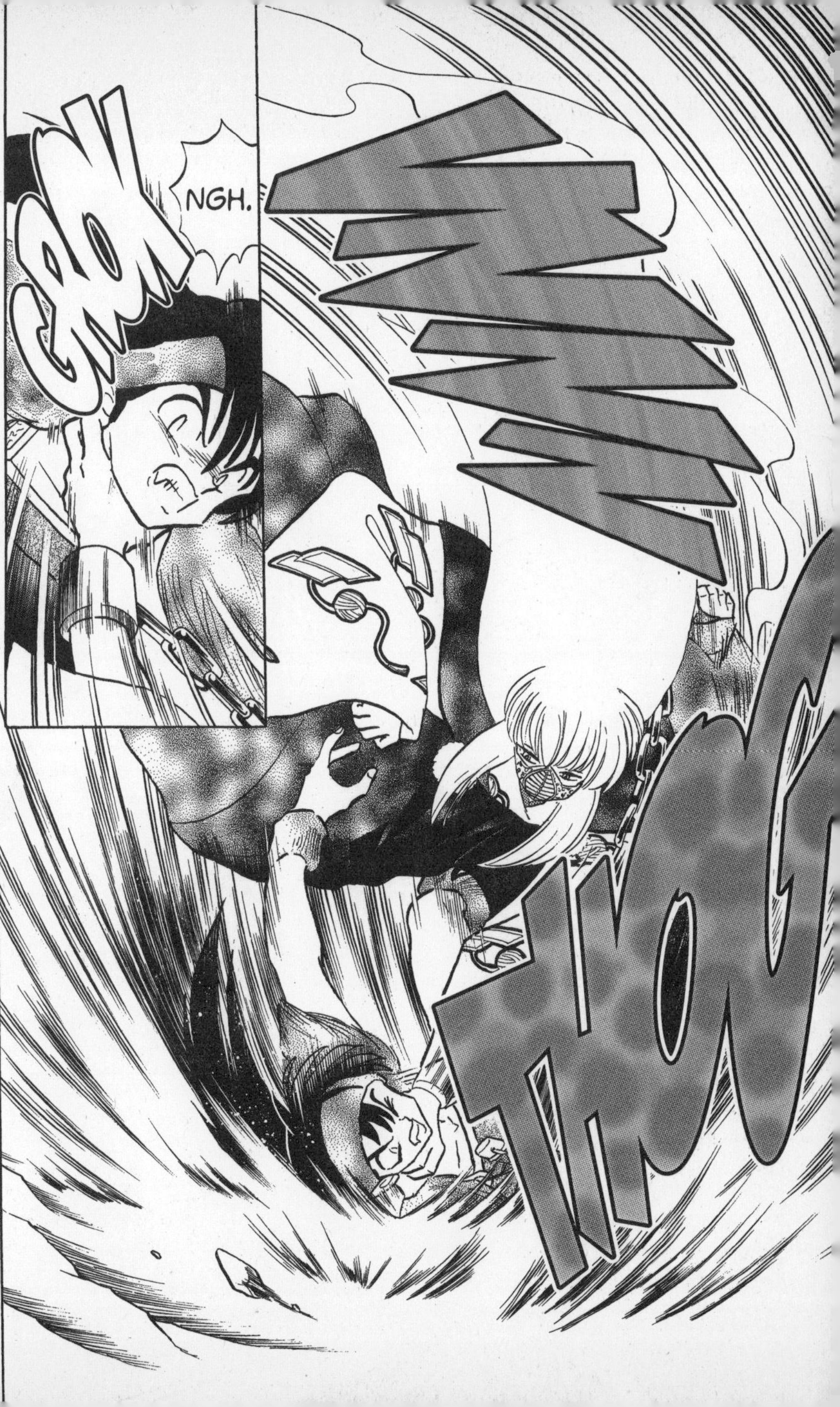
NGH.

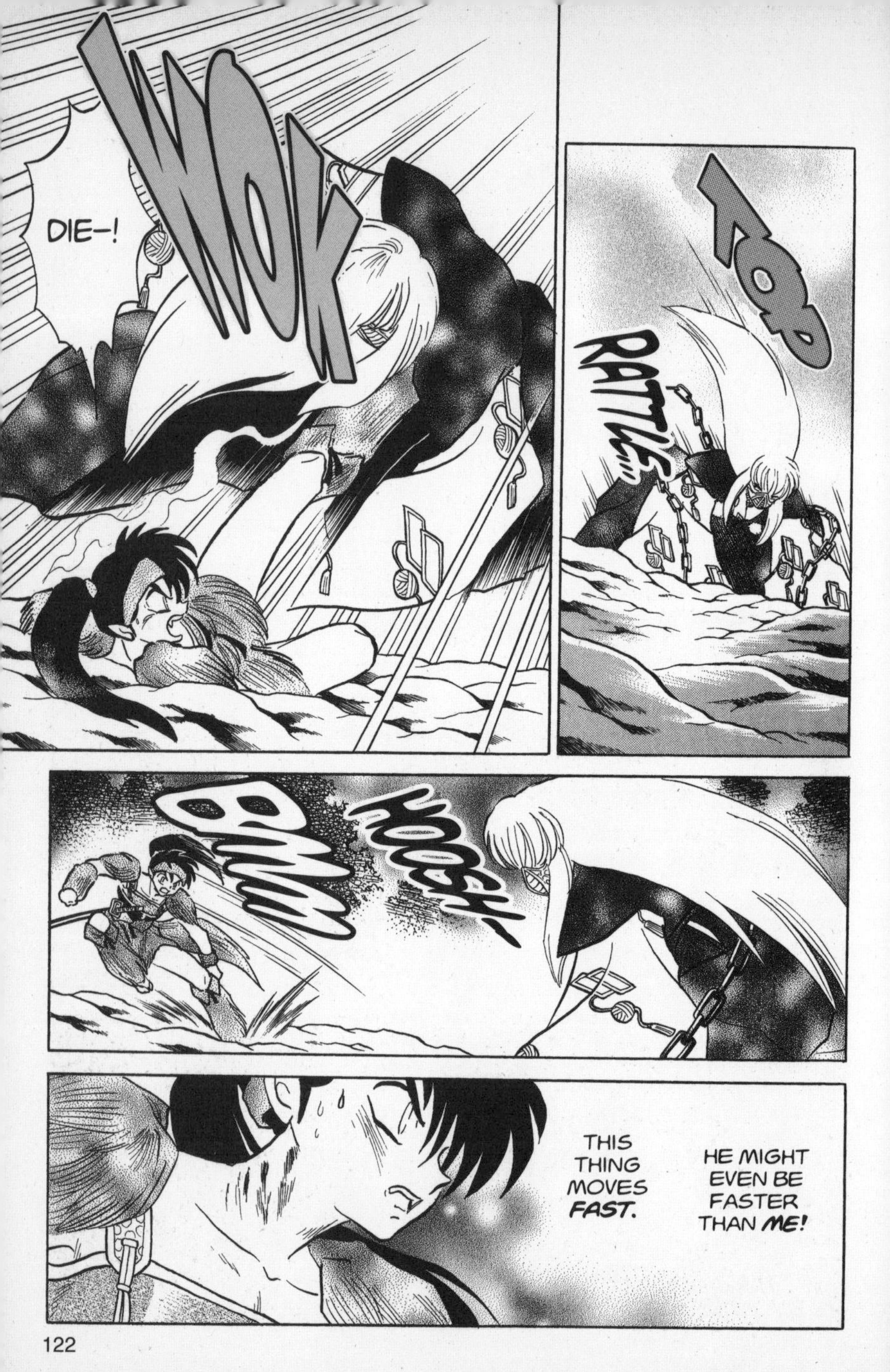
WOK
DIE–!
TOP
RATTLE...
BAM
WHOOSH
THIS THING MOVES FAST.
HE MIGHT EVEN BE FASTER THAN ME!

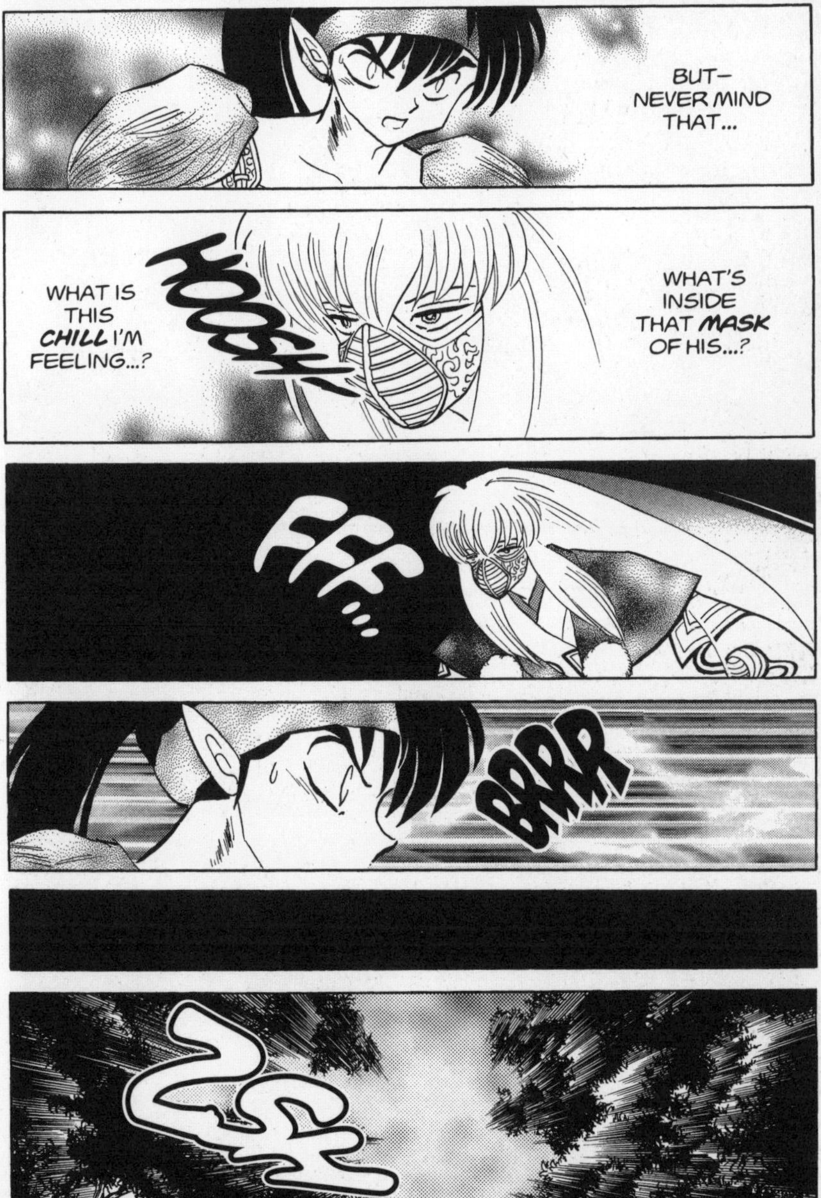
BUT—
NEVER MIND
THAT...
WHAT IS
THIS
CHILL I'M
FEELING...?
HOOSH!
WHAT'S
INSIDE
THAT MASK
OF HIS...?
FFF...
BRRR
ZSH

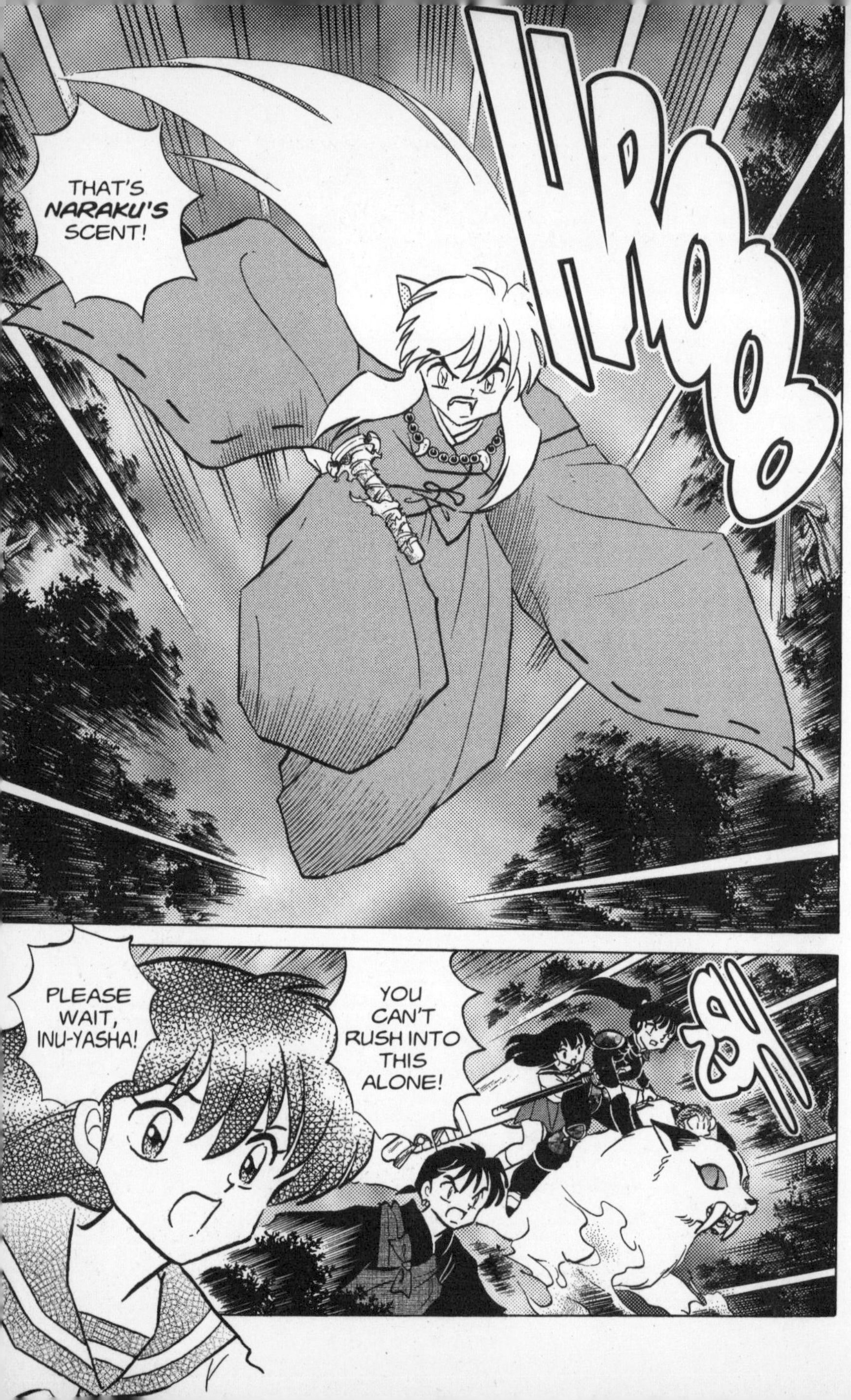
THAT'S *NARAKU'S* SCENT!
PLEASE WAIT, INU-YASHA!
YOU CAN'T RUSH INTO THIS ALONE!

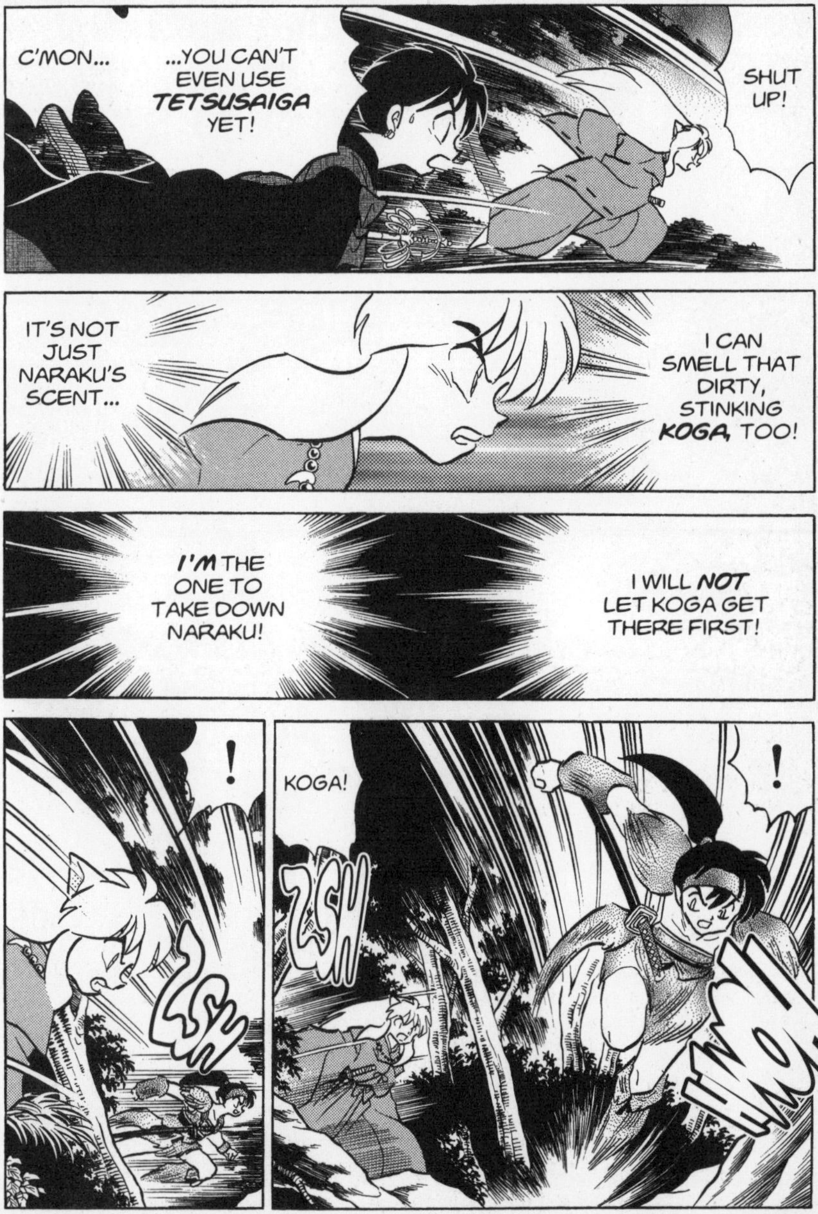
C'MON...
...YOU CAN'T EVEN USE TETSUSAIGA YET!
SHUT UP!
IT'S NOT JUST NARAKU'S SCENT...
I CAN SMELL THAT DIRTY, STINKING KOGA, TOO!
I'M THE ONE TO TAKE DOWN NARAKU!
I WILL NOT LET KOGA GET THERE FIRST!
!
ZSH
KOGA!
ZSH
!

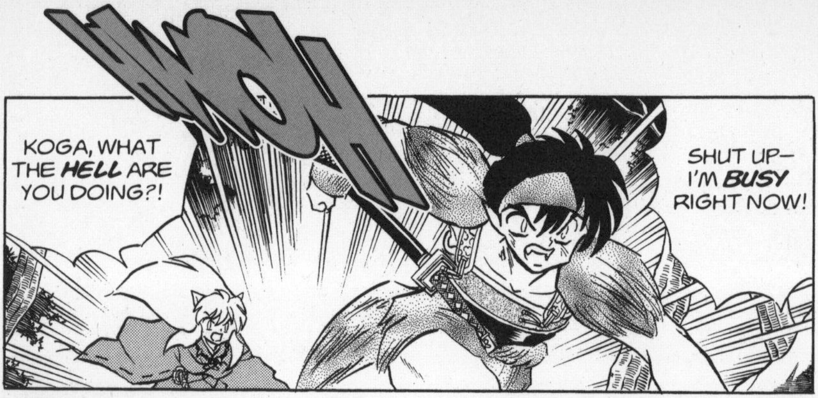
KOGA, WHAT THE **HELL** ARE YOU DOING?!
SHUT UP— I'M **BUSY** RIGHT NOW!

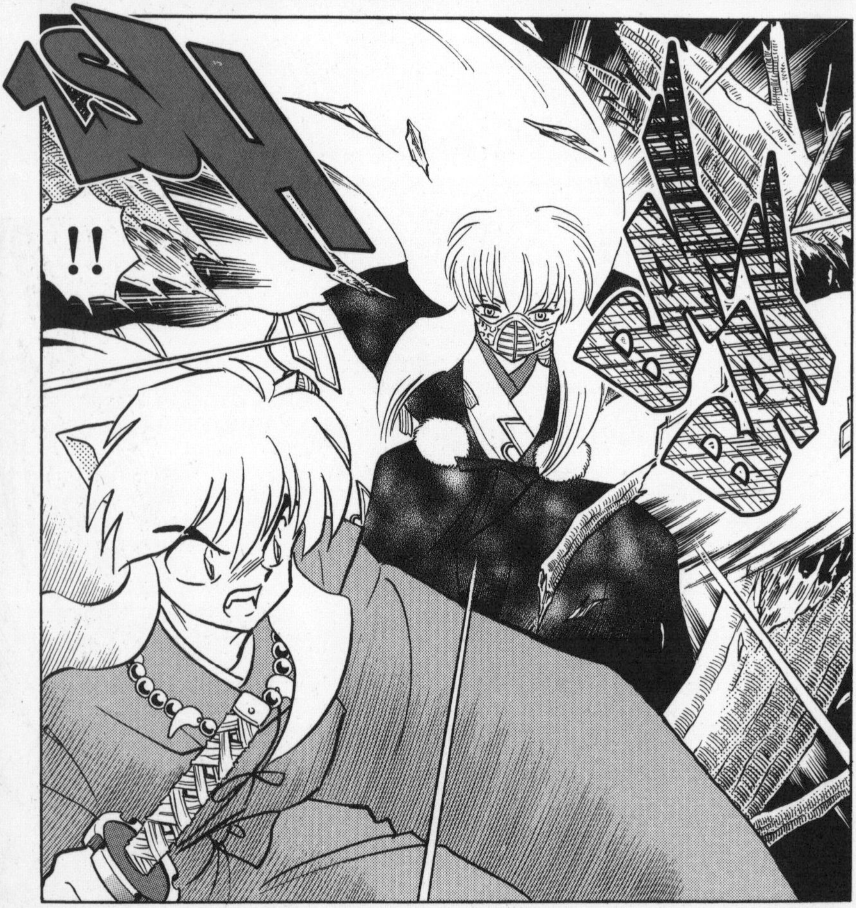
!!

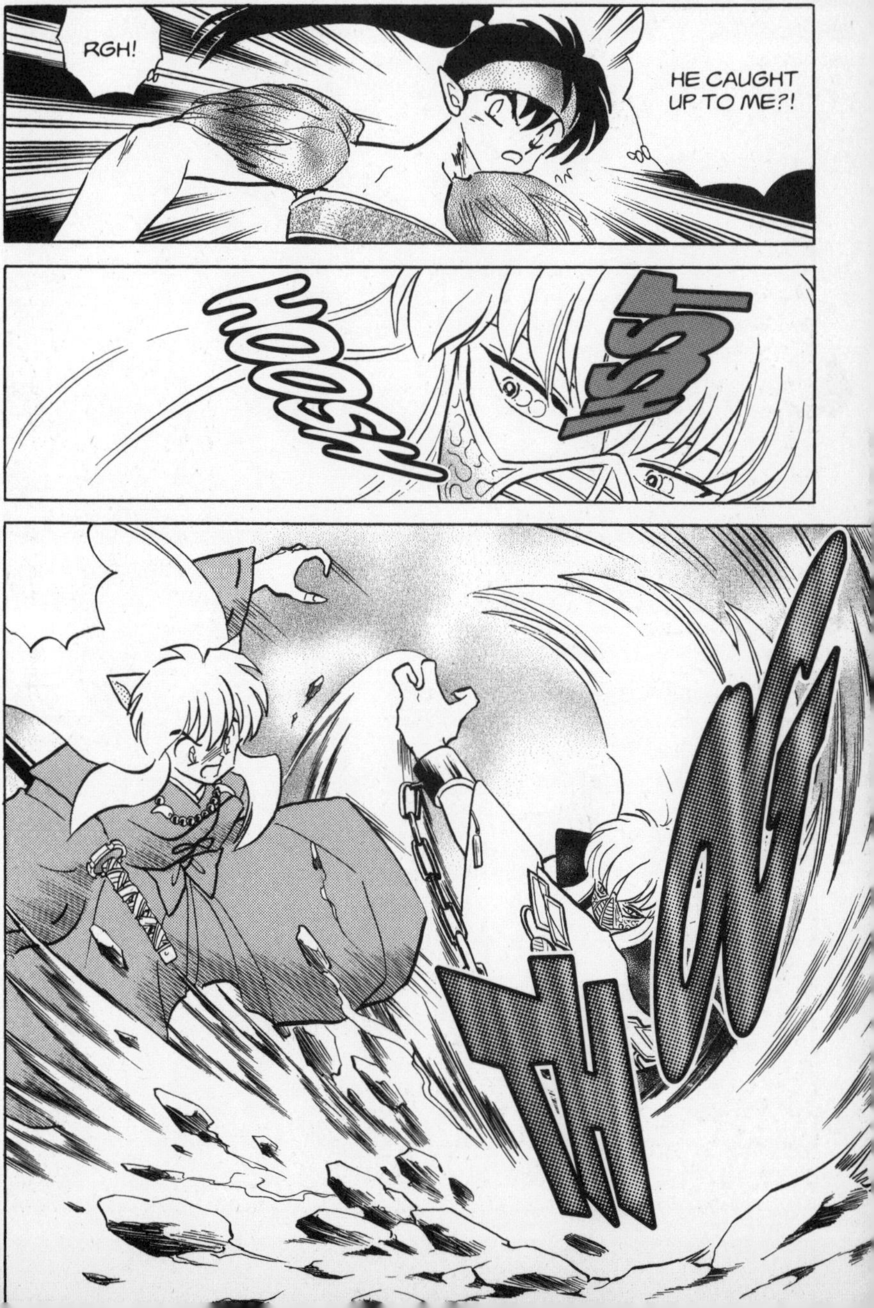
RGH!
HE CAUGHT UP TO ME?!
WHOOSH

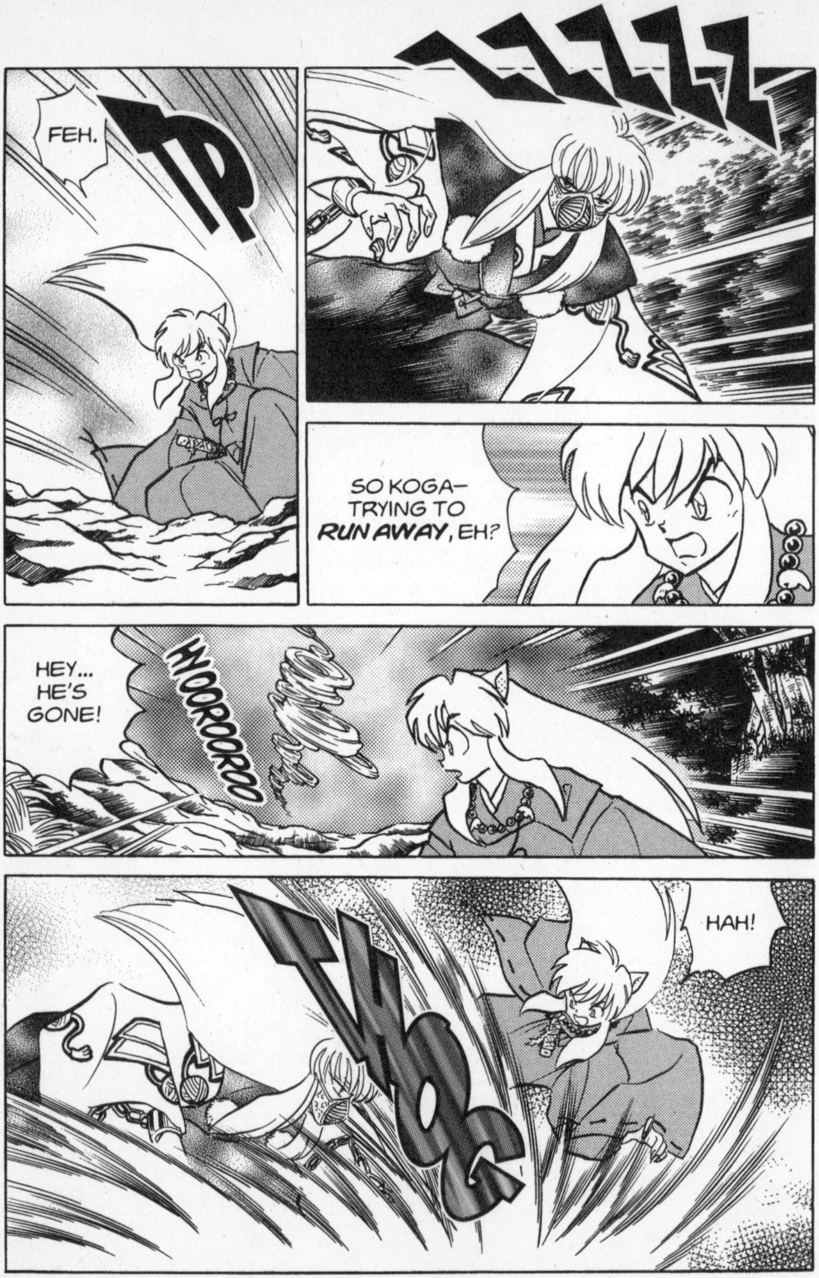
FEH.
TP
SO KOGA—
TRYING TO
RUN AWAY, EH?
HEY...
HE'S
GONE!
HYOOROOROO
HAH!

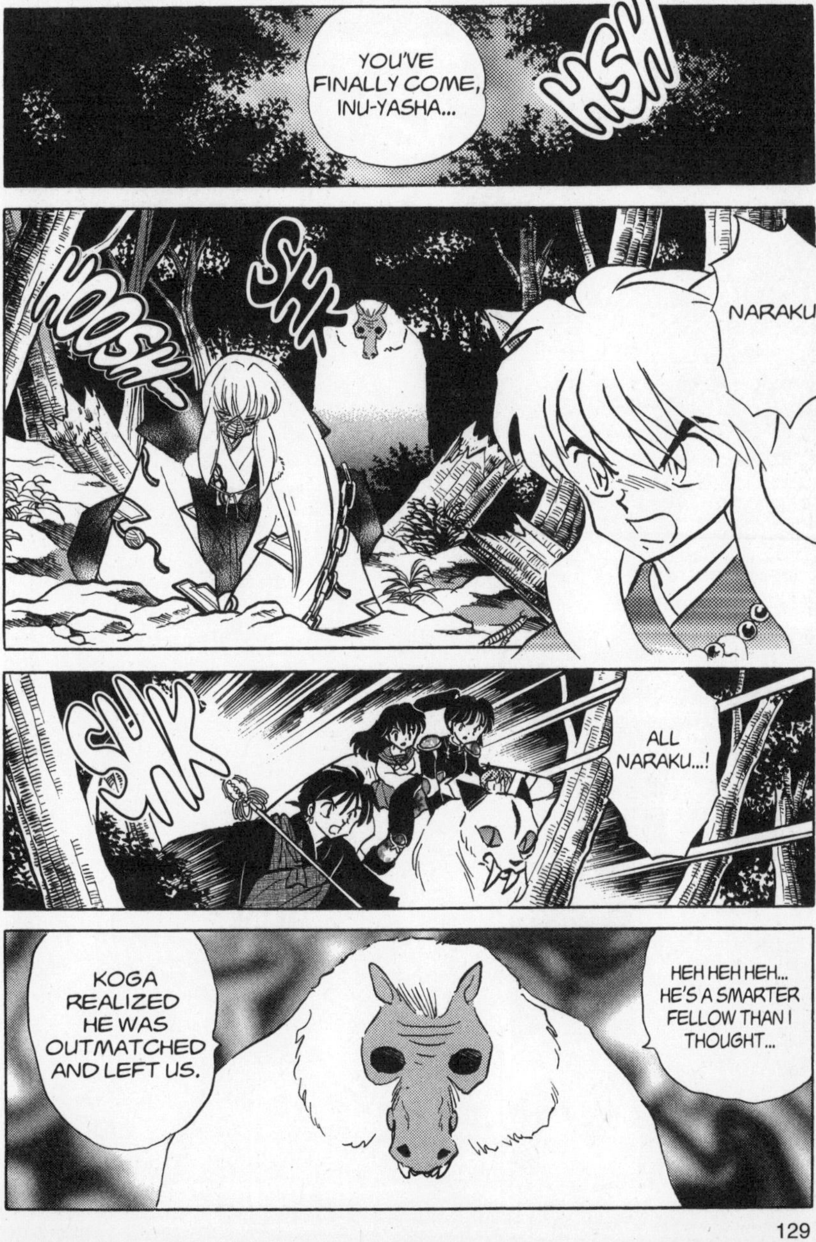
YOU'VE FINALLY COME, INU-YASHA...
HSH
HOOSH
SHK
NARAKU!
SHK
ALL NARAKU...!
KOGA REALIZED HE WAS OUTMATCHED AND LEFT US.
HEH HEH HEH... HE'S A SMARTER FELLOW THAN I THOUGHT...

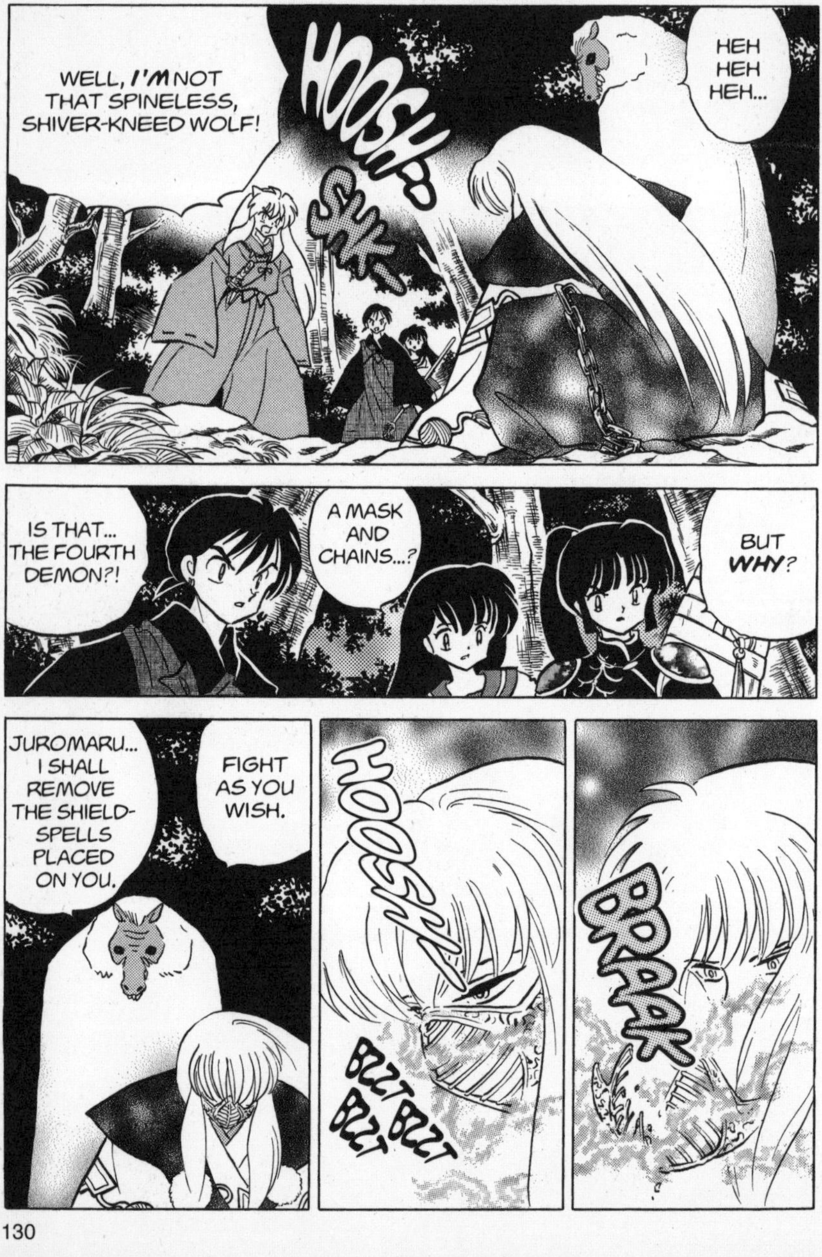
WELL, I'M NOT THAT SPINELESS, SHIVER-KNEED WOLF!
HOOSHPP
SHK
HEH HEH HEH...
IS THAT... THE FOURTH DEMON?!
A MASK AND CHAINS...?
BUT WHY?
JUROMARU... I SHALL REMOVE THE SHIELD-SPELLS PLACED ON YOU.
FIGHT AS YOU WISH.
HOOSH
BZZT BZZT BZZT
BRRAAK

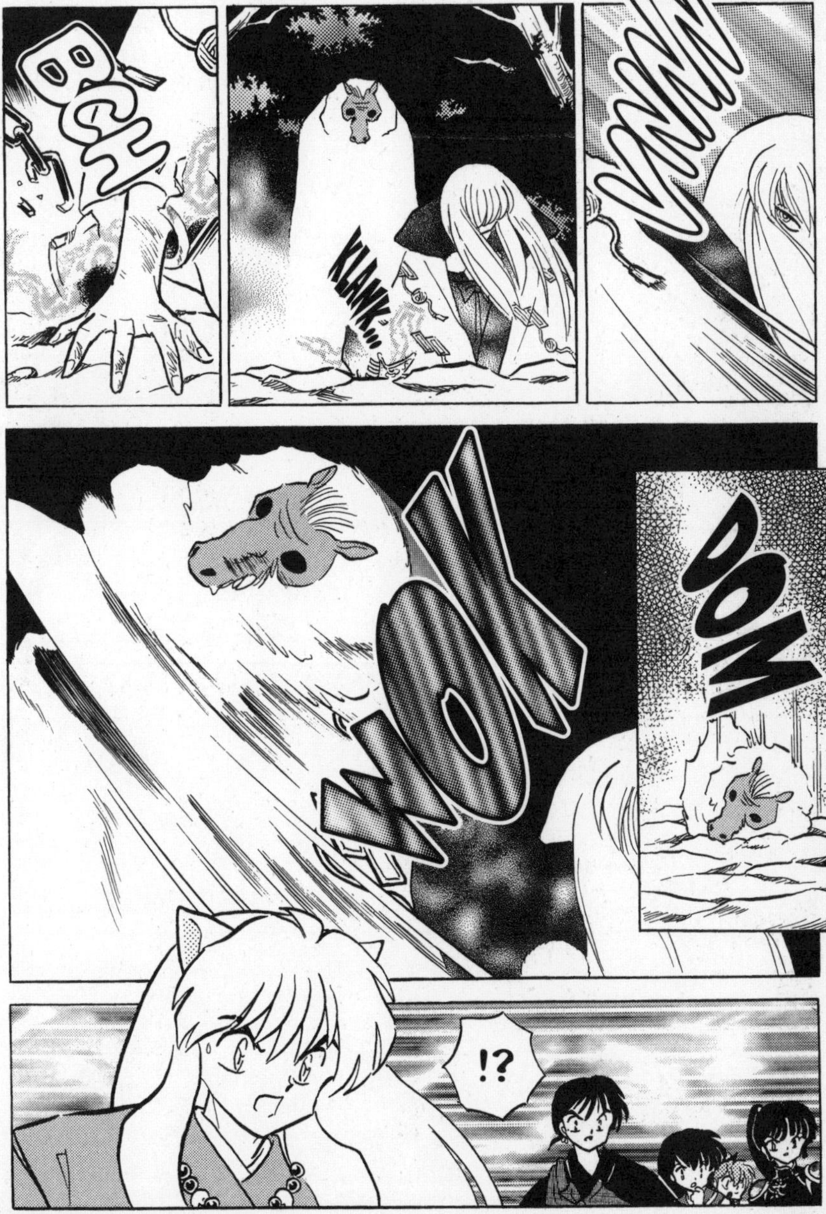
BCH
KLANK...
VMMM
WOK
DOM
!?

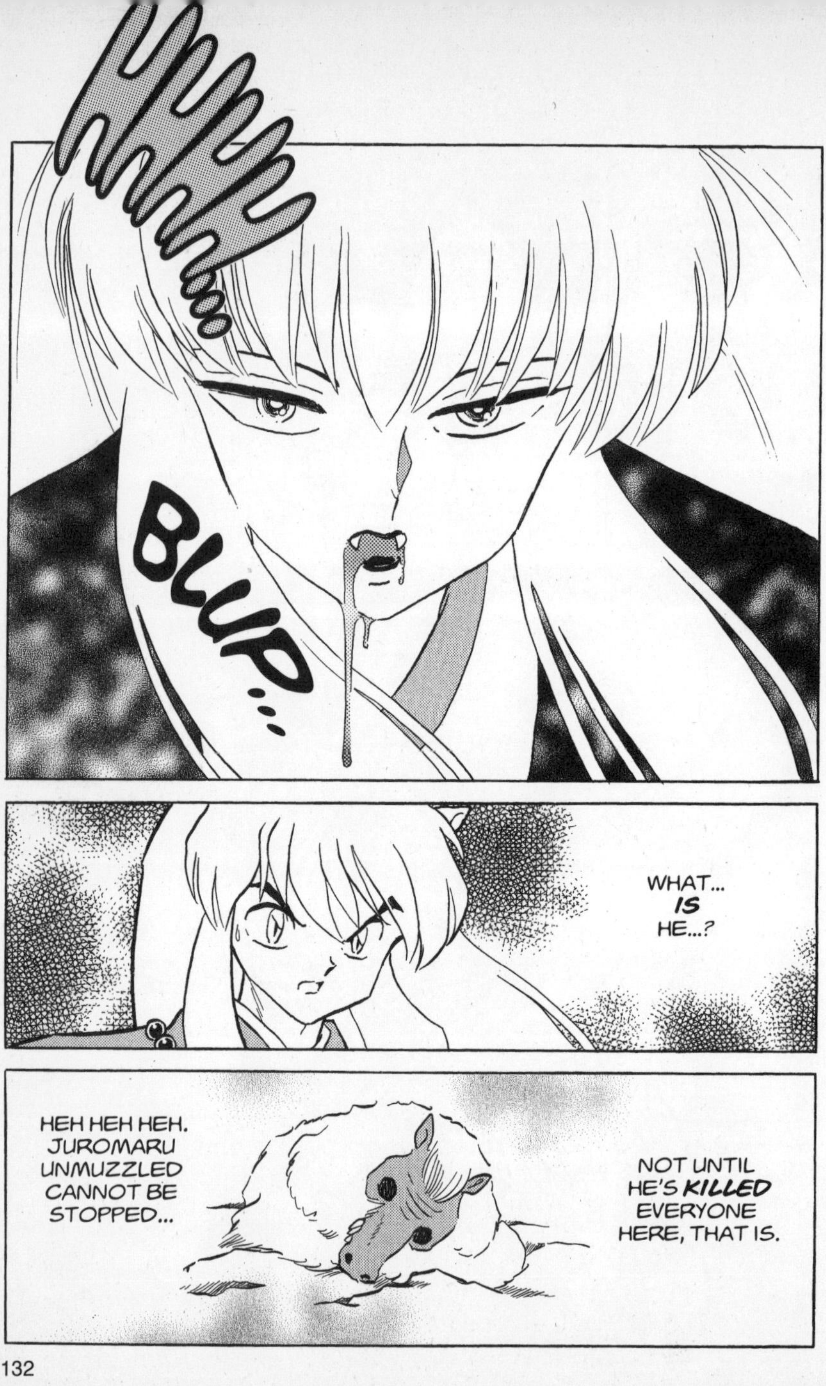
BLUP...
WHAT... *IS* HE...?
HEH HEH HEH. JUROMARU UNMUZZLED CANNOT BE STOPPED...
NOT UNTIL HE'S *KILLED* EVERYONE HERE, THAT IS.

SCROLL EIGHT

WITHOUT SHIELDS

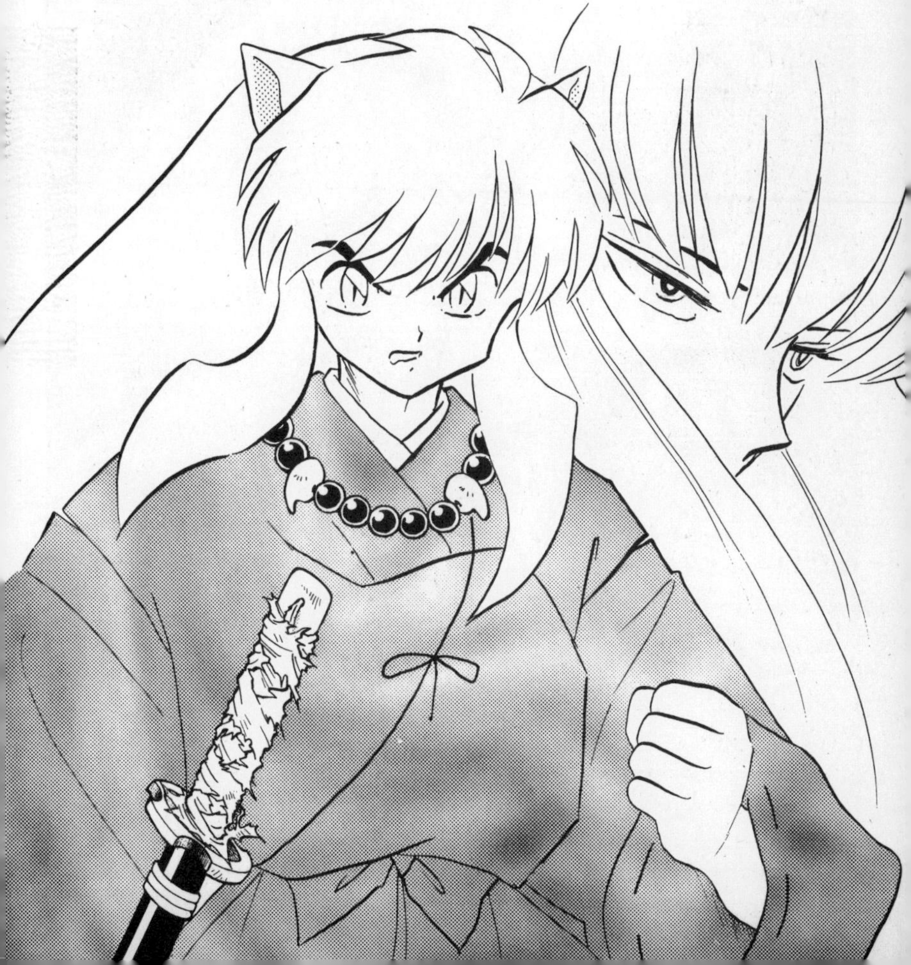

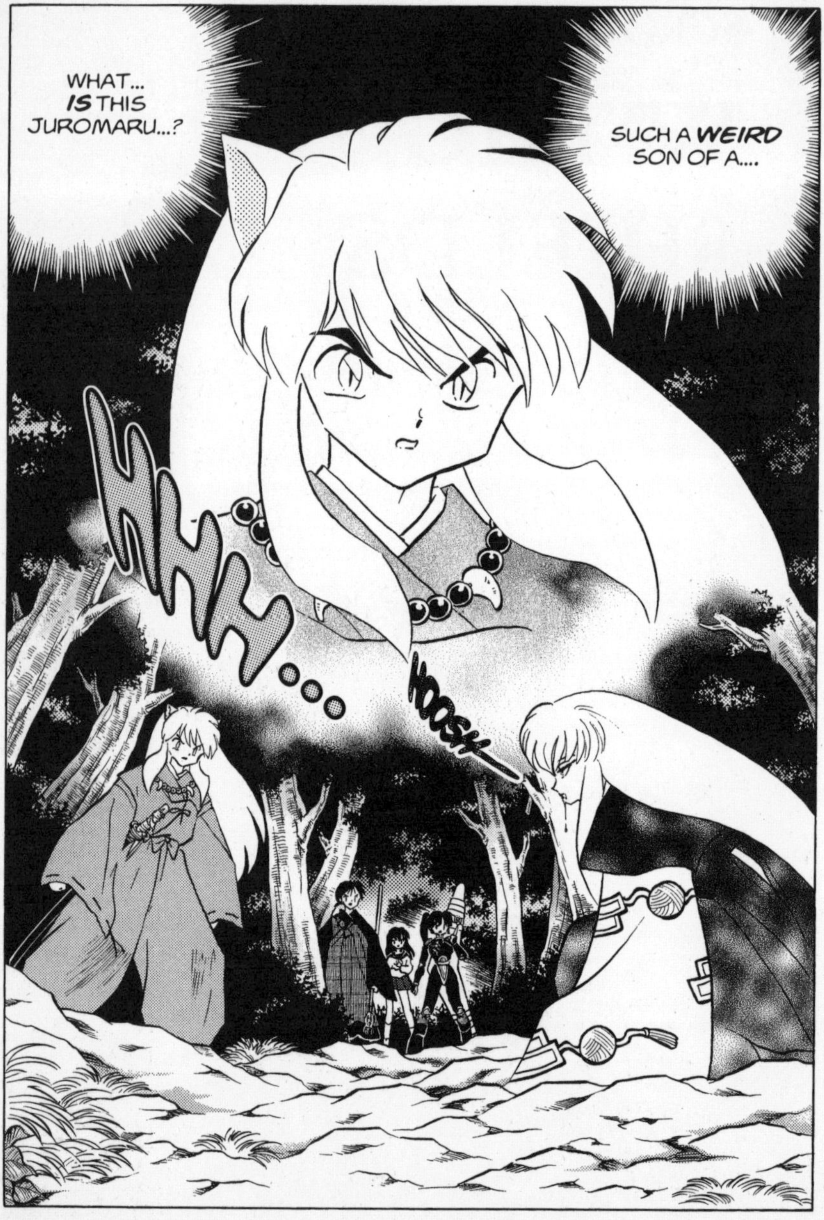
WHAT... **IS** THIS JUROMARU...?
SUCH A **WEIRD** SON OF A....
HWWH...
WOOSH

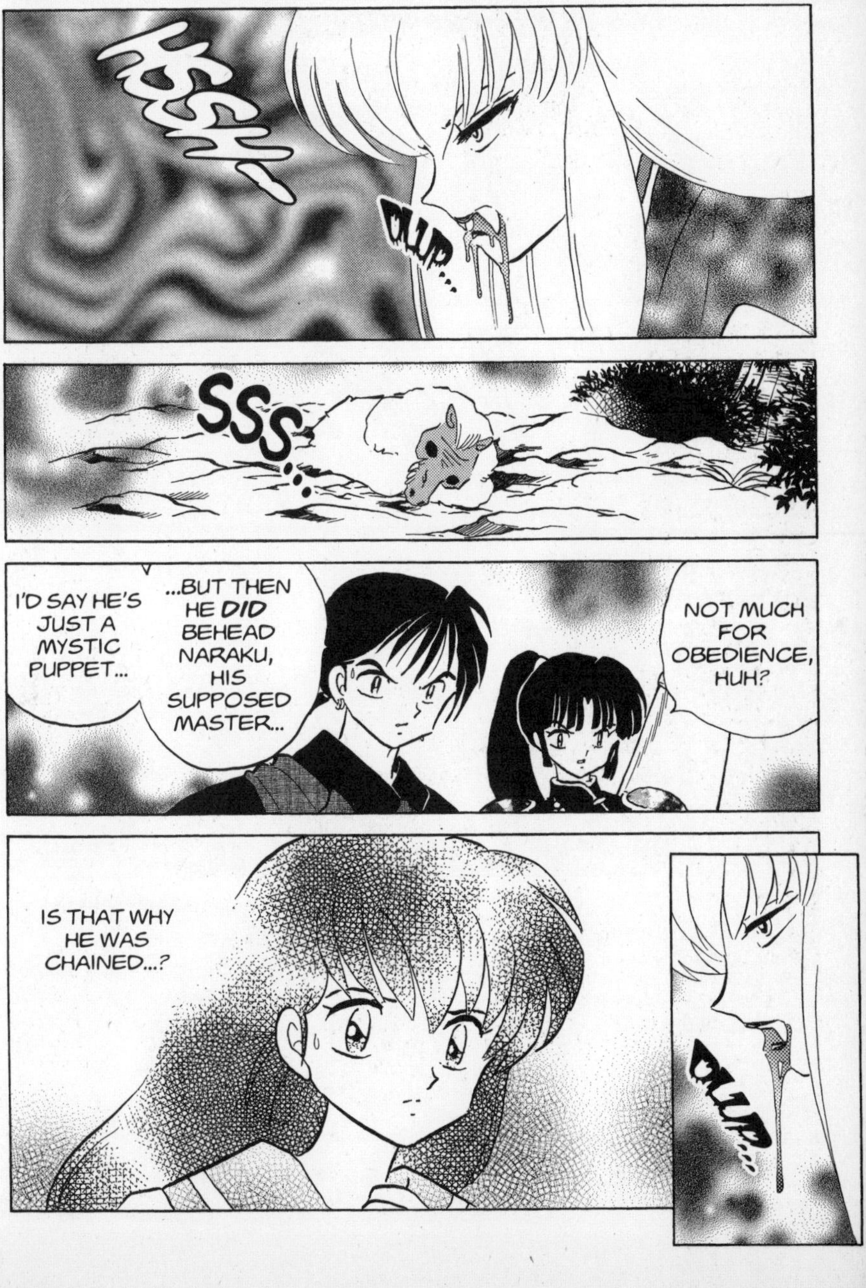
HSSH!
DLUP...
SSS...
I'D SAY HE'S JUST A MYSTIC PUPPET...
...BUT THEN HE *DID* BEHEAD NARAKU, HIS SUPPOSED MASTER...
NOT MUCH FOR OBEDIENCE, HUH?
IS THAT WHY HE WAS CHAINED...?
DLUP...

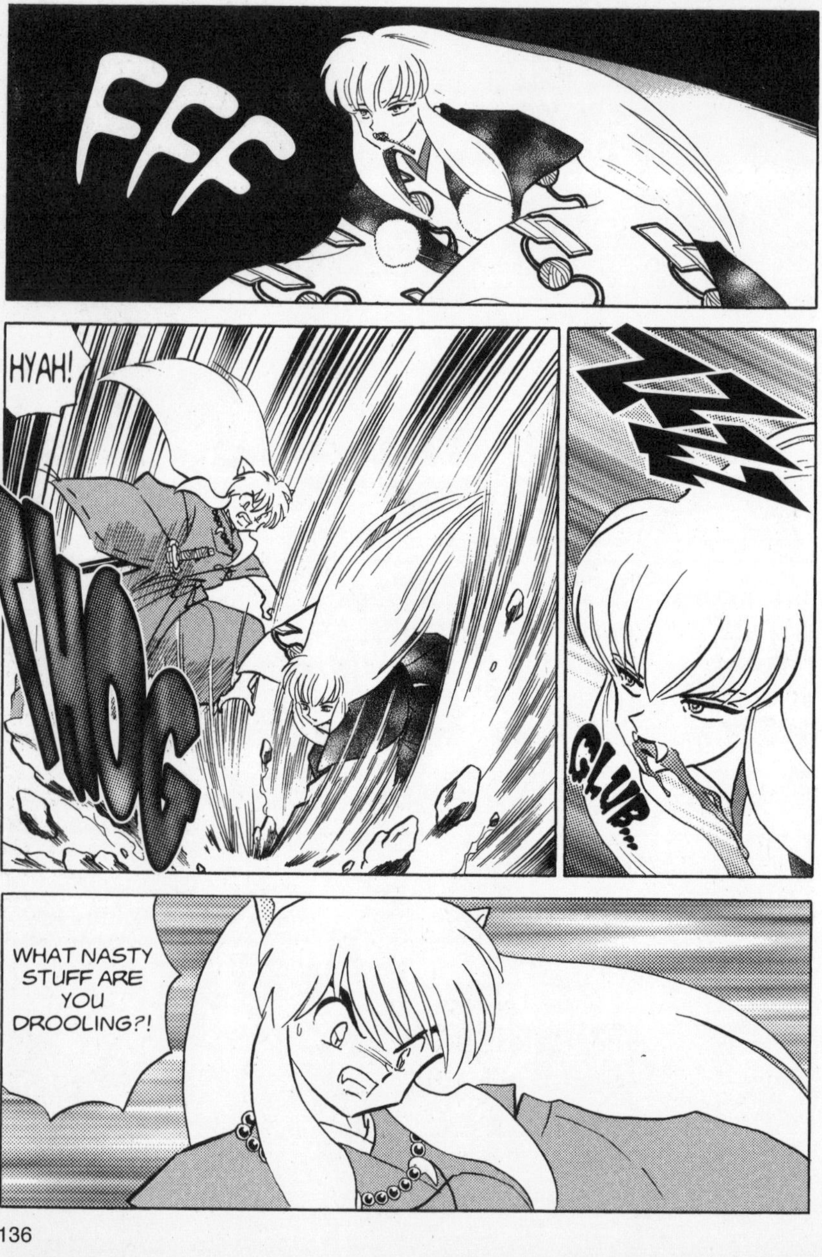
FFF
HYAH!
THOG
GLUB...
WHAT NASTY STUFF ARE YOU DROOLING?!

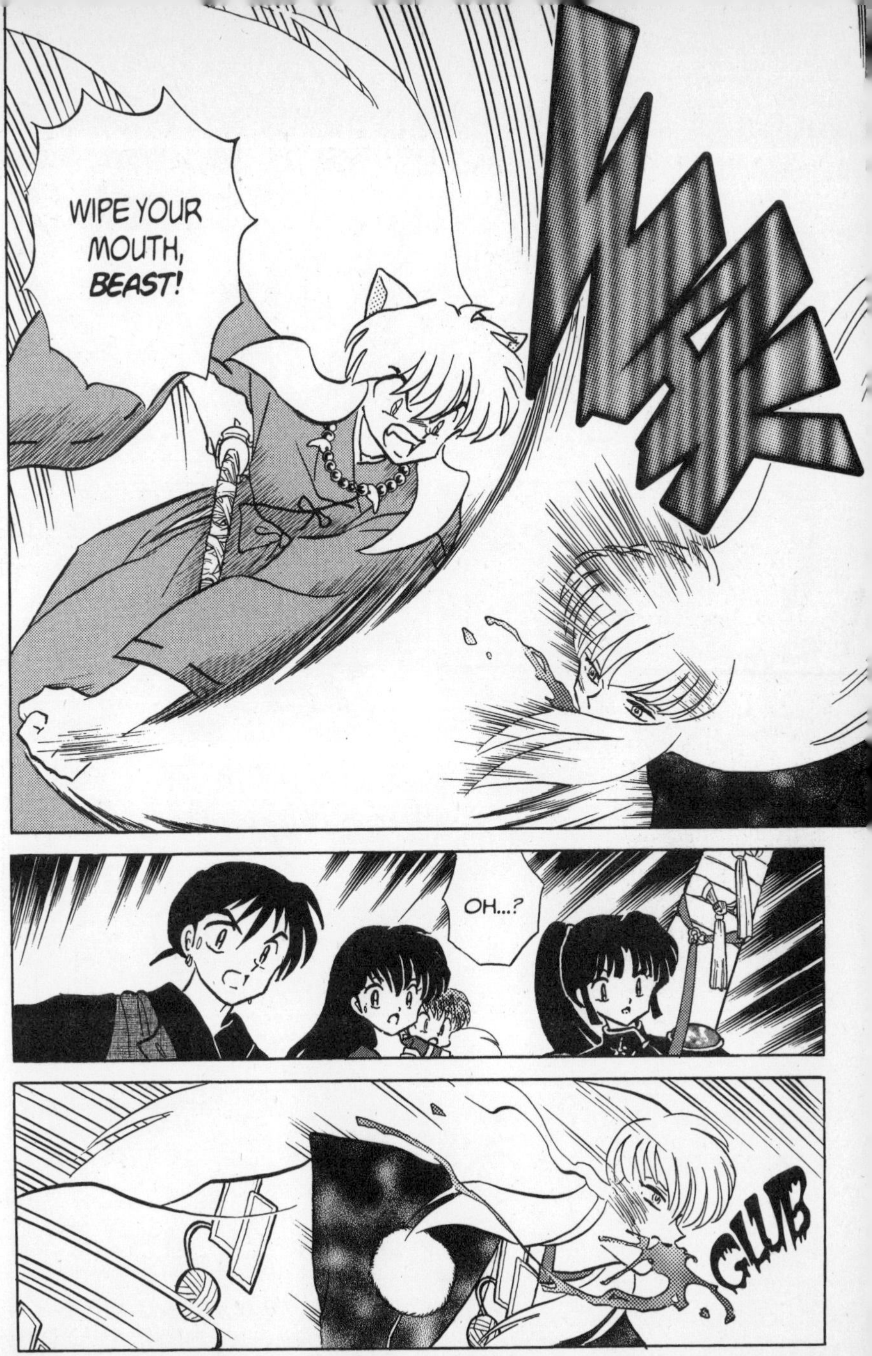
WIPE YOUR MOUTH, BEAST!
OH...?
GLUB

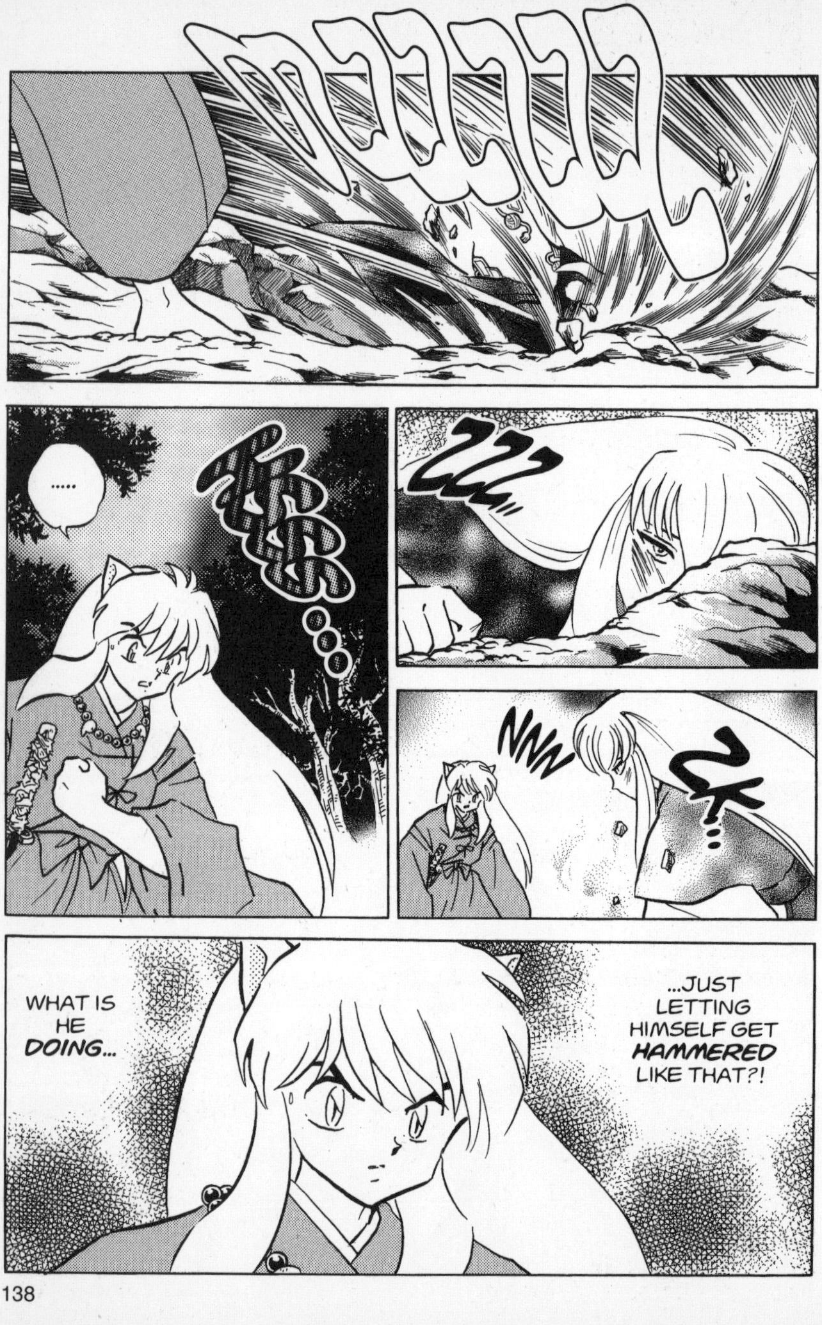
......
WHAT IS HE DOING...
...JUST LETTING HIMSELF GET HAMMERED LIKE THAT?!

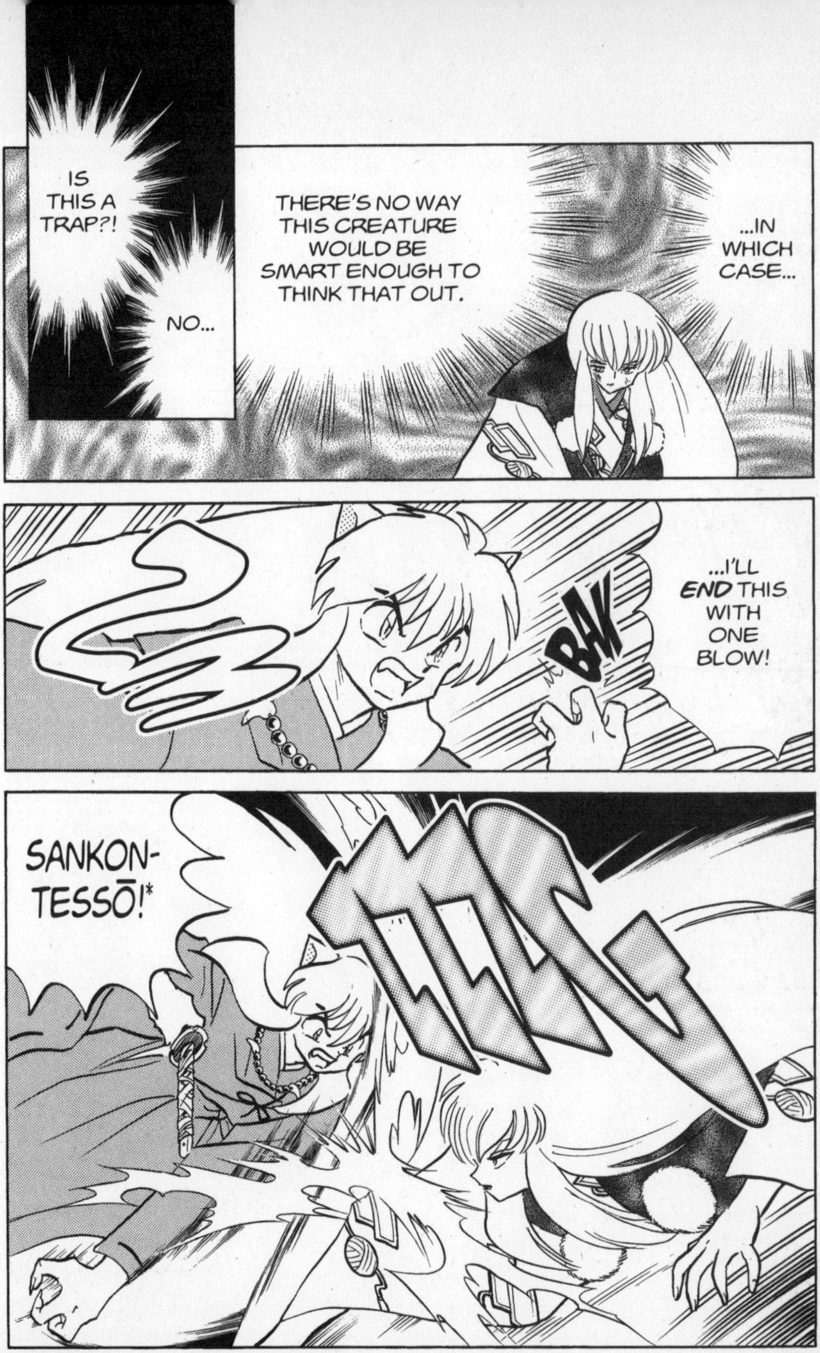
IS THIS A TRAP?!
NO...
THERE'S NO WAY THIS CREATURE WOULD BE SMART ENOUGH TO THINK THAT OUT.
...IN WHICH CASE...
BAK
...I'LL **END** THIS WITH ONE BLOW!
SANKON-TESSŌ!*

*IRON REAVER, SOUL STEALER

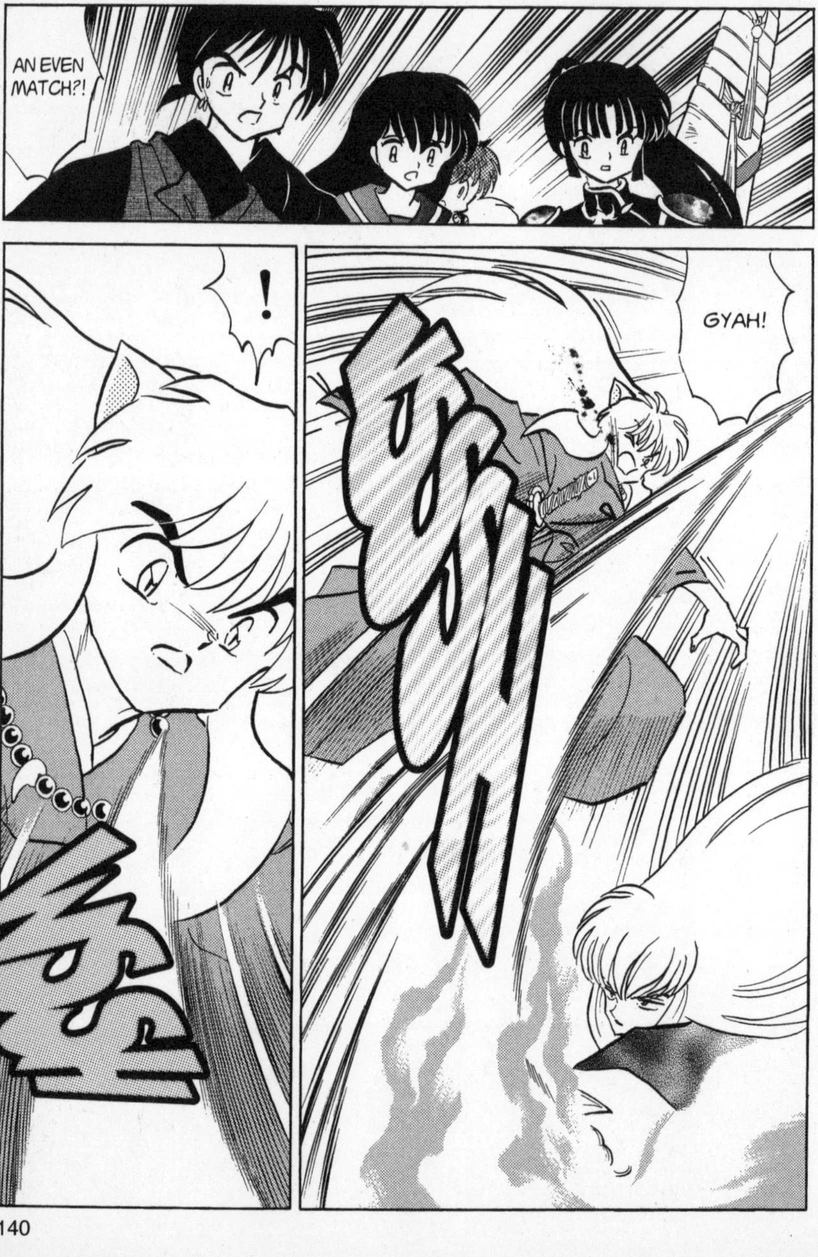
AN EVEN MATCH?!
!
GYAH!

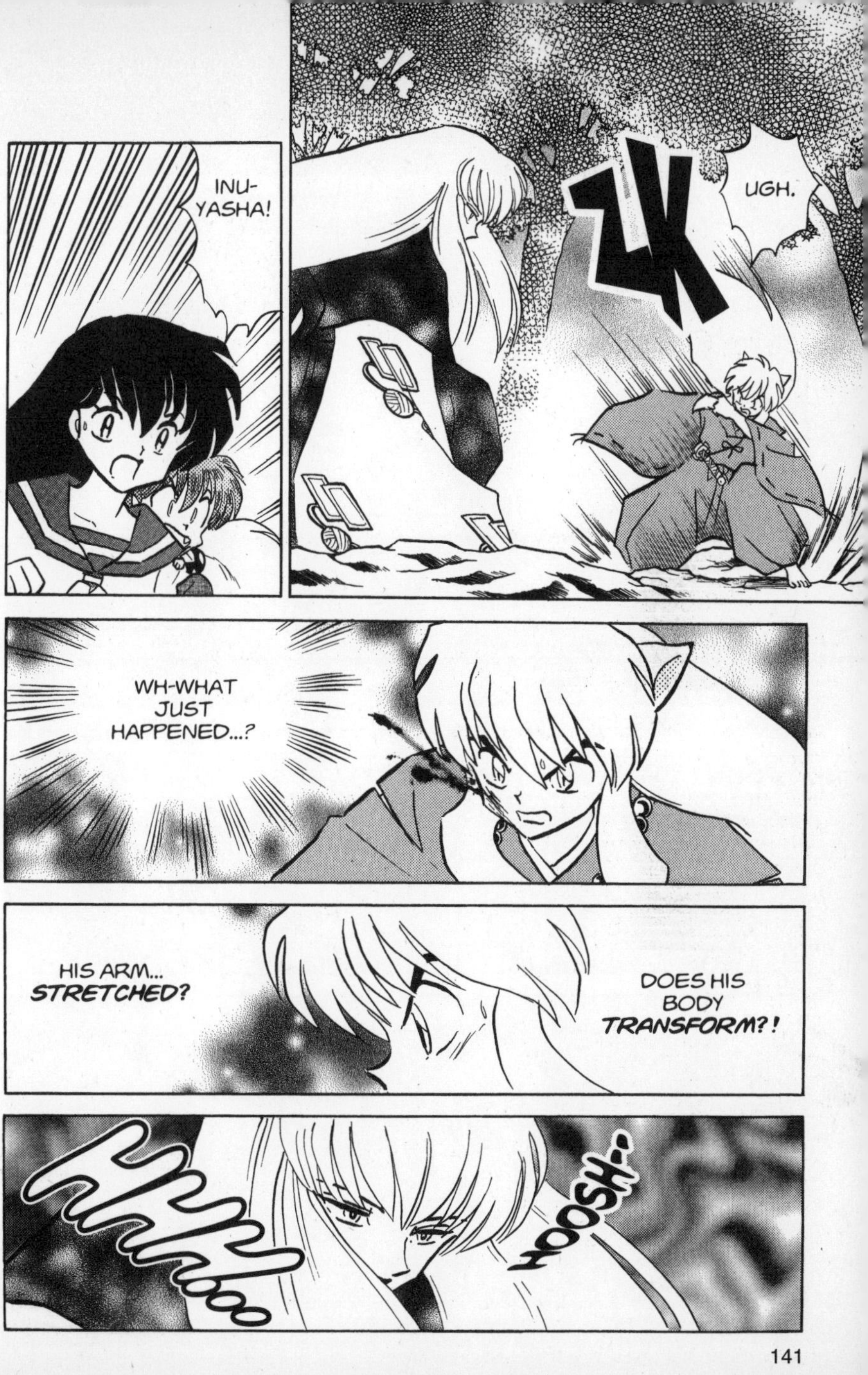
INU-
YASHA!
ZK
UGH.
WH-WHAT
JUST
HAPPENED...?
HIS ARM...
STRETCHED?
DOES HIS
BODY
TRANSFORM?!
WHOOSH

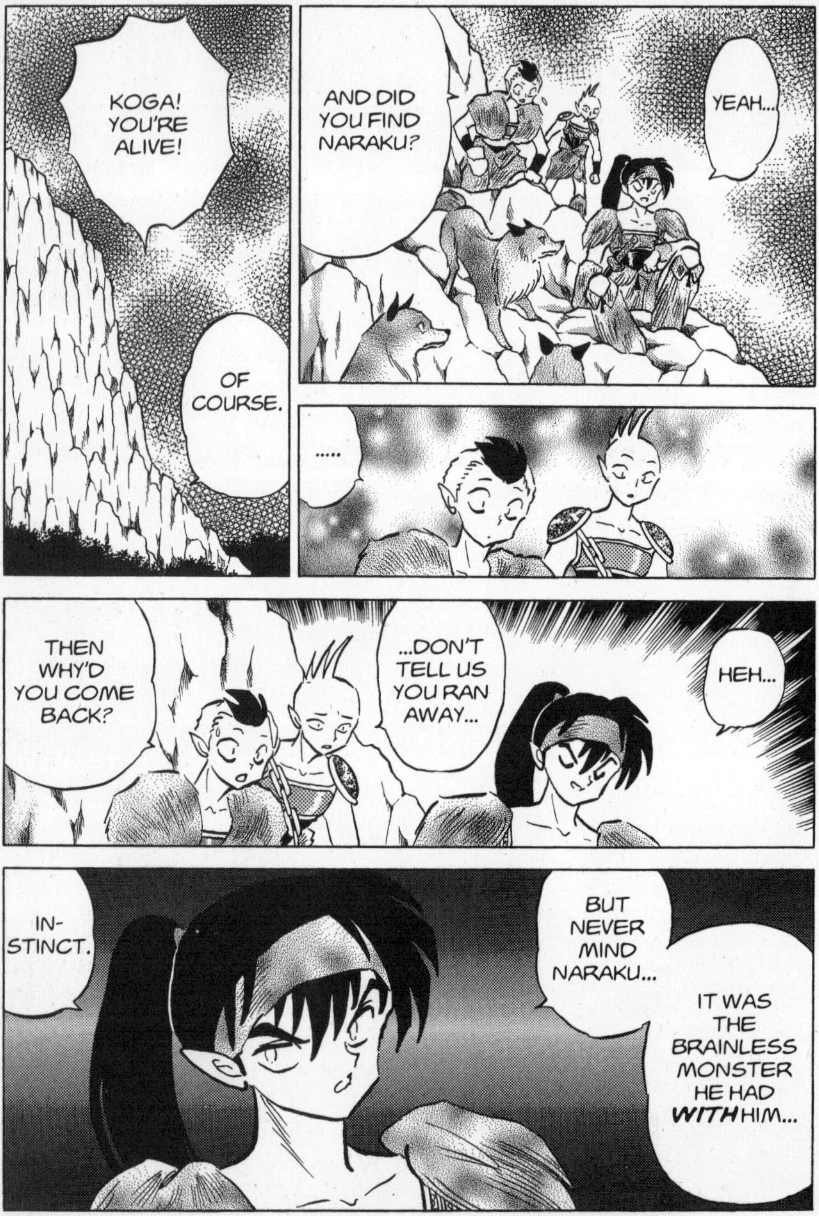
KOGA! YOU'RE ALIVE!
OF COURSE.
AND DID YOU FIND NARAKU?
YEAH...
......
THEN WHY'D YOU COME BACK?
...DON'T TELL US YOU RAN AWAY...
HEH...
IN-STINCT.
BUT NEVER MIND NARAKU...
IT WAS THE BRAINLESS MONSTER HE HAD **WITH** HIM...

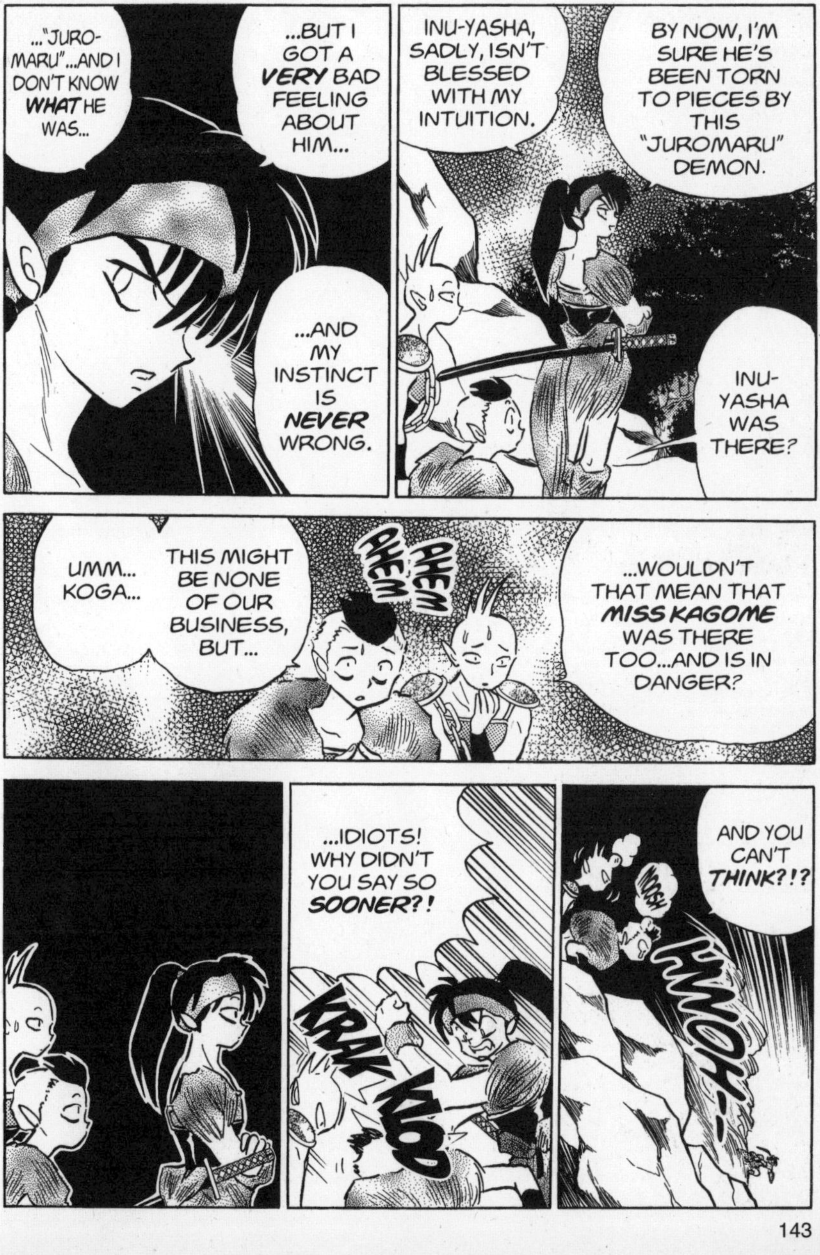
..."JURO-MARU"...AND I DON'T KNOW **WHAT** HE WAS...
...BUT I GOT A **VERY** BAD FEELING ABOUT HIM...
...AND MY INSTINCT IS **NEVER** WRONG.
INU-YASHA, SADLY, ISN'T BLESSED WITH MY INTUITION.
BY NOW, I'M SURE HE'S BEEN TORN TO PIECES BY THIS "JUROMARU" DEMON.
INU-YASHA WAS THERE?
UMM... KOGA...
THIS MIGHT BE NONE OF OUR BUSINESS, BUT...
AHEM AHEM
...WOULDN'T THAT MEAN THAT **MISS KAGOME** WAS THERE TOO...AND IS IN DANGER?
...IDIOTS! WHY DIDN'T YOU SAY SO **SOONER**?!
KRAK KLOB
AND YOU CAN'T **THINK**?!?
WOOSH
HWOOH--

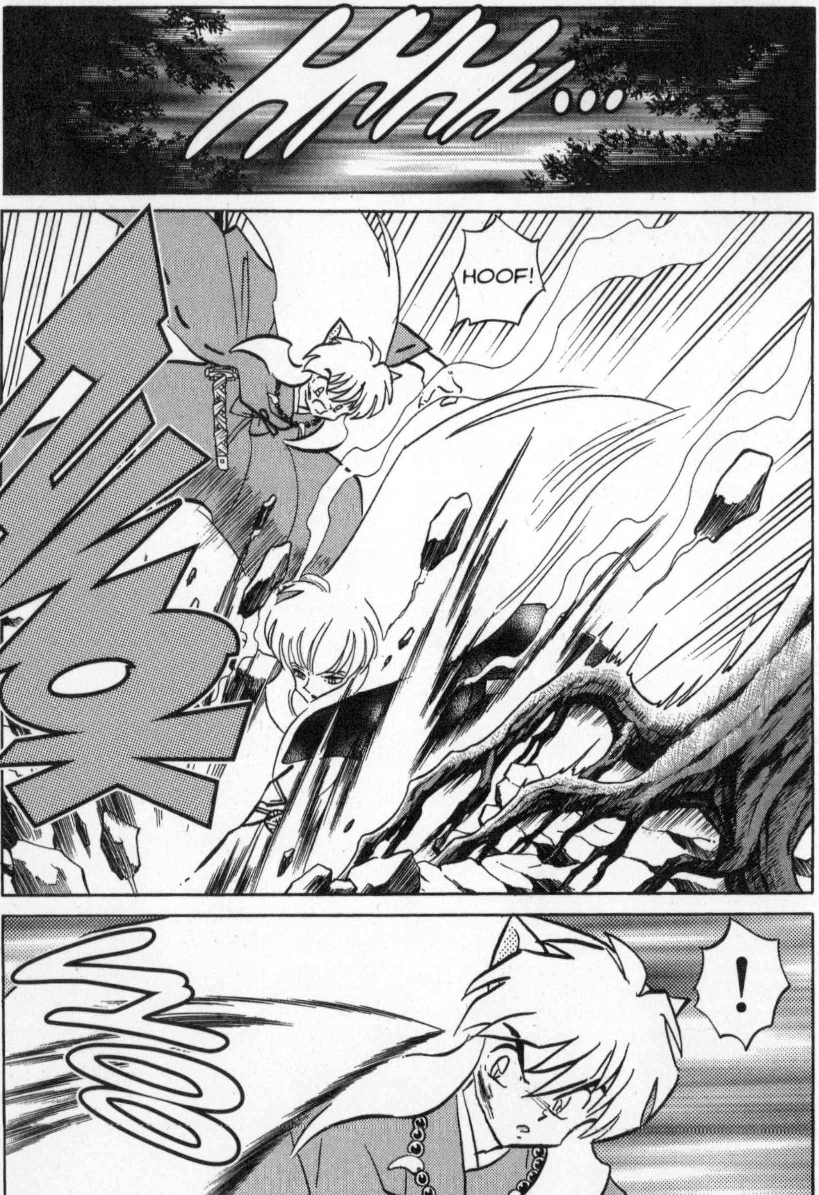
HOOF!
!

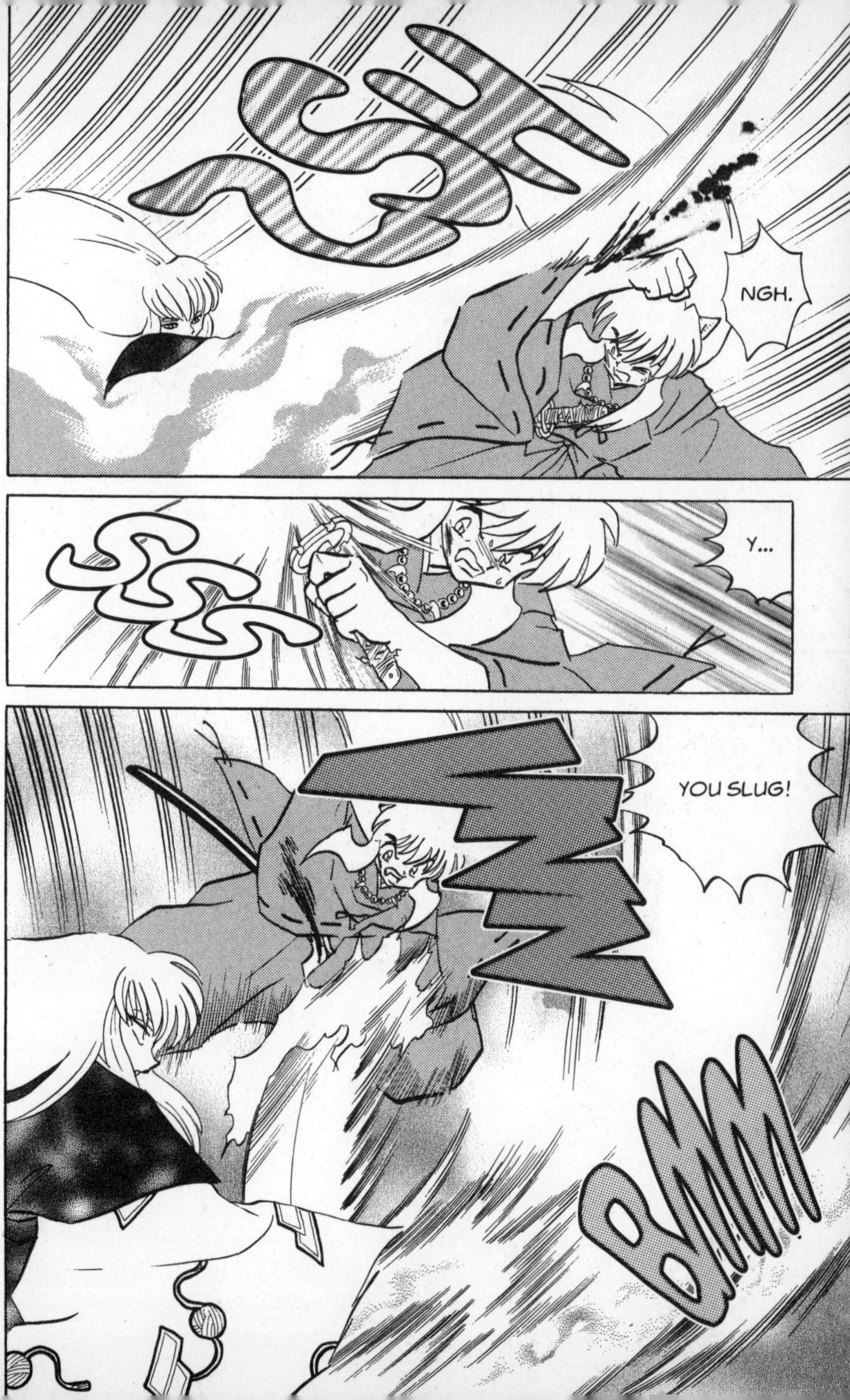
SSH
NGH.
SSS
Y...
YOU SLUG!
BMM

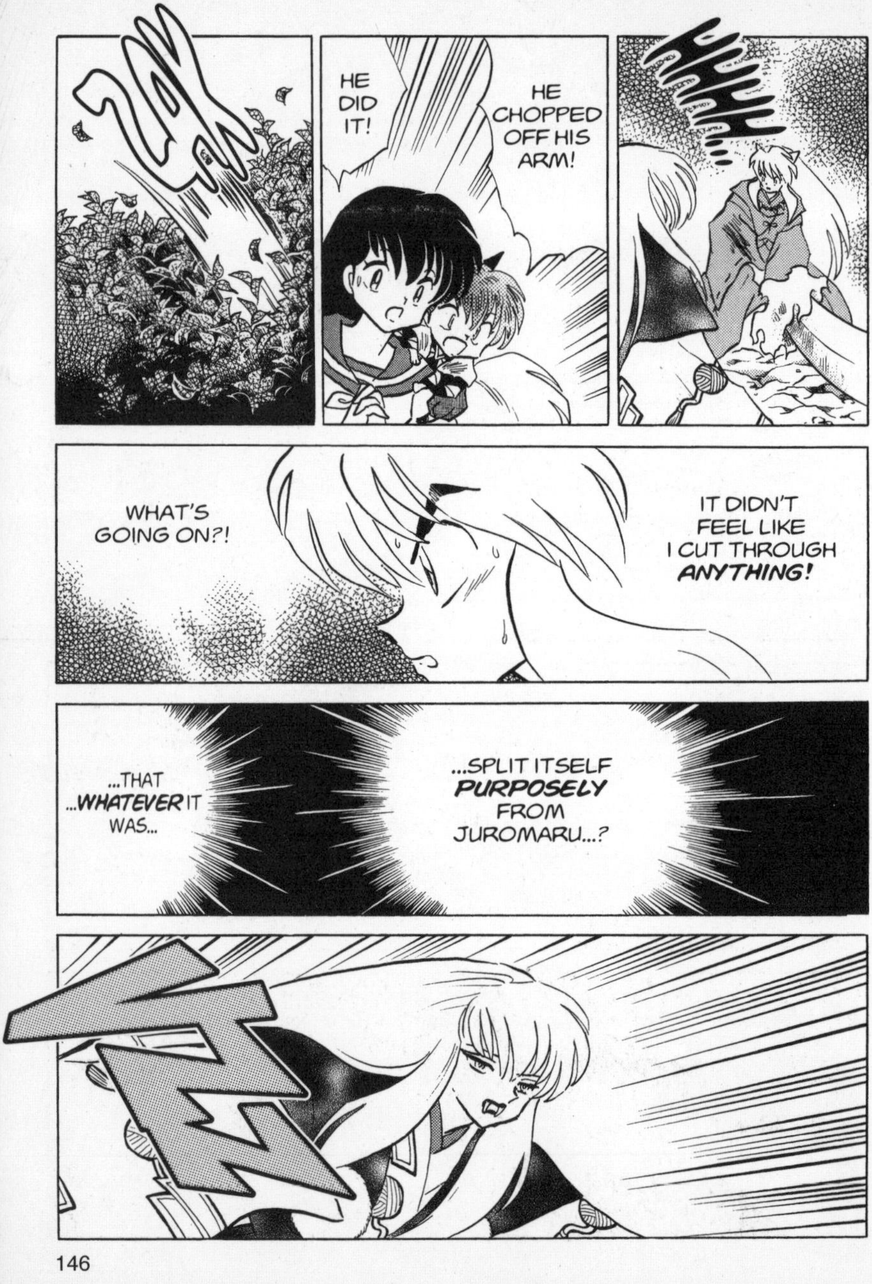
HE DID IT!
HE CHOPPED OFF HIS ARM!
WHAT'S GOING ON?!
IT DIDN'T FEEL LIKE I CUT THROUGH **ANYTHING!**
...THAT ...**WHATEVER** IT WAS...
...SPLIT ITSELF **PURPOSELY** FROM JUROMARU...?

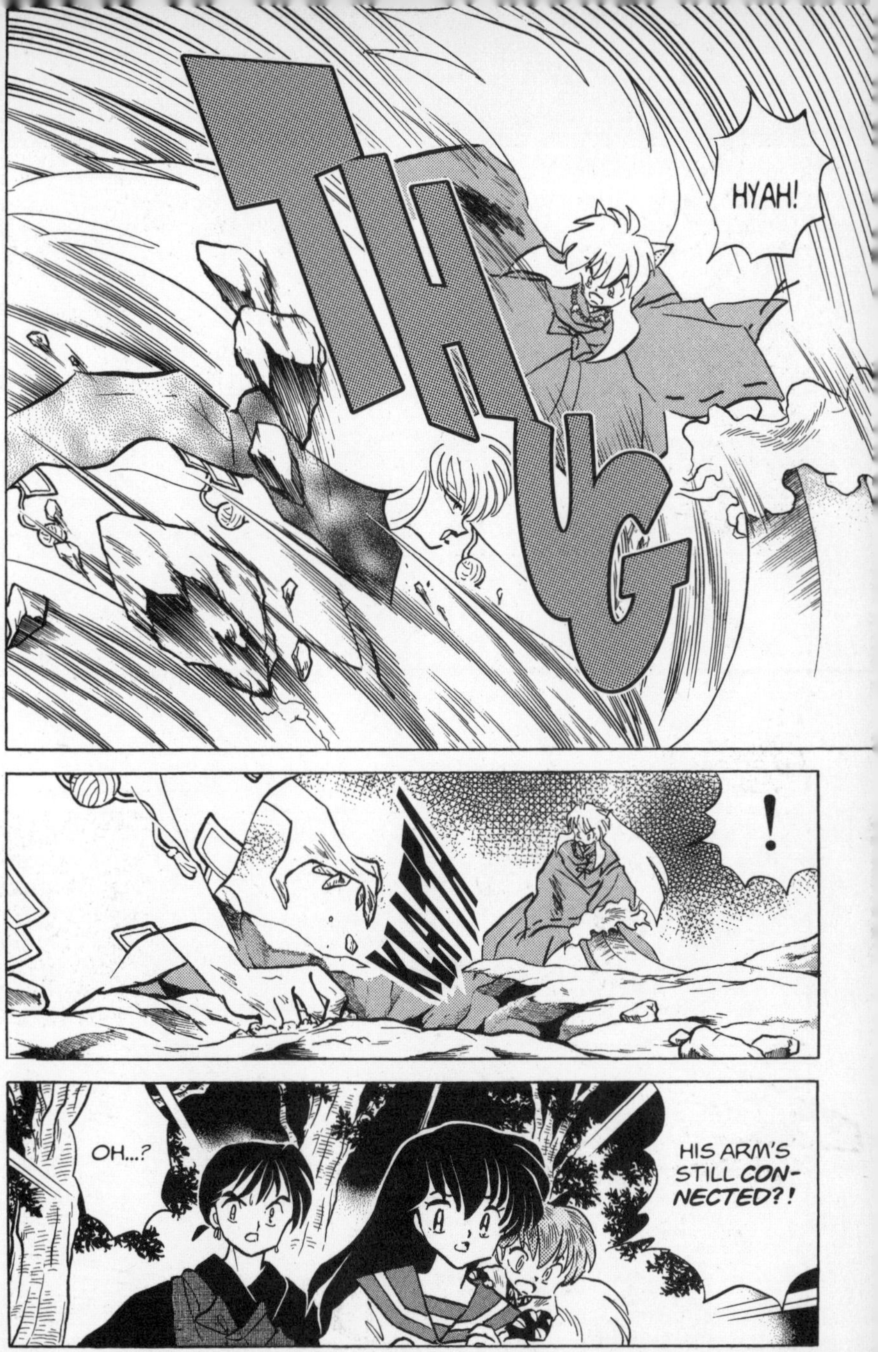
HYAH!
!
HIS ARM'S STILL CONNECTED?!
OH...?

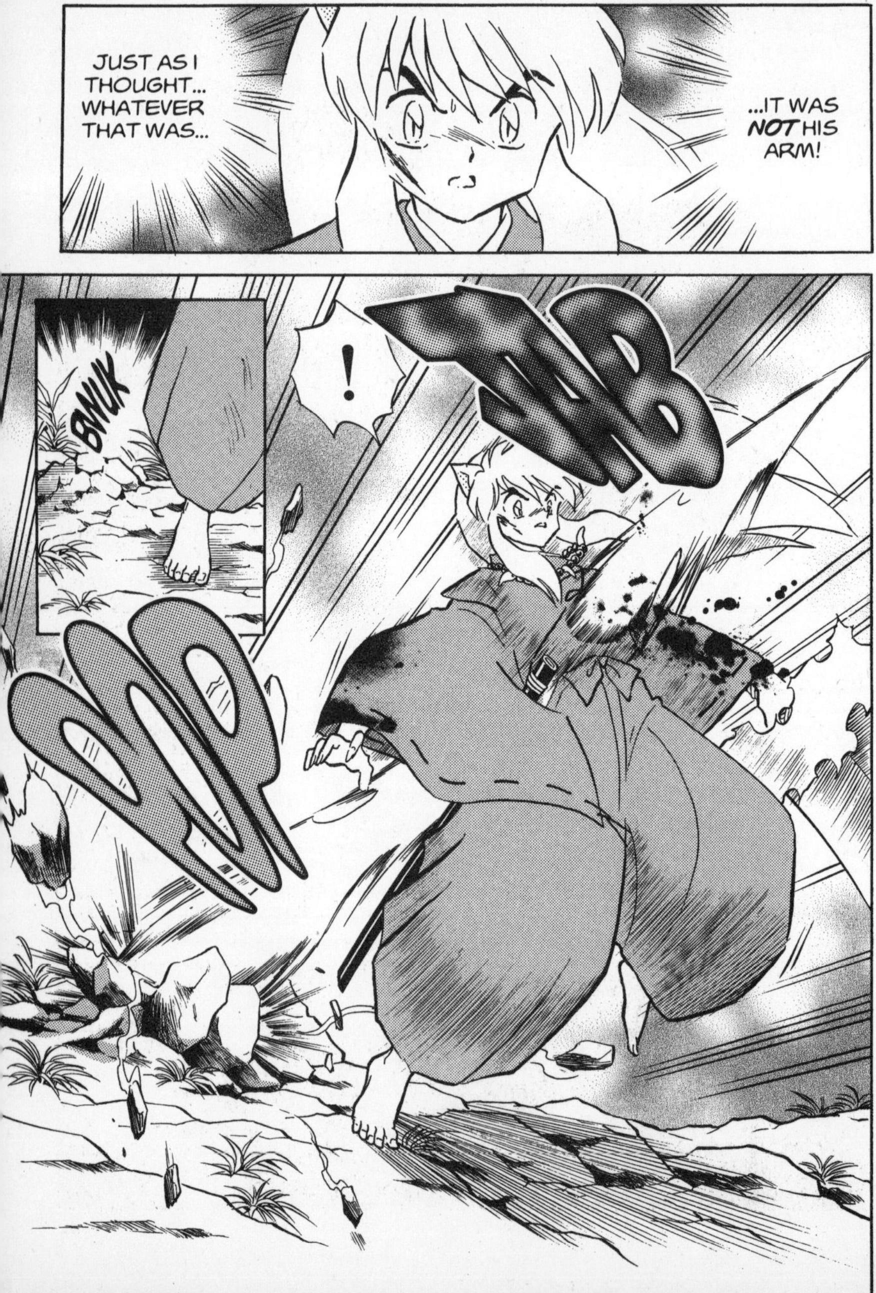
JUST AS I THOUGHT... WHATEVER THAT WAS...
...IT WAS **NOT** HIS ARM!
BWUK
!

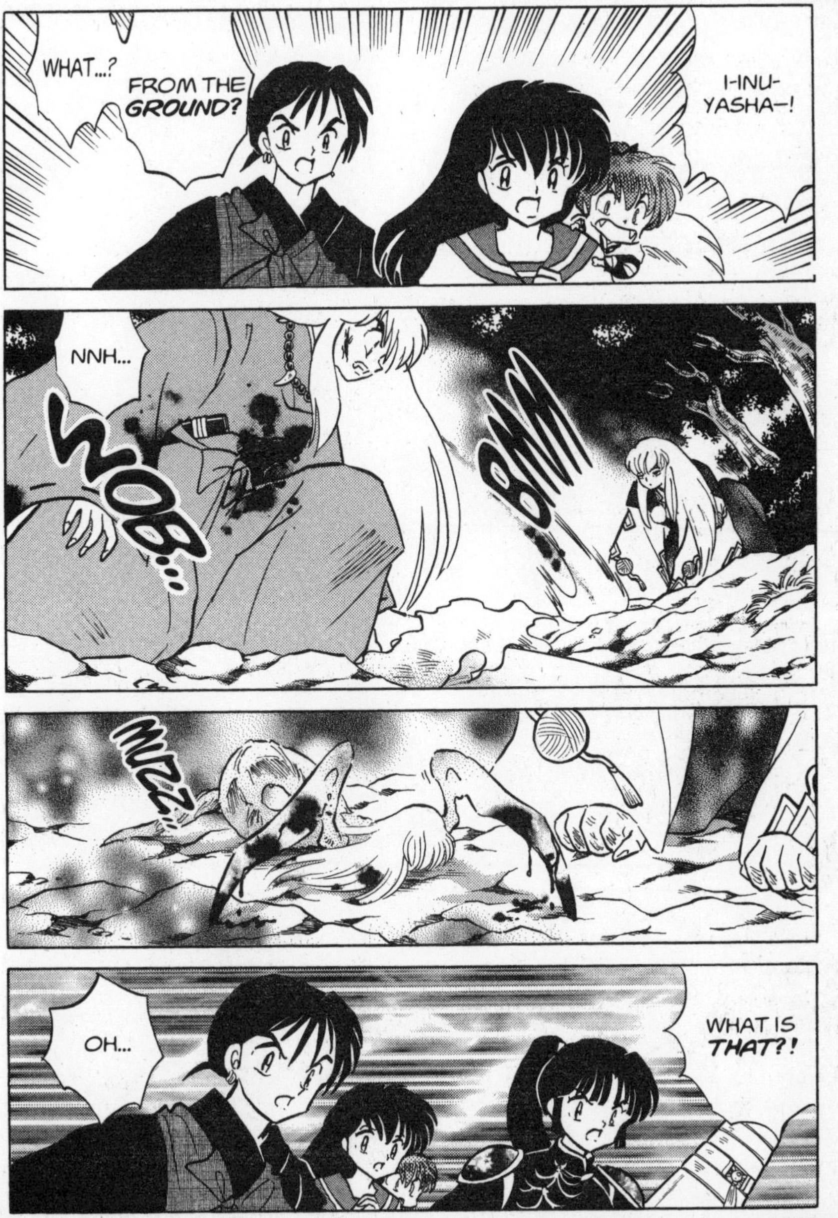
WHAT...?
FROM THE GROUND?
I-INU-YASHA--!
NNH...
WOB...
BMM
MUZZ...
OH...
WHAT IS THAT?!

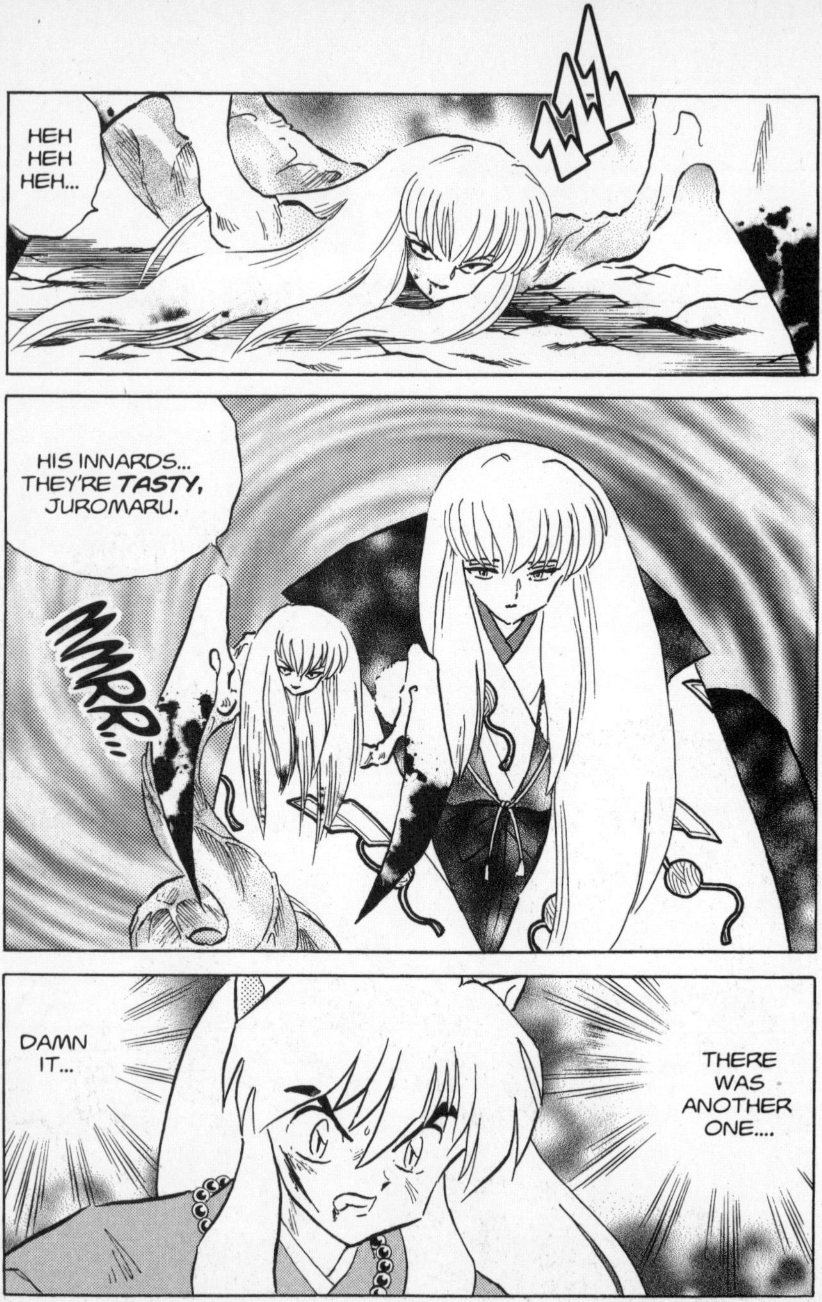
HEH HEH HEH...
HIS INNARDS... THEY'RE *TASTY*, JUROMARU.
MMRR...
DAMN IT...
THERE WAS ANOTHER ONE....

SCROLL NINE

SHADOW BOY

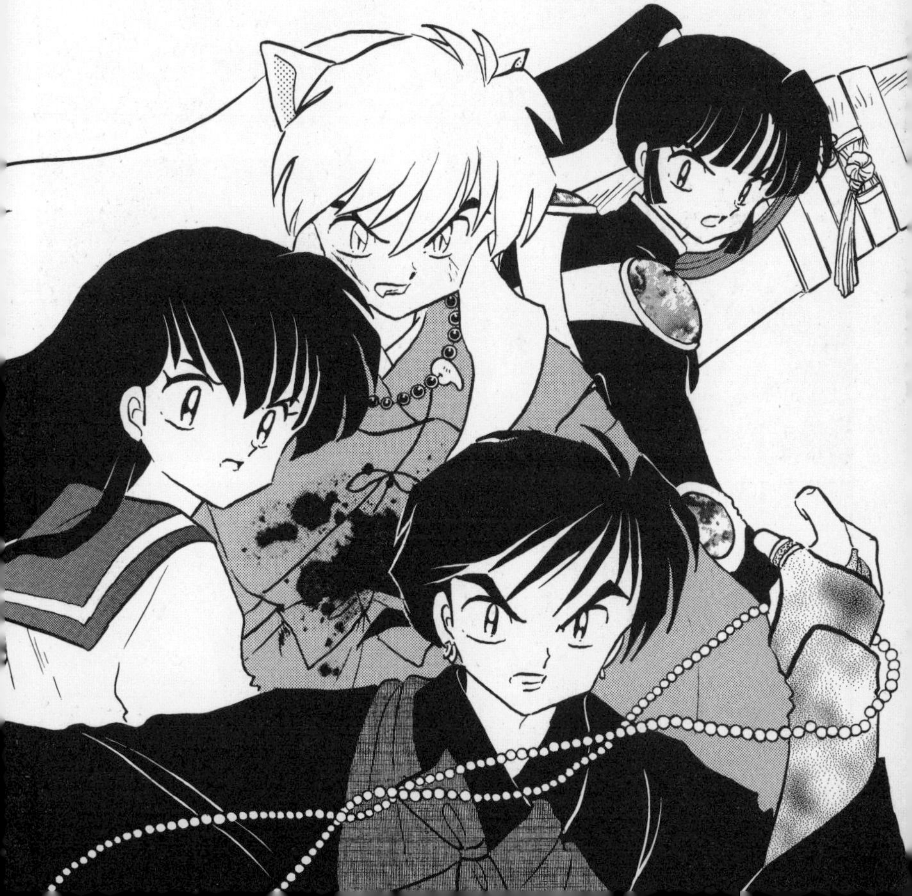

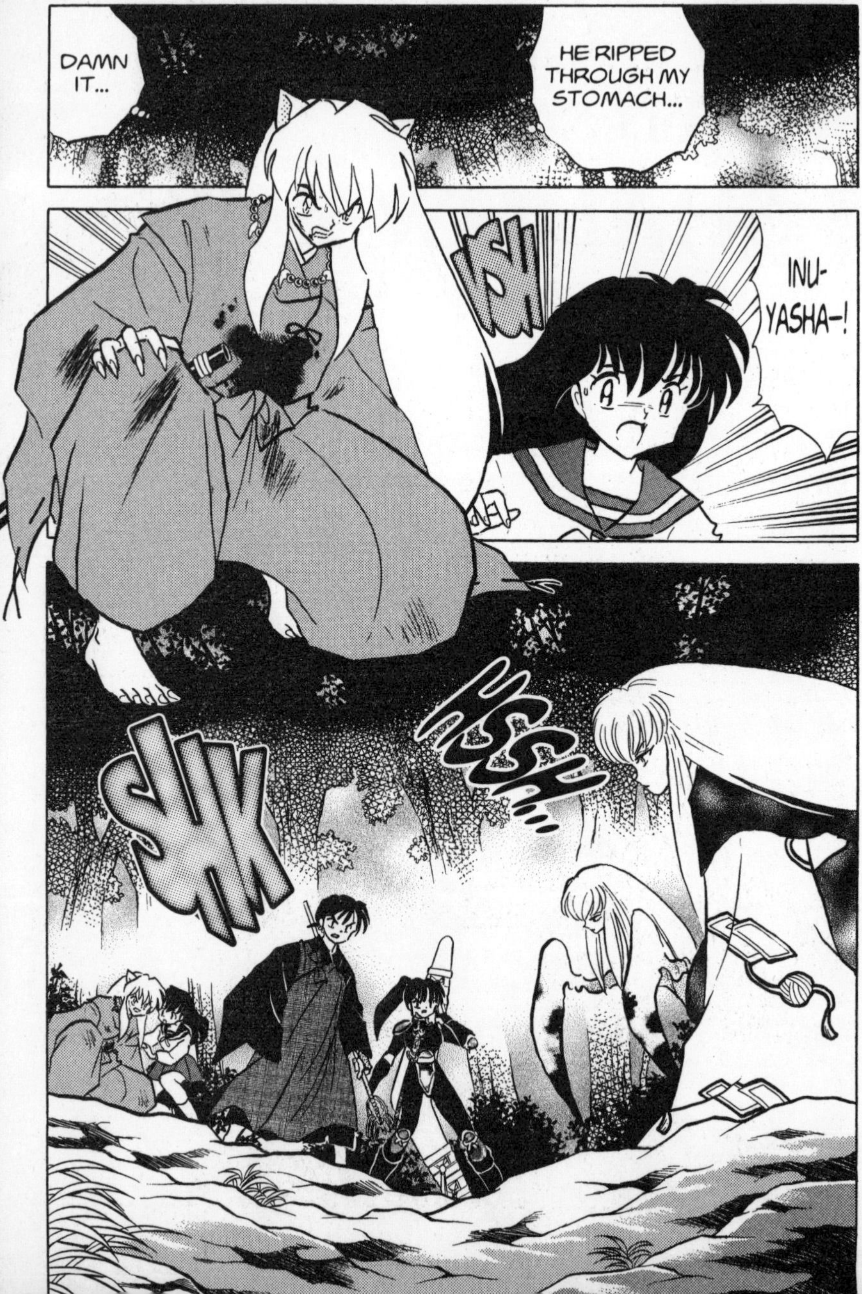
DAMN IT...
HE RIPPED THROUGH MY STOMACH...
INU-YASHA-!
SHK
WSSH...

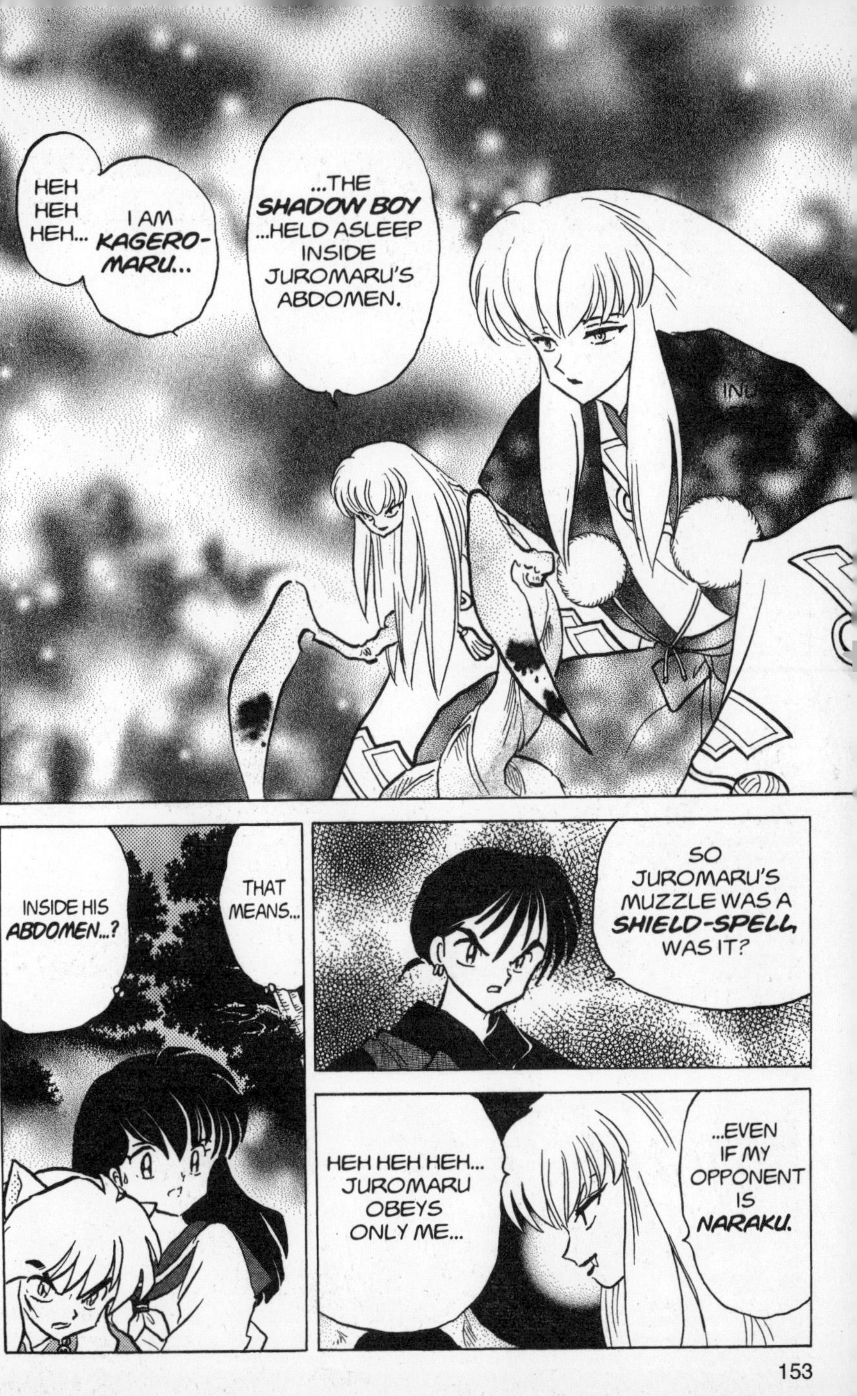
HEH HEH HEH... I AM KAGERO-MARU...
...THE SHADOW BOY ...HELD ASLEEP INSIDE JUROMARU'S ABDOMEN.
INSIDE HIS ABDOMEN...?
THAT MEANS...
SO JUROMARU'S MUZZLE WAS A SHIELD-SPELL, WAS IT?
HEH HEH HEH... JUROMARU OBEYS ONLY ME...
...EVEN IF MY OPPONENT IS NARAKU.

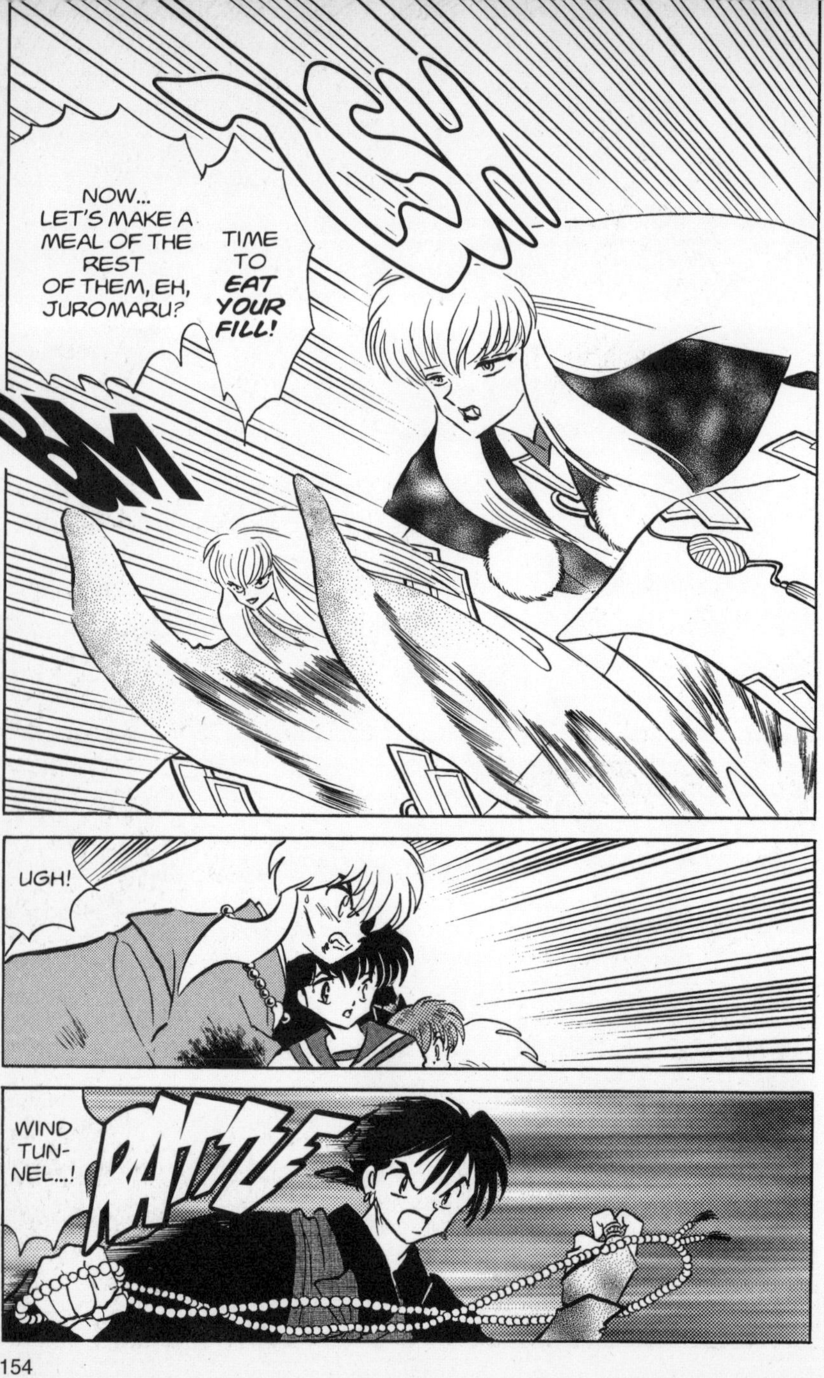
NOW... LET'S MAKE A MEAL OF THE REST OF THEM, EH, JUROMARU?
TIME TO *EAT YOUR FILL!*
UGH!
WIND TUN-NEL...!
RATTLE

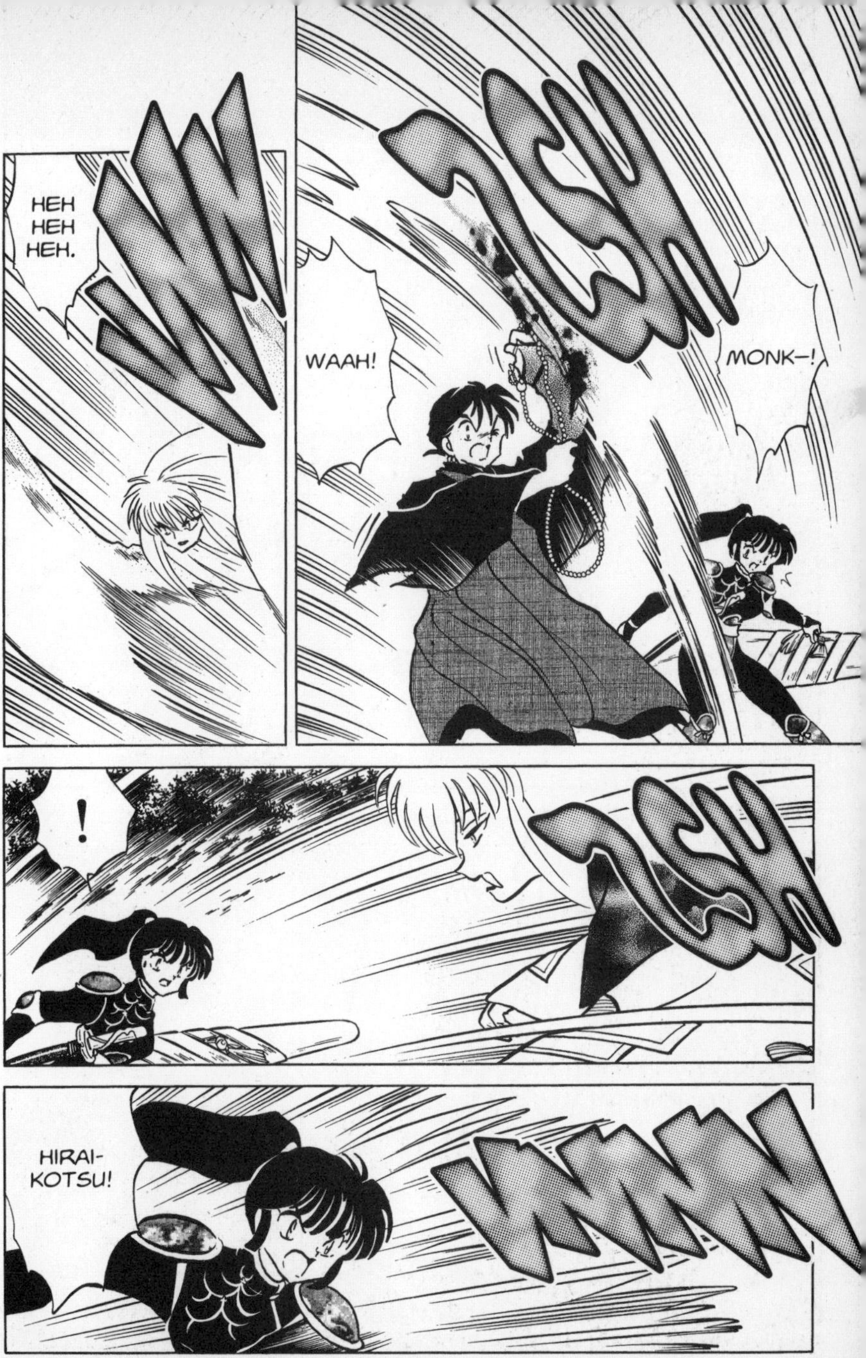
HEH HEH HEH.
WAAH!
MONK–!
!
HIRAI-KOTSU!

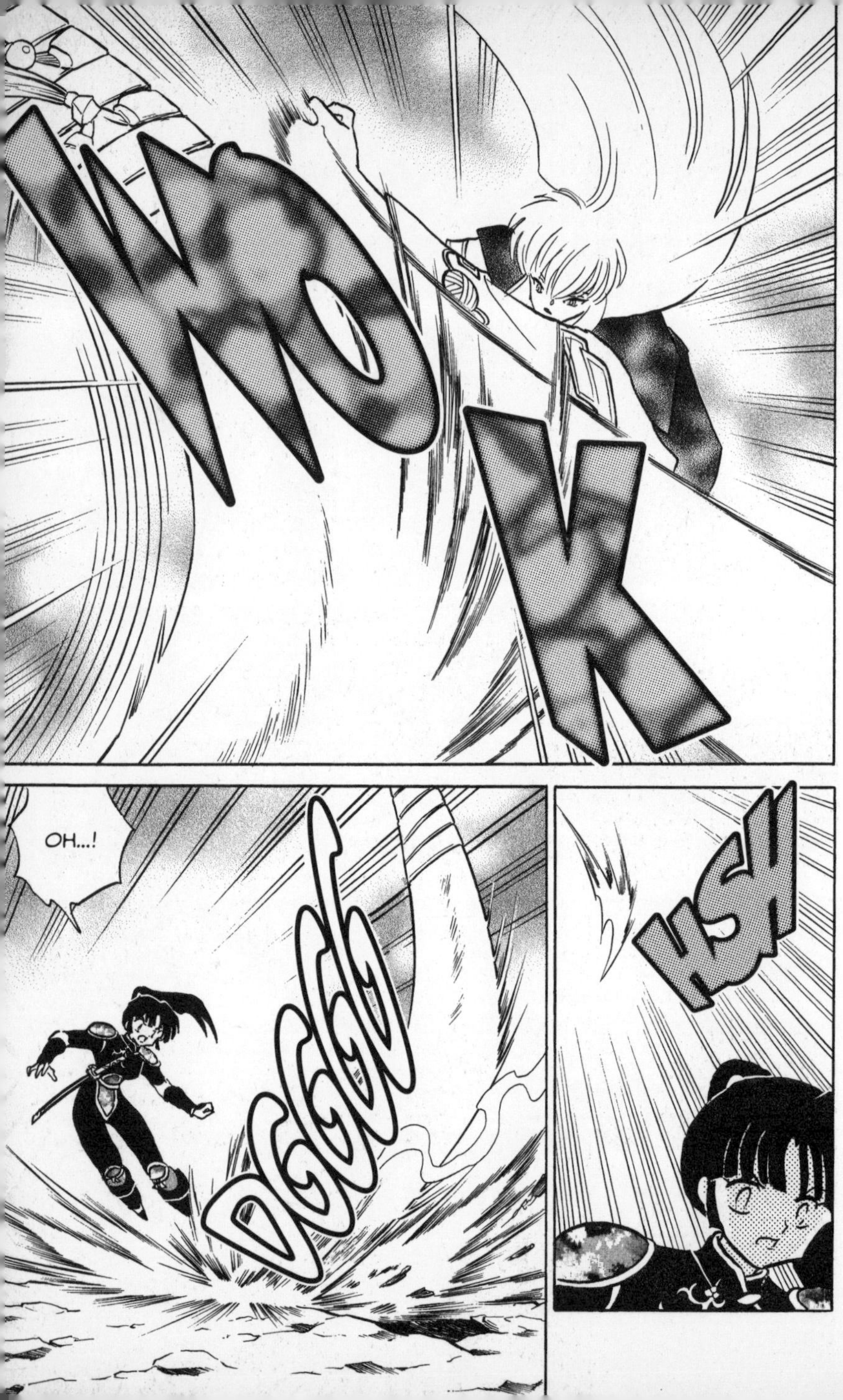
OH...!

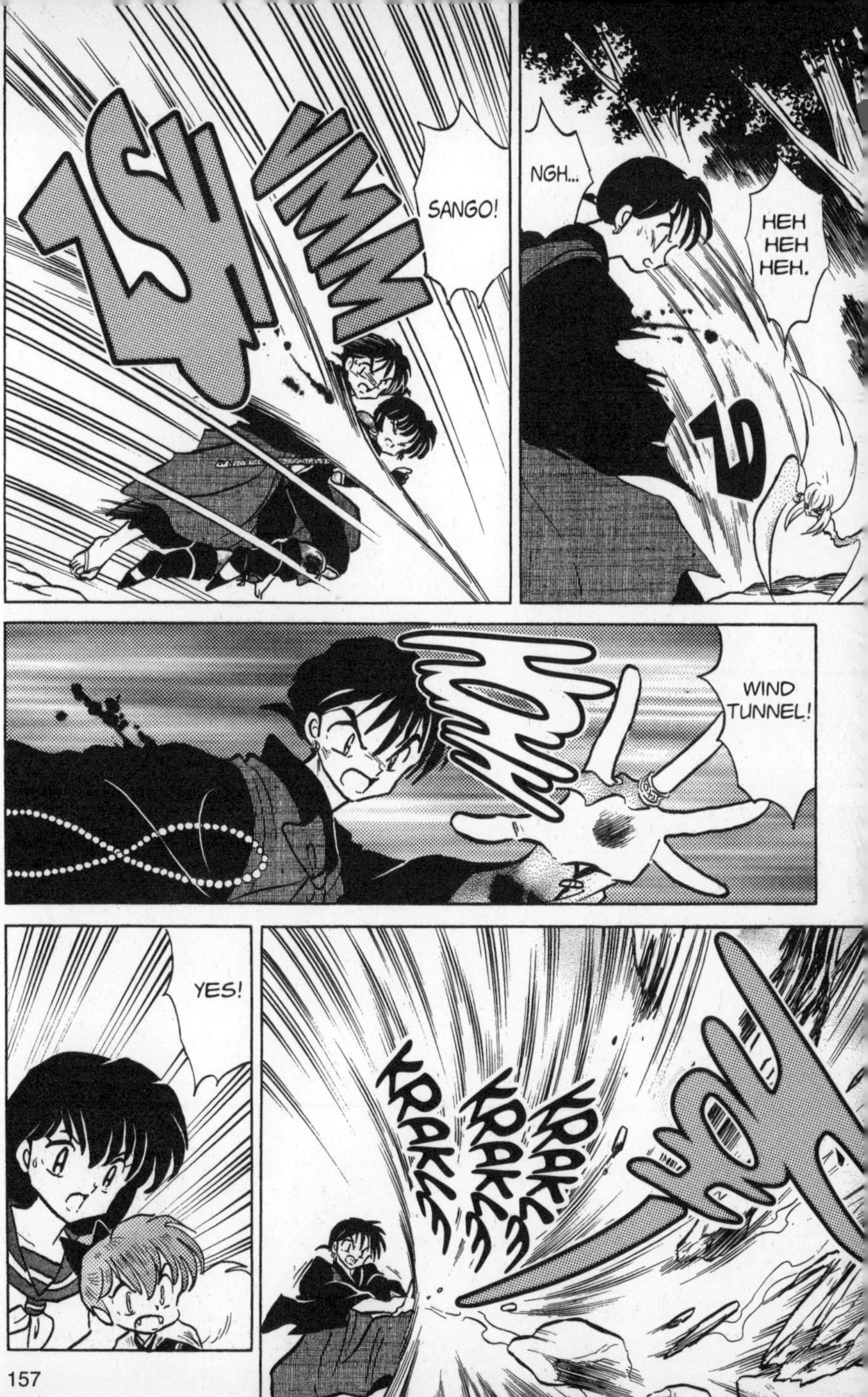
ZSHH
VMMM
SANGO!
NGH...
HEH HEH HEH.
WIND TUNNEL!
YES!
KRAK
KRAK
KRAK

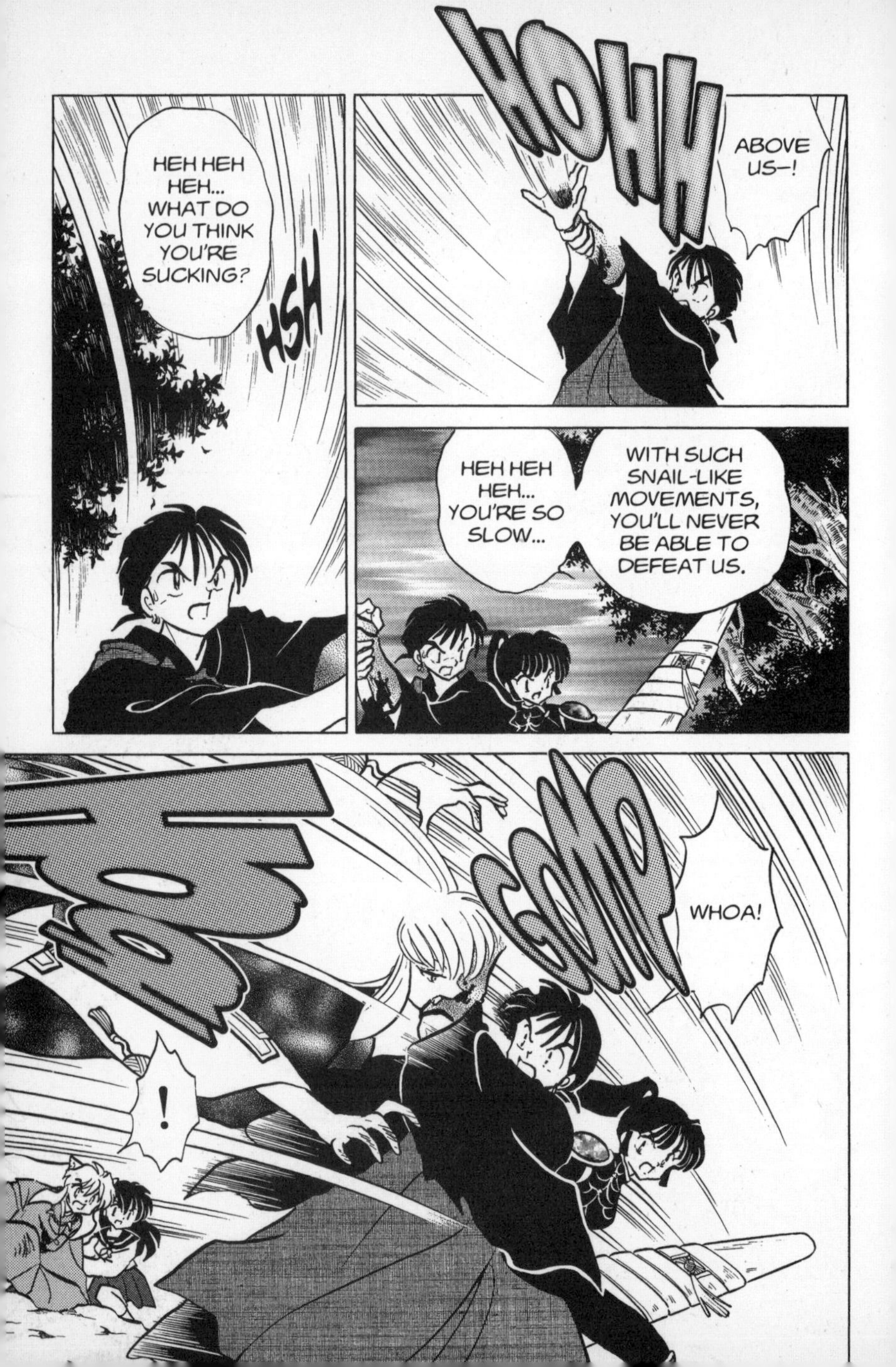
HEH HEH HEH... WHAT DO YOU THINK YOU'RE SUCKING?
HSH
HOHH
ABOVE US–!
HEH HEH HEH... YOU'RE SO SLOW...
WITH SUCH SNAIL-LIKE MOVEMENTS, YOU'LL NEVER BE ABLE TO DEFEAT US.
WHOA!
!

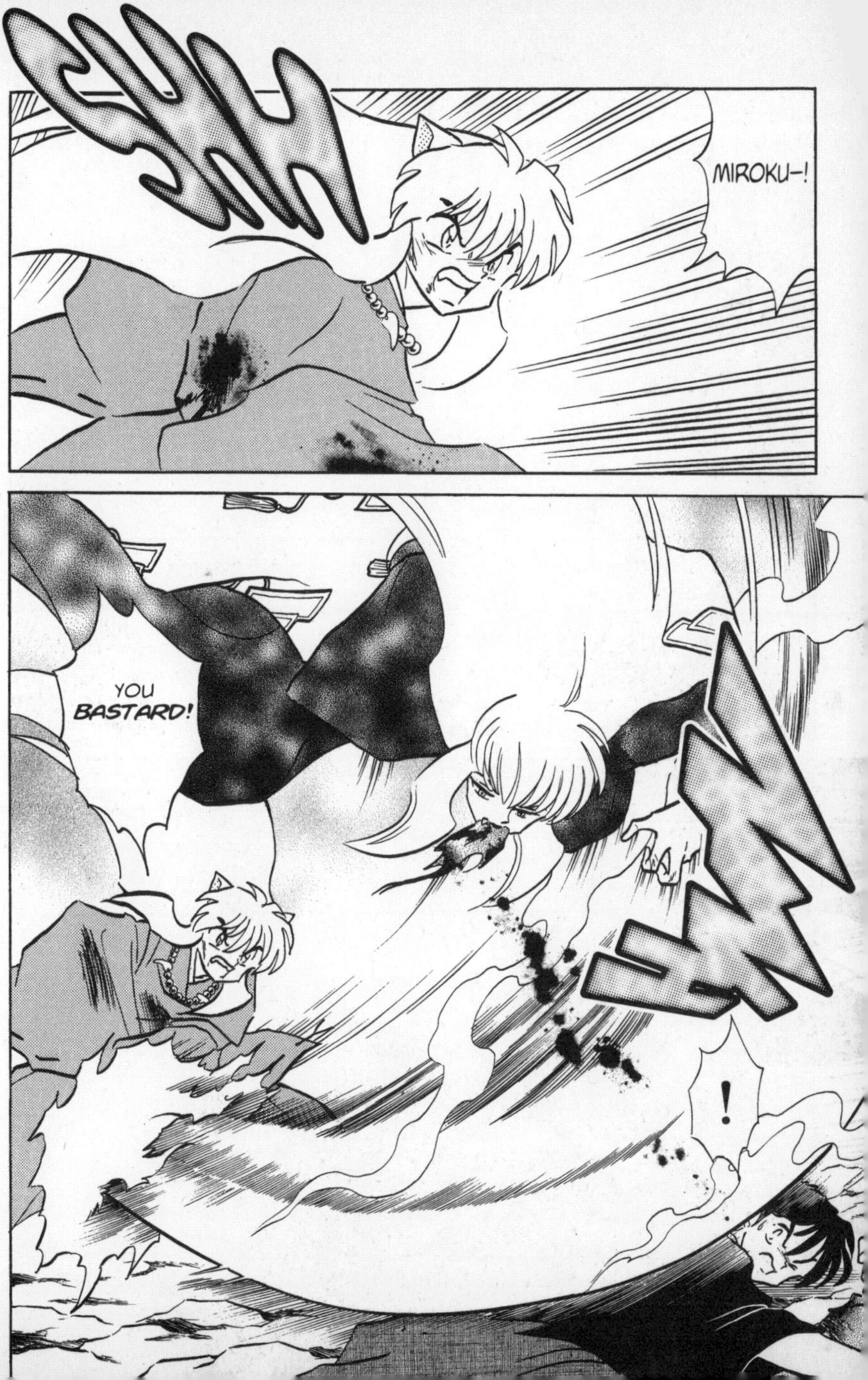
MIROKU-!
YOU BASTARD!
!

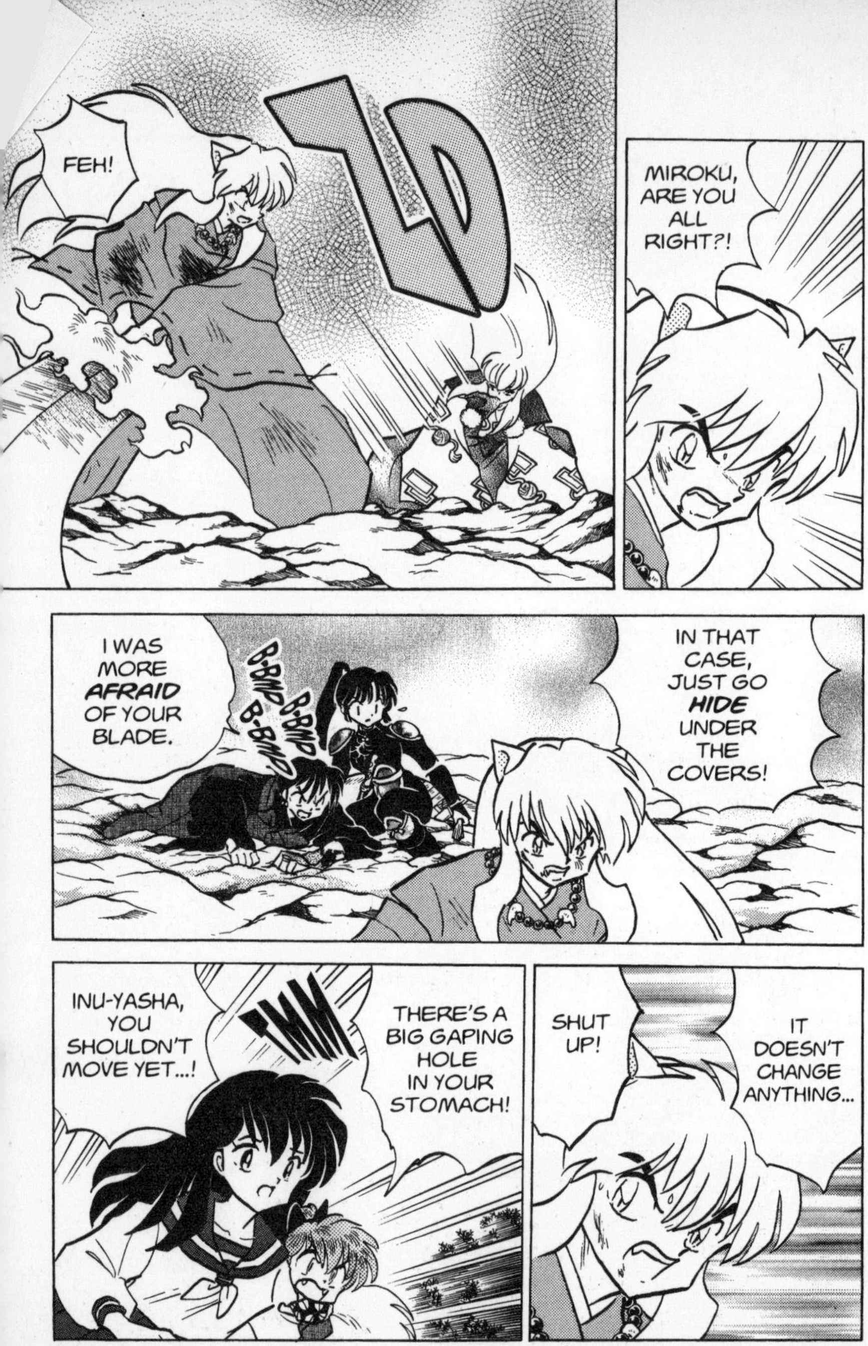
FEH!
MIROKU, ARE YOU ALL RIGHT?!
I WAS MORE AFRAID OF YOUR BLADE.
B-BMP B-BMP B-BMP
IN THAT CASE, JUST GO HIDE UNDER THE COVERS!
INU-YASHA, YOU SHOULDN'T MOVE YET...!
THERE'S A BIG GAPING HOLE IN YOUR STOMACH!
SHUT UP!
IT DOESN'T CHANGE ANYTHING...

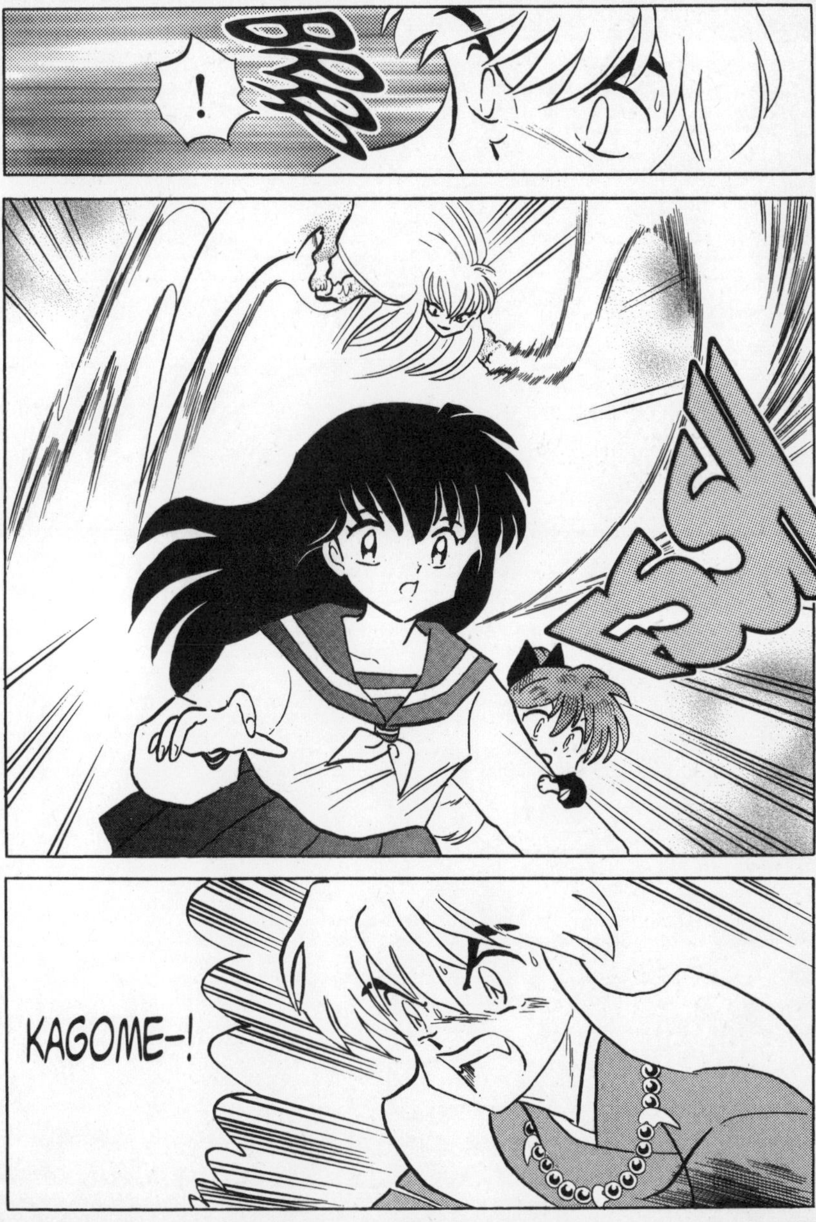

!
BRRR
KAGOME-!

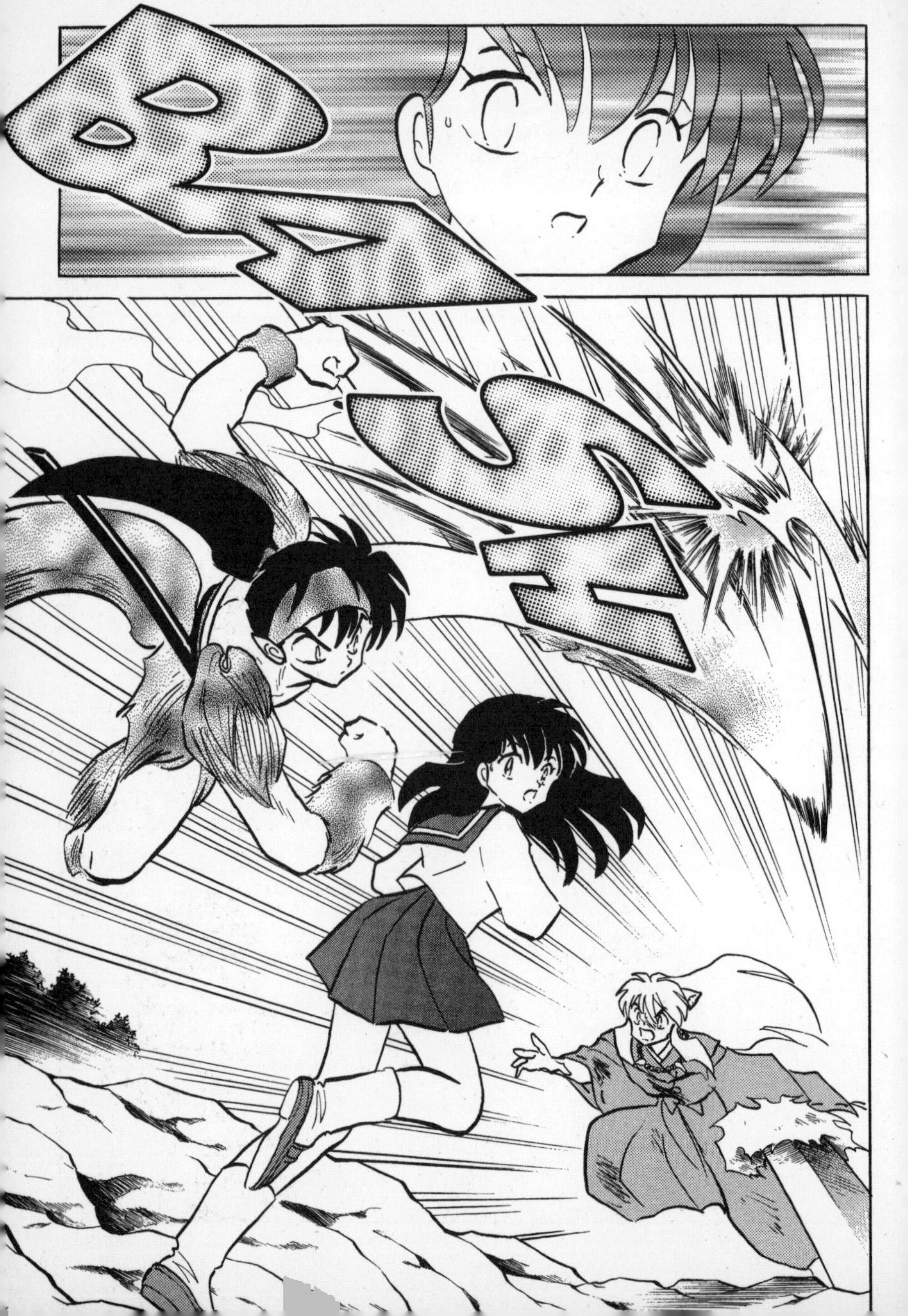
BASH

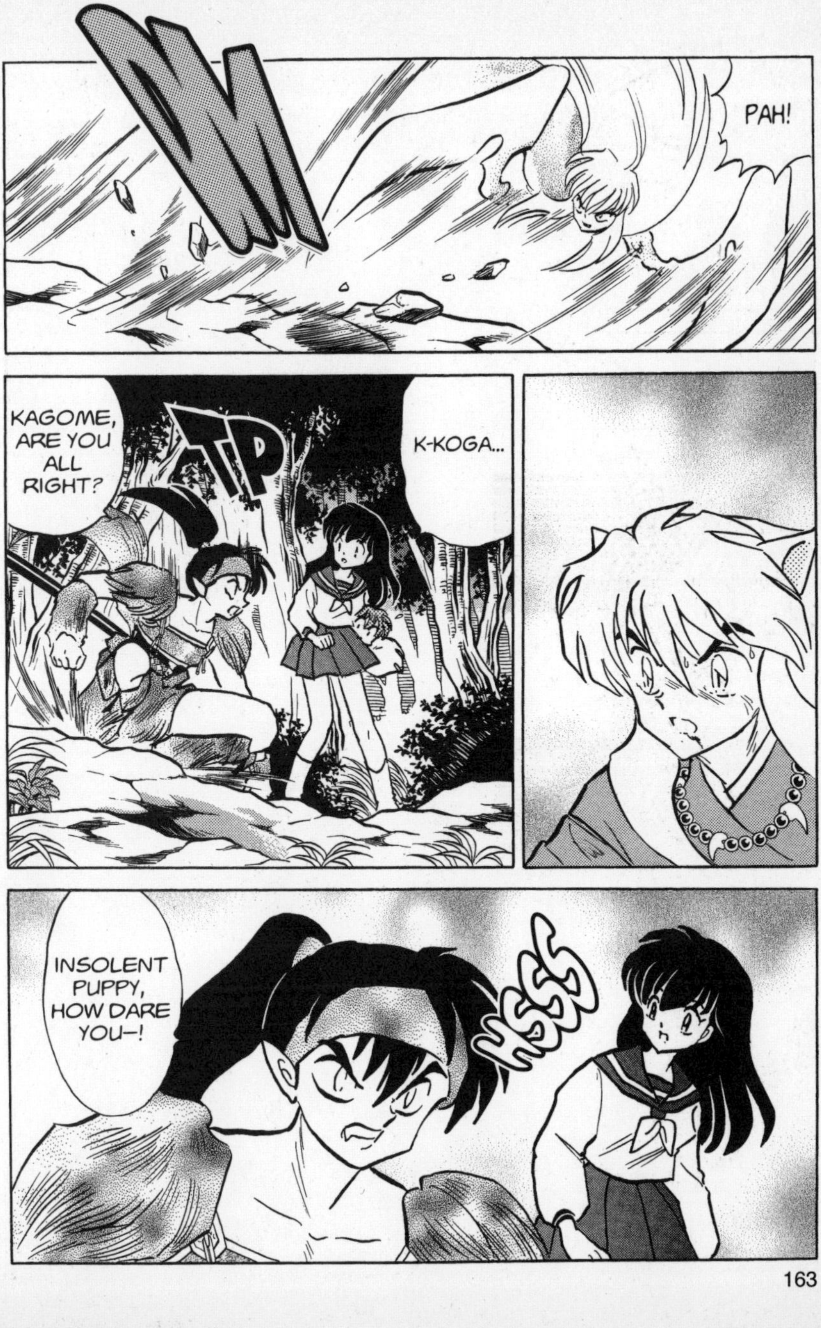
DWM
PAH!
KAGOME, ARE YOU ALL RIGHT?
TP
K-KOGA...
INSOLENT PUPPY, HOW DARE YOU–!
HSSS

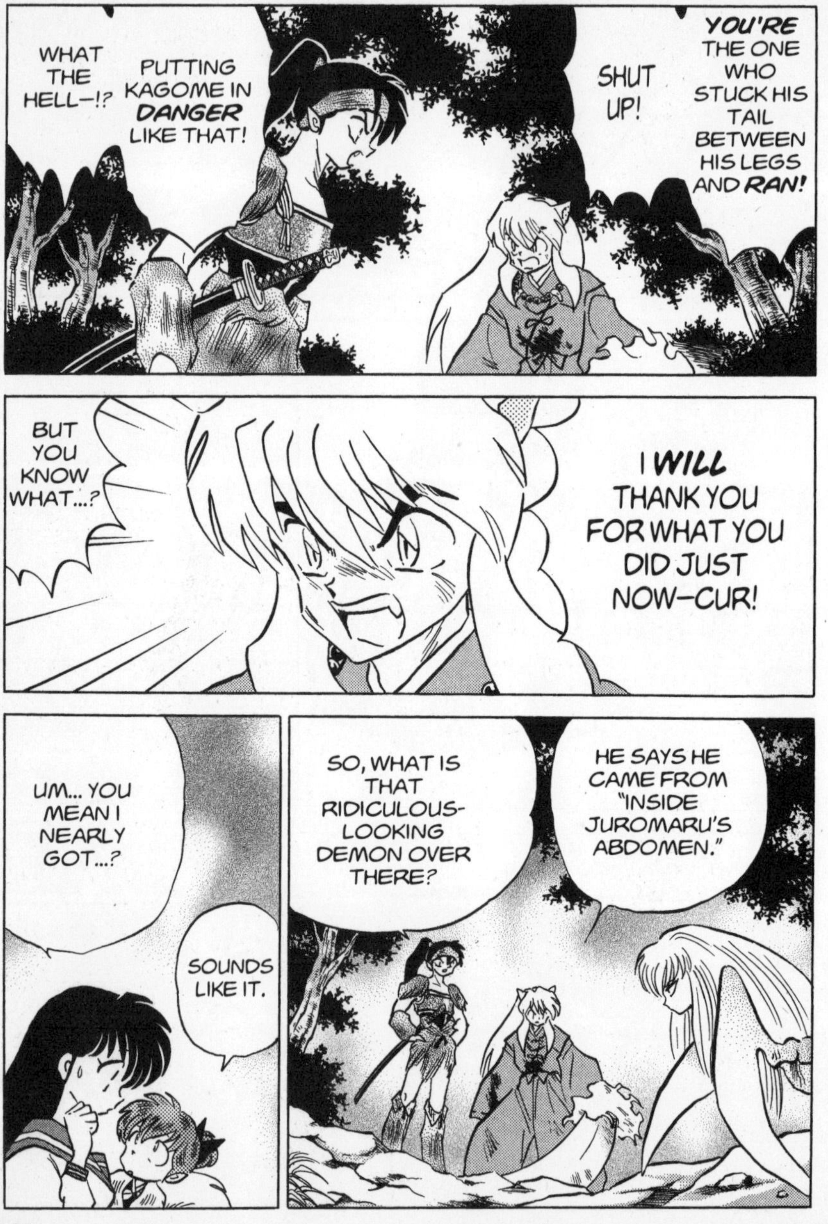
WHAT THE HELL—!?
PUTTING KAGOME IN DANGER LIKE THAT!
SHUT UP!
YOU'RE THE ONE WHO STUCK HIS TAIL BETWEEN HIS LEGS AND RAN!
BUT YOU KNOW WHAT...?
I WILL THANK YOU FOR WHAT YOU DID JUST NOW—CUR!
UM... YOU MEAN I NEARLY GOT...?
SOUNDS LIKE IT.
SO, WHAT IS THAT RIDICULOUS-LOOKING DEMON OVER THERE?
HE SAYS HE CAME FROM "INSIDE JUROMARU'S ABDOMEN."

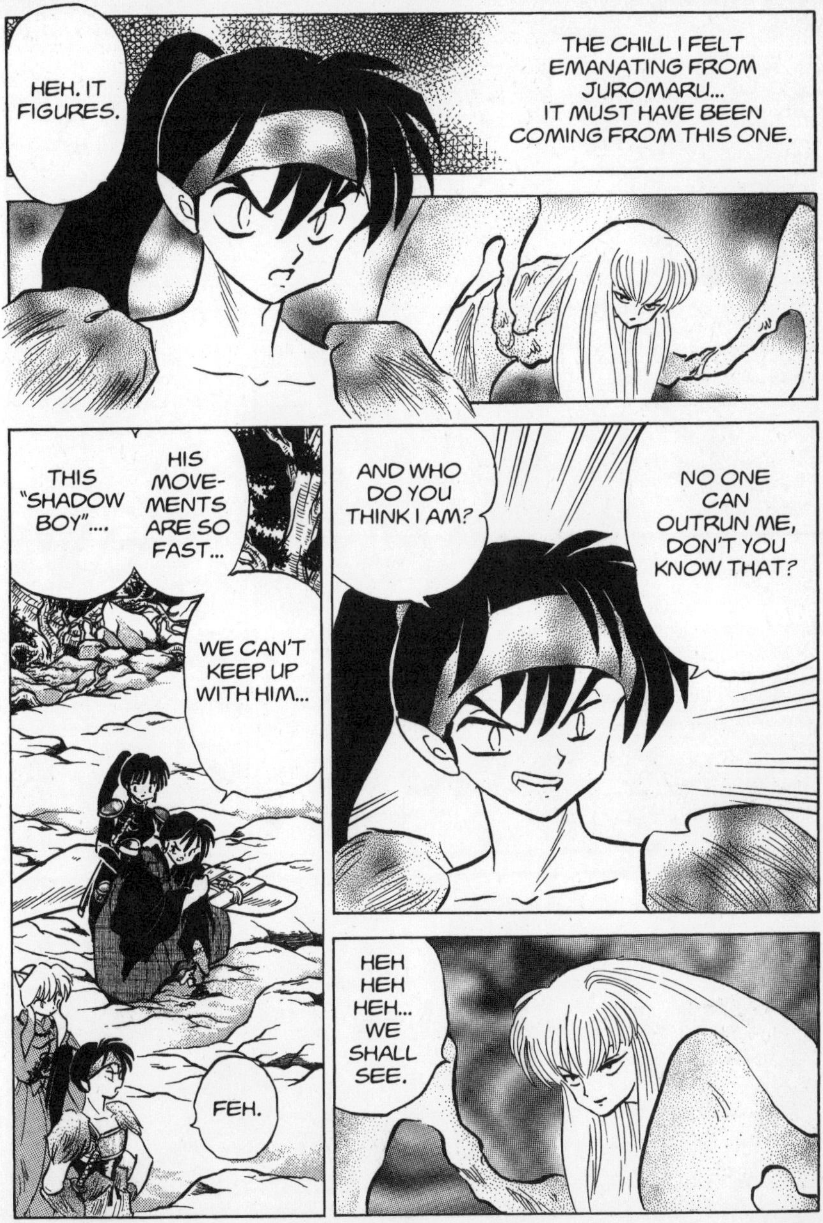
HEH. IT FIGURES.
THE CHILL I FELT EMANATING FROM JUROMARU... IT MUST HAVE BEEN COMING FROM THIS ONE.
THIS "SHADOW BOY"....
HIS MOVEMENTS ARE SO FAST...
WE CAN'T KEEP UP WITH HIM...
FEH.
AND WHO DO YOU THINK I AM?
NO ONE CAN OUTRUN ME, DON'T YOU KNOW THAT?
HEH HEH HEH... WE SHALL SEE.

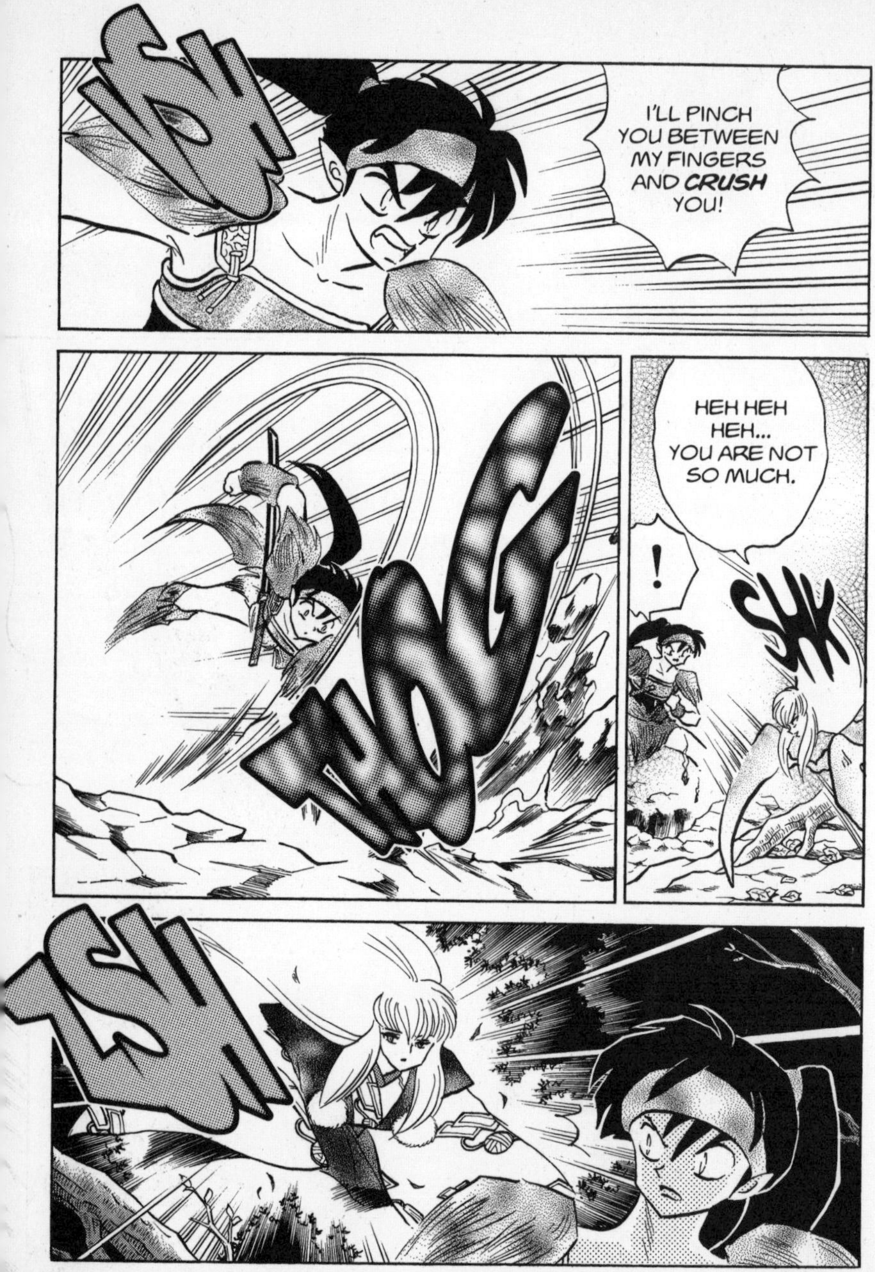
I'LL PINCH YOU BETWEEN MY FINGERS AND **CRUSH** YOU!
HEH HEH HEH... YOU ARE NOT SO MUCH.
!
SHK

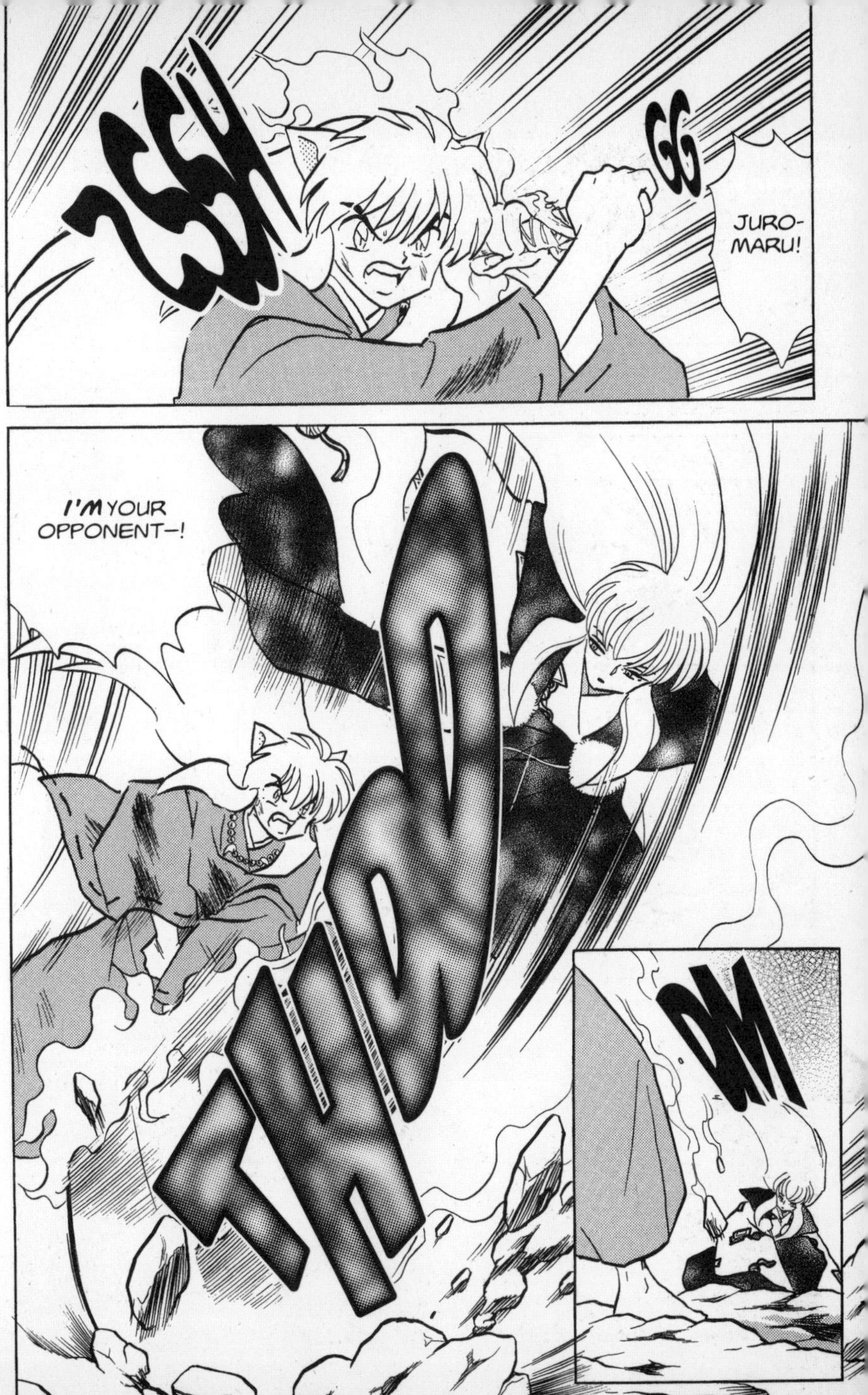
ZESH
GG
JURO-MARU!
I'M YOUR OPPONENT–!
THUD
DM

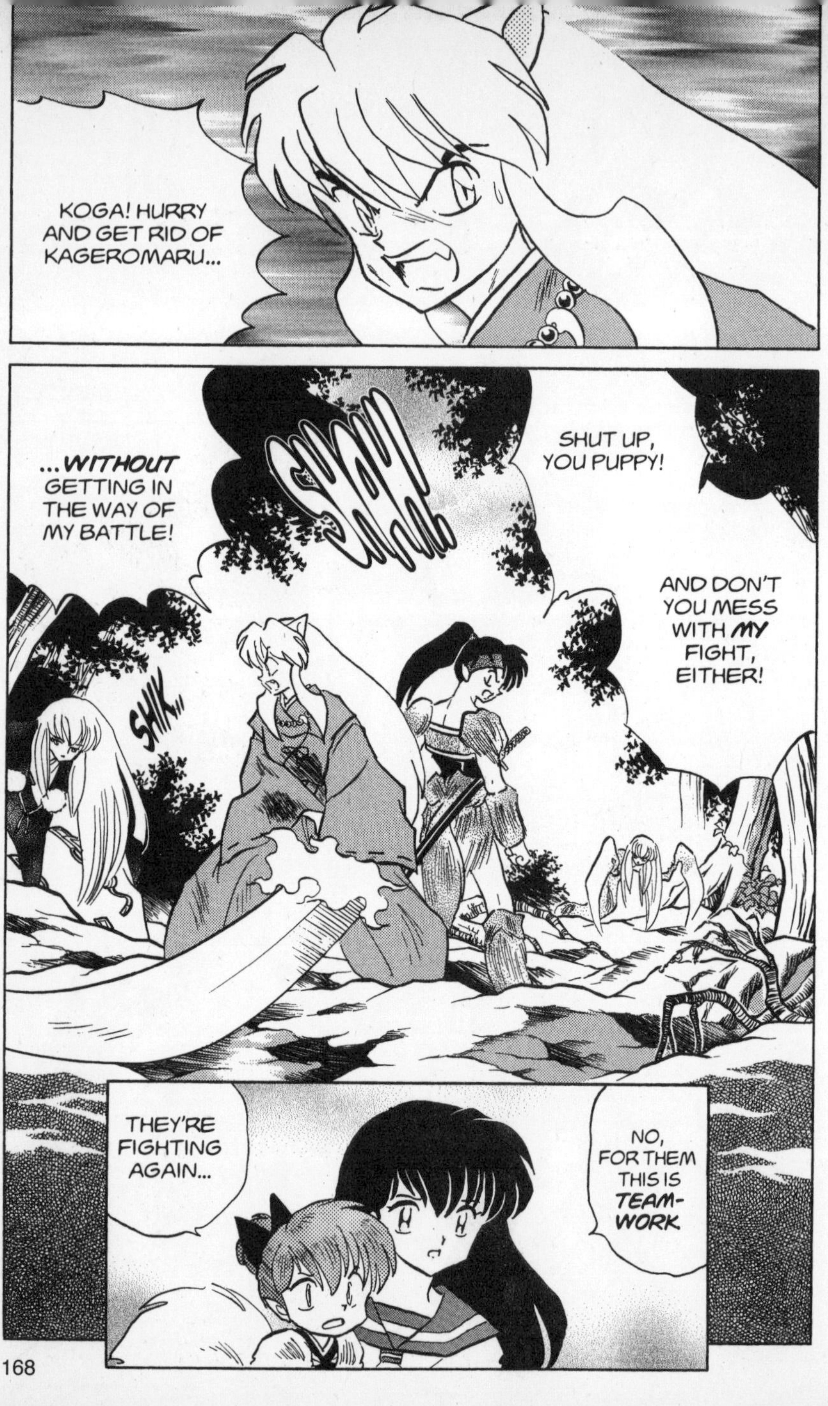
KOGA! HURRY AND GET RID OF KAGEROMARU...
...*WITHOUT* GETTING IN THE WAY OF MY BATTLE!
SHUT UP, YOU PUPPY!
AND DON'T YOU MESS WITH *MY* FIGHT, EITHER!
SHIK...
THEY'RE FIGHTING AGAIN...
NO, FOR THEM THIS IS *TEAM-WORK*

SCROLL TEN

TWO AGAINST TWO

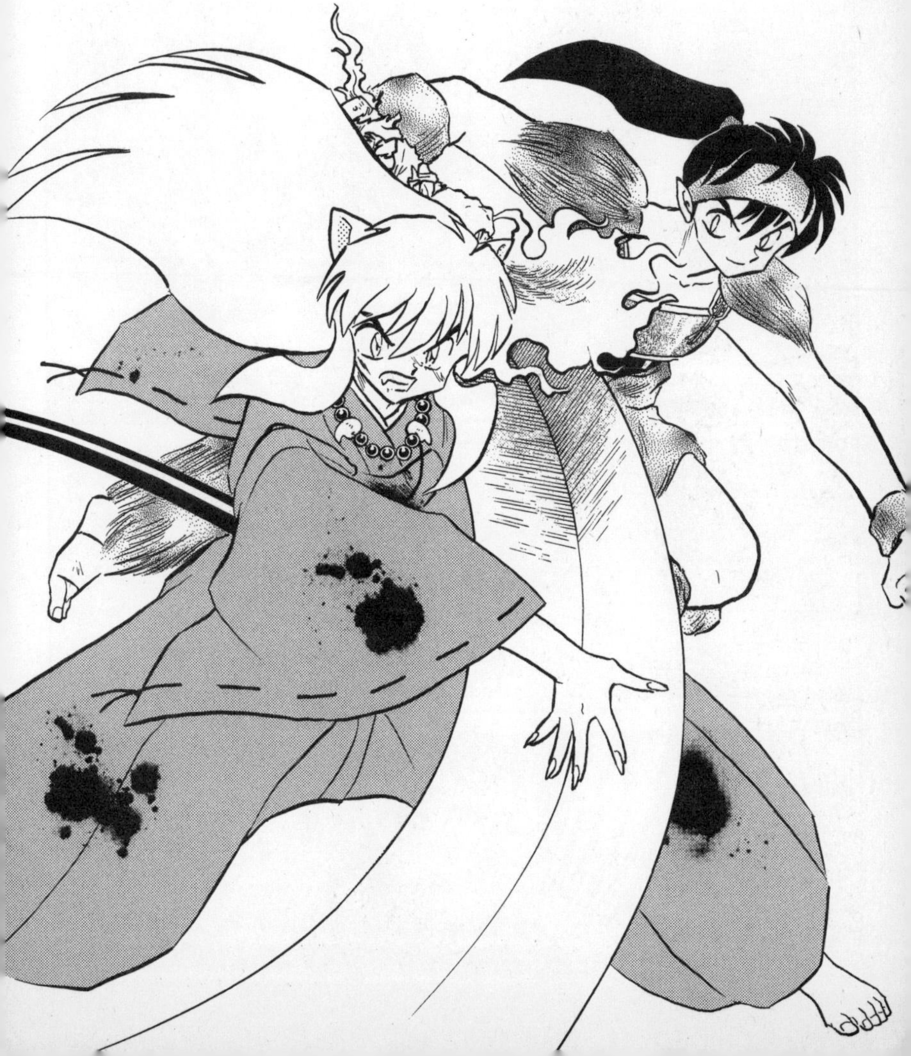

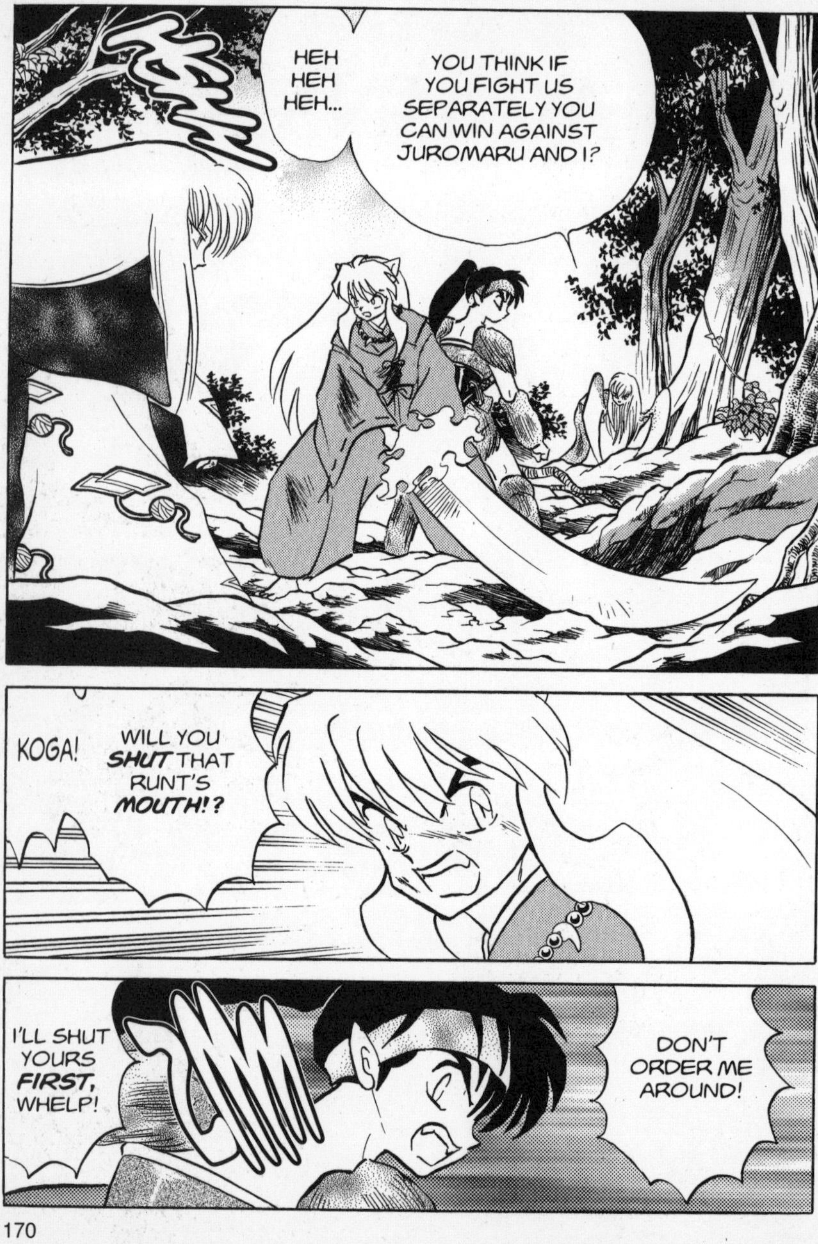
HEH
HEH
HEH...
YOU THINK IF YOU FIGHT US SEPARATELY YOU CAN WIN AGAINST JUROMARU AND I?
KOGA!
WILL YOU **SHUT** THAT RUNT'S **MOUTH!?**
I'LL SHUT YOURS **FIRST**, WHELP!
DON'T ORDER ME AROUND!

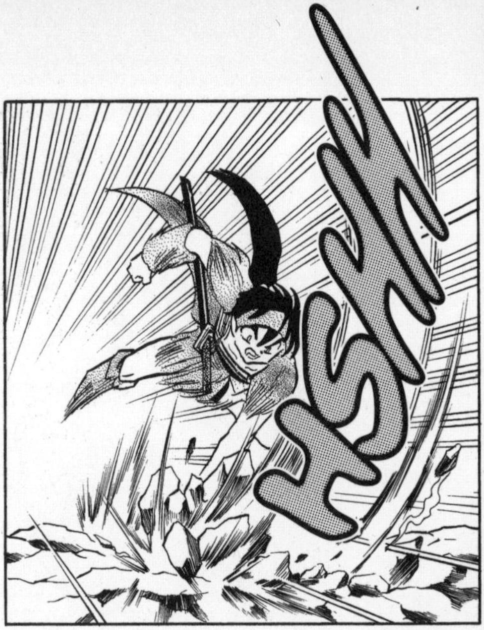

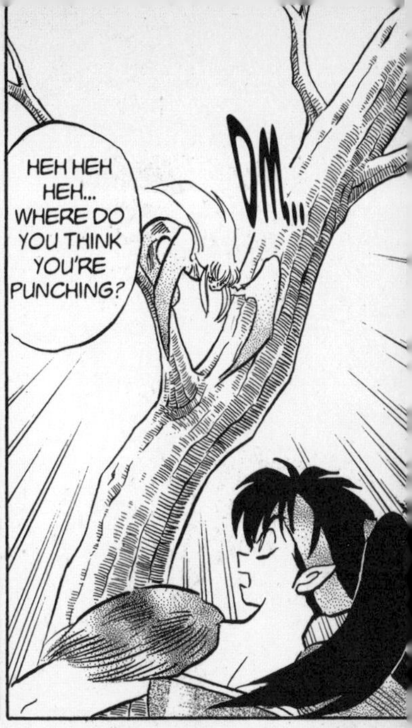
HEH HEH HEH... WHERE DO YOU THINK YOU'RE PUNCHING?
DM...

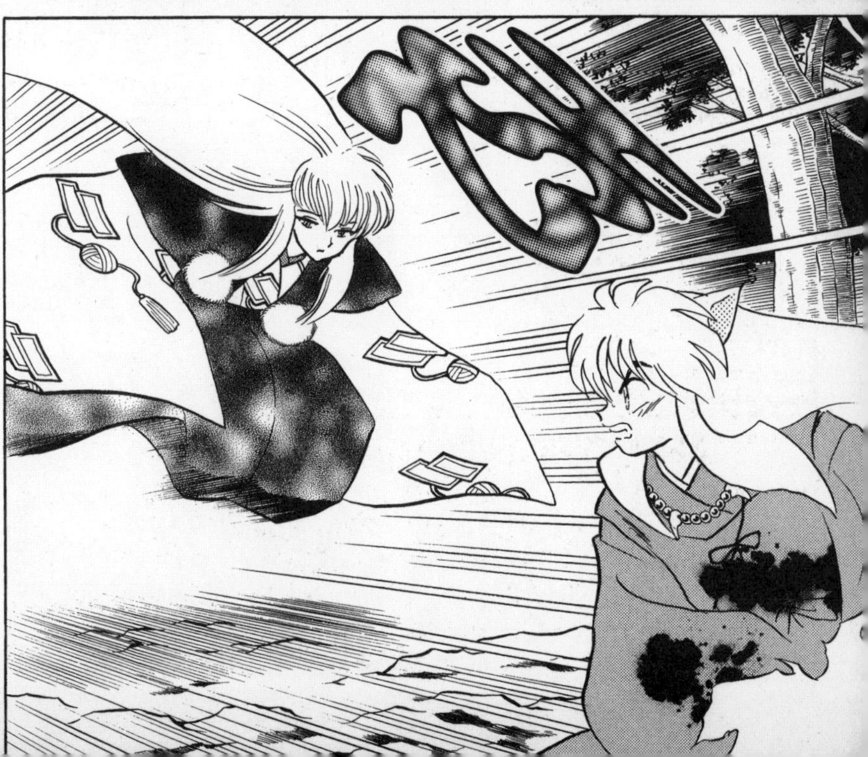

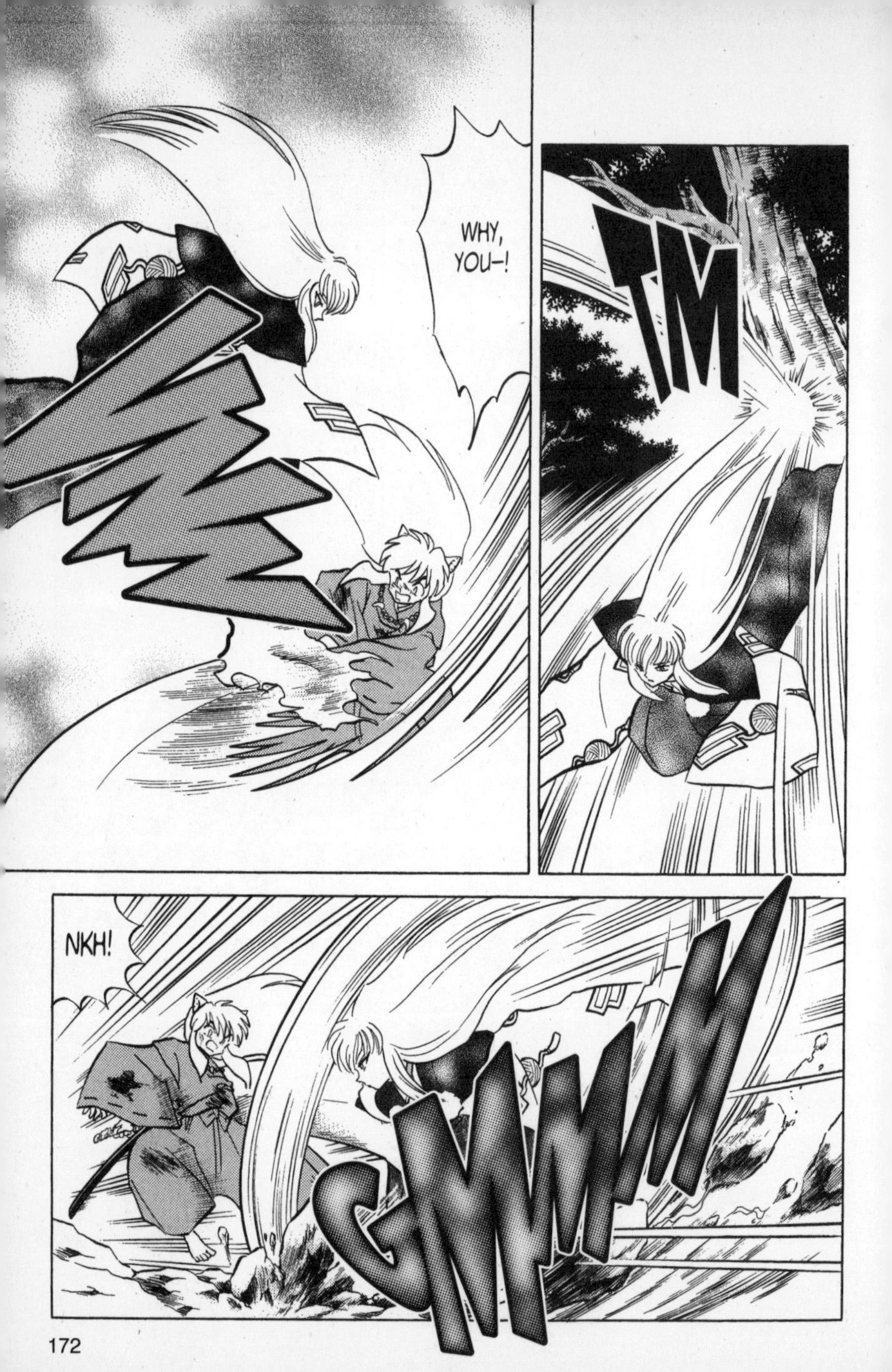
WHY, YOU-!
TM
NKH!

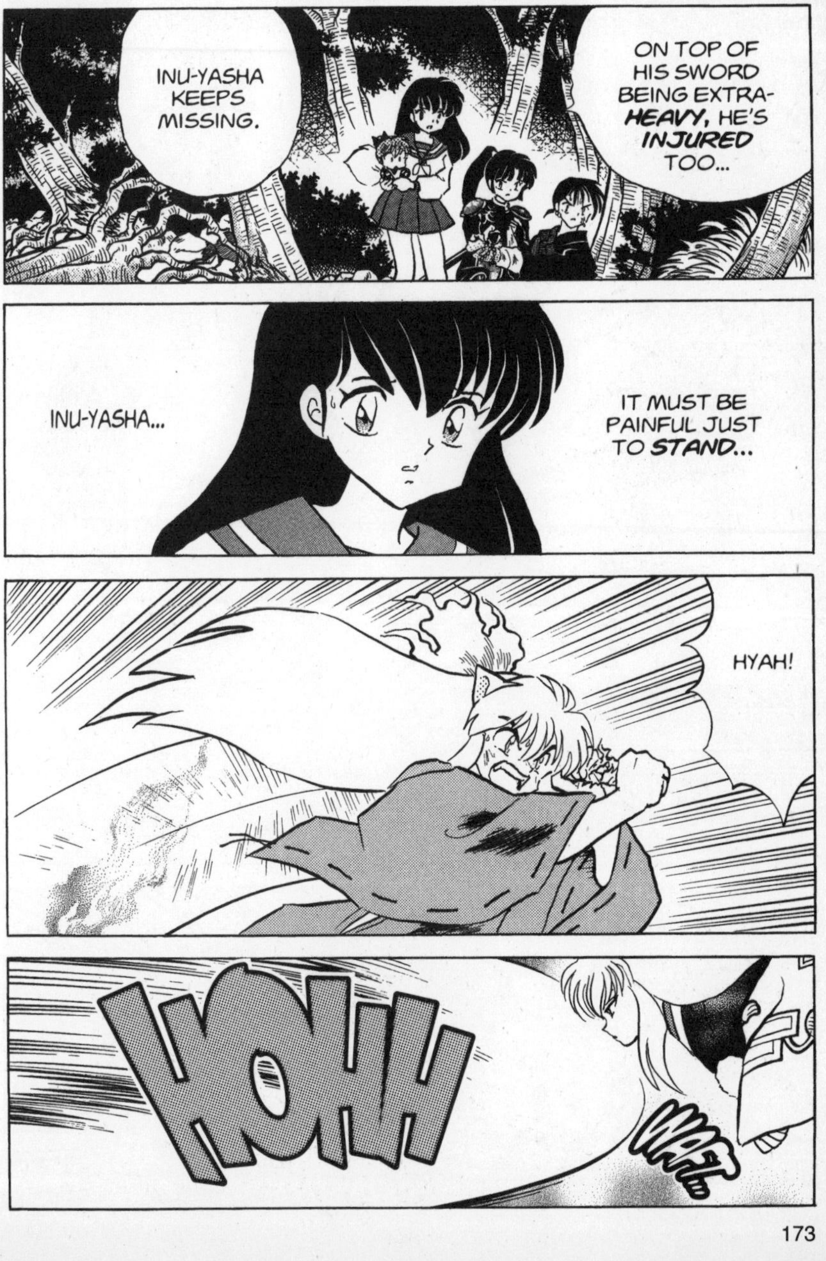
INU-YASHA KEEPS MISSING.
ON TOP OF HIS SWORD BEING EXTRA-**HEAVY**, HE'S **INJURED** TOO...
INU-YASHA...
IT MUST BE PAINFUL JUST TO **STAND**...
HYAH!
WOHH
WAFT

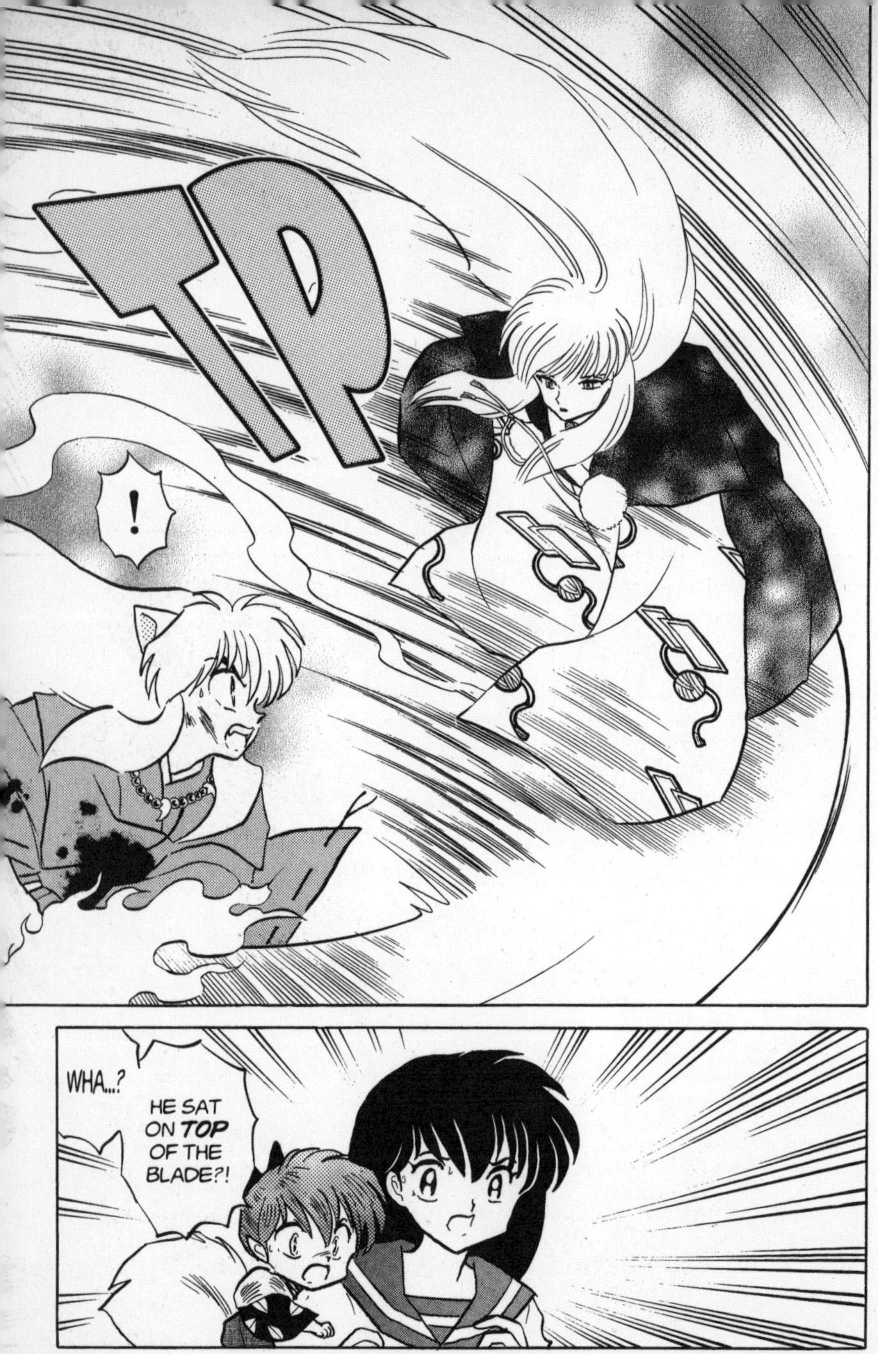
TIP
!
WHA...?
HE SAT ON *TOP* OF THE BLADE?!

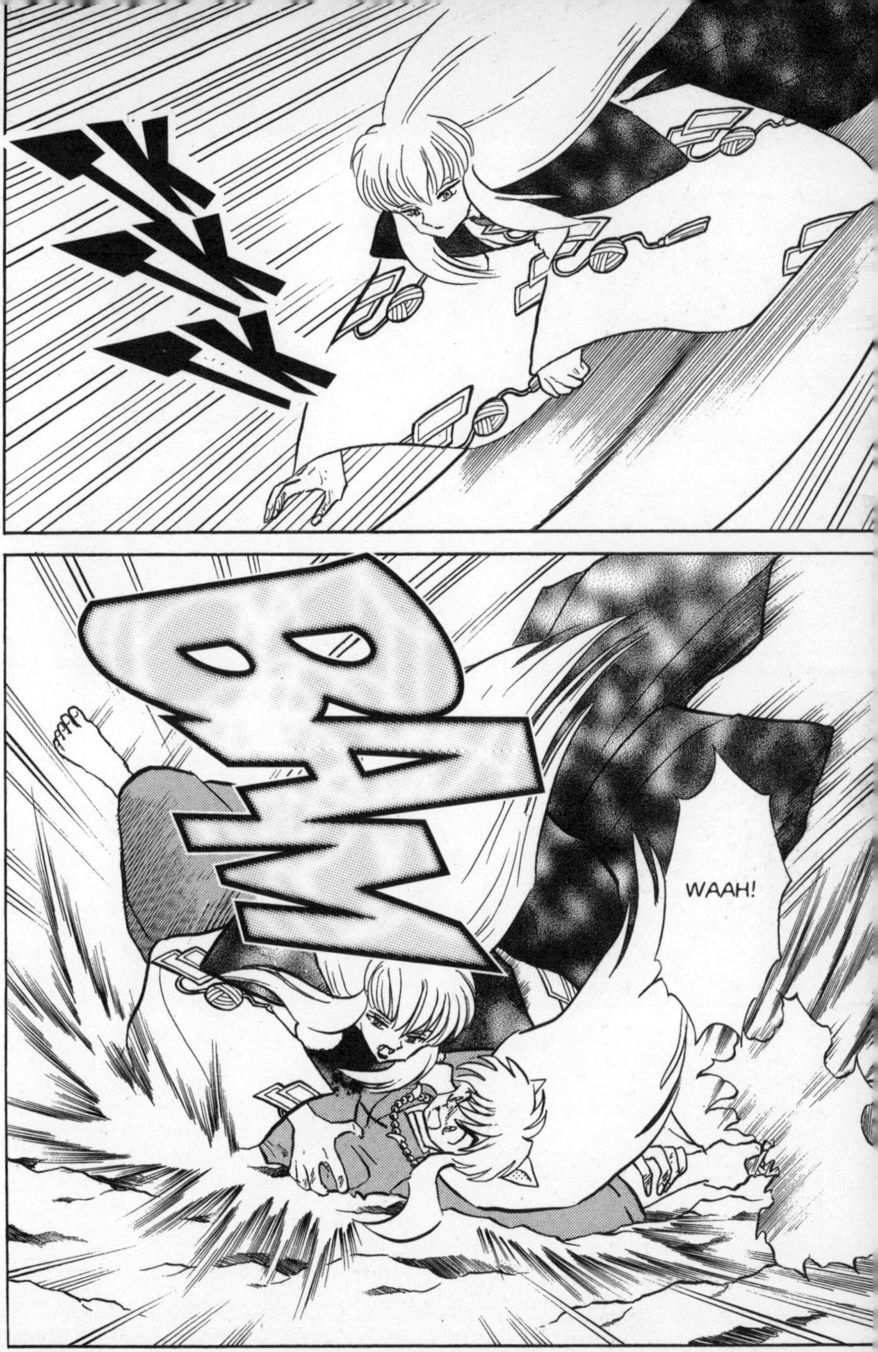
BAM
WAAH!

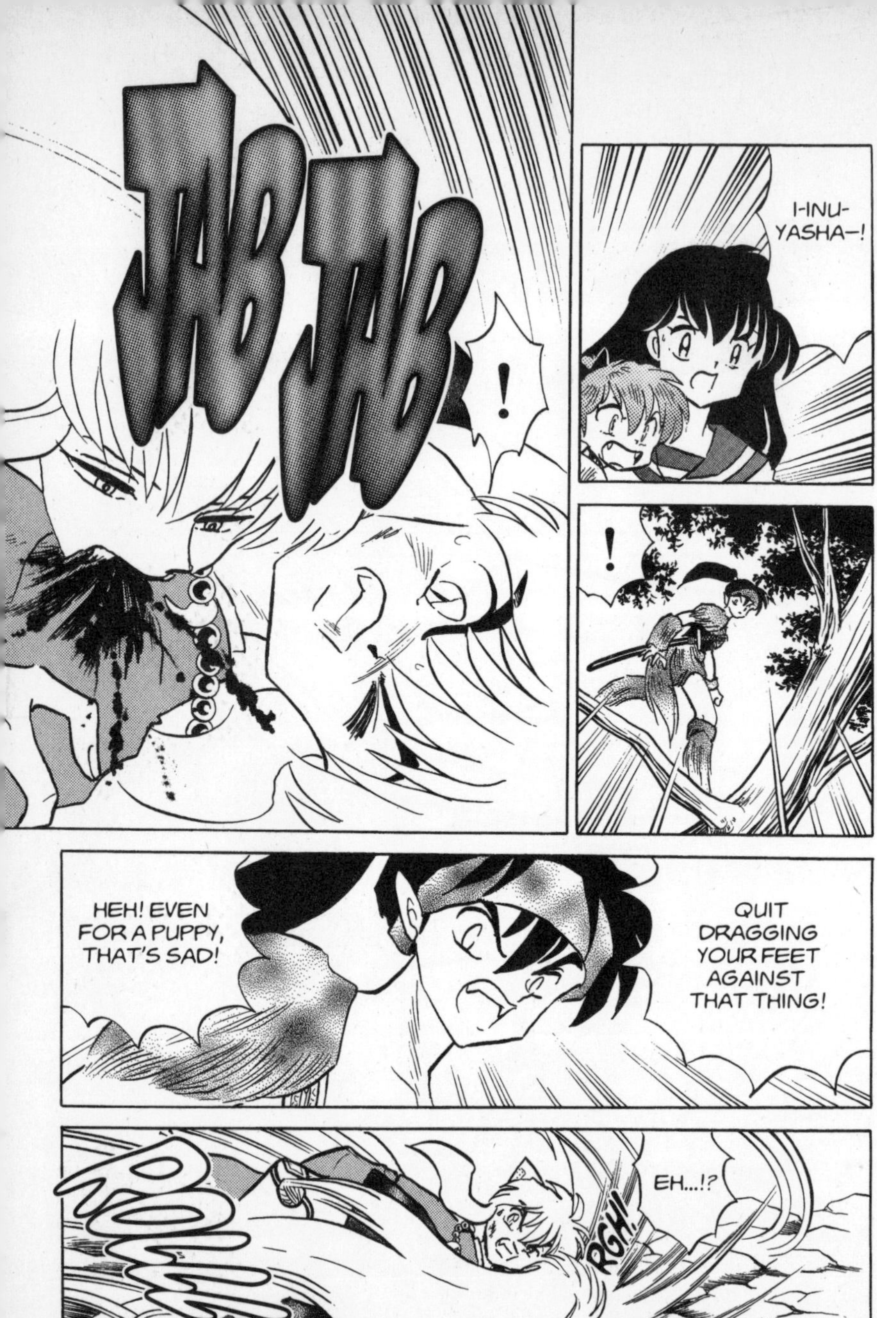
JAB JAB
!
I-INU-YASHA—!
!
HEH! EVEN FOR A PUPPY, THAT'S SAD!
QUIT DRAGGING YOUR FEET AGAINST THAT THING!
RGH!
EH...!?

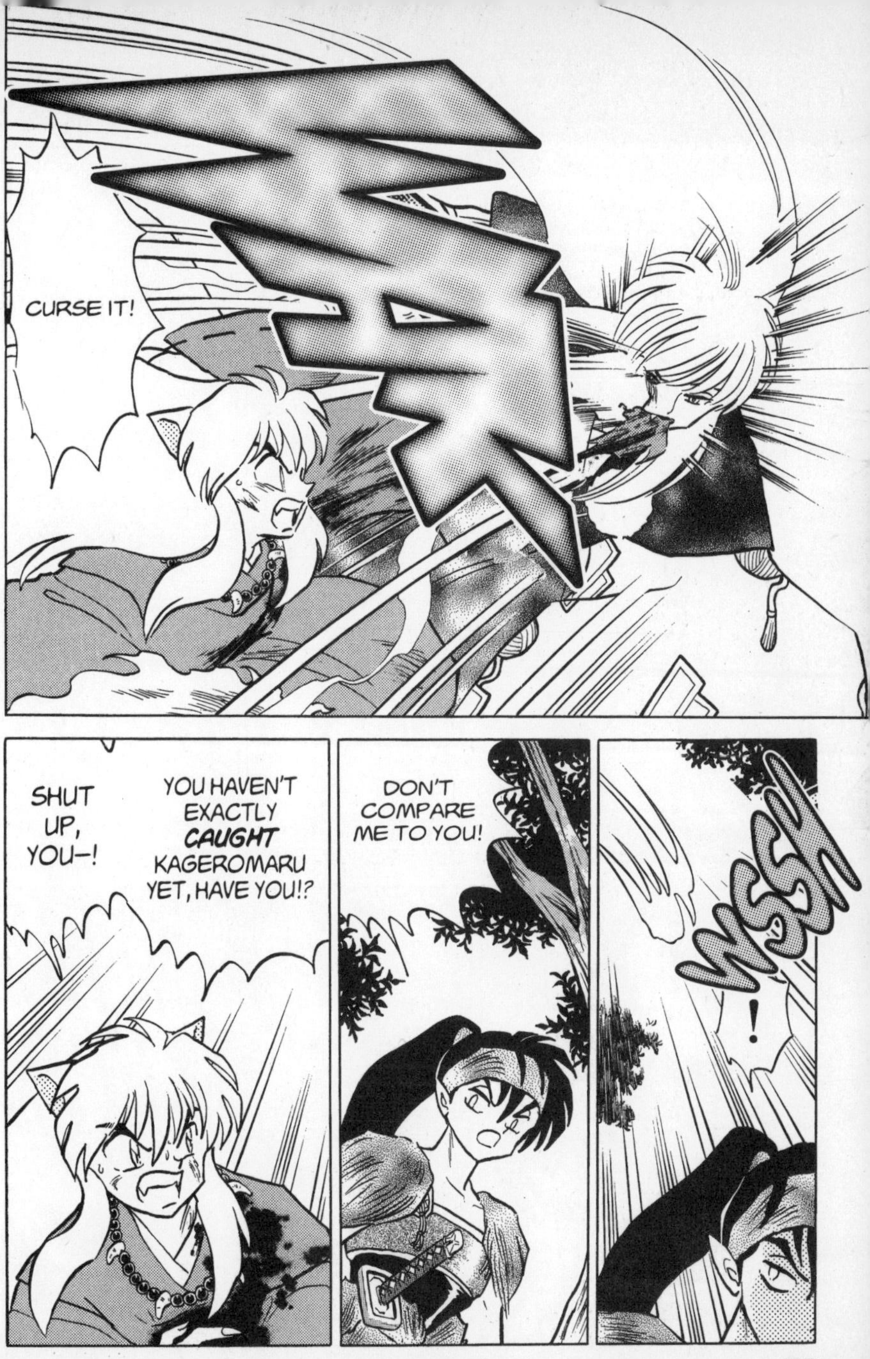
CURSE IT!
SHUT UP, YOU–!
YOU HAVEN'T EXACTLY CAUGHT KAGEROMARU YET, HAVE YOU!?
DON'T COMPARE ME TO YOU!
WSSH
!

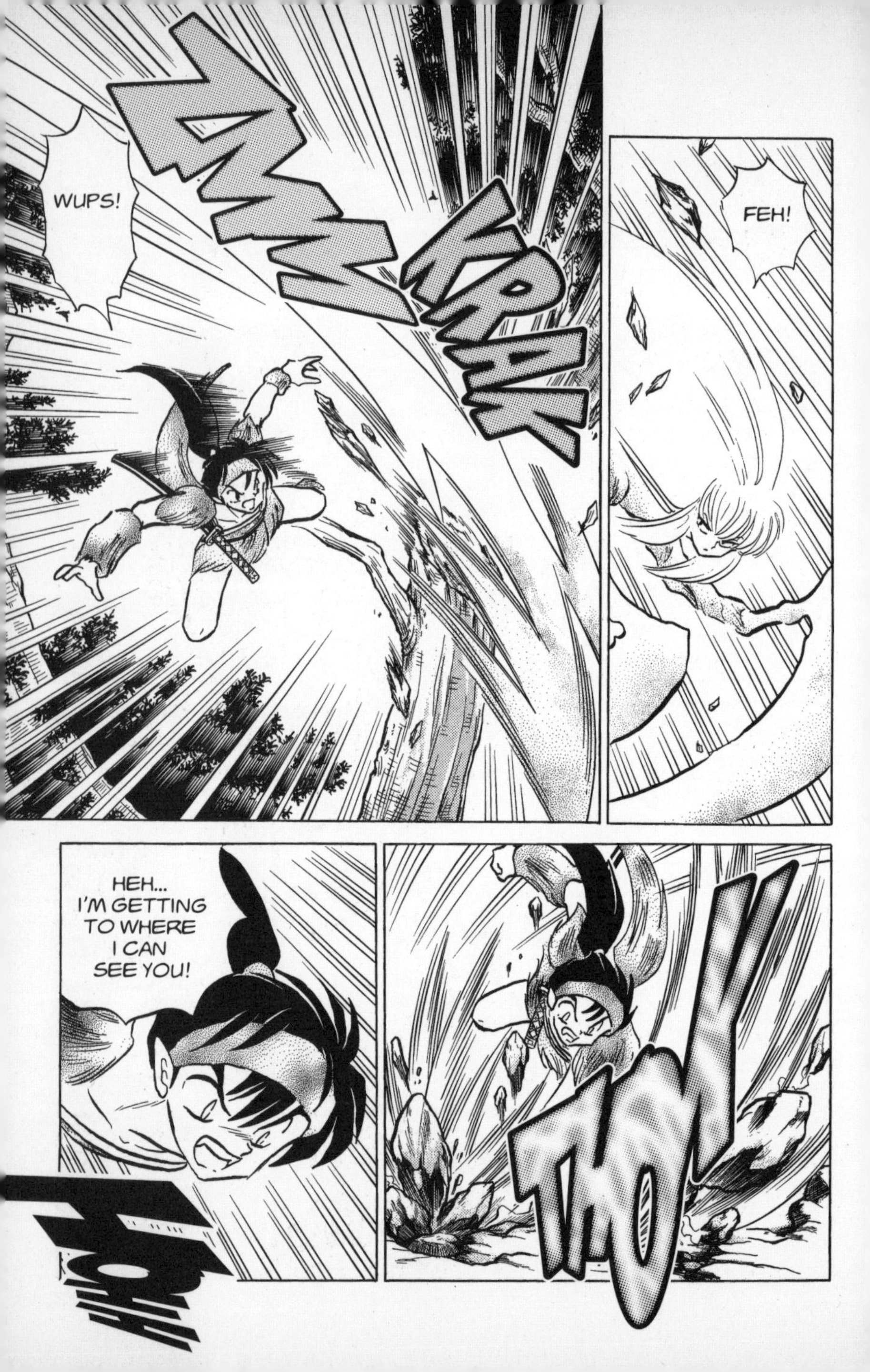
WUPS!
ZANN
KRAKK
FEH!
HEH... I'M GETTING TO WHERE I CAN SEE YOU!
THOM

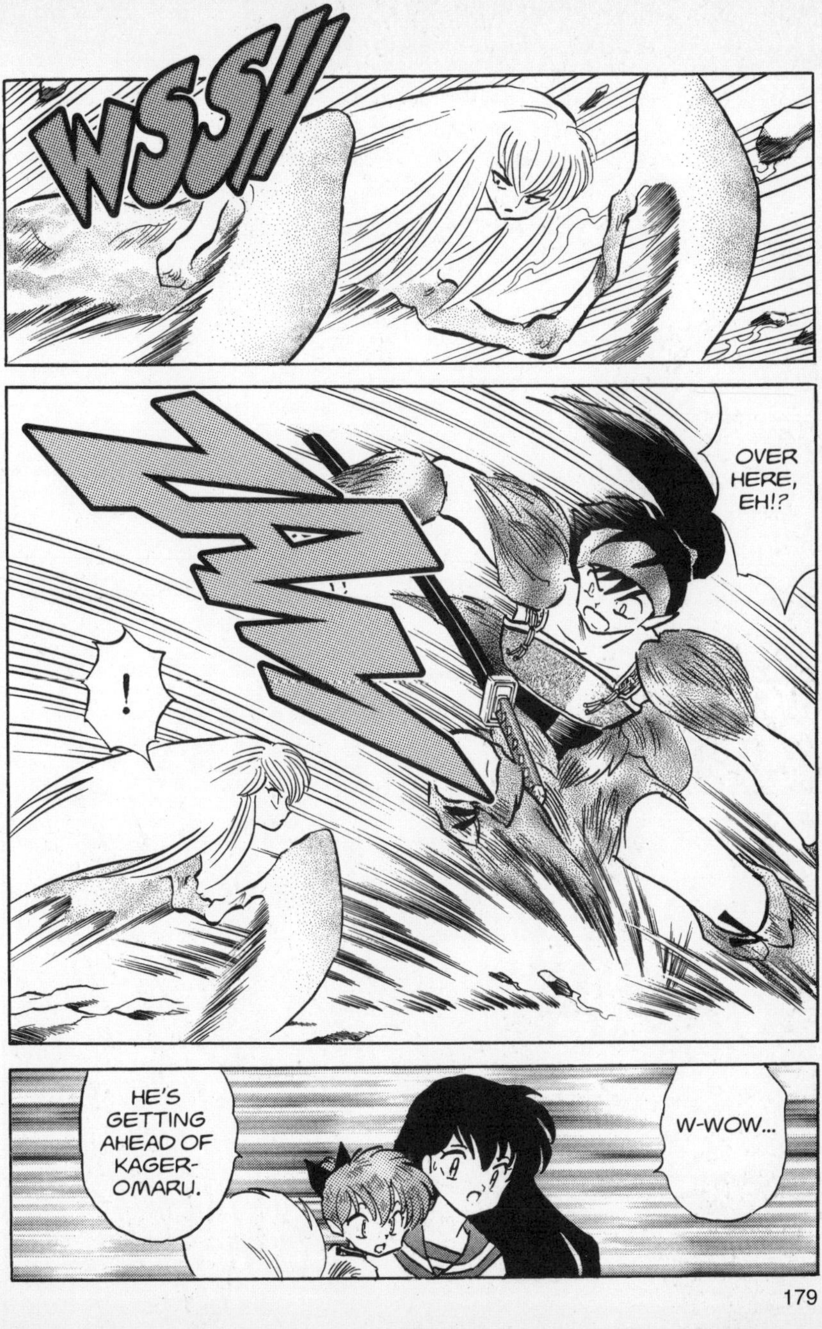
WSSH
ZAN
OVER HERE, EH!?
!
HE'S GETTING AHEAD OF KAGER-OMARU.
W-WOW...

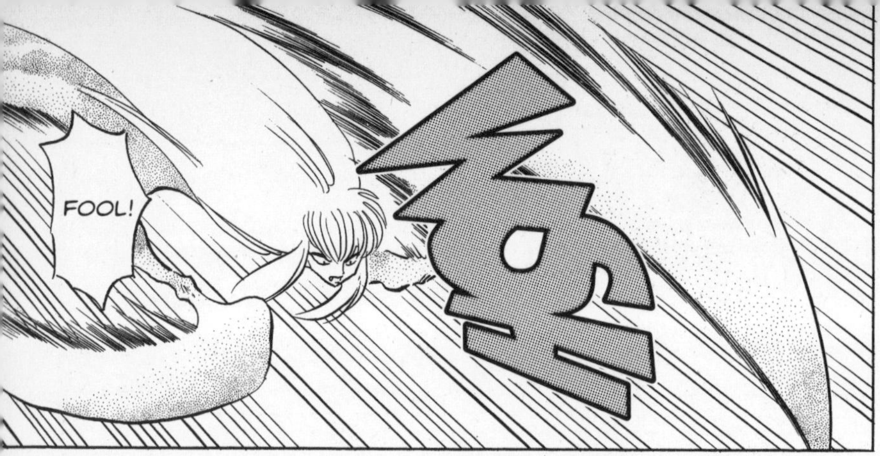
FOOL!
WOSH

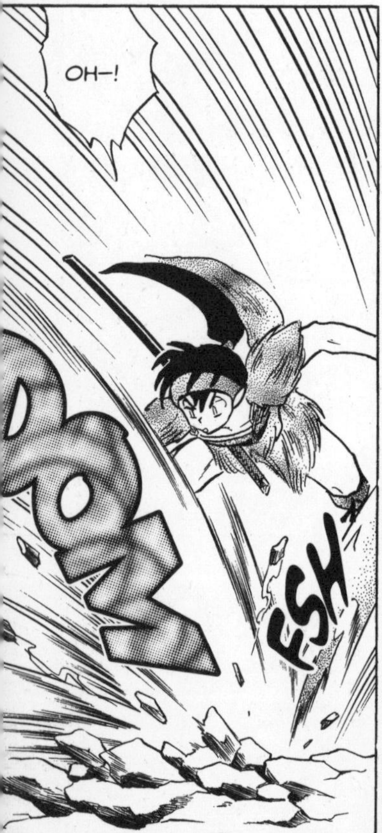
OH–!
FSH

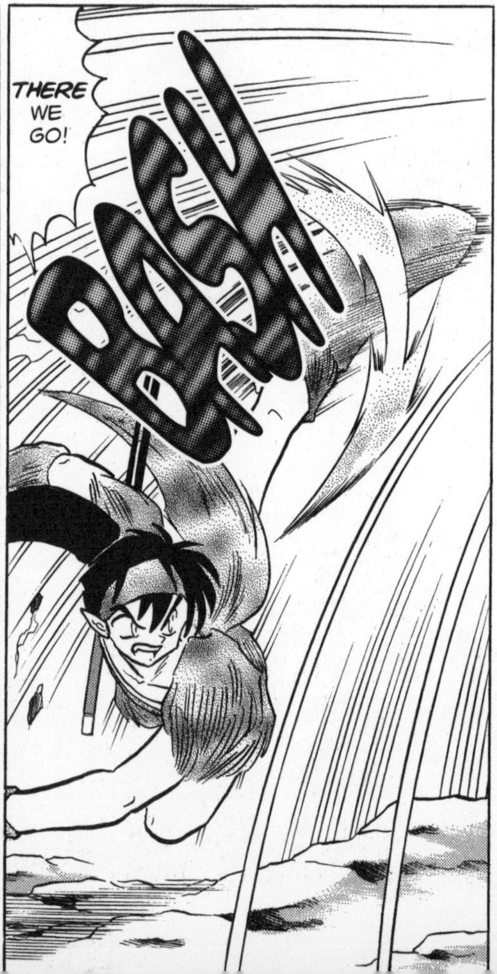
THERE WE GO!
BASH

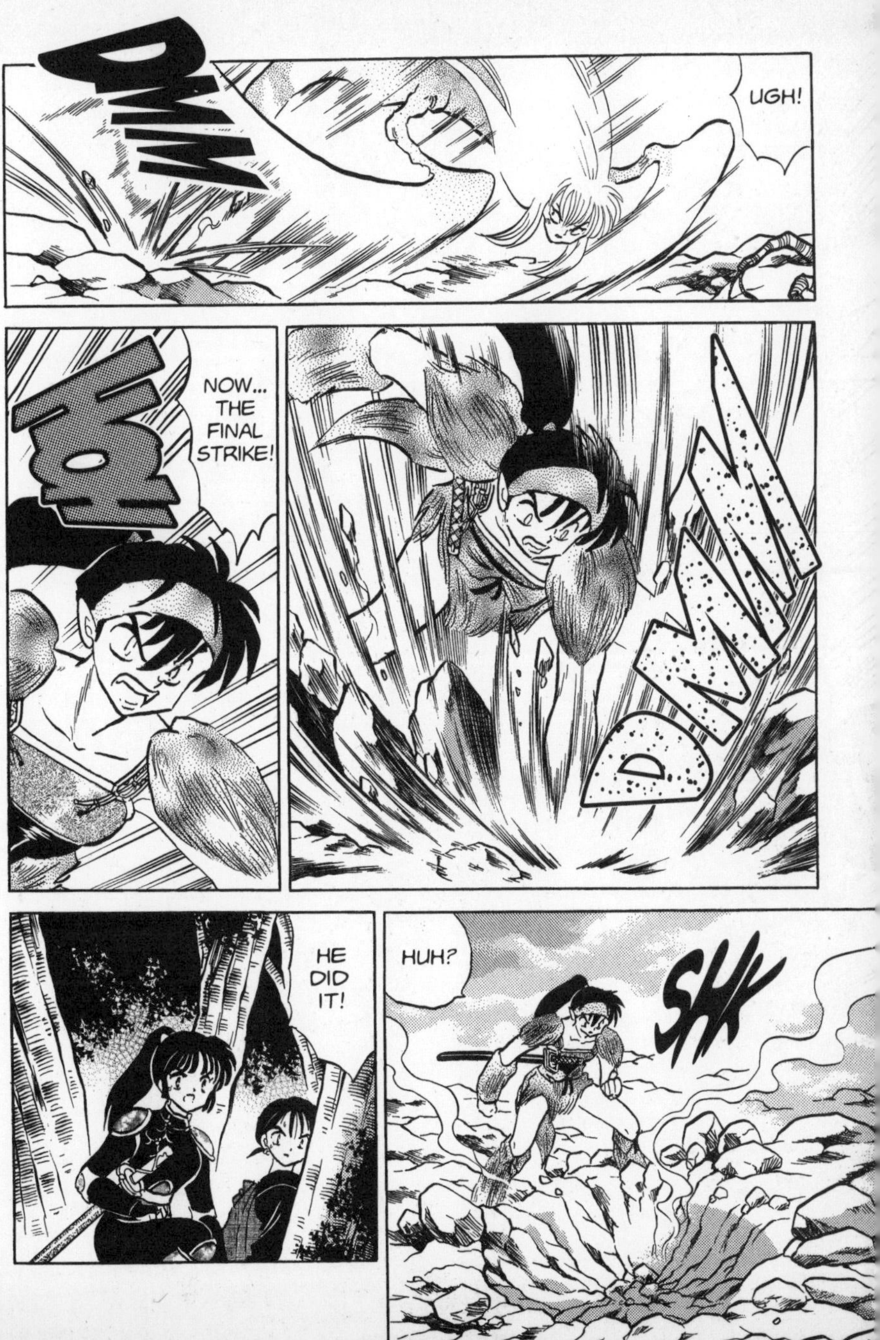
UGH!
NOW... THE FINAL STRIKE!
DMMM
HE DID IT!
HUH?
SHK

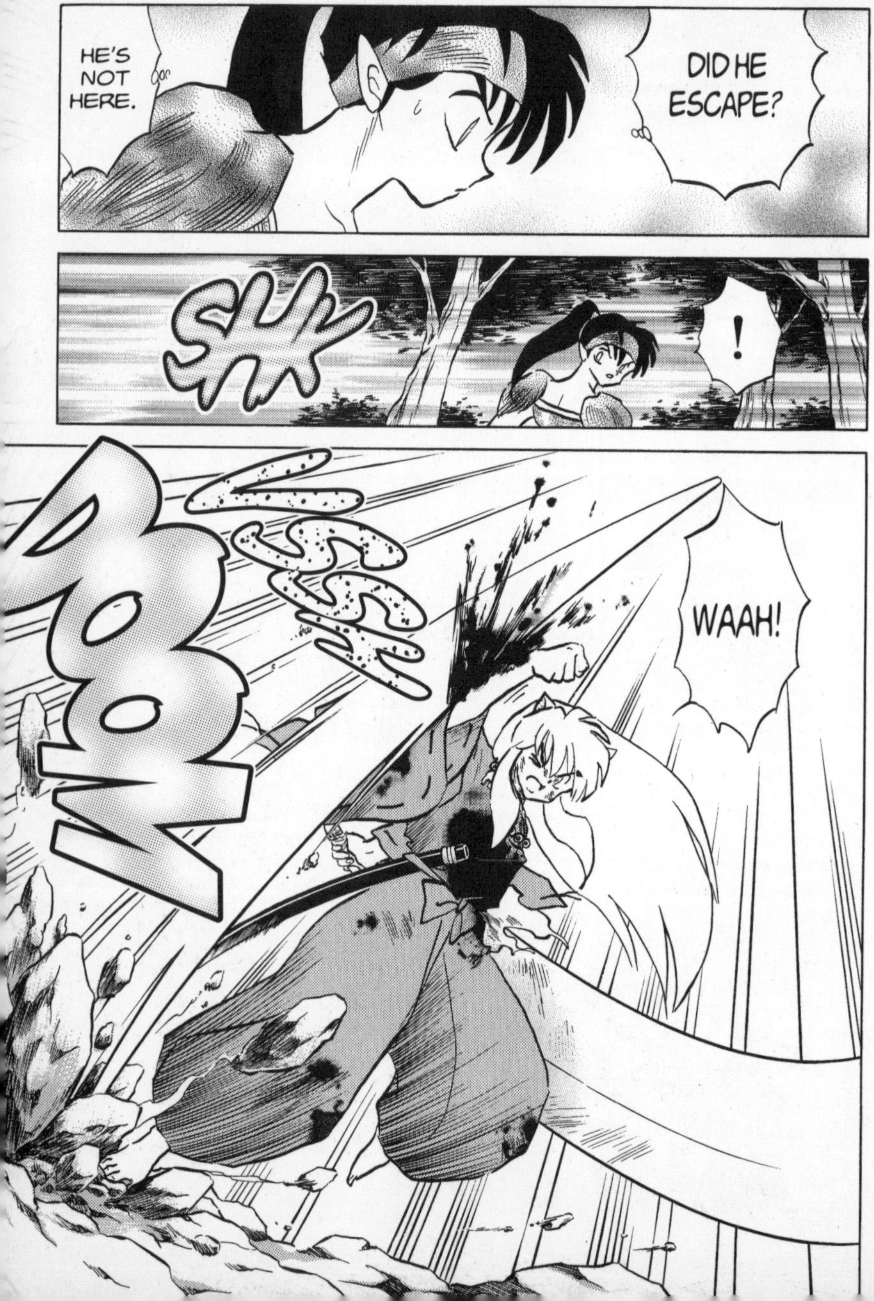
HE'S NOT HERE.
DID HE ESCAPE?
SHK
!
VSSH
WOOSH
WAAH!

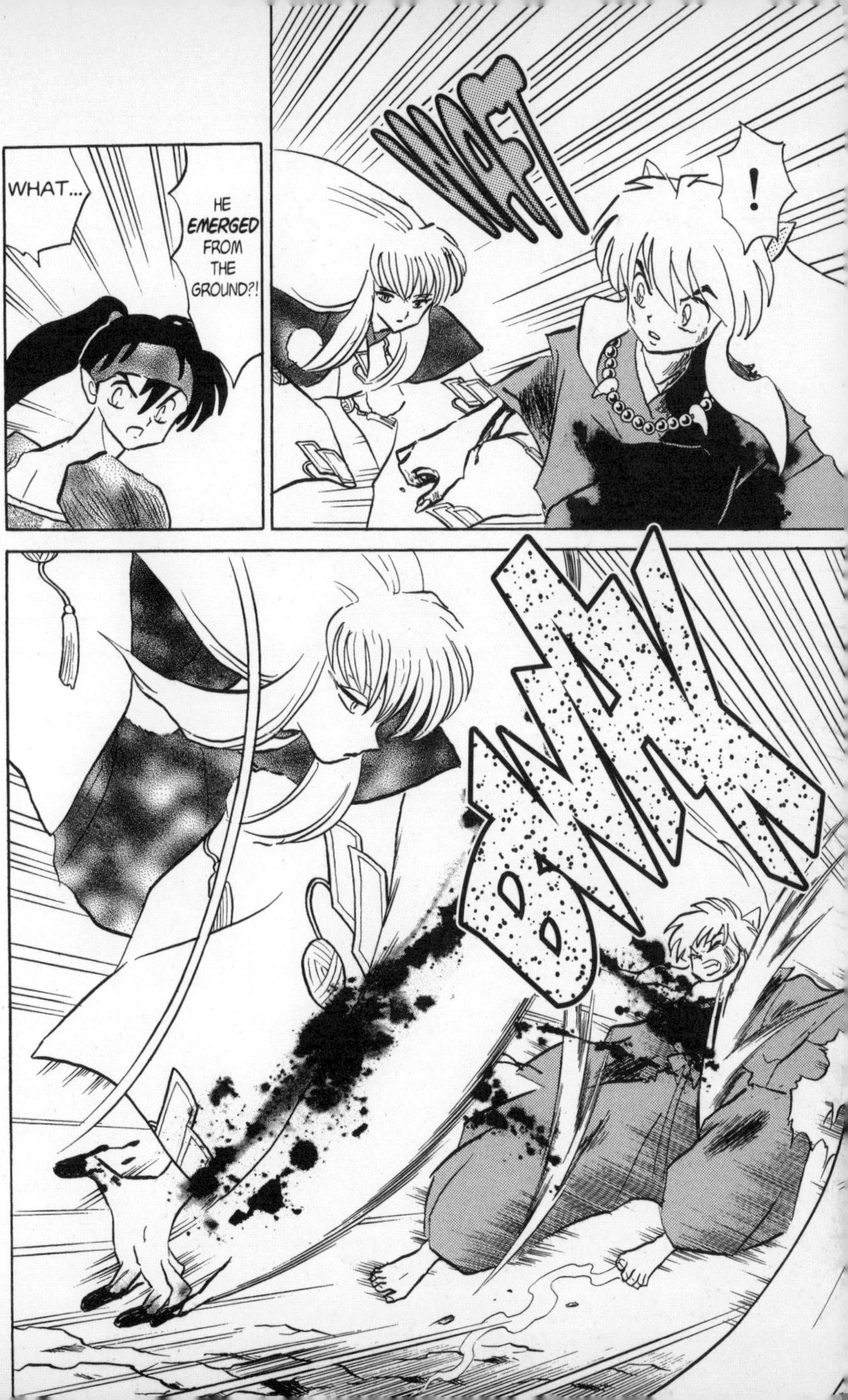
WHAT...
HE EMERGED FROM THE GROUND?!
WHAFT
!

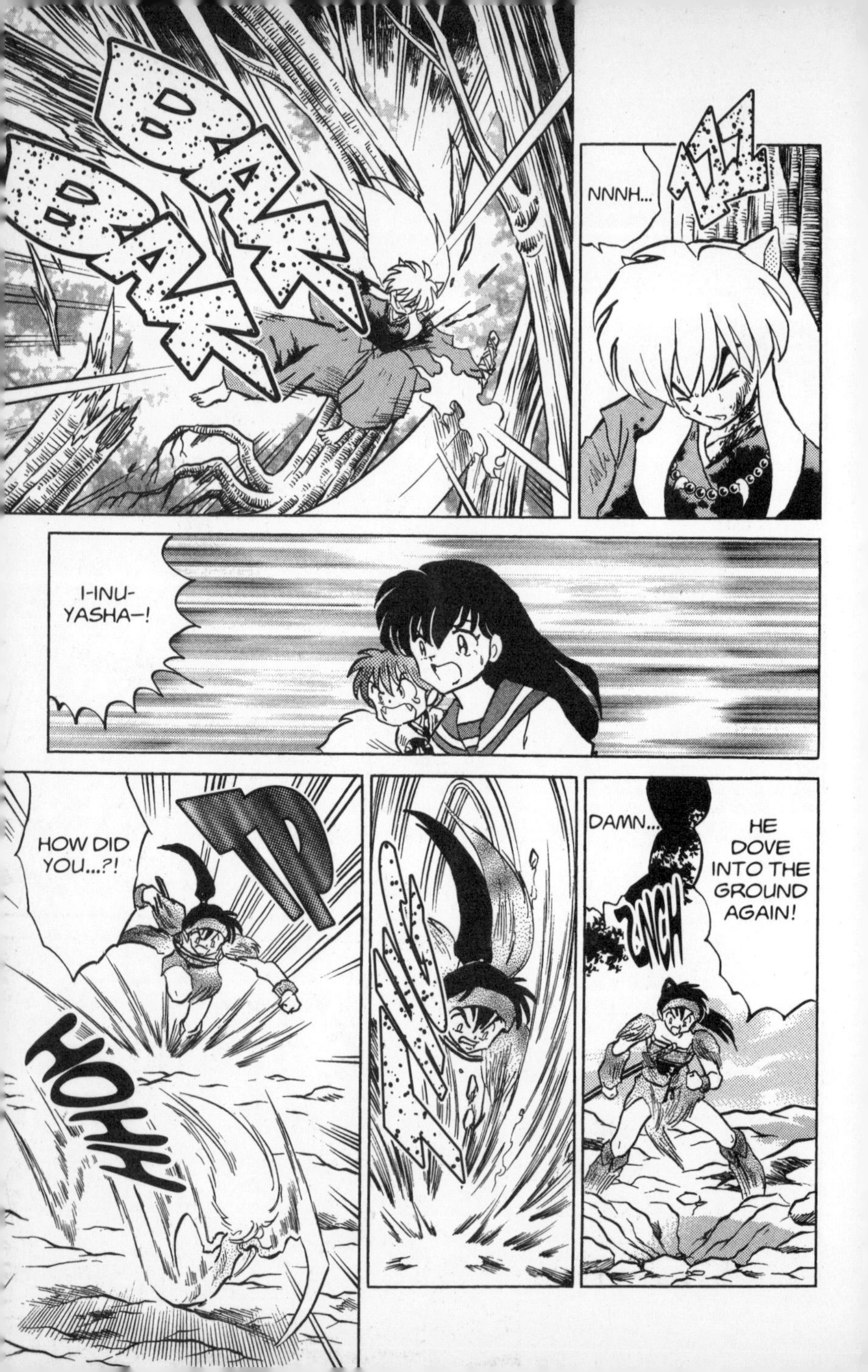
NNNH...
I-INU-YASHA-!
HOW DID YOU...?!
DAMN...
HE DOVE INTO THE GROUND AGAIN!

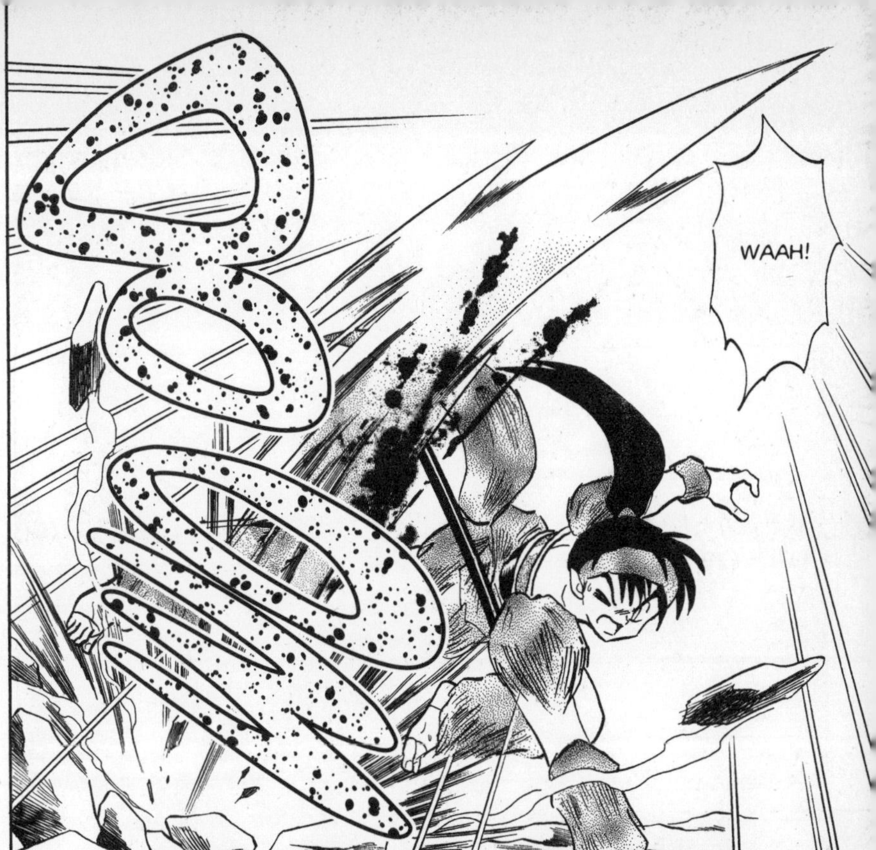
WAAH!
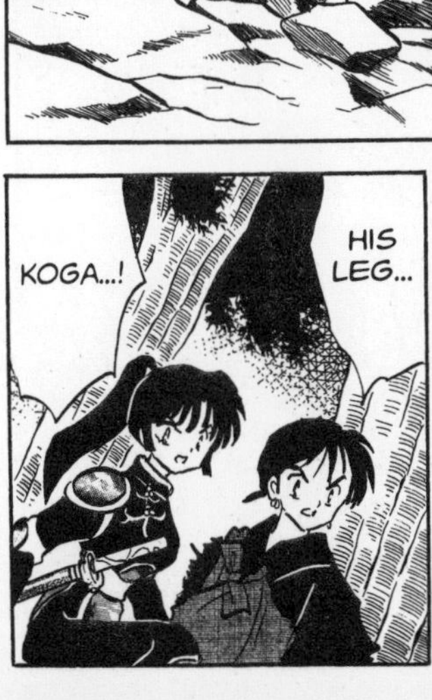
KOGA...!
HIS LEG...
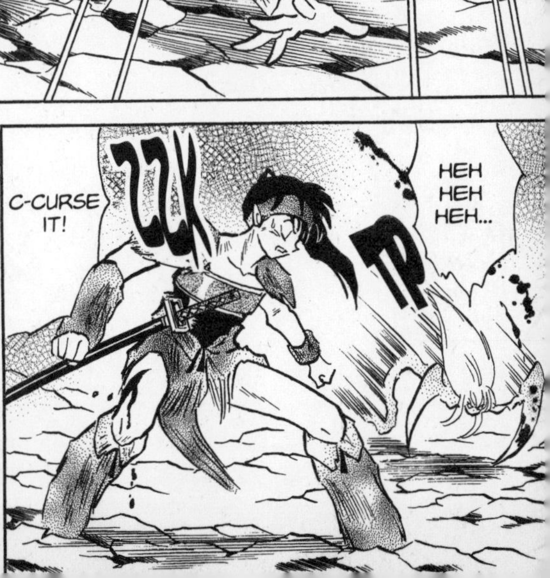
C-CURSE IT!
ZZK
HEH HEH HEH...
TP

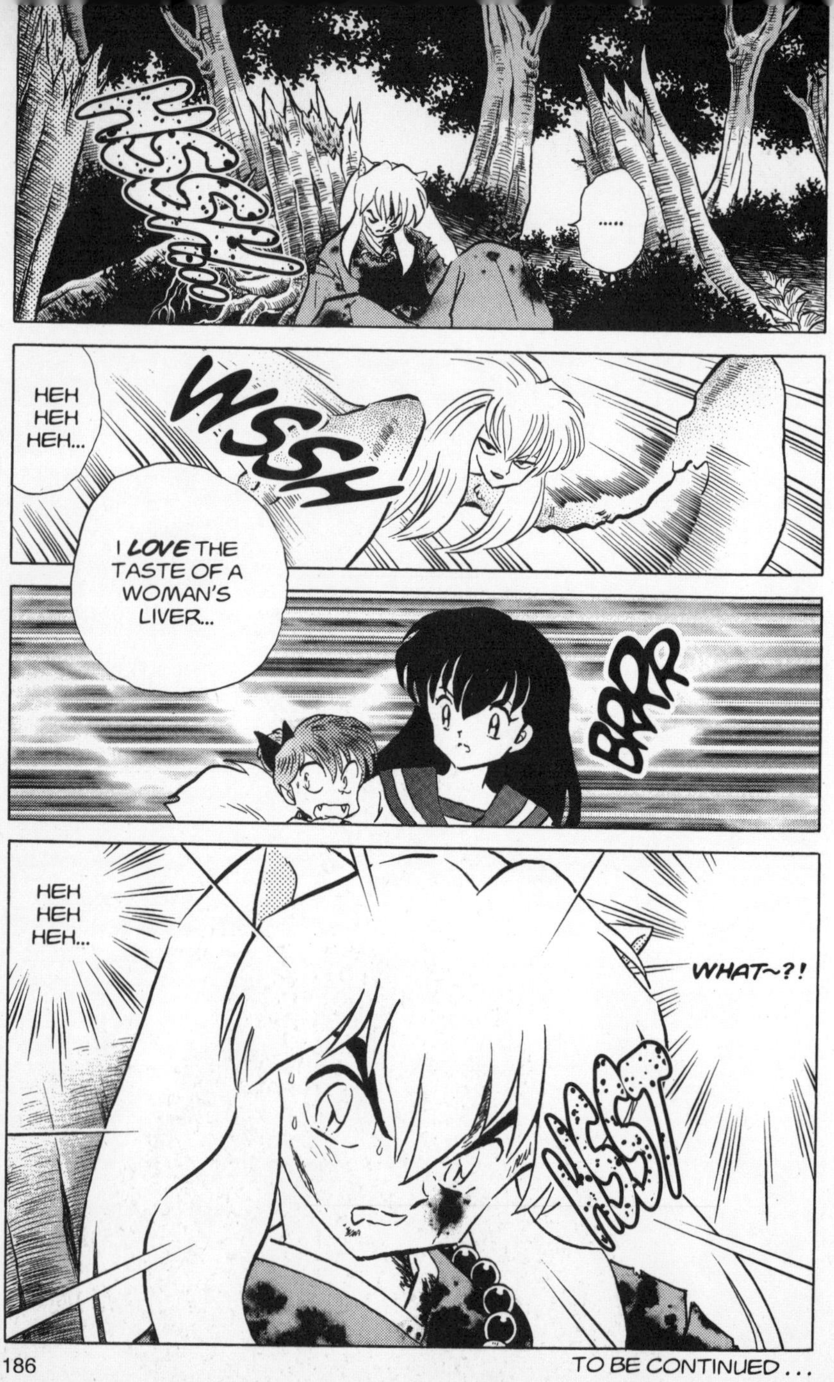
WSSHooo
......
HEH HEH HEH...
WSSH
I LOVE THE TASTE OF A WOMAN'S LIVER...
BRRR
HEH HEH HEH...
WHAT~?!
HSSST

TO BE CONTINUED . . .

Rumiko Takahashi

Rumiko Takahashi was born in 1957 in Niigata, Japan. She attended women's college in Tokyo, where she began studying comics with Kazuo Koike, author of *Crying Freeman*. In 1978, she won a prize in Shogakukan's annual "New Comic Artist Contest," and in that same year her boy-meets-alien comedy series *Lum*Urusei Yatsura* began appearing in the weekly manga magazine *Shônen Sunday*. This phenomenally successful series ran for nine years and sold over 22 million copies. Takahashi's later *Ranma 1/2* series enjoyed even greater popularity.

Takahashi is considered by many to be one of the world's most popular manga artists. With the publication of Volume 34 of her *Ranma 1/2* series in Japan, Takahashi's total sales passed one hundred million copies of her compiled works.

Takahashi's serial titles include *Lum*Urusei Yatsura*, *Ranma 1/2*, *One-Pound Gospel*, *Maison Ikkoku* and *Inu-Yasha*. Additionally, Takahashi has drawn many short stories which have been published in America under the title "Rumic Theater," and several installments of a saga known as her "Mermaid" series. Most of Takahashi's major stories have also been animated, and are widely available in translation worldwide. *Inu-Yasha* is her most recent serial story, first published in *Shônen Sunday* in 1996.

EDITOR'S RECOMMENDATIONS

Did you like INUYASHA? Here's what we recommend you try next:

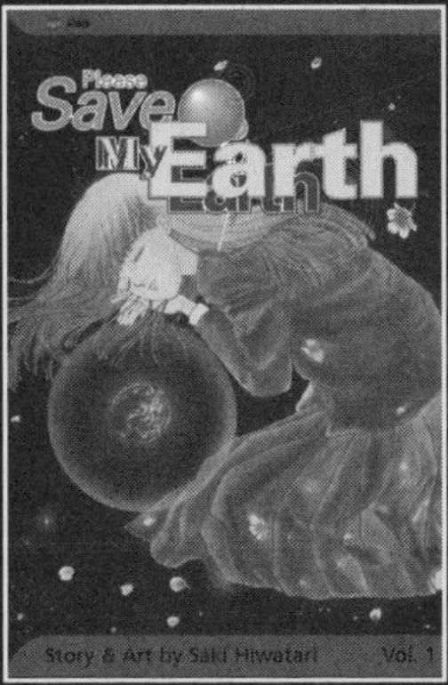
Please Save My Earth
Story & Art by Saki Hiwatari
Vol. 1

PLEASE SAVE MY EARTH

A sensitive high school student has recurring dreams that she's part of a team of seven alien scientists from the moon. She doesn't believe this could possibly be true until she meets other people who've been having these dreams as well. Fragments of a past life eventually come to light in an intricate, fascinating story of reincarnation, psychic powers, and eternal, tragic love.

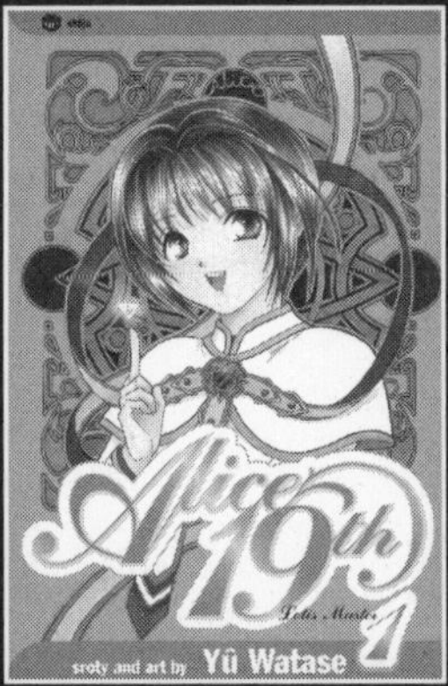
Alice 19th
Yû Watase

ALICE 19TH

Alice was a typical young girl—hopelessly in love and bored, until she follows a magical rabbit that literally jumps in front of her life. In a shôjo twist on Alice in Wonderland, this new story by the artist of *FUSHIGI YÛGI* and *CERES, CELESTIAL LEGEND* features two sisters: one who's been pulled into a world of darkness, and another (Alice) who must become a master of the Lotis Words to save her.

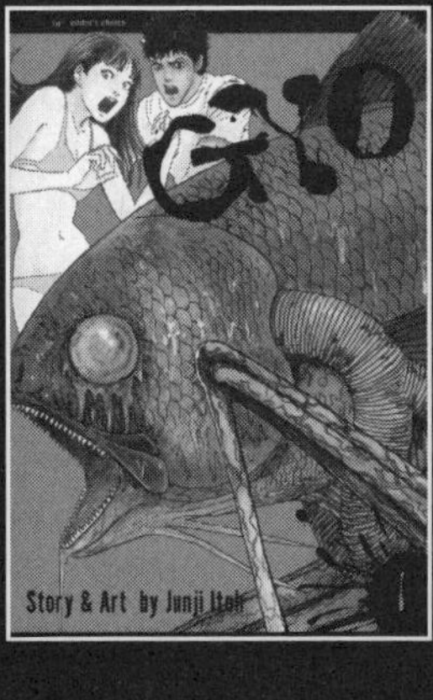
Story & Art by Junji Itoh

GYO

This horror manga by *UZUMAKI* artist Junji Ito dredges up a nightmare from the deep—monstrous, mutant fish and sea creatures that invade an Okinawa town. Ito's artwork is gorgeous and unforgettable—if you're looking for something completely different in manga, this is it.

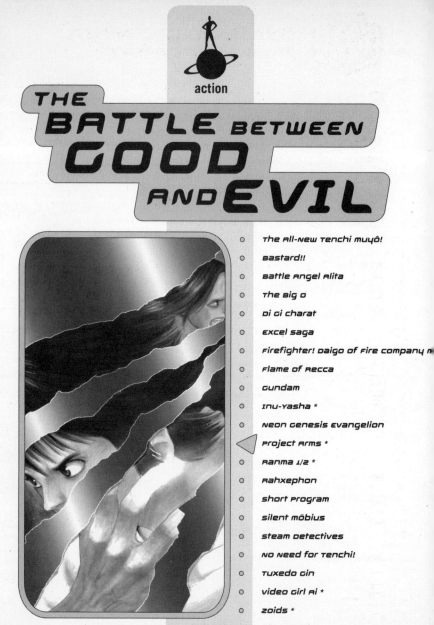

COMPLETE OUR SURVEY AND LET US KNOW WHAT YOU THINK!

☐ Please check here if you DO NOT wish to receive information or future offers from VIZ

Name: _____

Address: _____

City: _____ State: _____ Zip: _____

E-mail: _____

☐ Male ☐ Female Date of Birth (mm/dd/yyyy): ___ / ___ / ___ (Under 13? Parental consent required)

What race/ethnicity do you consider yourself? (please check one)

☐ Asian/Pacific Islander   ☐ Black/African American   ☐ Hispanic/Latino

☐ Native American/Alaskan Native ☐ White/Caucasian   ☐ Other: _____

What VIZ product did you purchase? (check all that apply and indicate title purchased)

☐ DVD/VHS _____

☐ Graphic Novel _____

☐ Magazines _____

☐ Merchandise _____

Reason for purchase: (check all that apply)

☐ Special offer   ☐ Favorite title   ☐ Gift

☐ Recommendation   ☐ Other _____

Where did you make your purchase? (please check one)

☐ Comic store   ☐ Bookstore   ☐ Mass/Grocery Store

☐ Newsstand   ☐ Video/Video Game Store ☐ Other: _____

☐ Online (site: _____)

What other VIZ properties have you purchased/own? _____

_____

How many anime and/or manga titles have you purchased in the last year? How many were VIZ titles? (please check one from each column)

ANIME
- ☐ None
- ☐ 1-4
- ☐ 5-10
- ☐ 11+

MANGA
- ☐ None
- ☐ 1-4
- ☐ 5-10
- ☐ 11+

VIZ
- ☐ None
- ☐ 1-4
- ☐ 5-10
- ☐ 11+

I find the pricing of VIZ products to be: (please check one)
- ☐ Cheap
- ☐ Reasonable
- ☐ Expensive

What genre of manga and anime would you like to see from VIZ? (please check two)
- ☐ Adventure
- ☐ Comic Strip
- ☐ Science Fiction
- ☐ Fighting
- ☐ Horror
- ☐ Romance
- ☐ Fantasy
- ☐ Sports

What do you think of VIZ's new look?
- ☐ Love It
- ☐ It's OK
- ☐ Hate It
- ☐ Didn't Notice
- ☐ No Opinion

Which do you prefer? (please check one)
- ☐ Reading right-to-left
- ☐ Reading left-to-right

Which do you prefer? (please check one)
- ☐ Sound effects in English
- ☐ Sound effects in Japanese with English captions
- ☐ Sound effects in Japanese only with a glossary at the back

THANK YOU! Please send the completed form to:

NJW Research
42 Catharine St.
Poughkeepsie, NY 12601

All information provided will be used for internal purposes only. We promise not to sell or otherwise divulge your information.